CRIMINAL LAW AND THE RIGHTS OF THE CHILD IN MUSLIM STATES: A COMPARATIVE AND ANALYTICAL PERSPECTIVE

NISRINE ABIAD
and
FARKHANDA ZIA MANSOOR

British Institute of International and Comparative Law

Published and Distributed by
British Institute of International and Comparative Law
Charles Clore House, 17 Russell Square, London WC1B 5JP

© 2010

British Library Cataloguing in Publication Data
A Catalogue record of this book is available from the British Library

ISBN 978–1–905221–45–5

Typeset by Cambrian Typesetters
Camberley, Surrey
Printed in Great Britain by MPG Books Group, UK

Contents

Foreword

The British Institute of International and Comparative has developed an expertise over a number of years in the interface between Islamic law and international law. It has undertaken research projects, organized events and produced publications in this area using a comparative legal approach. It has done this in order to foster knowledge and dialogue between international and Islamic legal scholars, practitioners, judges, civil society and others on international and Islamic human rights standards, and to assist in legal and policy developments. It has been fortunate in its work to have established, in particular, an effective engagement with scholars and others in the Islamic Republic of Iran.

This publication arises from a research project on Criminal Law and the Rights of the Child Muslim States. This research considers the protection of the human rights of children within the criminal justice system of a selection of Muslim States and the extent to which those States have implemented international human rights legal protections. This is to enable an overview of the diverse ways in which Islamic criminal law (the Sharia) is applied across the world today. The research examines the internal national laws and practices of these States, including the State's constitutional responsibilities towards juvenile justice, the role of the judiciary and the application of the law within States. This includes considering the legislative and judicial actions in relation to non-discriminatory laws in criminal matters, and the age of criminal responsibility, as well as judicial and non-judicial processes. Its aim was to establish the legal and policy framework, and the actual substantive impact on the rights of children in the criminal justice systems in those States. With many recent changes in some States' legislation, this research provides an analysis of legal developments in the area of child rights in criminal justice in Muslim States that have not been discussed in detail in the existing international legal literature.

In undertaking this research, the researchers benefitted from national rapporteurs in each State. These experts completed questionnaires about the issues and provided important information and insights on the ground. The materials provided by the experts have been edited by the authors and together with the scholarly knowledge of the authors, are included in the middle chapters in this book. The context of these State laws and practices are set out in two substantive chapters dealing with the key issues concerning child offenders, and the ideas and roles of Islamic law within the criminal justice systems. The latter chapter considers the Islamic perspectives on the nature of child rights, the fundamental elements of what is considered a crime within Islamic jurisprudence, and the age of criminal responsibility as understood by Islamic jurists. The concluding chapter brings all this research together in offering a comparative analysis of these laws and practices, and comments on good practices.

This research project was enhanced by the organization of a workshop for a number of people from the selected States. This included a group of judges and lawyers from Egypt, Lebanon, Iran, Turkey and the United Arab Emirates, and took place in London in June 2010. During this workshop the participants and other experts shared their views in a collegially comparative way, and discussed the successes and potential shortcomings of the different criminal processes applied to young offenders.

The authors and I want to thank all those who assisted them in this research, especially as there were many obstacles and challenges that were faced. We thank the interns at the Institute who devoted their time for the project: Zahra Al Tai, Priscilla Dudhia, Hudda Khaireh, Umeda Khudoikulovana, Ritika Patni Lulwa Rizkallah, and Safoora Saremi. Our many thanks to the national rapporteurs: Musa Usman Abubakar, Dr Amir Ardeshir Arjomand, Dr Georges Assaf, Dr Mohamed Badar, Magda Boutors, Dr Farah Dusuki, Dr Mehmet Hakan Hikri, Behrooz Javanmard, Ayla Karmali, and Monica Sanchez.

In addition, we thank Professor Mashood Baderin, who reviewed the research and gave valuable comments on it, Dr Reza Eslami, Dr Seyed Mohammad Hosseini and Judge Yuksel Erdogan for commenting on different chapters, Alexa van Sickle, who carefully edited the entire book which was not an easy task at all, Kristin Hausler who largely organized the workshop, and Dr Sergey Ripinsky for doing a special painting as a book cover, as well as those members of the Institute staff who were invaluable in ensuring that the research and events progressed so well.

It was also a special pleasure for me to supervise this research, which was directed under the excellent management and insight of Dr Nisrine Abiad and with the depth of research of Dr Farkhanda Zia Mansoor. My warmest thanks to them.

Professor Robert McCorquodale
Institute Director
British Institute of International and Comparative Law

Explanation of Terms

Al Aqilah: The term includes all the kinsmen and relations on the father's side, however remote they may be

Al Wilayatu Alal Maal: Guardianship Concerning Property

Aqil: Reason; Rational thought

Baliq: Anyone who has attained puberty

Baliq Wa Rashid: A mature person

Dhimmis: Members of other Faith communities who are under the protection of the Islamic State

Diyah: Blood Money

Diyah Mugalazah: Heavy Blood Money

Diyah Al Mukhafafa: Light Blood Money

Fiqh: Islamic Jurisprudence

Hadith: Written documentation of the sayings, conduct or the traditions of the Prophet Mohammed

Hadana: Guardianship; Child Custody and Care

Hudood: Boundary, Limits, fixed punishment in Criminal Offence

Idrak: Understanding

Ijtihad: Juridical interpretation of a qualified Islamic jurist

Ikhtiyar: Free will

Kaffara : Expiation

Maroof: Right

Mubah: Permissible

Munkar : Wrong

Musalah Murssila: Consideration of common good

Qadi: Judge

Qasad Aljanai: *mens rea*; Guilty Mind; Criminal Intention

Qiyas: Analogy

Qisas: Islamic Law of Retribution

Qudra: The power to commit or not to commit an act

Sabiy Ghar Mumayiz: A child with indiscrete understanding

Sabiyy Mummayyiz: A child with weak understanding

Sharia: Way or path; basic sources of Islamic Law

Sunnah: The practice or practical life of the Prophet Mohammed according to the Quran

Tadib: Discipline

Tazeer: Discretionary penal punishment

Urf: Customs

Wilayat Al Tabiyya: Guardianship concerning education

PART I

CHAPTER 1

Introduction

The 1924 Geneva Declaration on the Rights of the Child was the first attempt to create an international standard recognizing children as individual rights holders. Today, the United Nations Convention on the Rights of the Child (UNCRC) sets the international benchmark for the provision and protection of child rights across the world. It is the most ratified international convention in the history of the United Nations. However, the issue of child rights with respect to children who break the law has not had uniform application within States. In many instances, when children come into contact with the national criminal justice systems, it demonstrates whether their rights are protected in practice.

This book considers the protection of the rights of children within the criminal justice system and the extent to which States have implemented international human rights legal protections. It focuses on States with Muslim majority populations, and States that are members of the Organisation of the Islamic Conference (OIC). A range of Muslim States are examined, governed by a huge variety of political systems, from religious States (Iran) to multi-religious democracies (Malaysia) and to States where Islamic criminal law plays a limited role (Egypt). This is to ensure a robust overview of the diverse ways in which Islamic criminal law (Sharia) is applied across the world today. It considers both State compliance with international human rights obligations, as well as domestic laws and practices as expressed by State legislation. This includes exploring a State's constitutional responsibilities towards juvenile justice, State law and the application of law within States. With many recent changes in some State's legislation, this research provides an analysis of legal developments in the area of child rights in criminal justice in Muslim States that have not been discussed in detail in the existing international legal literature. It also provides some consideration of the nature of judicial discretion—its pattern and its substantive impact on the rights of children in criminal justice areas—within Muslim States.

II. SELECTED STATES

The Muslim States included in this research are Afghanistan, Egypt, Iran, Lebanon, Malaysia, Nigeria, Pakistan, Turkey and United Arab Emirates

(UAE). In addition two non-Muslim States are studied; Spain and the United Kingdom. There are several reasons behind the selection of these Muslim States for the research:

1. The legal systems chosen set a spectrum of ages for the minimum age of criminal liability, varying from seven to 18, allowing for a comprehensive study on this subject and its relationship within the child rights framework.
2. The States selected follow different administrative systems. There is a federal model in the case of Pakistan, the United Arab Emirates, Nigeria and Malaysia, and in other cases, the legal system is structured around a central government (Egypt, Afghanistan and Turkey). Lebanon is a republic within the overall framework of confessionalism. The UK is a constitutional monarchy, and a unitary State with a devolved system of government. Spain is a parliamentary representative democratic constitutional monarchy. This approach allows a nuanced analysis, using the legal landscape to understand differences between national legal considerations and Islamic principles, international law and the role and reach of each sphere within the jurisdictions.
3. The Muslim States selected use various different schools of Islamic jurisprudence. For example, the Shia Jaafari school of jurisprudence in Iran,[1] the Sunni Hanafi school of jurisprudence in Egypt and Pakistan, and the Sunni Shafi'i school of jurisprudence in Malaysia.[2] This will enable a more informed understanding of Islamic law and the different schools of Islamic jurisprudence.
4. The States selected differ in terms of the role Sharia plays in their legal system,[3] ranging from a general recognition without practical application, for example, Turkey—which operates a secular criminal justice system despite having a 99 per cent Muslim population—and States in which Sharia is an important source of legislation, such as Iran and Northern Nigeria.
5. States within the study also vary in the level of implementation of Islamic criminal law in particular. Only Iran, Northern Nigeria and Pakistan apply Islamic criminal law (regarding punishments).
6. The States selected have been undergoing legislative amendments with regard to the law relating to children in criminal matters. For example, in Egypt, specific reforms of the child law were carried out in 2008 in

---

[1] This school of jurisprudence is named after the name of its founder, Imam Jaffar Sadiq.
[2] Each of these Sunni schools of jurisprudence has also been named after its founder.
[3] See N Abiad, *Sharia, Muslim States and International Human Rights Treaty Obligations: A Comparative Study* (BIICL, London, 2008) 32–58.

an attempt to make its law more compatible with the international human rights norms expressed within the UNCRC, and in Afghanistan, the restructuring of the judicial criminal system was recently finalized to give specific consideration as to how children can be given better protection. In Turkey, efforts to accede to the European Union have triggered remarkable improvements to the Turkish juvenile justice system.

7.   The role of the judiciary in expanding the protection of juvenile offenders, particularly in the context of Islamic criminal law, is an important trend that required investigation and for which these States provided important instances. For example, in Northern Nigeria the Sharia Penal Code confers considerable discretion on judges to substitute sentences in that Code provided the guilty party is younger than 18 years old. In Iran and the UAE, judges also have a high degree of discretion in respect to young defendants.

The non-Muslim jurisdictions chosen for the study—Spain and the United Kingdom—represent two examples of legislation in non-Muslim States. The United Kingdom, despite having a very effective criminal justice system, has 10 as the age of criminal liability, whereas Spain places the age of criminal liability at 18. Through comparative research, the role of the age of criminal liability in offering protection to children in conflict with the criminal law is also explored.

III. METHODOLOGY

The research focuses on legislative and judicial actions in relation to non-discriminatory laws for children in general and criminal matters in particular. The research aims to provide an analysis of State legal instruments and their effective enforcement, with an exposition on their religious, socio-economic, cultural and political contexts. The analysis of legal protection of child rights on application within States included in the study includes possible ways of reconciling and harmonizing the requirements of international human rights laws with the complex national systems and religious considerations within each State. By having a solid foundation and grounding both in international human rights law and in the internal dynamics of each State and in the Sharia, and through comparative study, the recommended improvements suggested within the study intend to have universal, widespread applicability and utility across a variety of jurisdictions.

The research is broad in scope and required detailed analysis, not just of the criminal system but also of case law within jurisdictions, which was in many cases only available in the local languages and in many instances not published at all. For this reason, the study has relied on a multi-dimensional methodology, combining thorough theoretical research conducted by the authors in London and questionnaires completed by national rapporteurs, being local experts in the field in each jurisdiction.[4] These questionnaires sought to clarify the key areas and subjects, such as describing the national and international legal systems operating within a State with regard to children and the criminal law, and identifying important aspects such as the age of criminal liability, judicial protection granted to juveniles in courts, and the death penalty (when relevant). National rapporteurs were also requested to carry out interviews with judges and/or legal practitioners where possible. For the sake of harmonization, and due to the limited space in this book, the reports were then edited and short conclusions were added by the authors.[5]

The research also examines the Sharia (Islamic law) perspective regarding the minimum age of criminal responsibility. Therefore, to help the reader there is an explanation of the relevant Islamic law terms. Additionally, detailed explanations of the terms and concepts have been provided in Chapter 3.

IV. CONTENTS

This book raises specific issues: the factors which bring a child into conflict with law, the legal minimum age of criminal liability, and gender issues pertaining to the protection of child rights. It examines the extent to which Islamic considerations impact the legal context in these matters. Mechanisms for the integration of international law into national legal systems are discussed and the extent of this integration is analysed. Criminal cases that led to the death penalty or cases in which the death penalty was avoided, are discussed at length within the book, particularly the role and prescriptions found within Sharia law. At the national (domestic) level, the book highlights crucial issues concerning the adequacy of national laws related to the protection of child offenders, while exploring the gaps and the difficulties in their enforcement. It examines the divergence between law and practice and recommends a variety of initiatives for addressing child delinquency.

The various provisions of the relevant international instruments are considered. These are: the 1924 Declaration on the Rights of the Child; the 1959 Declaration on the Rights of the Child; the 1966 International

---

[4] With the exception of Pakistan and the United Kingdom, where research was done by the authors.

[5] With the exception of Spain and the United Arab Emirates, which were edited by the national rapporteurs who initially completed them.

Covenant on Civil and Political Rights (ICCPR); the 1985 Beijing Rules; the 1989 UNCRC; the 1990 United Nations Guidelines for the Prevention of Juvenile Delinquency (the Riyadh Guidelines); 1990 United Nations Rules for the Protection of Juveniles Deprived of their Liberty; the 1981 Universal Islamic Declaration of Human Rights; the 1990 Cairo Declaration of Human Rights; the 2005 Covenant on the Rights of the Child in Islam and the OIC Rabat Declaration on Child's Issues in the Member States of the Organization of Islamic Conference held in Rabat, November 2005.

Chapter 2 provides the background of the study. It provides an overview of the issues of child offenders. It addresses various questions, including who is considered a 'juvenile offender' (and why the choice of 'juvenile' rather than 'child' is made),[6] why there is a need to set a legal minimum age for child offenders, and how States' juvenile justice systems develop. It examines the development of the juvenile justice system and issues regarding the death penalty. Further, the chapter discusses international laws relating to the rights of juvenile offenders, with analysis of the various relevant provisions of the international Conventions discussed above.

Chapter 3 explores the role of Sharia law and the protection of the rights of children who encounter the criminal justice system. The chapter discusses the protection of children and provides relevant injunctions prescribed by the Quran and the *sunnah* (the traditions of the Prophet Mohammed) in this matter. It examines several verses of the Quran and *hadith* (sayings of the Prophet Mohammed) that are applicable to understanding the Islamic perspective on the nature of child rights in Islam and how the Sharia seeks to achieve this. It analyses the effectiveness of relevant Islamic instruments, based on core (basic) Islamic sources. This chapter also analyses the fundamental elements of what is considered a crime within Islamic jurisprudence. It examines the age of criminal responsibility and its interpretation by Islamic jurists. It presents the different stages of development and maturity as understood by the Sharia and juristic interpretations regarding the age of puberty in respect to the criminal age of responsibility and liability. It also explores whether there is any link between the age of a child and criminal accountability. The death penalty and other punishments under Islamic law are explored in the context of their applicability to juvenile offenders.

Part II of the book provides the State reports on each of the 11 States: Afghanistan, Egypt, Iran, Lebanon, Malaysia, Nigeria, Pakistan, Spain, Turkey, the United Arab Emirates, and the United Kingdom. Each report focuses on the legal background of criminal law concerning children in the Muslim States and the two non-Muslim States. The information is

---

[6] The term 'juvenile' includes anyone under the age of 18, and (commonly used for young people including children and adolescents). Beijing Rule 2.2.

comprised of the edited reports of the national rapporteurs, the findings of the national rapporteurs' interviews with stakeholders, as well as findings from the United Nations Committee for the Rights of the Child (CRC) reports and relevant NGO findings within the jurisdictions. This provides a comprehensive overview of the juvenile justice contexts. Key facts were gathered for each jurisdiction to enable a comparative study, which includes the relevant national laws relating to children within domestic criminal justice systems, the minimum age of criminal liability, the existence of special children's courts, the applicability of the death penalty to children, and the experience of children within the criminal system.

The final chapter sets out the conclusion of the research, and discusses the arguments raised in the State reports. This will also offer some comparative aspects and some recommendations for improving the protection of children in the criminal justice system.

CHAPTER 2

Juvenile Delinquency: An Overview of the Problem

I. INTRODUCTION

This chapter establishes the background to the following study concerning child delinquents. In order to provide an accurate overview of the problem, this chapter explores several core issues, notably the importance of setting a threshold age for child delinquents. Further, it examines the development of the juvenile justice system and issues regarding the death penalty. The research discusses the international legal protection and provides analysis of the various relevant provisions of international law. In this regard, it examines the United Nations Convention on the Rights of the Child (UNCRC) 1989 and other conventions, declarations and rules such as the International Covenant on Civil and Political Rights (ICCPR), the 1924 Declaration on the Rights of the Child, the 1959 Declaration on the Rights of the Child and the 1985 United Nations Standard Minimum Rules for the Administration of Juvenile Justice (known as the Beijing Rules), and the United Nations Rules for the Protection of Juveniles Deprived of their Liberty (the JDL Rules).

A. Juvenile Delinquency: the Importance of Setting a Threshold Age

1. Who is a juvenile delinquent?

Before looking into delinquency, it is appropriate to define the term 'juvenile'. One can define a juvenile as a child or young person, who due to their young age, if he or she commits an offence, may be legally tried in a manner different from the legal procedure adopted for adults.[1] According to the Beijing Rules, 'a juvenile offender is a child or young person who is alleged to have committed or who has been found to have committed an offence'.[2] Further, an 'offence is any behaviour (act or omission) that is punishable by law under the respective legal systems'.[3] It is difficult to define 'juvenile delinquency' with reference to law. Generally, laws are specific to serious offences committed by adults, such as robbery, murder, assault etc, whereas

---

[1] Beijing Rules, 2.2(a).   [2] Beijing Rules, 2.2(c).   [3] Beijing Rules, 2.2(b).

children are said to be delinquents when they are found guilty in a court of any offence under any law applicable to adults.[4]

In the Beijing Rules, consideration has been given to establishing the definitions of juvenile 'offence' and 'offender', although minimum and maximum age limits are left to the discretion of the States, influenced by the existing economic, social, political, cultural and legal systems of States. These differences have meant that a wide variety of minimum and maximum age limits, ranging from seven years to 18 years and in some cases, above 18 years, have been adopted. This age variation is due to different national legal systems which have evolved over centuries, which obviously cannot be ignored when establishing minimum standard rules at an international level. Such a variety seems inevitable when considering the different national legal systems, but should not diminish the impact of these Standard Minimum Rules.[5]

According to article 1 of the UNCRC, 'a child means every human being below the age of eighteen years unless under the law applicable to the child, majority is attained earlier'. The Beijing Rules define an offence as an act or behaviour of a person which is deemed punishable in the eyes of law under the legal system enforced in the State concerned. Keeping in mind the above internationally agreed age criteria in the Convention, this study considers that a 'juvenile or young person' is anyone under the legal adult age, that is, under the age of 18. Therefore, when a juvenile commits an offence, or is alleged to have done so, they are called a 'juvenile offender'.[6]

2. The importance of setting a threshold age

According to the above definition of a child under the UNCRC (unless under the law applicable to the child, majority is attained earlier) the age criteria set may differ from those prevailing in individual jurisdictions. For example, in the US the age of juvenility varies from state to state. In the District of Columbia and other Federal Districts, children under the age of 18 years are juveniles. Further, children under 16 years old are considered juveniles in New York, Connecticut, and North Carolina, among others. In Georgia, Illinois, Louisiana, Massachusetts, Michigan, Missouri, New Hampshire, South Carolina, Texas and Wisconsin, those under 17 years old are juveniles, yet in Wyoming, those under 19 years are considered juveniles.[7]

---

[4] RS Cavan, 'The Concepts of Tolerance and Contra Culture as Applied to Delinquency' in WE Thomon and JE Bynum, *Juvenile Delinquency: Classic and Contemporary Readings* (Allyn and Bacon, London, 1991) 11.

[5] Beijing Rules, Commentary to Rule 2.2.

[6] Beijing Rules, 2.2.

[7] See background of the development of the Juvenile Justice system at http://criminal.findlaw.com/crimes/juvenile-justice/juvenile-justice-background.html, accessed 10 April 2009.

These upper age limits are the age of criminal responsibility. This means that juveniles of various ages, ranging from seven to 19, are liable under the law for their acts and omissions. However, along with upper age limits, there is also a lower age limit that is under the age of six or seven when, due to lack of *mens rea* or criminal intent, a child cannot have criminal responsibility. This is the age when children or juveniles are considered unable to distinguish between right and wrong, or to use the Latin term, are considered *doli incapax*.

These upper and lower age limits are important when the court considers the jurisdiction for the purpose of trial, either under the juvenile court system or the adult court system. If the juvenile court assumes jurisdiction, then in most States, until the accused/defendant reaches his or her 21st birthday, they remain under this jurisdiction. However, criminologists and policy-makers are critical of the age criterion for the determination of juvenility and adulthood. They argue that the maturity level differs from person to person, as in some cases, 18-year-olds show more maturity than adults. Due to this 'maturity' criterion, the juvenile court judge has a wide discretion to waive juvenility and hand over the accused to the adult courts.[8] Age limits as a concept however reflect an understanding about childhood and children. Children above a certain age are assumed to possess the requisite attributes to hold them legally responsible for their actions, though courts are also assigned the task of assessing whether the child in question acted with intent. Therefore we can say that a child's age as well as their level of maturity along with additional considerations may contribute to the degree of criminal liability imposed on a child and the subsequent punishment they may face.[9]

Although the age of 'criminal responsibility' is managed differently in particular legal systems, those under the age of 'criminal responsibility' will not be held liable for the acts which, if committed by adults, would become offences. This legal term is kept in most legal systems; the age of criminal responsibility is specified and children above this age who commit an offence will be tried as adults.[10]

Some researchers dispute the notion that children under the age of criminal responsibility are presented as lacking in basic understanding and skills, or in other words as a group who do not understand criminal behaviour and cannot distinguish between right and wrong. They refuse to accept

---

[8] ibid. For further details about minimum age of criminal liability see D Cipriani, *Children's Rights and the Minimum Age of Criminal Responsibility: a Global Perspective* (Ashgate, Kent, 2009).

[9] Cipriani ibid 11.

[10] C McDiarmid, 'What Do They Know? Child-Defendants and the Age of Criminal Responsibility: A National Law Perspective' in K Arts and V Popovski (eds), *International Criminal Accountability and the Rights of Children* (Hague Academic Press, The Hague, Netherlands, 2006) 85.

it as a general rule and in individual cases in particular, and regard it as an excuse to exonerate individuals from criminal responsibility and liability.[11]

Similarly, to assign criminal responsibility is to determine that the juvenile is no longer subject to the provisions of juvenile justice system, and therefore he or she will be tried under the adult court or procedural system.[12] Undoubtedly, due to national particularities, cultural differences and more or less high sensibility of the laws to this problem, legislative models and legal systems are not homogeneous.[13]

In the US, once the minor in the juvenile justice system passes the age of criminal responsibility, he or she is subjected to a process known as the 'waiver procedure', where they go through the juvenile system and, on becoming an adult, receive the adult sentence for serious crimes because they then understand the offence. Other legal systems also have options to prosecute once the minor becomes of the age to assume criminal responsibility but is below the age where those proceedings are automatically applied.[14]

On the other hand, juveniles aged below the 'age of criminal responsibility' cannot be prosecuted for a crime. This immunity from prosecution is lifted once the child reaches the age of criminal liability, and the prosecution authorities are able to bring a case against an accused minor, for an offence committed when they were still a minor.[15] It is also a fact that very young children are not likely to understand the trial process and be able to defend themselves against a charge.

The European Court of Human Rights (ECtHR), in the case of Robert Thompson and Jon Venables[16] (juveniles convicted in the UK of murdering two-year-old James Bulger), held that the trial process for States party to the 1950 European Convention on Human Rights (ECHR) should be understandable to juvenile defendants.[17] The lack of advocacy skills of juveniles means that they are unable to answer to charges read to them effectively and therefore cannot adequately engage in trial without a lawyer.[18] Regarding the incapacity of committing an offence, (*doli incapax*) it was originally presumed that a child below the age of 14 was incapable of committing a crime within English law. Therefore it was the duty of the prosecution to prove, beyond reasonable doubt, that the defendant not only committed the offence (*actus reus*) but also possessed the relevant mental capacity or the element of fault, able to distinguish between right and wrong. The presumption of *doli incapax* is applied in South Africa and Australia. However, in English law it was abolished in 1998.[19] Therefore,

---

[11] ibid 86.   [12] ibid.
[13] R Ottenhof, 'Criminal Responsibility of Minors in National and International Legal Order—General Report (2004) 75 International Review of Penal Laws, 73.
[14] McDiarmid (n 10) 87.   [15] ibid.
[16] *V v United Kingdom*, Application No 24888/94, 30 EHRR 121, 16 December 1999.
[17] McDiarmid (n 10) 88.   [18] ibid.   [19] ibid 89.

the age of criminal responsibility can be defined as the age when children are able to know the difference between right or wrong. From the discussion, two questions are raised; when is a child considered to have the mental ability of committing a crime? At what age is he or she liable to be prosecuted and punished?[20]

The concept of a minimum age of criminal responsibility has been adopted almost universally. Key to this development has been the widespread acceptance of the reduced mental capability of children, and their mental, psychological, physical and emotional vulnerability. Given this assessment, the conventional adult criminal justice system is recognized as an inappropriate forum to address a child's behaviour.[21] The UNCRC can be seen as establishing the international consensus on the minimum age of criminal responsibility and a platform for States which seek to increase (or decrease) this age.[22] The Beijing Rules provides further guidance for States with regard to the setting of the minimum age of criminal responsibility. In that, for those legal systems which do adopt the notion of a minimum age of 'criminal responsibility' for juveniles, that age shall not be fixed 'too low', with consideration to 'the facts of emotional, mental and intellectual maturity'.[23] Supporters for the establishment of a minimum age of criminal responsibility note that if the age of criminal responsibility is fixed too low or if there is no lower age limit at all, the notion of responsibility would in itself become meaningless.[24] Efforts should therefore be made to agree on a reasonable lowest age limit that is applicable internationally.

The UN Committee on the Rights of the Child (CRC), when considering the question of minimum age, concluded that the failure of States to set a legal minimum age of criminal responsibility is a clear violation of the UNCRC. The CRC expressed this view in their Concluding Observations to the initial State Reports of Guatemala, Micronesia, Panama and Senegal, none of which have set a minimum age.[25] The second concern of the CRC regarding the minimum age of criminal responsibility was over States that have established an excessively low minimum age, which was in itself a violation of the UNCRC. In this regard, the CRC commented that setting an extremely low age concerning criminal responsibility highlighted that 'the State does not have a clear idea of what the criminal law can achieve with young children, and does not appreciate the harm it can cause'.[26] Hence, it is a legal and moral responsibility of States, after ratifying the UNCRC, to re-examine the minimum age for the criminal responsibility. In

---

[20] African Child Forum 'A Case for Raising Minimum Age of Criminal Responsibility' (May 2007) available at http://www.africanchildforum.org/Documents/age_of_cri_response. pdf, accessed 15 May 2009.
[21] ibid.   [22] ibid.
[23] Beijing, Rule 4(1).   [24] Beijing Rules Commentary to Rule 4(1).
[25] African Child Forum (n 20).   [26] ibid.

General Comment No 10 on Child Rights within Juvenile Justice, the CRC seemed to be inclined to consider the upper age of the *doli incapax* rule as helpful age of criminal responsibility and to observe this doctrine as a blanket measure for the improved protection of child rights.[27] The CRC also observed that '[q]uite a few States parties use two minimum ages of criminal responsibility'. In that case the children 'who at the time of the commission of the crime are at or above the lower minimum age but below the higher minimum age are assumed to be criminally responsible only if they have the required maturity in that regard'. However, the assessment of their mental 'maturity is left to the court, often without the requirement of involving a psychological expert.' The system of two minimum ages provides much discretion to the court and could affect the end of justice. Therefore, the CRC recommended that the States parties should provide clear guideline and recommendations 'regarding the minimum age of criminal responsibility'.[28]

In the case of Egypt, the CRC was not satisfied with level of protection to children and recommended that adequate protection needs to be provided for children who come into conflict with the law. Further, it pointed out the need for amendments to the Juveniles Act No 31 of 1974, to become compatible with the ICCPR, the Beijing Rules, the Riyadh Guidelines and the JDL Rules. The CRC further suggested taking into consideration the guiding principle: the best interest and dignity of the child and its role in society. As to the sentence, it recommended the deprivation of liberty as the last resort. It was suggested that rehabilitation, psychological care, and a positive approach focusing on social reintegration should be explored before this happens. Where offenders are sent to social care for rehabilitation, there is a need for a judge or an independent body to monitor the process.[29]

When considering the report of Libya, the CRC noted that the age of maturity is 10 for boys and nine for girls respectively, and the age of criminal responsibility is seven years, which is unacceptably low.[30] Further, the committee showed its concern as to the situation of administration of justice in Libya and its compatibility with articles 37 and 40 of UNCRC, Beijing Rules, Riyadh Guidelines and JDL Rules.[31]

The CRC responded to the UK's abolition of the doctrine and criticized the low minimum age of criminal responsibility, set at eight years in

---

[27] ibid; see also Committee on the Rights of the Child (44th Session) Geneva, 15 January–2 February 2007 Distr GENERAL CRC/C/GC/10, 25 April 2007, General Comment No 10 (2007) Children's rights in juvenile justice.

[28] Para 30.

[29] Concluding Observations of the Committee on the Rights of the Child: Egypt (18 February 1993) CRC/C/15/Add.5. (Concluding Observations/Comments) para 14.

[30] ibid para 16.   [31] ibid para 17.

Scotland and 10 years for the rest of the UK. It specifically voiced its concern about the abolition of the above-mentioned doctrine and recommended that the UK raise the age of criminal responsibility from 10 years.[32] For setting the minimum age for criminal responsibility, full consideration should be given to the mental capacity and maturity of a child. Once a child reaches 18 years they are subject to the full measure of the criminal justice system and not the juvenile justice system. Therefore, creating a juvenile justice system which recognizes and nurtures children's evolving capacities in turn creates a society that equips children for the world of adult rights and responsibilities. International standards already protect juveniles from excessive punishments and deprivation of liberty, maintaining the well-being of the child as paramount importance.[33]

Having a nuanced approach to criminal responsibility in respect to juveniles, factoring in their capability to understand the consequences of their behaviour to set a response that is reflective of both their developmental maturity and the actual offence committed, is a step to encourage children away from a life of criminality. Creating an environment in which children can understand and comprehend the consequences of their actions helps to develop a sense of responsibility and maturity in children that would make them less likely to re-offend. Conversely, by having a response to juvenile delinquency that is disproportionate to the mental faculties of the child or not responding at all to criminal activity, children are denied the opportunity to take personal responsibility for their actions. This is why the UNCRC states the need 'to ensure children are dealt with in a manner appropriate to their well-being and proportionate both to their circumstances'.[34]

B. The Development of the Juvenile Justice System

Shoemaker considers that 'the concern over youthful deviance stems from the thought that today's delinquent is tomorrow's criminal, if nothing is done to change the antisocial behaviour of youth'.[35]

Throughout human history, religion has played a large role in the foundation for the treatment of children within civil society—whether from the monotheistic religions of Judaism and Christianity in Europe and Islam in

---

[32] Committee on the Rights of the Child: 49th Session, Consideration of reports submitted by State Parties under Article 44 of the Convention, Concluding observations: United Kingdom of Great Britain and Northern Ireland, 20 October 2008, para 10, available at: http://www2.ohchr.org/english/bodies/crc/docs/AdvanceVersions/CRC.C.GBR.CO.4.pdf. accessed 4 March 2010; African Child Forum (n 20).

[33] Cipriani (n 9) 34.

[34] ibid 35.

[35] DJ Shoemaker, *Theories of Delinquency: An examination of Explanation of Delinquent Behavior* (OUP, New York, 2000) 4.

the Muslim world, or before that, the polytheistic religions of Babylonia, Greece, and Rome. Children were regarded as 'a proof of prosperity but not merely as a next generation'.[36] At the heart of the debate regarding juvenile justice are the different philosophical conceptualizations of childhood. Ideas regarding childhood delinquency and the punishment of young offenders vary significantly across history and across society. During the Middle Ages, the commonly-held position regarding child crime was that criminal and delinquent behaviour was caused by demonic possession. Later, classical criminology argued that 'people, adults and children, act according to free will ... and all persons, including children, are thought to weigh the costs and benefits of their proposed actions before they embark on them, and all persons, it is assumed, posses the ability to do so'[37] and 'all people possess the ability to reason and to act on their own volition'.[38] Pye notes that 'societies approached the treatment of delinquents from a common sense perspective, it is important to know that common sense exists in all cultures, but it is not the same from culture to culture'.[39]

In modern times there has been a development towards a more reformative conception of juvenile justice, which has been encouraged in large part by the prominence of an emerging view of childhood itself. Thomas Bernard typifies this understanding towards juveniles as 'vulnerable to the influences of other people, whether good or bad. They were "malleable" like clay—they could be shaped and moulded and formed into whatever was wanted. Once they grew up however, they "set" just like clay that was baked in the oven. The shape became permanent and, whether good or bad, it could no longer be changed.'[40]

The former prevalent view that people were largely unchangeable has given way to a newer conception that, while adults might be unchangeable, children were not yet 'fixed' into a set pattern and had an opportunity to reform. Shoemaker also notes the fact that the American legal system is based on the notion of 'free will' and individual responsibility. It recognizes that 'not all individuals have the same ability to reason the outcome of their behaviour, especially the mentally ill and children. This recognition has manifested itself in the development of a distinct juvenile justice system, and in the formulation of better policies of 'prevention and treatment of punishment'.[41]

Nevertheless, the classical idea of 'free will' has been challenged by criminology and in its place, a scientific determinism of deviance, criminologi-

---

[36] B Sims and P Preston (eds), *A Handbook of Juvenile Justice* (CRC Press, Taylor and Francis Group, 2006) 4.
[37] ibid 4–13.   [38] ibid 14.
[39] Cited in Sims and Preston (n 30) 20.
[40] TJ Bernard, *The Cycle of Juvenile Justice* (OUP, New York, 1992) 49.
[41] Shoemaker (n 29) 4.

cal research, and scientific study of offenders has sought to identify the factors that cause crime and delinquency. This school of thought posits that criminal behaviour was considered determined and not a choice. Therefore, instead of punishing the offenders, the central idea is to promote reform.[42]

Bernard's view is that modern conceptions on reform have given way to more classical interpretations. He notes the increase in referring to juveniles as 'hardened' criminals and not malleable, not able to be moulded and shaped into law abiding, God-fearing adults. This analysis rejects the conventional ideas about delinquency. In concluding his analysis, he argues that 'while the phenomenon of juvenile delinquency is still a part of our modern world, the idea of juvenile delinquency is under attack and could be abandoned in the near future.'[43]

The term 'juvenile justice' denotes the special procedures established by States for dealing with children. Juvenile courts deal with cases in which the accused is a juvenile, ie, a child.[44] The philosophy behind the operation of the first juvenile courts was that of *parens patriae*: that the State could act 'as a parent'. This legal doctrine of *parens patriae* first appeared in English Common law in the 1500s. It was used in the English courts for protection of Crown's interests regarding the property of orphans who had inherited an estate. In such cases, the role of the State was to take over and manage the property just like parents until the child gained majority.[45] Accordingly, for the best interest of the child, the courts held authority to intervene in matters when appropriate. With the passage of time, the philosophy of intervention became broader, becoming subject to debate in court. The explicit inclusion of child rights into the administration of juvenile justice is a relatively new development in international law.[46] Its first inclusion can be identified in the Geneva Declaration on the Rights of the Child, adopted on 26 September 1924 by the League of Nations. Rule 2 of the Declaration, among other protections, provide that: 'the delinquent child must be reclaimed', here, 'reclamation' seeming to point towards the rehabilitation and reintegration of child delinquents into society as law abiding subjects. Further, Rule 4 provided that a child must be 'protected against every form of exploitation'. These two provisions could be considered a good starting point towards further development of the protection of the rights of child

---

[42] J Rank Encyclopedia entry: 'Juvenile Justice: History and Philosophy The Progressive Juvenile Court available at http://law.jrank.org/pages/1490/Juvenile-Justice-History-Philosophy-progressive-juvenile-court.html#ixzz0IiJ7vTU9&C, accessed 22 June 2010.

[43] Bernard (n 34) 55.

[44] Juvenile Justice: Background at http://criminal.findlaw.com/crimes/juvenile-justice/juvenile-justice-background.html, accessed 10 July 2010.

[45] ibid; see also Cipriani (n 9) 6.

[46] G Van Bueren, *'Article 40, Child Criminal Justice': A Commentary on the United Nations Convention on the Rights of the Child* (Martinus Nijhoff Publishers, Leiden/Boston, 2006) 4.

delinquents.[47] However, the 1959 Declaration on the Rights of the Child contained no explicit provision concerning the protection of child delinquents,[48] though several of its principles could be invoked for the protection of such children. For example, Principle 8 of the Declaration provides that 'the child shall in all circumstances be among the first to receive protection and relief'.[49] In fact, particular provisions concerning the regulation of the administration of juvenile justice were first included in the International Covenant on Civil and Political Rights (ICCPR). Nevertheless, these provisions appear to be related with particular essential improvements 'rather than a move towards child centred criminal justice systems'.[50] Subsequently, a large number of States started to establish separate juvenile justice systems.[51] In order to offer extensive protection, many States have legislated specific laws regarding protection of the rights of juvenile offenders within the process of juvenile justice. For example, in Sri Lanka a statute on juvenile justice was introduced and described as a 'children's charter'[52] designed to stop exploitation of children within the commercial sector as well as affirm their central role in society. Likewise, in India the Juvenile Justice Act provides for decisions concerning deserted and abused children to be made by Juvenile Welfare Boards in a child-centred environment.[53]

At the international level then, a need was felt for a comprehensive legal framework for a juvenile justice system which could be used by States for seeking guidance in the setting up and proper working of their specific national juvenile justice systems.[54] With the aim of preparing such a baseline standard, in 1980 the Sixth UN Congress on the Prevention of Crime and the Treatment of Offenders was convened and in 1985, the General Assembly approved the UN Standard Minimum Rules (the Beijing Rules) for the Administration of Juvenile Justice. These rules offer a framework within which a national juvenile justice system should operate and the rights of children who come in conflict with the law are protected.[55] Efforts have also been made to explore proper methods to address the challenges confronted by legal and social systems, particularly the issue of fair treatment of juveniles in justice systems and helping to improve the system. For

---

[47] Geneva Declaration of the Rights of the Child (adopted 26 September 1924) League of Nations. http://www.unhchr.ch/html/intlinst.htm.

[48] Van Bueren (n 40) 4.

[49] Declaration of the Rights of the Child (adopted 20 November 1959) GA Res1386 (XIV) 14 UNGA OR Supp (No16) 19 UN Doc A/4354(1959).

[50] Van Bueren (n 40) 4.

[51] J Munice, *Youth and Crime* (2nd edn, Sage, London, 2004) 57.

[52] P Alston, *The Best Interests of the Child: Reconciling Culture and Human Rights* (Clarendon Press, Oxford, and UNICEF, 1994) 139. Provide reference also to the primary statute itself, if possible.

[53] ibid.

[54] Van Bueren (n 40) 4.

[55] ibid.

example, in December 2001 the Danish Institute of Human Rights (DIHR) collaborated with its NGO partners in Nepal, Malawi, Uganda and Tanzania to set up a juvenile justice platform.[56] It is clear that some efforts are being made at an international and national level, however it is also clear that much more still needs to be achieved to provide adequate protection to children.

C. Juveniles and the Death Penalty

Some States have abolished the death penalty outright, even for adult offenders. Many countries which still enforce death punishments, however, make provisions in their law to exclude child offenders from this punishment. A global survey of 145 States by Amnesty International on national death penalty laws found that until mid-1988, of 72 States and territories which retained the death penalty in their laws, half had provisions in national law which excluded child offenders. Similarly, 12 States that acceded to the ICCPR and the American Convention on Human Rights without reservation could be presumed to have excluded child offenders from the death penalty. Therefore, more than 84 States out of 145 exclude child offenders as a matter of law. [57]

In the same survey, 20 States—Barbados, Burma (Myanmar), Chile, China, Congo (Republic), Cyprus, Equatorial Guinea, Gambia, India, Israel, Mauritania, Morocco, Nigeria, South Korea, Thailand, Tonga, the US, Vietnam, Zaire (now the Democratic Republic of Congo) and Zimbabwe—were found to have an age limit of less than 18 years or no age limit for the death penalty. All those States except the US were signatories or parties to the UNCRC and most of them were parties to the ICCPR, the African Charter on the Rights and Welfare of the Child or the American Convention on Human Rights. However, Barbados and China have since increased the minimum age to 18 years.[58] It is also reported that Pakistan and Yemen have followed suit. According to the study, several States parties to the UNCRC who retained the death penalty did not enact explicit legislation that precluded its use against juvenile offenders. These States include Afghanistan, Argentina, Bangladesh, Burundi, the Democratic Republic of

---

[56] CF Pedersen, 'Support for the Implementation of Human Responses to Children In Conflict with Law in DIHR, Partner Countries' in E Jensen and J Jepson (eds), *Juvenile law Violators, Human Rights, and the Development of New Juvenile Justice Systems* (Hart, Oxford, 2006) 39.

[57] Amnesty International, 'The Exclusion of Child Offenders From the Death Penalty under General International Law' http://www.amnesty.org/ar/library/asset/ACT50/004/2003/en/dom-ACT500042003en.html, accessed 17 May 2009; Death Penalty Information Center http://www.deathpenaltyinfo.org/documents/FactSheet_7_6_2010.pdf last accessed 12 July 2010.

[58] ibid.

Congo, Egypt, India, Indonesia, Iran, Iraq, Malaysia, Morocco, Myanmar, Nigeria, North Korea, Saudi Arabia and the United Arab Emirates.[59]

The US, in its initial report under the ICCPR in 1994, while pointing towards article 6(5) of the ICCPR, recognized that in 'the United States the death penalty may be imposed on wrongdoers who were 16 or 17 years of age at the time of the offence.' The US report acknowledged that in the case of *Thompson v Oklahoma* (1988)[60] the Supreme Court ruled that imposing the death penalty on under-15s was unconstitutional. However, offenders aged 16 or 17 were not exempt in the case of *Stanford v Kentucky*, 1989[61] in which Kevin Stanford, who committed the crime when he was just 17, was sentenced to death,. [62]

In its comments on the sentencing of under-18s, the Human Rights Committee showed its concern

> about the excessive number of offenses punishable by the death penalty in a number of States, the number of death sentences handed down by courts, and the long stay on death row which, in specific instances, may amount to a breach of article 7 of the Covenant. The Committee urges the State party to take necessary steps so that over 18s are not sentenced to death for crimes which they committed when they were under 18.

Further, the HRC earlier noted the US's reservations with respect to article 6(5) of the ICCPR, and urged it to withdraw the reservation.[63] However in 2005, the Supreme Court abolished the death penalty for juveniles. The court held that the Eighth and Fourteenth Amendments forbid the execution of offenders who were under the age of 18 when their crimes were committed. [64]

In 1992, in a second periodic report under the ICCPR on the prohibition of the death penalty for juvenile offenders, Iran acknowledged that under article 49 of the Islamic Penal Law, 'children shall not bear penal responsibility for the offence they commit'. The CRC took note that a child was

---

[59] ibid.

[60] *Thompson v Oklahoma*, 487 US 815 (1988).

[61] *Stanford v Kentucky* 492 US 361 (1989); Amnesty International, 'United States of America: Indecent and Internationally Illegal—the Death Penalty Against Child Offenders' AMR 51/143/2002, September 2002, http://www.amnesty.org/en/library/asset/AMR51/143/2002/en/060e0781-d7e8-11dd-9df8-936c90684588/amr511432002en.pdf, 1–4.

[62] Amnesty International, ibid.

[63] Human Rights Committee (53rd Session) Comments on United States of America, UN Doc CCPR/C/79/Add 50 (1995) paras 16, 31, at http://www1.umn.edu/humanrts/hrcommittee/US-ADD1.htm

[64] Death Penalty Information Centre at www.deathpenaltyinfo.org, accessed 11 May 2009. *Roper v Simmons*, 543 US 551 (2005) at http://www.deathpenaltyinfo.org/u-s-supreme-court-roper-v-simmons-no-03-633.

defined as a person who has not attained religious maturity. [65] Thus, criminal 'majority' is to be determined according to Islamic law. The Iranian criminal code does not set any chronological age; instead it refers to the concept of religious maturity. The age of criminal 'maturity' is set by the Civil Code, which fixes the age at 15 for males and nine for females. [66] The Committee is seriously concerned that respect for the inherent right to life of a person under 18 is not guaranteed under the law. [67] According to Amnesty International, Iran executed three child offenders in 1992 and one each in 1990, 1999, 2000, and 2001. [68] Therefore, the CRC, in its concluding observation in 2000, referred to articles 6 and 37 of the Convention and urged Iran not to impose the death penalty on under-18s and also to enact law to abolish the death penalty, because the execution of under 18s is incompatible with the UNCRC. The CRC also noted that 'in all actions concerning children, the general principle of the best interests of the child contained in article 3 of the Convention is not a primary consideration' in Iran. [69]

Likewise, in the case of Saudi Arabia, while considering the 'right to life' the CRC expressed its concern and commented that since 'the age of majority is not defined' it was therefore possible that the death penalty could be imposed on under-18s or for offences committed while they were under 18 years old, which contravenes article 6 and 37(a) of the UNCRC. The CRC urged Saudi Arabia to stop executing child offenders and enact laws to abolish the death penalty for under-18s. Further, the CRC recommends that 'the State party review its legislation and administrative measures to ensure that article 3 (regarding the best interest of the child) of the Convention is duly reflected therein and taken into consideration'. [70]

---

[65] Concluding Observations of the Committee on the Rights of the Child: Iran (Islamic Republic of) 28/06/2000. CRC/C/15/Add.123 (Concluding Observations/Comments) (24th Session) paras 19, 29, 30.

[66] Ottenhof (n 13) 57.

[67] Concluding Observations of the Committee on the Rights of the Child: Iran (Islamic Republic of) 28/06/2000. CRC/C/15/Add.123. (Concluding Observations/Comments) para 27, at http://www.unhchr.ch/tbs/doc.nsf/(Symbol)/4448a41dab88b4da802569000034deb0? Opendocument.

[68] Amnesty International, 'The Exclusion of Child Offenders From the Death Penalty under General International Law' http://www.amnesty.org/ar/library/asset/ACT50/004/2003/en/dom-ACT500042003en.html accessed 17 May 2009; D Weissbrodt et al, 'International Human Rights: Law, Policy and Process' (3rd ed 2001) 709–710.

[69] Concluding Observations of the Committee on the Rights of the Child: Iran (Islamic Republic of) (28 June 2000) CRC/C/15/Add.123. (Concluding Observations/Comments) para 19,25, 29,30, available at http://www.unhchr.ch/tbs/doc.nsf/(Symbol)/4448a41dab88b4da 802569000034deb0?Opendocument.

[70] Concluding Observations of the Committee on the Rights of the Child (26th Session) Saudi Arabia, UN Doc CRC/C/15/Add.148,(2001) paras 27, 26, 28, 3–34, available at http://www.wfrt.net/humanrts/crc/saudiarabia2001.html.

With Pakistan, the CRC noted with concern the system of administration of juvenile justice and its incompatibility with articles 37, 39, 40 of the UNCRC, the Beijing Rules, the Riyadh Guidelines and United Nations Rules for the Protection of Juveniles Deprived of their Liberty, 1990 (JDL Rules).[71]

According to Amnesty International, despite the Juvenile Justice System Ordinance (JJSO) 2000 and its enforcement since 1 July 2000, in practice Pakistan under-18s are sentenced to death.[72] In contrast, the death penalty has been abolished in the UK. On 27 January 1999, the UK signed Protocol 6 of the European Convention on Human Rights (ECHR) and formally ratified it on 27 May 1999. Nevertheless, for committing very serious offences like murder, there is a mandatory sentence of detention even for under-18s.[73]

In response to a global campaign for a world free of executions, several other States have also abolished the death penalty. In June, the Philippines abolished the death penalty, being the 88th State to do so. Likewise, Moldova has ratified international treaties concerning the abolition of the death penalty and, to formalize the abolition, has amended its Constitution.

Despite this, in 2006 around 3,861 people were sentenced to death in 55 States and in some States, children have been executed.[74] The above cases of executions of juveniles under 18 are clear violations of various instruments, not only at international level but also at regional and domestic levels. This situation prevails, despite the fact that in October 2002 the Inter-American Commission on Human Rights (IACHR) declared that the prohibition of death penalty for under-18s should be a norm of customary international law and has also been acknowledged as a norm of *jus cogens*.[75] Customary international law is described in article 38 of the Statute of the International Court of Justice as 'international custom, as evidence of a general practice accepted as law', and a rule of customary international law is binding on all States. [76] Further, according to the IACHR:

---

[71] Concluding Observations of the Committee on the Rights of the Child: Pakistan (25 April 1994). CRC/C/15/Add.18. (Concluding Observations/Comments) para 20.

[72] Amnesty International (n 55).

[73] The Consolidated 3rd and 4th Periodic Report to the UN Committee on the Rights of the Child (2007), UK Government, Department for Children, Schools and Families, 174 para 8.120 and 121.

[74] Amnesty International, 'The Death Penalty' available at http://report2007.amnesty.org/eng/A-year-in-campaigning/The-death-penalty accessed 17 May 2009.

[75] Inter- American Commission Report on Human Rights No. 101/03CASE 12.412 Napoleon Beazley United States, December 29, 2003, paras 21, 84, at http://www.cidh.org/annualrep/2003eng/usa.12412.htm accessed 12 September 2010; Press Release No 7/02, IACHR calls upon the United States to postpone execution of juvenile offender Alexander Williams available at http://www.cidh.org/comunicados/english/2002/press7.02.htm accessed 12 September 2010.

[76] Amnesty International, 'The Death Penalty' (n 74).

As a jus cogens norm, this proscription binds the community of States' and therefore 'cannot be validly derogated from, whether by treaty or by the objection of a state, persistent or otherwise'. [77]

In addition to this, proper enforcement of the above-mentioned covenants and other instruments must be promoted in domestic law,[78] as this will make it possible to raise the standards of protection of children who come into conflict with the law.

II. INTERNATIONAL LEGAL PROTECTION AND JUVENILE OFFENDERS

A. Protection Offered Under International Law

International law has several instruments, as well as relevant provisions in certain conventions and basic principles, which provide a legal framework and foundation for the child criminal justice system.

1. Prevention of child delinquency and the UN Guidelines

First of all, the United Nations Guidelines for the Prevention of Juvenile Delinquency provide that 'the prevention of juvenile delinquency' should be an 'essential part of crime prevention in society'. For proper implementation of the present Guidelines, in accordance with national legal systems, the well-being of young persons from their early childhood should be the focus of any preventive programme, because through 'engaging in lawful, socially useful activities, and adopting a humanistic orientation towards society,' juveniles may build up 'non-criminogenic attitudes'.[79] The Guidelines call 'for progressive delinquency prevention policies and the systematic study and the elaboration of measures' and the 'provision of opportunities, in particular educational opportunities, to meet the varying needs of young persons and to serve as a supportive framework for safeguarding the personal development of all young persons, particularly those who are demonstrably endangered or at social risk and are in need of special care and protection'. These guidelines encourage the development of specialized philosophies and approaches for delinquency prevention, on the basis of laws, processes, institutions, facilities and a service delivery network aimed at reducing the motivation, need and opportunity for, or

[77] Inter-American Commission Report on Human Rights No. 101/03CASE 12.412 (n 79) para 85.

[78] Ottenhof (n 13) 73.

[79] Fundamental principles, 1–5, United Nations Guidelines for the Prevention of Juvenile Delinquency (The Riyadh Guidelines) Adopted and proclaimed by General Assembly resolution 45/112 of 14 December 1990.

conditions giving rise to, the commission of infractions. Nevertheless, 'for the interest of the young person official intervention could also be perused'.[80]

2. Protection of juveniles who come into conflict with the law

However, if a child comes into conflict with the law, the UNCRC and the Beijing Rules provide a sound foundation for the protection of children in the administration of criminal justice.[81] In fact, the Beijing Rules were a direct response to a call made by the Sixth United Nations Congress on the Prevention of Crime and the Treatment of Offenders, which convened in 1980. The Rules are the first international legal instrument to provide detailed norms regarding the administration of juvenile justice, with a development-oriented approach for child rights.[82]

The Beijing Rules operate within the framework of two other sets of rules: The United Nations Guidelines for the Prevention of Juvenile Delinquency (the Riyadh Guidelines) and the JDL Rules. These three sets of rules provide guidance for systematic progression. The Riyadh Guidelines provide social policies that should be applied for preventing and protecting young people from offending. The regulations regarding the establishment of a progressive justice system for juvenile offenders is provided by the Beijing Rules. Rules about the protection of fundamental rights and establishing measures for social re-integration of juveniles, once deprived of their liberty, whether in prison or other institutions, are provided by JDL Rules.[83] The JDL Rules 'establish minimum standards accepted by the United Nations for the protection of juveniles deprived of their liberty in all forms, consistent with human rights and fundamental freedoms, with a view to counteracting the detrimental effects of all types of detention and to fostering integration in society'.[84] They are also 'designed to serve as convenient standards of reference and to provide encouragement and guidance to professionals involved in the management of the juvenile justice system'.[85] According to the JDL Rules 'the juvenile justice system should uphold the rights and safety and promote the physical and mental well-being of juveniles. Imprisonment should be used as a last resort'.[86]

---

[80] ibid.
[81] Van Bueren (n 40) 11.
[82] G Van Bueren and A-M Tootell, United Nations Standard Minimum Rules for the Administration of Juvenile Justice, Beijing Rules, Defence for Children International, http://child-abuse.com/childhouse/childrens_rights/dci_be29.html, accessed 15 June 2010.
[83] ibid.
[84] A/RES/45/113,68th plenary meeting 14 December 1990 Rule 3.
[85] Rule 5.
[86] United Nations Rules for the Protection of Juveniles Deprived of their Liberty. Adopted by General Assembly resolution 45/113of 14 December 1990.

Nevertheless, the Rules are recommendatory in nature—they are merely guidelines and have no legally binding force.

At the international level, the UNCRC is a great legal and political achievement because it acknowledges a child not only as an object of law but also a subject of law, with individual rights. Further, the UNCRC recognizes that issues related to children should be placed at the centre of the mainstream human rights agenda—one could even consider it the *Magna Carta* for children's rights.[87]

The Beijing rules provide that, with the aim of protecting juveniles and the maintenance of a peaceful order in society, juvenile justice should be included as an essential 'part of the national development process of each State, within a comprehensive framework of social justice for all juveniles'.[88] Further, for the proper implementation of these Rules, consideration should be given to the socio-economic, cultural conditions prevailing in each Member State.[89] Furthermore, these Standard Minimum Rules should be equally applied to juvenile offenders, without any distinction of 'colour, sex, language, religion, political or other opinions, national or social origin, property, birth or other status'.[90] While explaining the aims of juvenile justice, the Beijing Rules provide that the juvenile justice system shall promote the well-being of juveniles and 'ensure that any reaction to juvenile offenders shall always be in proportion to the circumstances of both the offenders and the offence'. The rule provides two of the main objectives of juvenile justice. The first is related to the development of the well-being of the juvenile, while the second is related to 'the principle of proportionality'. It denotes that while considering the cases of juveniles, consideration should be given to the gravity of the offence as well as the personal circumstances of the juvenile. The rule urges that in cases of juvenile delinquency and crime, the reaction has to be just and fair.[91]

The Beijing Rules are recommendatory and not binding per se. Nevertheless, several of the fundamental principles have been incorporated into that Convention and they are expressly referred to in its Preamble. Further, certain principles enunciated within the Rules have also been encompassed in provisions of the UNCRC, a global treaty which is binding on all States Parties.[92]

---

[87] D Fottrell, *One Step Forward or Two Steps Sideways? Assessing the first Decade of the Children's Convention on the Rights of the Child, in Revisiting Children's Rights* (Kluwer Law International, The Hague, 2000) 1.
[88] Beijing Rule 1.4.
[89] Beijing Rule 1.5.
[90] Beijing Rule 2.1.
[91] Beijing Rule 5.1.
[92] Van Bueren and Tootell (n 80).

3. The right to fair trial and juvenile offenders

According to the UNCRC, States Parties should ensure that every child who has been implicated in or accused of a crime, or has violated penal law be 'treated in a manner consistent with the promotion of the child's sense of dignity and worth'. Further, special consideration should be given to age and 'the desirability of promoting the child's reintegration and the child's assuming a constructive role in society'.[93] With the aim of preventing juvenile delinquency, the UN has adopted guidelines which seek to assist children developing a sense of responsibility and a sense of belonging, resulting in the ability to assume a constructive role in society. Therefore, the Human Rights Committee, under the ICCPR, should interpret the term 'rehabilitation' as the means by which a child can assume a constructive role in society, and the States parties to the ICCPR and UNCRC should follow this example. In addition, States which are not party to the ICCPR or the UNCRC should be urged to adopt this 'higher and uniform standard of protection and rehabilitation'.[94]

In this regard, the approach adopted by the regional human rights tribunals could be very helpful for the UNCRC. For example, in the case of *Villagran Morales and others v Guatemala (1999)*, the Inter-American Court of Human Rights recommended that in cases where the offence is committed by minors, substantial efforts should be made to 'guarantee their rehabilitation in order to allow them to play a constructive and productive role in society'. Likewise, with regard to duties and responsibilities to children, Judge Morenilla of the European Court of Human Rights in *Nortier v The Netherlands (1993)*, while assessing the preamble and article 40(3) of the UNCRC, held that criminal justice systems dealing with children should be able to provide the required protection and assistance so that offenders know what they owe to the community and also how to live as individuals in a society. Further, to achieve all this, it is important for the authorities and institutions who deal with the juvenile offenders to further develop and reform the law and procedures in this regard.[95]

Additionally, States should specifically ensure that a child cannot be accused 'or recognized as having infringed the penal law by reason of acts or omissions that were not prohibited by national or international law at the time they were committed'. In this regard, full consideration should be given 'to the relevant provisions of international instruments'.[96] This non-retroactivity principle of criminal law can also be found in the other international instruments, for example, in article 15(1) of the ICCPR.[97]

---

[93] Convention on the Rights of the Child (adopted 20 November 1989, entered into force 2 September 1989) GA Res 44/25, annex 44 UN GOAR Supp (No 49) UN Doc. A/44/49,CRC 1577 UNTS 43, reprinted in 28 ILM, art 40(1).

[94] Van Bueren (n 40) 12–13.   [95] ibid 13.

[96] Art 40 (2) (a).   [97] Van Bueren (n 40) 13–14.

According to the UNCRC, a child accused of violating criminal law should be provided with the minimum guarantee of being 'presumed innocent until proven guilty according to law'.[98] This provision provides protection against frivolous charges and the benefit of doubt will go in favour of the juvenile. Further, the accused should be informed immediately about the charge, and if it is more suitable then the information about the charge or allegations can be passed on through parents or legal guardians. Furthermore, accused juveniles should be provided with the opportunity for seeking legal assistance through a lawyer.[99]

As explicitly mentioned, the guarantees provided in article 40 are the minimum guarantees. Therefore, the protections offered by the other international and regional human rights instruments equally apply to children and adults.[100] Accordingly, the principle of equality before the law will apply to children as well as adults on the same footing. According to the UNCRC, matters concerning juveniles should be determined 'without delay'. Article 10(2) (b) of the ICCPR also provides the concept of undue delay. Further, the UK Privy Council determined that, in the case of a juvenile, the provision concerning 'without delay' in the ECHR had to be interpreted in the light of the UNCRC and the Beijing Rules.[101] The relevant Beijing Rule is that: 'Detention pending trial shall be used only as a measure of last resort and for the shortest period of time.'[102]

However this rule is often violated by many States. For example, according to Amnesty International's report, many juveniles have been detained, pre-trial, for more than two years in Pakistan. Undue delay means children are held in so-called pre-trial for years, in explicit breach of international as well as national laws. The Pakistan Juvenile Justice System Ordinance (JJSO) provides that trials concerning juveniles should be decided within a period of four months.[103] In reality, over three quarters of children in detention are on pre-trial remand.[104]

According to the Beijing Rules, 'upon the apprehension of a juvenile, her or his parents or guardian shall be immediately notified'. However, in cases where 'immediate notification is not possible, the parents or guardian shall be notified within the shortest possible time thereafter'.[105] The provision does not set any specific time limit; therefore, setting the time has been left to the discretion of the authorities concerned, who must set the criterion of reasonableness according to the circumstances of each case. For example, in

---

[98] Art 40 (2) (b) (i).
[99] Art 40 (2) (b)(ii).
[100] Van Bueren (n 40) 12–13.
[101] Van Bueren (n 40) 19.
[102] 13(1) for the details regarding the right to fair trial, see FZ Mansoor 'Reassessing Packer in the Light of International Human Rights Norms' (2005) 4 Connecticut Public Interest Law Journal 2, 287–307 available at http://lsr.nellco.org/uconn/cpilj/papers/32/, accessed 15 June 2010.
[103] S 4 (6).
[104] Amnesty International (n 55).
[105] Beijing Rule, 10.1

Epeli Seniloli Anor v Semi Voliti,[106] where a 14-year-old-boy was hand-cuffed to a post at the police station and not informed of reason for his arrest, the Fijian High Court considered the act as false imprisonment and violation of article 27 of the Constitution as well as the UNCRC and awarded aggravated damages as well as punitive damages.[107] However, it is worth noting that a juvenile's right to have his/her parents or legal guardians informed of the charges is linked to the phrase 'if appropriate'. This check is an extra measure and a safeguard to ensure that the best interests of child is of first and foremost importance. However, in cases where in the opinion of the authorities such information might not be in the best interest of a child, the State Party has to consider the desire of the child. [108]

The authority having charge of the juvenile has to put the case before a neutral authority or judicial body for a fair hearing, set up for this purpose, and he or she might be provided with legal and other assistance as may be needed, keeping in mind the best interests of the juvenile, along with other factors, such as 'age or situation'.[109] Article 40 of the UNCRC admits the right to fair trial of children who come into conflict with the law. In *Nortier v Netherlands*, which was heard before the European Court of Human Rights, Judge Walsh said '[j]uveniles facing criminal charges and trial are as fully entitled as adults to benefit from all the Convention requirements for a fair trial. Fair trial and proper proof of guilt are absolute conditions precedent'.[110] Judge Morenilla, while referring to the UNCRC and article 25 of the Universal Declaration of Human Rights, highlighted that the child should be entitled to additional protection beyond the guarantees set out in the European Convention of Human Rights and stated that 'minors are entitled to the same protection of their fundamental rights as adults but that their developing state of personality—and consequently their limited social responsibility—should be taken into account in applying article 6 of the Convention'. [111]

The above-mentioned provision is further strengthened by article 37(d) of the UNCRC which provides that 'every child deprived of his or her liberty shall have the right to prompt access to legal and other appropriate assistance'. Further, the Beijing Rules provides that the 'judge or other competent official or body shall, without delay, consider the issue of release'.[112] The phrase used in the UNCRC is 'appropriate assistance'. However, in practice in a number of cases it was found that serious flaws in the provision of legal assistance cause prolonged detention of children. It

---

[106] Epeli Seniloli Attorney-General of Fiji v Semi voliti, On behalf of Poasa Ravea Oawaoawa Voliti HIGH COURT, Fiji (Appellate Jurisdiction) Civil Appeal No: HBA 0033 of 1999
[107] Van Bueren (n 40) 15.   [108] ibid.
[109] Art 40 (2) (b)(iii).   [110] Van Bueren (n 40) 18.
[111] ibid.   [112] Beijing Rule, 10.2.

is not necessarily the situation that these juveniles are initially treated as criminals. For example, in Pakistan, under the Juvenile Justice System Ordinance (JJSO) juveniles are eligible to be provided legal assistance by the State. In this regard the arresting officer is duty bound to tell the juveniles and their parents about free legal aid.[113] Nevertheless, according to Amnesty International, despite this specific and clear provision, there is ignorance about this within the police system and even in the judiciary. Moreover, JJSO section 3(2) intends to provide expert legal assistance, by requiring five years practical experience to represent juveniles. However, the on-the-ground reality is that lawyers with such experience generally avoid taking up State cases, because of the low fees. Therefore, the cases attract those lawyers who do not have five years experience or NGOs and inexperienced lawyers. Another factor is that in State cases, the costs of the case are payable after the case is finally decided, which can take several months or years.[114] Therefore, emphasizing the quality of representation rather than legal or non-legal qualifications seems to be much more effective. Since the main objective of this provision is that a juvenile should feel confident, satisfied and less exposed to stress, it is preferable that representation by a well informed trained independent professional is available.[115]

Apart from admitting the right to legal representation, the UNCRC also sets out the right of a child 'who is capable of forming his or her own views' to freely express such views, particularly in matters which affect him or her. Further 'the views of the child' should be duly considered 'in accordance with the age and maturity'.[116] With this aim, 'the child shall in particular be provided the opportunity to be heard in any judicial and administrative proceedings affecting the child, either directly, or through a representative or an appropriate body, in a manner consistent with the procedural rules of national law'.[117] The same right has been provided by article 14(2)(d) of the ICCPR.[118] According to the UNCRC, the procedure followed creating these substantive rights have been consistent with the national laws of individual States.

According to the UNCRC, the case has to be presented before a judicial body or authority. Hence, the provision stresses the competence, impartiality and independent nature of the proceedings rather than that the body determining the charge must be judicial. Further, the structure of the body is not a main concern, as long as the procedure adopted by the authority is consistent with the protections offered by the UNCRC.[119] The UNCRC admits that there are differences among States in the types of juvenile

---

[113] S 3(1).
[115] Van Bueren (n 40) 19.
[117] ibid.
[119] ibid 16.

[114] Amnesty International (n 55).
[116] CRC art 12(1)(2).
[118] Van Bueren (n 40) 20.

proceedings, which could make it difficult to determine the criminal liability and responsibility of juveniles. For example, the juvenile proceedings system in Scandinavian States consists of administrative bodies, while those in the US evolved from the adult court system.[120] There are States that do not have a specialized juvenile court for juveniles involved in serious crimes; child defendants are instead tried in adult courts and are even subject to the same laws as adults, except perhaps when it comes to sentencing, where they would face a reduced penalty with respect to the age of the child. In contrast, for petty crimes many jurisdictions operate specialized child courts.[121]

Similarly, in some States, due to the lack of juvenile courts or because of difficulty in accessing such courts in far-flung cities, the criminal courts also have jurisdiction over juvenile offences. It is pertinent to note that, although juvenile codes are applied, in criminal trials the judge considers juveniles cases no differently than adult criminal cases. Hence no leeway is given to take into consideration the fact that defendants are children. Further, the CRC has often pointed out the shortcomings on the part of the State parties with regard to failing to make provisions regarding the minimum age and to take steps towards the reintegration of the child delinquents, in the reports submitted under article 40.[122] For example, regarding the second periodic report of Pakistan, the CRC welcomed the promulgation of the Juvenile Justice System Ordinance (JJSO, 2000). It nevertheless observed:

> [The] high number of children in prisons, who are detained in poor conditions, often together with adult offenders and thus vulnerable to abuse and ill-treatment. Further, the Committee is deeply concerned about the reports of juvenile offenders sentenced to death and executed, which have also occurred after the promulgation of the Juvenile Justice System Ordinance.[123]

---

[120] ibid. For example in the England and Wales for an 'indictable' or 'eitherway' offences juveniles are tried within the adult Crown Court. Juvenile defendants may even face the same charges as adult such as life imprisonment if the juvenile is considered sufficiently dangerous and sentencing is to protect members of the public see Criminal Justice Act 2003, s 226; http://www.statutelaw.gov.uk/content.aspx?LegType=All+Legislation&title=Criminal+Justice +Act+2003&searchEnacted=0&extentMatchOnly=0&confersPower=0&blanketAmendment =0&sortAlpha=0&TYPE=QS&PageNumber=1&NavFrom=0&parentActiveTextDocId=902 928&ActiveTextDocId=903219&filesize=4718. Also http://www.yjb.gov.uk/en-gb/yjs/Courts/ CrownCourt.htm, accessed 15 June 2010.

[121] ibid. For example in the England and Wales for an 'indictable' or 'eitherway' offences juveniles are tried within the adult Crown Court. Juvenile defendants may even face the same charges as adult such as life imprisonment if the juvenile is considered sufficiently dangerous and sentencing is to protect members of the public; see Criminal Justice Act 2003, s 226 (n 120).

[122] Van Bueren (n 40) 16–17.

[123] Concluding Observations of the Committee on the Rights of the Child: Pakistan CRC/C/15/Add.217 (27 October 2003) (Concluding Observations/Comments) para 80.

In Pakistan, the minimum age for criminal responsibility is set at seven years of age;[124] this means that any children above seven are presumed to be able to understand the legal repercussions of their actions and so can be charged in accordance with the law. However, section 83 of the Pakistan Penal Code (PPC) states: 'Nothing is an offence which is done by a child above seven years of age and under twelve, who has not attained sufficient maturity of understanding to judge of the nature and consequences of his conduct on that occasion'. Hence, if a child is between seven to 12 years of age, the judge in authority has the discretion to establish that the child has attained 'sufficient maturity' before he or she can be charged and stand trial as an accused adult. The CRC pointed out that a minimum age of seven is extremely low and recommended that it be raised to internationally acceptable standards. [125]

Further, the UNCRC provides that an accused juvenile may not be forced to stand witness or confess guilt, neither 'be compelled to examine or have examined adverse witnesses and [has the right] to obtain the participation and examination of witnesses on his or her behalf under conditions of equality'.[126]

Furthermore, the Beijing Rules also provide basic procedural safeguards regarding the rights of the juveniles, such as:

> [T]he presumption of innocence, the right to be notified of the charges, the right to remain silent, the right to counsel, the right to the presence of a parent or guardian, the right to confront and cross-examine witnesses and the right to appeal to a higher authority shall be guaranteed at all stages of proceedings.[127]

In the Commentary of the Beijing Rules it has been explained that at international level there are recognized standards for a fair and just trial, which are embodied in human rights documents. On the one hand, human rights documents such as article 11 of the UDHR and article 14(2) of the ICCPR stress on the presumption of innocence, and also prohibit compulsion to testify. However, ironically, if the accused juvenile remains silent or refuses to give an answer, this may lead to a negative inference against the juvenile while he or she is in custody. In this regard, a Defence for Children International study highlighted maltreatment during the time juveniles were in custody.[128] Although article 37 of the UNCRC prohibits the use of torture or other cruel, inhumane or degrading treatment or punishment on children/juveniles, according to Amnesty International there is evidence of

---

124 S 82, The Pakistan Penal Code, 1860 (PPC).   125 Amnesty International (n 55).
126 Art 40 (b)(iv).   127 Beijing Rule 7(1)(Rights of Juveniles).
128 Van Bueren (n 40) 21.

arresting officers using torture against juveniles. In many States police stations' culture is made or developed for hardened adult criminals. However, children, unfortunately, also go through the same experience as adults, at the hands of police officers, who do not have training in dealing with children.[129] With regard to this situation, the Human Rights Committee recommended that the national laws of each State should guarantee that any evidence secured by breaching international human rights standards should be made inadmissible in court. Therefore, States, if sincere, should incorporate the Beijing Rules to recognize the right of silence on the part of children.[130]

The UNCRC provides that in cases where it has been decided that a juvenile is found breaking the criminal law, they have the full right to get the decision reviewed by a 'higher competent, independent and impartial authority or judicial body according to law'.[131] Moreover, a juvenile has a right to receive 'the free assistance of an interpreter' if he or she is not able to understand the court language.'[132] This is an important issue in multilingual societies, where the official language may be different from the commonly spoken languages. Therefore, ICCPR article 14(3)(a) requires that the accused juvenile be informed of the charge against him in the language he understands.[133] Otherwise, all proceedings against the juvenile will be legally null and void from the start.[134]

The UNCRC also provides that the privacy of a juvenile should be protected and fully respected at all stages of the proceedings.[135] Similar protection is also offered by the Beijing Rules, which provide for the aim of protecting juveniles from harm 'by undue publicity or by the process of labelling'. Their 'right to privacy shall be respected at all stages' of the proceedings and principally, any 'information that may lead to the identification of a juvenile offender' may not be published.

In the Commentary to the Beijing Rules, it is explained that this rule is important because juveniles are particularly susceptible to stigmatization. In fact the Rule seems to emphasize the significance of protecting young children from the deleterious effects of publication in the mass media, for example, their names being associated with being a juvenile delinquent, accused or convicted. The deleterious effects which arise from the permanent identification of a young person as 'delinquent' or 'criminal' have been established by criminological research into labelling processes.[136] In order to further strengthen the privacy provision, the rules provide that records concerning 'juvenile offenders shall be kept strictly confidential' and may not be disclosed to third parties. Further, only 'the persons who are directly

---

129 Amnesty International (n 55).
131 Art 40 (b)(v).
133 Van Bueren (n 39) 9.
135 Van Bueren (n 39) 9.

130 Van Bueren (n 39) 21.
132 CRC Art 40 (b)(vi).
134 Art 40 (b)(vii).
136 Beijing Rules, Rule 8.

concerned with the disposition of the case at hand or other duly authorized persons' should have access to the record. Additionally, the use of such records is also not allowed in a subsequent proceeding against the same juvenile as an adult for another case. This rule tries to retain a balance between differing interests concerning the records and files of the police, prosecution and other authorities on the one hand and the interests of the young offender on the other.[137] Hence the previous character of a child delinquent cannot be used as evidence in a subsequent case as an adult.

To ensure the rights of a litigant and to protect them from arbitrary decisions, a public hearing of the case is extremely important.[138] In this regard, the ICCPR provides that in the determination of any criminal charges everyone shall be 'entitled to a fair and public hearing by a competent, independent and impartial tribunal'. Further, 'the press and the public may be excluded from all or part of a trial' due to reasons of morality and public order, or national security and the interests of justice. Any judgement rendered in a criminal case or in a suit at law shall be made public except where the interest of juvenile persons otherwise requires.[139] Hence, in a case where the security of a juvenile is at risk, a trial could be held in private. Similarly, the interest of the juvenile would have priority at every step. Therefore, the proceedings or judgment will be made public if it is in the interest of juvenile; if not, they should remain private. In the case of James Bulger's murder, it was stated by the Commission that the public trial of the accused, along with enormous media coverage, could threaten the fairness of the trial and be prejudicial to fact-finding.[140] Further, a public trial might have consequences that extend beyond the childhood of the juveniles involved. Therefore, juveniles convicted of murder can be granted lifelong anonymity. However, the main reason for keeping them anonymous was the severity of threat to their lives if the identity of those juveniles was ever exposed.[141] Hence, in the best interest of the children involved, their identity was not exposed.

There are a number of reasons why children's best interests are to be primary consideration. Article 40(3) of the UNCRC specifically calls on State Parties to work specifically to establish child-centred laws, procedures, authorities and institutions in order to deal with offences in which children are involved; further, to establish a minimum age for criminal

---

[137] Beijing Rules, Rule 21.
[138] P Van Dijk and GJH Van Hoof, *Theory and Practice of the European Convention on Human Rights* (2nd edn, Kluwer Law and Taxation Publishers, 1990) 325; Mansoor (n 96) 296–297 available at http://lsr.nellco.org/uconn/cpilj/papers/32, accessed 15 June 2010.
[139] International Convenant on Civil and Political Rights (adopted 16 December 1966, entered into force 23 March 1976) 999 UNTS 171, art 14(1).
[140] C Dyer, 'Bulger Killers 'Were Denied Fair Trial' *The Guardian* (London England 16 March 1999) 2; Mansoor (n 96).
[141] Van Bueren (n 40) 23–24.

responsibility, below which one can presume that children cannot commit a crime, or the law cannot take cognisance of the act. States are required to act against such law-breakers without resorting to judicial proceedings. This could mean taking mentoring measures or rehabilitatory measures to prevent criminality. Moreover, if such proceedings are initiated, they must be in accordance with the fundamental human rights or legal safeguards provided generally to all.[142]

While the specific target of this provision seems to be a minimum age, it is likely intended to juveniles a chance for rehabilitation and to return to a normal life. The UNCRC's provision regarding the minimum age of criminal responsibility is further strengthened by the Beijing Rules. The Rules provide that in legal systems that have recognized the notion of a minimum age of criminal responsibility for children, 'the beginning of that age shall not be fixed at too low an age level, bearing in mind the facts of emotional, mental and intellectual maturity'.[143] Hence, the rule acknowledges the 'protective aspect of evolving capacities' of children and provides that due to young age, children might not be capable of understanding the consequences of their actions. Children are still developing their capacity to understand right from wrong. Assigning them a high degree of criminal liability at a young age unfairly penalizes them.[144] The commentary to this Rule also explains that due to history and cultural diversity, clear differences could be found concerning the minimum age of criminal responsibility among different States.[145]

In fact, discrepancies in the minimum age for criminal responsibility are found at global as well as continental level.[146] In Ghana and Uganda, following the rule of *doli incapax,* it is considered that a child below the age of seven does not have a criminal capacity. As a comparison, higher age limits are set by other African States. For example Senegal and Burkina Faso set it at 13, Sudan at 15 and Libya at 14. Most African States set the minimum threshold age at 13. To follow the guidelines of the Beijing Rules, in 1996, the age related to *doli incapax* has been raised to 12 by the Ugandan Children's Statute. Similarly in 1998, Ghana raised it to 14.[147] Disparity concerning the minimum age is also found among European States. For example, Denmark, Sweden and Finland set it at 15, the Netherlands set it at 12, Germany and Italy at 14, Cyprus at seven and the UK at 10.

In fact, uniformity in the minimum age would appear to be helpful in setting an international standard,[148] since variations related to minimum

---

[142] ibid.

[144] Cipriani, (n 9) 32.

[146] Van Bueren (n 40) 27.

[147] African Child Forum 'A Case for Raising Minimum Age of Criminal Responsibility' (n 20).

[148] ibid.

[143] Beijing Rule 4.

[145] Beijing Rule 4.

age limit render juveniles more vulnerable to exploitation, the CRC has called upon countries to raise the minimum age of responsibility.[149] While the minimum age of criminal responsibility in the case of Malaysia, provided in the Penal Code (Act 574) is 10 years, it noted the disparity between the Penal Code, and the interpretation of the Muslim Jurists in the Sharia (Islamic Law) Court and the Sharia Criminal Procedure (Federal Territories) Act 1984. The Committee recommended increasing the minimum age to 12 with a further increase to a higher age. It also requested a study on discrepancies between the minimum age among current criminal laws.[150]

Like other provisions of the UNCRC, this provision aims high for the best interest of the child and provides a general guideline to States, so that there remains no possibility of default on the part of States responsible for the well-being of the juveniles or young persons. This could be in the course of care, guidance and supervision orders, counselling, probation, foster care, education and vocational training programmes and other alternatives to institutional care. It is worth noting that the article requires States to consider the reason or cause behind the committing of the offence, along with the circumstances of the offence. Therefore, it seems to protect juveniles physically, as well as spiritually.[151] The variety of choices in the article enables the State to adopt a suitable approach according to its culture and the social needs and entitlements of each individual child. [152]

Undoubtedly, the UNCRC takes a holistic approach to protect children's rights. In addition to article 40, article 37 and article 39 also explicitly deal with the protection of the juvenile delinquents and criminal justice system in this regard.[153] The UNCRC is both ambitious and far-reaching and the potential exists within the UNCRC to advance considerable protection to the rights of children globally.[154] The UNCRC is highly successful in the protection of the rights of the child generally. However, the strength of the UNCRC is not being fully realized in its protection to children. Juvenile justice appears to be a neglected area.[155] One of the reasons could be that children who come into conflict with the law might not receive as much sympathy as other children. A juvenile delinquent is often considered as one who spreads fear, thus adversely affecting peace and the quality of life in the society and this could lead to the failure of penal reforms.[156] Another reason for the lack of support for penal reforms is that where the word

---

[149] Van Bueren (n 39) 6.
[150] Committee on the Rights of the Child (44th Session) Concluding Observations, Malaysia UNCRCCRC/C/MYS/CO/1, paras 103, 104 (25 June 2007) available at http://www.unhchr.ch/tbs/doc.nsf, accessed 15 June 2010.
[151] Art 40(4).   [152] Van Bueren (n 40) 30.
[153] ibid 5.   [154] Fottrell (n 85) 1.
[155] B Abramson, 'Juvenile Justice: the Unwanted Child' in Jensen and Jepson (n 50) 21.
[156] ibid 23.

'child' is used, it carries connotations of innocence, vulnerability, helplessness and victimization and not of delinquency.[157] In contrast, when a child commits an offence, this soft approach towards them changes. However, it is also noticeable that there are many cases in which these juvenile offenders are themselves victims, not only of physical but also of sexual and emotional abuse.[158] Another reason behind juvenile behaviour could be fear and recollections of incidents of abuse, which could urge them to take revenge on the society that failed to save them from it. Therefore, this abuse makes them a victim and thus causes a change in behaviour which leads them to commit crime. Therefore there is a dire need that these juvenile offenders, before receiving any punishment, are first subject to an investigation into the causes of their behaviour.

III. CONCLUSIONS

Article 1 of the UNCRC considers anyone who is under the age of 18 a child. This threshold age appears logical. However, the exception provided by the same article through inclusion of the phrase 'unless majority is attained earlier', weakens the solid definition of a child and has been invoked by several States to justify their use of a lower age of criminal responsibility, while taking into consideration their history, culture and religion. This situation resulted in setting various thresholds for considering an individual as a child and affects the minimum age for criminal responsibility, leaving children less protected in the criminal justice systems at national and international levels. Consequently, the loophole that has been provided by the exception adversely affects the approach of childhood that might be linked to mental, physical, and psychological components of criminal responsibility. Hence, in order to offer more protection to juveniles at international level, a reasonable minimum age limit has to be set. A uniform age limit of 18 seems to offer more protection. Nevertheless, this limit could adversely affect the core concept of the juvenile justice system, which is meant to provide for children under the age of 18. Therefore, the reasonable minimum age should not be too low, nor too high—the latter may render the concept of juvenile justice system meaningless.

As discussed in the introduction, criminal justice systems across the world reflect the indigenous values of States, and no more is this apparent than in Muslim majority States that practise Sharia law. Having discussed the international framework in the current chapter and before addressing

---

[157] ibid.   [158] ibid.

how these States responded to the child rights movement in respect to their own juvenile justice systems through the country reports, the following chapter will examine the Sharia in regard to child rights within its criminal justice system. It will look at whether it is possible to harmonize the exigencies of both Islamic and international systems with regard to young offenders.

CHAPTER 3

Juvenile Delinquency and Islamic Criminal Law

I. INTRODUCTION

This chapter explores the role of Islamic law and the protection of the rights of children who break the law. It highlights and discusses the relevant injunctions prescribed by the Quran[1] and the *sunnah*,[2] and examines several verses of the Quran and *hadith* (the traditions of the Prophet) applicable to the protection of the rights of the child. The chapter also explores the adequacy of protection offered by relevant 'Islamic' human rights instruments, such as the 1981 Universal Islamic Declaration of Human Rights, the 1990 OIC Cairo Declaration of Human Rights and the 2005 OIC Covenant on the Rights of the Child in Islam, and the OIC Rabat Declaration on Child's Issues in the Member States of the Organization of Islamic Conference held in Rabat, November 2005.

Furthermore, it provides analyses of the fundamental elements of a crime, and their relevance to the minimum age of criminal responsibility. The chapter examines the Islamic views on the different stages of development of understanding and maturity. It provides the juristic interpretations regarding the age of puberty and criminal responsibility under Islamic law. In the final section, this chapter will explore the available tools in Islamic jurisprudence, assessing their effectiveness in providing protection to child offenders. It will explore the role and impact of *ijtihad*[3] and interpretation of criminal law and punishments under changing circumstances by raising several crucial issues, including whether *ijtihad* and 'analogy' are permitted in matters of crimes and punishment. The chapter discusses the death penalty under *hudood* and *qisas*[4] and other punishments under Islamic law and their applicability to child offenders. It will then address the rules

---

[1] Muslims believe the Quran is the literal word of Allah (God), revealed to Mohammed by the archangel Gabriel around 610 AD. It is the first and main source of Islamic law and is the foundation for legal, political and cultural life.

[2] Practices of the Prophet Mohammed.

[3] A technical term of Islamic law that describes the juridical interpretation by a qualified Islamic jurist; a legal decision through independent interpretation.

[4] The term means 'retaliation' and follows the principle of 'an eye for an eye' or *lex talionis*. In the case of murder for example the legal heirs of the victim can demand execution of the murderer.

related to the imposition of *diyah* (blood money) in the case of children and explore the disparities between Islamic law and practice in this regard by evaluating the role of *diyah* in avoiding the death penalty for offenders including child offenders.

II. PUNISHMENT UNDER ISLAMIC LAW AND CHILD OFFENDERS

A. Hudood

Islamic criminal law recognizes three categories of crimes; *hudood, qisas* and *tazeer*. The first category, *hudood*, includes those crimes for which fixed punishments are prescribed in the Quran and/or the *sunnah*. These are *zina* (adultery or fornication), *qadhf* (false accusation of adultery or fornication) alcoholism, theft, highway robbery, apostasy, and rebellion.[5] Once these crimes are proven, it is mandatory to enforce the prescribed punishments for these offences, which are found in the Quran and the *sunnah*.[6] Therefore, *hudood* punishments are different from *tazeer* punishments, which fall under the discretion of the judge for the intended purpose of rehabilitation or warning.[7] Under *hudood* cases, the judge or person in authority has no discretion to decrease the punishment or to forgive. Once a *hudood* crime is proven, no consideration is given to the personality of the offender. This is due to the fact that in those cases the purpose of the Sharia (Islamic law) is focused on safeguarding society against crime.[8] The Sharia's aim in this regard is compatible with Herbert Packer's crime control model. In his framework, he suggested that criminal tendencies be evaluated by means of crime control and due process.[9] According to this model, the fundamental aim is to repress criminal conduct, or the society will suffer

---

[5] Wahbah-Al-Zuhayli, *Fiq-al-Isalami-wa-Adilatuhoo* (Darul-Fiker, Beirut, 1985) 13; for more on *hudood* see Mohammad-bin-Ismail Al Asqalani, *Subal-Assalam-Sharah-Baloogh-Almaram* (Dar Al-Kutab-Al Islamia, Pakistan, Maktabah Atif, Azhar 19591379 Hijra) vol 4, 267; Imam Allaudin Abi-Baqar Bin Masood, *Badai-us-Sanaiy* (Educational Press Karachi, Egypt 1910) vol 7, 33; M Cherif Bassiouni, *The Islamic Criminal Justice System* (New York, Oceana, 1982) 198.

[6] Al-Mawardi, *Al-Ahkam-Al-Sultania,* (Dar-al kutub al Ilmia, Beirut, 1406 AH) 221; Abi-Yalla, *Al-Ahkam-Al-Sultania* (Dar-al kutub al Ilmia, Beirut, 1406 AH) 260; Dr Ahamed Hemid, *Muqwamat-Al- Jareema-wa-Dawafiaohaa* (Amara-al-sor, Kuwai, 1982) 77.

[7] M Cherif Bassiouni (n 5) 203; Imam Allaudin Abi-Baqar Bin Masood, *Badai-us-Sanaiy* (Educational Press Karachi, Egypt, 1910) 33; Ibn-Al-Qayam-Al-Jowzia, *Aelam-Almoqeain* (Darul Jaleel, Beirut and Motaba al-kuliyat al Azhareya 1968) vol 2 29; M Lippman, S McConville and M Yerushalmi, *Islamic Criminal Law and Procedure* (Praeger, New York, 1988) 49; AQ Awdah, *Criminal Law of Islam:Volume 2* (International Islamic Publishers, Karachi, Pakistan, 1987) 337.

[8] TM Khan and MH Syed, *Criminal Law in Islam* (Pentagon Press, New Delhi, 2007) 342; Imam Abu Zahara, *Falsafah-tul-Aquba-fee-Fiqahalislami,* (Mahad Darasat Al-Arabia Al-alamia, 1963) s 31–32.

[9] HL Packer, *The Limits of Criminal Sanction* (Stanford UP, Palo Alto, 1969) 153.

and the criminal justice system will not be trusted.[10] In the absence of such control, a general disregard for criminal law would develop, and citizens would live in constant fear. According to Packer, '[t]he failure of law enforcement to bring criminal conduct under tight control is viewed as leading to the breakdown of public order and hence to the disappearance of an important condition of human freedom.'[11]

Although the main aim of the criminal justice system is to control crime and protect the society as a whole, Islamic law and practice has attempted to strike a balance by protecting the rights of individuals through stringent requirements for evidence for proving serious crimes. An example is the requirement of a specific number of witnesses for particular crimes, along with the method of *tazkiya tul shohood*—the purgation of witnesses for giving evidence—by persons who are well acquainted with the circumstances of the case.[12] For the implementation of these punishments, certain conditions have to be met. For example the offender has to be both *aqil* (a person with full, mature understanding) and *balig* (an adult). Under Sharia, a child is therefore exempt from *hudood* punishments.

B. Qisas

Qisas punishments cover the crimes of homicide and injury. It has five subdivisions: homicide (wilful homicide or murder), voluntarily causing death, involuntarily causing death,[13] physically injuring someone, and maiming.[14]

For these types of crimes, two modes of punishments have been prescribed; these are *qisas* (retribution) and *diyah* (blood money).[15] If these crimes are committed intentionally, the offender is liable to be punished under *qisas* and if the act is unintentional, the offender will be liable only to *diyah*.[16] These punishments are prescribed in cases involving adults.[17] If

---

[10] ibid 158. See also A Sanders and R Young, *Criminal Justice* (OUP, Oxford, 1994) 22; FZ Mansoor, 'Reassessing Packer in the Light of International Human Rights Norms' (2005) 4 Connecticut Public Interest Law Journal 2 263, available at http://lsr.nellco.org/cgi/viewcontent.cgi?article=1033&context=uconn/cpilj.

[11] ibid.

[12] M Asad, *The Message of The Qur'an* (Translation) (Oriental Press, Dubai, 2003) 995.

[13] Imam Mohammed Ameen, *Rad-al-Mohtar-Ala-Dur-al-Mukhtar,Hasheia-Ibn-e-Abedeen*, (3rd edn, Mustapha Al-Babi Al-Halbi, Cairo, 1984) 375; Allamah Shamsh-ud-Din Muhammad Bin Abi-Al-Abbas Ahmed Bin Hamza Shahab-ud-Din Al-Ramali, *Nihayat-ul-muhtaj ala-sharhil-minhaj* (Mustapha Al-Babi Al-Halbi, Cairo, 1938) vol 7, 235; Syed Sabiq, *Fiq us sunnah* (Dar-ul-Fiqr, Beirut, 1985) vol 2, 518; Imam Allaudin Abi-Baqar Bin Masood, *Badai-us-Sanaiy*, (Educational Press Karachi, Egypt, 1910) 233–234;

[14] Dr Wahaba Al-Zuhayli (n 5) vol 4, 11; Cherif Bassiouni (n 5) 203; Lippman, McConville and Yerushalmi (n 7) 49; Awdah (n 7) 138; MS El-Awa, *Punishment in Islamic Law* (American Trust Publications, Plainfield, 1993) IN 46168.

[15] *Diyah* in Islamic law can be given in lieu of *qisas* with the consent of the heirs of the victim in case of intentional murder.

[16] Khan and Syed (n 8) 342.   [17] ibid 343.

the victim or legal heir forgives a willful offence, the punishment under *qisas* is annulled and it will be replaced by *diyah* if the victim or legal heirs agree to that. However, if the offender has been forgiven without any monetary compensation then no *diyah* will be payable and it stands void. In such cases, courts need to ensure they take into account other circumstances and to ensure the act of pardoning or compensation has not been made under coercion. In the case of nullification of *qisas* for willful offences, and *diyah* in cases of unintentional offences, the court's inherent powers to punish the accused under penal law could be invoked, taking into consideration the circumstances of the victim.[18] In such cases the Sharia empowers the victim or legal heirs affected, rather than the community or society. [19]

Sharia recognizes that the acts of a person are linked to their will or intention; it takes into account the offence and also the offender's will.[20] Furthermore, offences that can legitimately be attributed to a person who is accountable, due to understanding and free choice, may be divided into two categories.[21] The first includes offences which were committed with the intention of violating the command of the law-giver. The second category includes offences committed erroneously and without having any intention of violating these commands.[22] Based upon this distinction, the Sharia distinguishes between the extent of an offender's accountability. Therefore, the accountability of the intentional offence is severe because in this case the offender commits the offence willingly. In contrast, the accountability for committing a crime in error is lenient. The Quran itself differentiates between the two kinds of offenders: '... and there is no blame on you concerning that wherein you made a mistake, but concerning that which your hearts do purposely'.[23] Also, the Prophet Muhammed says: 'My *Ummah* is not accountable for what it does by mistake and forgetfulness or under coercion'.[24]

The Quranic verse and the Prophet's tradition (*hadith* and *sunnah*) cited above do not have the purpose of completely removing accountability; rather, they merely distinguish between offences committed in error and those committed with full intention or awareness. This is borne out by the fact that the Quran prescribes *qisas* as the penalty for deliberate murder,[25] while laying down *diyah* and expiation as penalties for murder committed in error. But the Quran does not remove accountability of the latter altogether.[26] On this topic it says: 'O you who believe! Retaliation is prescribed

---

[18] ibid.   [19] ibid.   [20] ibid 139.
[21] ibid.   [22] ibid.   [23] Q33:5.
[24] *Sunan-ibn-maja*, vol 1, 347: 'Divorce under coercion'. (*Sunan-ibn-maja* is one of the six canonical *hadith* collections).
[25] However, diyah can also apply even in premeditated murder if the victims heir decides to accept diyah as a substitute for qisas.
[26] Khan and Syed (n 8) 140.

for you in the matter of the murder'.[27] 'And we prescribed for them therein the life for the life.' [28] A further verse states:

> And it is not conceivable that a believer should slay another believer, unless it be by mistake. And upon him who has slain a believer by mistake there is the duty of freeing a believing soul from bondage and paying an indemnity to the victim's relations, unless they forgo it by way of charity. Now if the slain, while himself a believer, belonged to a people who are at war with you, [the penance shall be confined to] the freeing of a believing soul from bondage; whereas, if he belonged to a group of people to whom you are bound by a covenant, [it shall consist of] an indemnity to be paid to his relation in addition to the freeing of a believing soul from bondage. And he who does not have the wherewithal shall fast [instead] for two consecutive months. [This is] the atonement ordained by God: and God is indeed all-knowing, wise. [29]

Hence the verse lays down the principle that *qisas* is not permitted in cases of murder by error. However, the blood money has to be paid.[30] In short, criminal accountability and its degrees vary with the numerous degrees and diversity of offences. It is, therefore, necessary to be familiar with the variety and degrees of offences in order to be familiar with degrees of accountability.[31] The offender violates the command of the law-maker either intentionally or by mistake. Further, willful offences are also distinguished by being willful and 'semi-willful'.[32] Accordingly, there are four levels of accountability. As accountability is grounded in the offence, the severity of punishment corresponds to the 'level' of the offence.[33]

C. Tazeer

The third category of crimes, *tazeer* (penal punishment) are those crimes which are not dealt with in Islamic law under *hudood* or *qisas*. Therefore, any offence for which no prescribed punishment is available can be included under *tazeer*.[34] As outlined above, in *hudood* cases the court has no power to increase or decrease the prescribed punishment if both intention and age of the offender meet the prescribed requirements for having

---

[27] Q2:178.   [28] Q5:45.
[29] Q4:92.   [30] El-Awa (n 14) 72.
[31] Khan and Syed (n 8) 140.
[32] For example, if A wilfully attacks B with the intention of merely causing hurt, but instead his act results in B's death.
[33] Khan and Syed (n 8) 141.
[34] Mawardi (n 6) 238; , Abi-Yalla (n 6) 224; Dr Muhammed Rushdi Muhammed Ismael, *Al-Janayat-fi-Shariah-Al-Islamia* (Dar ul Ansar, 1983) 84; Asqalani (n 5) 234; Al-Ramali (n 13) vol 8, 18; Ibn-Al-Qayam-Al-Jowzia, Aelam-Almoqeain, vol 2, 118; El-Awa (n 14) 96–107.

committed this crime. In contrast, under *tazeer* the court is empowered to use its discretion in penalizing the offender from among the provided punishments, as justified by the circumstances of the case. Hence, most of the offences committed by children might be better considered to fall under *tazeer*. However, if the judge, after evaluating the evidence and other factors such as motive, is not satisfied that these circumstances benefit the accused, the judge may award him or her appropriate punishment seen fit in the eyes of the court, which could be minimum or maximum penalties, with or without a financial penalty. Moreover, if the circumstances of the case offer enough evidence to remit punishment, the court will award a lighter punishment paying regard to personality, character, behaviour, and age of the offender.[35]

Sharia deals with *tazeer* crimes according to the principles of justice, bearing in mind all the circumstances and particular aspects of the case.[36] Therefore, reformatory punishment falls under this category and appears to provide a good means of handling crimes committed by children. Similarly, the position of the victim as a pardoning party cannot be solely relied upon, as the fact that the victim has pardoned does not itself make the punishment void. However, if the court is satisfied it may accept and consider it as a mitigating factor in favour of the offender.[37]

In the cases of crimes liable to *hudood*, *qisas* and *diyah*, punishment in Sharia sources is prescribed expressly, and in the cases of *tazeer* it is left to the discretion of a ruler or a judge to prescribe it in the relevant circumstances.[38] However, in order to achieve more clarity the provisions regarding crimes liable to *tazeer* should exist prior to the punishment of the criminal for act that falls under this category. That could be done, as Anwarullah proposed, 'whether in the form of a codified law or in the form of a compiled collection like books, magazines and publications. However, the details of the punishments in such cases need not to be provided but that these acts are punishable must be known to the person who commits any such act'.[39] In the Islamic legal framework, *tazeer* provides a forum for further legislation, under which full consideration could be given to the circumstances in which the crime has been committed, and personality of the offender. This area of flexibility seems to provide much room for comprehensive reformative and rehabilitative legislation with regard to juvenile offenders.

---

[35] Khan and Syed (n 8) 279.

[36] ibid 344–345; Dr Mohammed Rushdie Muhammad Ismail, *Al-Janayat fi Shariah-Al-Islamia* (Dar-Al Ansa 1983) 86.

[37] Khan and Syed (n 8) 345.

[38] Shams-Al-Aiama-Alsarkhsi, *Almabsut,* vol 4 (Dar-al-Mahrifah, Beirut, Lebanon) 64.

[39] Dr Anwarullah, *The Criminal Law of Islam* (Kitab Bhavan, New Delhi 2006) 6.

The motive behind fixed punishments for *hudood* offences is the notion these crimes harm the very fabric of society and are considered dangerous to the social order. Therefore, the nature of the Sharia in this regard is to guard the values of the society—by safeguarding the morals of the society, it seeks to maintain social order and peace. Hence Sharia punishments objectively seem to be concerned with the public good, not the individual. By prescribing harsh punishments under *hudood* offences, the public good has been given primacy over individual interest.[40]

III. LEGAL FRAMEWORK FOR THE PROTECTION OF CHILD OFFENDERS IN ISLAMIC LAW

The legal framework of Islamic criminal law can be divided into two parts, one substantive and the other procedural. Its substantive portion falls under the remit of Sharia, and the procedural part is dealt with under *fiqh* (Islamic jurisprudence), which evolved through a process of juristic thought. In Islamic law, the two fundamental sources of legislation are the Quran and the *sunnah* (the practices of the Prophet Mohammed). Therefore, these sources define crimes, prescribe punishments, state commandments, and direct substantive justice. By nature, these commandments are constitutional or objective resolutions, and other regulatory or procedural issues, such as how to make arrests, detain, investigate, prosecute, hear the case and make a judicial review, are not outlined.[41] Therefore, substantive justice is dealt with by Sharia, and the legislative formulation regarding procedural matters is left to the State, so that it can make rules to secure what is in the 'best interest of the society'.[42]

Due to this evolutionary process, Islamic law progressed to a comprehensive legal system.[43] The evolutionary process of Islamic law began almost 1400 years ago with the Quran as the foundation of Islam and the teachings of the Prophet Mohammed establishing Islamic law through his own practices (the *sunnah*). This evolutionary process continues. On the one side, the substantive part has been kept intact, and on the other, a legal system has grown to fulfil the demand of the Sharia, that is, to apply it to every aspect of the individual Muslim's life, as well as society across the ages, adapting to the requirements of changing times. The core aspects are

[40] Dr Ahmad Hemed, *Muqwamat Al Jareema wa Dawafi-o-ha* (Kuwait, 1982) 88.

[41] MA Baderin, *International Human Rights and Islamic Law* (Oxford, New York, 2003) 98.

[42] ibid; for details regarding the best interest of society see MB Utaiba, *Mohadarat-Fi-Alfiah-Al-Janai Al Islami* (Mahad Darasat al Islamia, 1998) 17–22; Imam Muhammad Abu Zarah, *Falsifah tul Aquba fil Fiqh al Islami* (Mahad Darasat Al-Arabia Al-Alamia, 1963, Beirut) 30–32.

[43] IAK Nyazee '*Theories of Islamic Law*' (Islamic Research Institute, Islamabad, 1993) 111.

fixed, but the extensions of this law attempt to meet the demands of historical changes in society.[44]

A. *Juvenile Offenders and Protection Offered under the Quran and the Sunnah*

A formal Juvenile Justice System and in particular a procedural law to protect young offenders have yet to be fully developed and codified within Islamic law. However, there are several protections offered by the UN Convention on the Rights of the Child (UNCRC) that are touched upon in the Quran. For example, the UNCRC's principle of the 'best interests of the child' appears to be found in certain aspects of the Sharia and interpreted in several verses of the Quran, for example, concerning guardianship of the property of a child held in trust.[45] The Quran says: 'And they will ask thee about [how to deal with] orphans. Say: 'To improve with their condition is best.'[46]

The implication is that if one shares the life of an orphan in one's charge, one is permitted to benefit by such an association, for instance, through a business partnership, provided this does not damage the orphan's interests in any way.[47] Hence, the Quran acknowledges, while dealing with matters related to orphans, that their best interests have to be kept in mind. However, this essential principle with regard to the guardianship of property (*al wilayatu alal maal*) might equally apply to the guardianship of the infant (*hadana*) as well as to various other areas, such as guardianship regarding education (*wilayat al tarbiyya*).[48]

One of the basic principles of Islamic criminal law is the establishment of justice and equity. This principle is mentioned in several verses of the Quran.[49] In this regard the Quran says '... And [thus gave you] a balance [wherewith to weigh right and wrong], so that men behave with equity ...'.[50] Regarding justice and kindness the Quran also says 'Behold, God enjoins justice and the doing of good. ...'[51] Elsewhere it says '... and whenever you judge between people, to judge with justice...'[52]

---

[44] ibid.
[45] M Siraj Sait, 'Islamic Perspectives on the Right of the Child' in D Fottrell, *Revisiting Children's Rights* (Kluwer Law International, the Hague, 2000) 42.
[46] Q2:220
[47] Asad (n 12) 59.
[48] Siraj Sait (n 45) 42.
[49] SS Hussain, *Human Rights in Islam* (Kitab Bhavan, New Delhi, 2001) 65.
[50] Q57:25.
[51] Q16:90.
[52] Q4:58.; Justice has also been enjoined in verses 65, 105, 135 of the same surah and in other places in the Quran ie 5:8, 42–50; 7:29; 10:47; 49:9; 57:25; 60:8.

Islamic law has also prescribed equity and justice as a general principle for the Islamic State, in which no distinction should be made between individuals except in terms of righteousness. In Islamic criminal law, the killing of any innocent human being is akin to the killing of the whole human race.[53] Children, who are vulnerable, deserve more protection and just and fair treatment.

Further, general Quranic principles could also be invoked to protect a child from harm.[54] For example, with regard to the issue of child labour, reference might be made to the Quran, which specifies that the family or parents have responsibility as the breadwinners and should not force a child to work. Similarly, on protecting children during armed conflict, the Prophet Mohammed prohibited execution of children and women during war.[55] Furthermore the Sharia prohibits harming children in any manner and children were excluded from war campaigns during the era of Prophet Mohammed.[56] Some Islamic principles offer full protection against child labour and their involvement in armed conflicts,[57] since both of them are detrimental and dangerous practices and adversely affect the physical and mental health and overall development of the children involved. The same protection could be invoked to protect specifically children from harsh punishments, and cruel, inhuman and degrading treatment.

There are a number of examples where the Prophet Mohammed made allowances for the inappropriate behaviour of children, due to their immaturity. For example, a *hadith* demonstrates the leniency of Mohammed with children's wrongdoing; Anas bin Malik said:

> When Allah's Apostle arrived at Medina, Abu Talha took hold of my hand and brought me to Allah's Apostle and said, 'O Allah's Apostle! Anas is an intelligent boy, so let him serve you.' Anas added, 'So I served the Prophet at home and on journeys; by Allah, he never said to me for anything which I did: 'Why have you done this like this' or, for anything which I did not do: 'Why have you not done this like this?'[58]

The above *hadiths* touch on the theme that children need to be treated differently from adults.

Ideally this should extend to criminal justice. Children are exempt from liability for their acts according to the following *hadith* of the Prophet: 'Three persons are not accountable: a child until he or she reaches the age of puberty, a person in sleep until he awake and an insane person until he

---

[53] Q5:32.   [54] Siraj Sait (n 45) 43.

[55] *Sahi Al Bukhari* vol 2, 'Qutal Nisa Fil-Herb' 362.

[56] Siraj Sait (n 45) 43.   [57] ibid.

[58] Abi Abdullah Bin Ismael Al-Bokhari, *Sahi Al-Bukahari*, vol 9, book 83, no 46.

becomes normal.'[59] The *hadith* points towards exemption of a child's acts and waiving the liability of the insane—indicating that accountability is based on puberty and maturity. Therefore, persons can only be held responsible and accountable for their acts once they attain both these qualities. Children are exempt from capital punishment.[60] While considering the issue of criminal liability, equal consideration should be given to the age as well as mental capacity of a juvenile offender.

Although the evolution of Islamic criminal law and procedures focus on the best interest of the individual and needs of society, its principal focus is on individual responsibility. Therefore, in Islamic criminal law, individuals are liable for their own illegal actions. However, if the offender is a child, due to lack of *mens rea*, (the 'guilty mind') he or she is exempt from the consequences.[61]

B. Protection of Juvenile Offenders under the Instruments Based on the Fundamental Islamic Sources

1. Protection offered by the OIC Covenant on the Rights of the Child in Islam

This Covenant on the Rights of the Child in Islam was adopted by the Organisation of Islamic Conference (OIC), which consists of 57 Muslim States.[62] The Covenant was adopted by the OIC States on the 32nd Islamic Conference of Foreign Ministers in Sana'a, Republic of Yemen, in June 2005.[63] In its preamble, the Covenant affirms previous international covenants including the Dhaka Declaration on Human Rights in Islam (1983), the Cairo Declaration on Human Rights in Islam (1990) and the

---

[59] Al-Hafiz Abi Essa Mohammed Bin Essa Al-Tirmazi, *Sunnan Tirmazi*, 'Regarding persons who are exempted from hudood Punishments' vol 2 64. Imam Abi Daood Suleman Bin Al-Ashhas, *Sunaun Abi Daood*, 4399.

[60] Imam Allaudin Abi-Baqar Bin Masood, Badai-us-Sanaiy (Educational Press Karachi, Pakistan, 1910) 134; Ibn-e-Quddama, *'Aalmughni'* vol 8 (Maktabatul Quliat Al-Azharia Egypt 620 AH) 124; Sabiq (n 13) 396; R Peters, *Crime and Punishment in Islamic Law* (CUP, Cambridge, 2005) 20.

[61] Mohammed Bahjat Utabah, *Muhadarat Fe Fiqah Al Janahi Al Islami* (Mahad Al Darasatal Islamia, 1998) 68; Peters ibid 20.

[62] The OIC is an international organization with a permanent mission to the United Nations. Members States as of June 2010: Afghanistan, Albania, Algeria, Azerbaijan, Bahrain, Bangladesh, Benin, Brunei, Burkina Faso, Chad, Côte d'Ivoire, Djibouti, Egypt, Gabon, Gambia, Cameroon, Comoros, Guinea, Guinea-Bissau, Guyana, Indonesia, Iran, Iraq, Jordan, Kazakhstan, Kuwait, Kyrgyzstan, Lebanon, Libya, Malaysia, Maldives, Mali, Mauritania, Morocco, Mozambique, Niger, Nigeria, Oman, Palestine, Pakistan, Qatar, Saudi Arabia, Senegal, Sierra Leone, Somalia, Sudan, Suriname, Syria, Tajikistan, Togo, Tunisia, Turkey, Turkmenistan, Uganda, United Arab Emirates, Uzbekistan, Yemen Arab Republic.

[63] Covenant on the Rights of the Child in Islam OIC/9-IGGE/HRI/2004/Rep. http://www.unhcr.org/refworld/docid/44eaf0e4a.html, accessed 6 June 2010.

Declaration on the Rights and Care of the Child in Islam (1994). It considers the protection of the rights of the child in Islamic Sharia and also takes into account the domestic laws of States within the Organization of Islamic Conference (OIC).

The Covenant is considered a legally binding document in the OIC States that have ratified it, but enforcement and implementation mechanisms are not fully explained. Article 24 of the Covenant outlines the implementation mechanisms of the Covenant, including the creation of the Islamic Committee on the Rights of the Child. The Committee is to examine the progress of the implementation of the Covenant, but enforcement mechanisms or other powers this Committee might have to ensure compliance are not set out and its mandate is only vaguely drafted.[64]

Article 4 of the Covenant sets out the obligations of the States Parties to this Covenant: they are obliged to respect the rights stipulated and to take the necessary steps to enforce it in accordance with their domestic regulations. Further, the States Parties shall 'end action based on customs, traditions or practices that are in conflict with the rights and duties stipulated in this Covenant'.[65] It provides general protection of children's rights, although some of its provisions within the Covenant could be particularly relevant for the protection of the rights of children who come in conflict with the law. According to article 1 of the Covenant, a 'child means every human being who, according to the law applicable to him/her, has not attained maturity'.[66] However the provision does not mention a specific age and leaves it at the discretion of States to set ages of majority, leaving juveniles less protected because States may set the minimum age for criminal responsibility, according to their interpretation, and might set it too low.

Article 11 protects the right of a child to a 'sound upbringing'. In this regard, 'parents or legal guardians' are responsible for the child's proper upbringing. Further, in fulfilling this responsibility 'institutions of the state within their means shall assist them'. The main focus of the upbringing of the child should be development of their 'personality, religious and moral values, and sense of citizenship and Islamic and human solidarity of the child and to instil in him/her a spirit of understanding, dialogue, tolerance, and friendship among peoples'.[67] Further, the child should be encouraged to acquire 'skills and capabilities to face new situations and overcome negative customs, and to grow up grounded in scientific and

---

[64] UN Chronicle, 'International Human Rights Law: A Short History' http://www.un.org/wcm/content/site/chronicle/cache/bypass/home/archive/Issues2009/internationalhumanrightslawashorthistory?print=1, accessed 22 June 2010.

[65] Covenant on the Rights of the Child in Islam OIC/9-IGGE/HRI/2004/Rep, art 4—Obligations of States: http://www.oic-oci.org/english/convenion/Rights%20of%20the%20Child%20In%20Islam%20E.pdf, accessed 22 June 2010.

[66] Covenant on the Rights of the Child in Islam OIC/9-IGGE/HRI/2004/Rep.

[67] ibid.

objective reasoning'.[68] This provision provides an overview and suggestions for the development of balanced personality which could be considered a prerequisite for avoiding anti-social behaviour and most probably juvenile delinquency.[69]

In addition it states a child should be 'protected from all forms of torture or inhumane or humiliating treatment in all circumstances and conditions…'. The Covenant also provides protection against 'all forms of abuse'.[70] As such it aims to provide full protection against physical and mental torture and all sorts of exploitation and abuse. The protection offered under this provision could play a significant role in blocking the path to juvenile delinquency.

Article 19 of the Covenant specifically deals with children who come into conflict with the law. It stipulates that '[N]o child shall be deprived of his/her freedom, save in accordance with the law and for a reasonable and specific period'. Again, the specification of reasonable time has been left for the State to define. Children deprived of their freedom 'shall be treated in a way consistent with dignity, respect for human rights and basic freedoms'.[71] Furthermore, a child should be dealt with according to the 'needs of persons of his/her age'.[72] This concept is touched upon in the Quran, which says: 'Allah tasks not a soul beyond its scope'.[73] It is understood that their physical vulnerability and mental immaturity leave children unable to cope with harsh treatment or hard and dangerous work.[74]

According to the Covenant a juvenile 'deprived of his/her freedom shall be separated from adults'.[75] Keeping children with adult criminals may have an adverse impact on their development and personality, thus leaving them vulnerable to abuse or exposing them to more hardened criminals. Hence, proper enforcement of this provision offers full protection against the impacts of keeping children with adult criminals.

---

[68] ibid.

[69] The Covenant also acknowledges the right of a child to education and culture. Its art 12 provides that a 'child has a right to free compulsory basic education by learning the principles of Islamic education and to the provision of the necessary means to develop his/her mental, psychological and physical abilities, to allow him/her to be open to the common standards of human culture'. For the provision of the right to education the state should provide equal opportunities for 'free and compulsory primary education for all children'. The States shall provide 'in accordance with the education system in each State effective treatment of the problem of illiteracy, drop-outs and those who miss basic education'. Proper implementation of these provisions might provide a safeguard against involvement of children in delinquent activities and in controlling these activities.

[70] Covenant on the Rights of the Child in Islam OIC/9-IGGE/HRI/2004/Rep.

[71] ibid.

[72] ibid.

[73] *Surah Al-Baqarah*, verse 286.

[74] UNICEF, *Children in Islam, their Care, Development and Protection* (International Islamic Centre for Population Studies and Research, Al-Azhar University, 2005) 5.

[75] Art 19 (3)(a)Covenant on the Rights of the Child in Islam OIC/9-IGGE/HRI/2004/Rep.

Similar to the UNCRC, the Covenant on the Rights of the Child in Islam protects the child's right to a fair trial and provides that a child should be directly and immediately informed about the 'charges against him/her upon his/her summoning or apprehension, and his/her parents, guardian or lawyer shall be invited to be present with him/her'. Legal and humanitarian assistance should be provided 'where needed including access to a lawyer and an interpreter if necessary'.[76]

Cases of juvenile crime should be tackled by 'a specialized juvenile court, with the possibility of the judgement being contested by a higher court, once the child is convicted'.[77] A juvenile should not 'be compelled to plead guilty or to offer testimony'.[78] Further, 'punishment shall be considered as a means of reform and care in order to rehabilitate the child and reintegrate him/her into the society'.[79] This provision of the Covenant is compatible with article 14 of the International Convention on Civil and Political Rights (ICCPR) and article 40 of the UNCRC, which, rather than stigmatizing juvenile offenders with criminality and focusing on their punishment, promote their rehabilitation and reintegration 'back onto the path of socially acceptable conduct'.[80] This is supported by the Islamic teachings on the proper upbringing and training of children. In fact, as shown above, the Prophet Mohammed exonerated immature persons from responsibility.[81] Further, for the protection of life and reputation of the juvenile offender 'assurance is provided through all the stages of the proceedings'.

2. Protection offered under the Universal Islamic Declaration of Human Rights

General protection for the juvenile offenders is also covered by the Universal Islamic Declaration of Human Rights (UIDHR). This Declaration is the second fundamental document proclaimed by the Islamic Council to mark the beginning of the 15th century of the Islamic era (the first was the Universal Islamic Declaration). The UIDHR was announced at the International Conference on the Prophet Muhammad and his Message, held in London from 12–15 April 1980.[82]

The UIDHR is based on the Quran and the *sunnah,* and was compiled by eminent scholars and jurists from the Muslim world. It was a response to the Universal Declaration of Human Rights, which was criticized by Muslim States for not taking into account the cultural and religious context of Muslim States and cultures. It is not internationally binding, but is declamatory in nature.

---

[76] ibid art 19(3)(b).
[78] ibid.
[80] Baderin (n 41) 109.
[77] ibid.
[79] ibid.
[81] ibid.
[82] The Universal Islamic Declaration of Human Rights, Paris 21 Dhul Qaidah 1401 Salem Azzam 19 September 1981, at http://www.ntpi.org/html/uidhr.html, accessed 15 March 2010.

Article I of the Declaration provides the right to life. It states that 'human life is sacred and inviolable and every effort shall be made to protect it. In particular no one shall be exposed to injury or death, except under the authority of the Law'. [83] This provision, which provides a general protection, could be equally invoked for the protection of the right to life of adults as well as children. Moreover, with regard to the right to life, children under Islamic law are offered more protection, as they have been exempt from the death penalty in cases of *hudood* and *qisas*. [84]

Article IV of UIDHR protects the individual's right to justice and provides that 'every person has the right to be treated in accordance with the law and only in accordance with the Law'. He or she shall also have the right not to be treated under law which contradicts the Sharia. Further, everyone has the right 'to self-defence against any charges that are preferred against him and to obtain fair adjudication before an independent judicial tribunal in any dispute'. Here again, the general nature of protection to all applies to the case of the juveniles who come into conflict with the law.

When anyone comes into conflict with the law, article V of the Declaration stipulates their right to a fair trial. Accordingly, no one 'shall be adjudged guilty of an offence and made liable to punishment except after proof of his guilt before an independent judicial tribunal'. Likewise, no one should be presumed guilty 'except after a fair trial and after reasonable opportunity for defence has been provided'. In meting out punishment, the circumstances in which the crime was committed should be considered. Moreover, a balance has to be kept between punishment and the severity of the crime. Furthermore, an act should not be 'considered a crime unless it is stipulated as such in the clear wording of the Law'. The Declaration also provides protection against torture. Article VII states that no one should be 'subjected to torture in mind or body, or degraded, or threatened with injury either to himself or to anyone related to or held dear by him, or

---

[83] ibid.

[84] If we examine art 7(a) of the Revised Arab Charter on Human Rights, in the light of art 1 of the UIDHR, the Charter specifically mentions the prohibition of the death penalty for persons who are under 18 years of age, an age which is compatible with the UNCRC. However, it also mentions 'unless otherwise stipulated in laws in force at the time of commission of the crime'. This directly conflicts with art 37(A) of the UNCRC and 6(5) of the ICCPR, since the prohibition mentioned in the latter international instruments is absolute and does not refer to national laws. A notable point is that almost all members of the Arab League are State parties to the UNCRC and most of them are parties to the ICCPR, and none of these States have entered reservations to art 37(a) UNCRC and 6(5) of the ICCPR. In fact, the provisions and spirit Charter seems, in practice, to be followed by few countries. Saudi Arabia and Yemen are among those States who are still executing under-18s. However, it is noted that the reservation in art 4 regarding prohibition of the death penalty in case of a state of emergency, is a break from and a denial of art 5 of the Charter, wherein right to life is guaranteed. It also adversely affects the protection of international human rights law in Arab countries, M Rishmawi, 'The Revised Arab Charter on Human Rights: A Step Forward?' (2005) 5 Human Rights Law Review 2, 371–372.

forcibly made to confess to the commission of a crime, or forced to consent to an act which is injurious to his interests'.

Undoubtedly all these rights offer equal protection to children who are under 18 and who come into conflict with the law. Further, the individual's right to found a family and related matters is provided by article XIX which states that everyone is 'entitled to marry, to found a family and to bring up children in conformity with his religion, traditions and culture'. A husband is obliged to 'maintain his wife and children according to his means' and 'every child has the right to be maintained and properly brought up by its parents, it being forbidden that children are made to work at an early age or that any burden is put on them' which could adversely affect their natural development. However, if due to whatever reasons, if parents are 'unable to discharge their obligations towards a child it becomes the responsibility of the community to fulfil these obligations at public expense'. Everyone has the right to 'material support, as well as care and protection, from his family during his childhood, old age or incapacity'. When children grow up, parents also have the right 'to material support as well as care and protection from their children'.[85] By this token, the duty to protect children is not only legal, but religious. The Declaration provides dual protection to vulnerable children. In the case of failure by parents in the duty of financial protection of their children, responsibility could be handed over to the State. Although this provision does not explicitly mention the protection of juvenile delinquents and offenders, it offers implicit protection to such children.

3. Protection offered under the OIC Cairo Declaration on Human Rights in Islam

The 19th Islamic Conference of Foreign Ministers, held in Cairo (31 July–5 August 1990), agreed to issue the Cairo Declaration on Human Rights in Islam to serve as a general guidance for Member States in the field of human rights and to serve as a guide for Member States in all aspects of life.[86] It was adopted by the (then) 45 members of the Organisation of the Islamic Conference on 5 August 1990. It provides an overview of the Islamic perspective on human rights—in 1982, the Iranian representative to the United Nations, Said Rajaie-Khorassani, argued that the Universal Declaration of Human Rights was a 'secular' understanding of Judeo-Christian traditions which could not be implemented by Muslims without

---

[85] The Universal Islamic Declaration of Human Rights (n 82).

[86] Cairo Declaration on Human Rights in Islam, 5 August 1990, UN GAOR, World Conference on Human Rights (4th Session) Agenda Item 5, UNDoc A/CONF.157/PC/62/Add.18 (1993) [English translation] http://www1.umn.edu/humanrts/instree/cairodeclaration.html, accessed 10 June 2010.

contradicting Islamic law. In 1993, Iran and several other Muslim States pressed for the acceptance of the Cairo Declaration as an alternative to the Universal Declaration of Human Rights, which was partially achieved in 1997 when the Cairo Declaration was included by the Office of the High Commissioner for Human Rights as the last document in *Human Rights: A Compilation of International Instruments: Volume II: Regional Instruments* (OHCHR, New York and Geneva, 1997).

On 30 June 2000, OIC members officially resolved to support the Cairo Declaration on Human Rights in Islam, which protected the freedom and right to life in accordance with Sharia law. The Cairo Declaration is not a United Nations-governed Covenant (like the Universal Declaration on Human Rights) falling under international law, but rather serves as a general guideline for Muslim States, with no body ensuring or promoting enforcement.

Certain provisions of the Cairo Declaration on Human Rights in Islam could be invoked to improve protection of juvenile offenders. While protecting the right to life, article 2 of the Cairo Declaration states that 'life is a God-given gift and the right to life is guaranteed to every human being. It is the duty of individuals, societies and states to protect this right from any violation, and it is prohibited to take away life except for a *Sharia* prescribed reason'. The right protected under this provision is equally applicable to children. Article 3 of the Declaration offers specific protection to children and states that 'in the event of the use of force and in case of armed conflict, it is not permissible to kill non-belligerents such as old men, women and children'. This provision reflects the vulnerable position of children in society.

Article 19 of the Declaration provides some rules regarding fair trial. It provides that 'All individuals are equal before the law, without distinction between the ruler and the ruled.' Everyone has equal right to access to justice. Further, 'there shall be no crime or punishment except as provided for in the *Sharia*'. An accused should be considered 'innocent until his guilt is proven in a fair trial in which he shall be given all the guarantees of defence'. Article 20 of the Declaration provides that no one should be arrested 'without legitimate reason to arrest an individual, or restrict his freedom, to exile or to punish him. It is not permitted to subject him to physical or psychological torture or to any form of humiliation, cruelty or indignity'.[87] All these rights are equally available to children who break the law because the protection offered by the provisions is without any specification of age.

---

[87] The Cairo Declaration on Human Rights in Islam Adopted and Issued at the 19th Islamic Conference of Foreign Ministers in Cairo on 5 August 1990, available at http://www.religlaw.org/interdocs/docs/cairohrislam1990.htm accessed 15 March 2010.

Along with the above-mentioned instruments, the OIC Rabat Declaration on Child's Issues in the Member States of the Organization of Islamic Conference 2005 also ensure the protection of the rights of each child 'without discrimination of any kind, irrespective of race, colour, sex, language, religion, political opinion or social status'.[88] It provides that consideration has to be given to 'the best interests of the child, non discrimination, participation, survival and development, which provide the framework for all action concerning children and adolescents alike'.[89] The declaration urges the 'Member States to take all appropriate measures to prevent and protect children from all forms of exploitation, abuse, torture and violence.[90] It also recommends the development of mechanisms to promote the exchange of expertise in the development and implementation of policies pertaining to child rights among OIC Member States.

All these provisions could be generally invoked for the better protection of the rights of children, including development and reformation of the juvenile justice system. Although the above instruments of Islamic law contain several general provisions which could offer protection to juvenile offenders, these provisions, however, cannot be considered adequate. The UIDHR and the Cairo Declaration are only Declarations and as such are not legally binding documents. Nevertheless, the Covenant on the Rights of the Child in Islam (2005), which is a binding document, also provides similar protection with regard to children who come into conflict with the law. Therefore, proper enforcement of the Covenant could lead towards better protection.

IV. ISLAMIC LAW: FUNDAMENTAL ELEMENTS OF A CRIME AND THE QUESTION OF AGE

According to Islamic criminal law, an act can only be considered a crime if the following three fundamental elements are present. The first element (which is known as a *legal* element of the crime), is existence of a clear provision for prohibition of an act that constitutes a crime and also of specific punishment for it. The second element (*substantial* element of a crime) is the actual commission of an illegal act or omission of an act enjoined or legal duty. The maturity and responsibility of the offender is the third element of a crime (known as the *cultural* element). Consequently, if

---

[88] Rule 1, OIC Rabat Declaration on Child's Issues in the Member States of the Organization of Islamic Conference held in Rabat, November 2005 available at http://www.isesco.org.ma/english/confSpec/MinistresEnfance/Documents/Final%20Agreed%20Declaration.pdf accessed 13 September 2010.

[89] Rule 2.   [90] Rule 9.

any of these elements are missing, an act cannot be considered a crime.[91] One of the characteristics of a crime is that the person committing the prima facie criminal act, as understood within the Islamic criminal law, is *aqil* and *balig,* that is, they should have maturity of understanding and be an adult. If these conditions are met then a person is considered capable of bearing the responsibility for the crime and thus be liable for the punishment for the crime.[92]

According to Muslim jurists, for the implementation of punishment prescribed in Islamic criminal law some other prerequisites have also to be fulfilled. The first is *qudra* (the offender must have the power to commit or not to commit the act) and *ikhtiyar* that is, a free will element. The third element is that the offender must have intended the committal of the crime (*qasad aljanai*).[93] This can be thought of as the foundation of the Islamic criminal law framework regarding the theory of *mens rea* in offences punishable with *qisas* (retribution) and *hudood* (fixed punishment*).*[94] Accordingly, the personal responsibility ascertained shall be proportionate to the individual's capacity or capability.[95] The Quran says that 'Allah does not burden any human being with more than he is well able to bear …'.[96] Hence, Islamic law does not allow the punishment under *qisas* and *hudood* on offenders who acted under duress, or lacked awareness of the criminal act, due to their young age or for any other reason.[97] Accordingly, a person is considered responsible in relation to his understanding and age. Therefore we can see that for accruing the criminal responsibility both of the elements, ie age and full understanding, are equally important.

To summarize, under Islamic criminal law, criminal responsibility and accountability are based on three elements, which are the committing of a prohibited act, free consent, and that the person who commits the offence has to be an adult and be able to differentiate between right and wrong (*idrak*).[98] If the first element is missing there can be no criminal responsibility and thus the question of penalty cannot arise. Compared to cases where there is an absence of the second and the third elements, there will

[91] AQ Awdah, *Criminal Law of Islam: Volume 1*(International Islamic Publishers, Karachi) 124–125; Mohammed Bahjat Utabah, '*Muhadarat Fe Fiqah Al Janahi Al Islami*' (Mahad Al Darasatal Islamia) 68; Anwarullah (n 39) 1.

[92] Besides this, for the implementation of punishment prescribed in Islamic criminal law there are distinct prerequisites for a specific crime to have been committed, for example, theft is taking away movable property , which belongs to another, stealthily. Awdah ibid 131, 125.

[93] ibid; Mohammed Bahjat Utabah, *Muhadarat Fe Fiqah Al Janahi Al Islami, Mahad Al Darasatal Islamia,* 68; Peters (n 60) 20.

[94] Peters ibid.

[95] Awdah (n 91) 133.

[96] Q2:286.

[97] Mohammed Bahjat Utabah, *Muhadarat Fe Fiqah Al Janahi Al Islami, Mahad Al Darasatal Islamia,* 68; Khan and Syed (n 8) 121,124.

[98] Anwarullah (n 39) 28.

be no punishment, however criminal responsibility for the act would still remain. [99]

Although the conditions discussed above might be the basis for exempting the offender from the punishment, it does not prevent the courts from taking 'appropriate measures' under the rubric of '*tazeer*'—considered necessary to save the community or that are in the interest of society in general. For example, a young child offender involved in a murder may be handed over to a reformatory for the purpose of reformation. Further, if a juvenile delinquent cannot face punishment under Sharia but they are still doing things that are a danger to society, in order to protect others from these actions alternative measures may be taken. These measures can include recommending admission for hospital treatment in cases of mental illness, or admission to a reformatory facility. In this situation children finish their treatment when it is found they have sufficiently reformed their destructive behaviour.[100] Under Sharia, these preventive and reformatory methods are a kind of penal punishment,[101] for instance, the reformation of juvenile delinquents.[102]

V. THE AGE OF CRIMINAL LIABILITY IN ISLAMIC LAW

According to Islamic law, the step from being a minor to the age of maturity is a physical one, that is, when the boy or girl show signs of sexual maturity. In Islamic jurisprudence it is, however, an 'irrefutable presumption' that boys and girls cannot have attained puberty before a 'certain' age. Further, there is also an age after which there cannot be any other presumption except that of 'puberty'.[103]

The Islamic schools of thought (of which there are four) have fixed the upper and lower levels for the age of puberty for boys and girls. The age before which puberty cannot be established in the case of boys, according to the Hanafi school of thought is 12, for the Malikis and Shafis nine years, and the Hanbali school fixes it at 10 years.[104] Only the Shia school of thought[105] does not fix any lower limit. Similarly, the upper level age after which puberty cannot be denied for boys according to Hanafis, Shafis,

---

[99] ibid 29.
[101] Nihaya-tul-Mohtaj vol 8, 22.
[103] Peters (n 60) 21.

[100] Khan and Syed (n 8) 124.
[102] Khan and Syed (n 8) 124.

[104] These are four Sunni schools of Islamic Jurisprudence, named after Imams (religious scholars). Hanafis are named after founder of this school of jurisprudence. Imam Abu Haneifa Numan bin Sabit, Haneifa, was his Kunya, ie his first-born child; Malikis are named after Malik ibn Anas; Shafies are named after Abu Abdullah Muhammad ibn Idris al Sajafi; the Hanbali school is named after Imam Ahmad ibn Hunbal.

[105] The Shia school of jurisprudence isdifferent from Sunni in the use of reason for interpretation of Islamic laws, in matters regarding inheritance, and in permitting temporary marriage.

Hanbalis and Shias is 15. However, Malikis fix it at 18 or in some cases 19 years.[106] For girls, Hanafis and Shafis fix it at 15 years, Shias at nine and Malikis at 18 years old.[107] Imam Abu Hanifa fixed it 17 for girls and 18 for boys.[108] These are the ages for physical maturity.

Although the Shia school of thought does not fix a lower age limit for boys or girls, it has fixed an age limit of 15 years in case of boys and nine in the case of girls, after which the status of having reached puberty cannot be denied. [109] When the *qadi* (judge) is satisfied that these conditions are met, and that the individual acted wrongly, the *qadi* may decide to discipline (*ta'dib*) them.[110] Hence, the logical outcome of the above appears to be that for criminal responsibility, physical maturity and awareness of the act is equally important. A key question at this stage is whether becoming physically adult makes a person mentally mature enough to understand their acts and deeds, or whether other factors such as education or experience further affect this awareness.

A. Juristic Interpretations and Age of Puberty

Islamic jurists base the age of puberty and its relationship to accountability on the above-mentioned *hadith* of the Prophet Mohammed regarding the exemption of children from criminal responsibility.[111] Accordingly, responsibility for a boy starts when he has a nocturnal discharge of semen, one of the signs of puberty,[112] as pointed out in the Prophet's *hadith*. Along with puberty, it is expected that prudence, maturity and care are developed, indicating an individual is fully grown. Once grown up he is able to use all organs of his body with consciousness, and nocturnal emissions show his coming of age and of his ability to impregnate a woman.[113] In the case of girls, the signs of puberty are menstruation, nocturnal emissions and the ability to become pregnant. However, these signs of puberty may occur early or may be delayed. Hence it becomes necessary to fix the age limits in order to consider an individual responsible enough for the purpose of equality and justice. The majority of Islamic jurists fix the age limit for boys

---

[106] ibid; M Waqar-ul-Haq, *Islamic Criminal Laws [Hudood Laws & Rules]* (Nadeem, Law Book House, Lahore, 1994) 124.

[107] Peters (n 60) 21.

[108] Mohammed Bahjat Utabah, Muhadarat Fe Fiqah Al Janah-097 Al Islami, Mahad Al Darasatal Islamia, 68; Anwarullah (n 39) 25.

[109] N Hussin, 'Juvenile Delinquencies in Malaysia: Legal Provisions and Prospects for Reforms' http://www.childjustice.org/docs/hussin2005.pdf, 11.

[110] Peters (n 60) 21.

[111] *Tirmazi* (n 59) 'Chapter regarding person who are exempted from hudood punishments' vol 2 64.

[112] Awdah (n 7) 335.

[113] ibid 336; Mohammed Bahjat Utabah, Muhadarat Fe Fiqah Al Janahi Al Islami, Mahad Al Darasatal Islamia, 1998, 69.

and girls at 15 years. These jurists rely on the argument that fundamentally, prudence comes with puberty and that responsibility and accountability spring from this. Therefore, in Sharia puberty is the age limit at which the child leaves childhood and enters adulthood. Nocturnal emissions normally occur by the age of 15 years, and if it does not occur, then the presumption would be that a child has some physical problem. Such a physical problem does not seem to have any adverse effect on reason or mental maturity, and therefore a young person's reasoning is assumed to be fully developed and criminal injunctions will begin to apply.[114] However, those jurists who set the age of puberty at 18 or 19 years suggest that nocturnal emissions could occur at any point up to the age of 18 or 19 years, and until then, the application of Sharia law is inappropriate. A physical problem is only presumed possible when a boy has reached the age of 18 or 19 years; nocturnal emissions are expected by this age at the latest.[115]

Muslim jurists' thoughts on this fall broadly into two categories. The first is in favour of placing puberty at the age of 15, when physical signs appear. They argue that the application of the relevant injunctions cannot be suspended on the basis of doubt. The second group give the maximum benefit of doubt until the age of 18 or 19, the latest age for puberty, ie in cases when a child has reached a certain age but has not yet reached physical puberty. Accordingly the symptoms of puberty could be delayed until 18 or 19 years. Similarly, in the case of women, menstruation is the primary sign of a girl coming of age, but if a woman's period stops, it is necessary to wait until the age of 18 since it is possible that menstruation may start again. In both cases, the principle seems to be to give the individual the benefit of the doubt rather than to take action with potentially serious consequences on the basis of what may prove to be a temporary or anomalous situation.[116]

In the Shia school of thought, the judiciary spokesman of the Islamic Republic of Iran confirmed in 2009 that a legal opinion (*estefsa*) was provided by Shia scholars stating that:

> If a person in the age group of under 18 is different from the average under 18s with regards to mental maturity, it is necessary for the judge to avoid *hudood* and *qisas* punishments for them. The main criterion remains the standards level of mental maturity of the offender and not the simply being of a certain age.[117]

This distinction between the different levels of maturity of a child is reflected in the new bill on Investigation of Crimes of Juvenile Offenders

---

[114] Awdah (n 7) 336.   [115] ibid 336–337.
[116] ibid 336–337.   [117] Iranian Judicial Gazette, Maa'va website, 10 May 2009.

which was ratified in 2006 by the Parliament of the Islamic Republic of Iran.[118] This legislative text is currently awaiting the approval of the Guardian Council in order to become effectively valid. Articles 29, 30 and 31 of this draft law consider persons (both boys and girls) between the age of nine to 18 years as a child, classifying them in three different categories: seven to 12, 12 to 15, and 15 to 18 years old. According to this classification, the severity of punishment would depend on age group; punishments range from being shadowed by social workers, sent to special schools, offered specific psychological treatments, and being kept in young offenders' institutions for up to five years.

According to article 90, in cases of *hudood* or *qisas* punishments for offenders under the age of 18, and despite the physical maturity of the person, the sentence could be transformed to a discretionary punishment awarded by the judge when there are doubts regarding the mental maturity of the offender and doubts in as to his understanding of the nature of his crime.

B. Reciprocity between Age and Criminal Accountability under Islamic Law

Islamic law divides the mental development and understanding of a person into three stages. Accordingly, criminal accountability starts once the human has passed those three stages of development: at the first stage, a child is considered to lack awareness in these matters. At the second stage, a child is still considered to have a weak understanding and lack of comprehension. At the third stage, a child emerges into a fully grown adult with a mature understanding.[119] For this reason, criminal responsibility of a child seems not be based just on physical majority, but also mental maturity. The following subsections explore in more detail these stages of development.

1. Islamic criminal law and the liability of a child who is unable to understand

The first stage is known as *sabiy ghayr mumayiz*. At this stage, due to their age, children are unable to understand their actions and cannot be presumed to be able to distinguish between right and wrong. This stage refers to the time from birth until the age of seven.[120] Of course, mental and physical capacities vary from child to child and this capacity can be developed after or even before the age of seven, depending upon on their envi-

---

[118] ibid.
[119] Awdah (n 7) 333; Mohammed Bahjat Utabah, Muhadarat Fe Fiqah Al Janahi Al Islami, Mahad Al Darasatal Islamia, 69.
[120] Hussin (n 109) 11–12.

ronment and other factors. However, with the aim of avoiding contention, and to assist the court in its duties, Islamic jurists have fixed an age limit.[121] Furthermore, this limitation is based on average occurrence/experiences, so that the judge when giving judgment may have an agreed-upon standard. Therefore, children under this age are protected from being punished and are considered incapable of understanding the consequences of their actions. This concept is compatible with the doctrine of *doli incapax*.[122]

Consequently, a child might be termed as 'not understanding', even if it develops the necessary consciousness before the age of seven years, because a judgment might not be applied to the exceptions but to the majority of cases. For this reason, if a child commits an offence while below the age of seven years, he or she will not be punished. For example, if a child commits theft, which is a *hudood* crime, he will not be liable for *hudood*. Similarly, if a child wounds or kills a person they will not be liable to *qisas*, nor to *tazeer*.[123]

2. Criminal liability of a child with weak understanding

The second stage is called *sabiyy mummayyiz* (a child with weak understanding). It starts over the age of seven and lasts until a child is 15. At this stage a child has a developing awareness, and is to some extent able to distinguish between right and wrong but not fully.[124] However this weak understanding will not make a child directly responsible for crimes.[125] Therefore, legally, it may be that this liability is not of the same level as that of an adult, which would attract the punishments of *hudood* or *qisas*. However, for maintaining discipline (*tadib*) the court may take appropriate action under *tazeer*, for example, warning and admonition.[126] In this stage of life a child may be punished for repeat offences, but will not be considered or labelled a criminal. Hence, for cases of *sabiy mumayyiz* even the punishments of the second category may not exceed a reprimand. This lesser degree of punishment is because of the child only has a weak understanding as to the consequences of their actions or immature and impulsive decisions.[127]

---

[121] Awdah (n 7) 333–334; Mohammed Bahjat Utabah, Muhadarat Fe Fiqah Al Janahi Al Islami, Mahad Al Darasatal Islamia, p 69.
[122] Hussin (n 109) 11–12.
[123] Awdah (n 7) 334.
[124] Hussin (n 109) 12.
[125] This age could be considered the minimum age of criminal responsibility, but not the penal majority. At this stage their responsibility is diminished.
[126] Awdah (n 7) 335.
[127] Hussin (n 109) 12.

3. Liability of a person with fully mature understanding

The third stage is called *balig wa rashid* (a mature person), that is when a person is presumed to have enough understanding to satisfy legal conditions that they know the consequences of their actions with no doubt that they can distinguish between their actions. Regarding puberty and maturity of understanding the Quran says '… and test the orphans [in your charge] until they reach a marriageable age; then, if you find them to be mature of mind, hand over to them their possession; and do not consume them by wasteful spending, and in haste, ere they grow up …'[128]

This is in fact the age when a person should be able to know or understand the nature of what, how, when, why, and where. This stage starts at the age of 15 according to some schools of thought. However Hanafi jurists, along with the majority of Malikis jurists, agree on the age of 18 to mark the beginning of this third category of maturity. At this age individuals are liable for punishment, whether *hudood, qisas* or *tazeer*.[129] In general, jurists set the age of puberty at 15.[130] However, according to Imam Abu Hanifa, it is 18 years for boys and 17 for girls. The view of the Malikis, often quoted, accords with that of Imam Abu Hanifa, setting puberty at 18 years.[131]

At this stage a person becomes criminally accountable for the committal of any kind of offence, such as *hudood* or *qisas*. Under Islamic criminal law this could be considered the age of penal majority. [132] The above-mentioned verse of the Quran regarding the maturity of mind for handing over the possession of the property to orphans, and the *hadith* about the exemption of a child from criminal responsibility, provide a basis for interpretation in relation to the minimum age of criminal responsibility and penal majority. No specific age has been mentioned in either of these basic sources—this further opens the door for *ijtihad*. Consensus (*ijma*) among jurists should be achieved for setting a uniform threshold age. Consensus is set out in the Quran and *sunnah*. Therefore, consensus of the Muslim jurists on a specific issue is considered binding.[133]

---

[128] Q4:6.

[129] Hussin (n 109) 12–13.

[130] Awdah (n 7) 334.

[131] ibid 334–35.

[132] ibid 335.

[133] AQ Oudah, *Criminal Law of Islam* Vol 214–215; in this regard the Quran says 'O you who have attained to faith! Pay heed unto God, and pay heed unto the Apostle and unto those from among you(Muslim Jurist and Scholars) who have been entrusted with authority! …'. Q4:59. 'And If any matter pertaining to peace or war comes … refer it unto the Apostle and unto those who have been entrusted with authority …' Q4:83. The above mentioned verses of the Quran points out that for a solution of problems either generally or specifically the Muslims have to refer those to the Prophet and those who have been entrusted with authority(the person entrusted with authority include Muslim Jurists, scholars who have deep insight and knowledge in the primary sources of Sharia).

Additionally, at national level better protection can also be offered through the consolidation of laws regarding child offenders in one single, legally binding code. Some Islamic States, such as Malaysia, have attempted to do just that. This code first seeks to establish criminal liability, by first proving that the act committed is unlawful. If it is established, it must be found that the unlawful act was carried out with free consent, by an adult and mentally sound person who is able to distinguish right from wrong. Before imposing a punishment it has to be established that the act was committed with criminal intent and that the accused has the mental capacity to understand the nature as well as the consequences of his act. However, the level of punishment depends on the age of the accused.[134]

According to the Malaysian Sharia Criminal Offences (Federal Territories) Act 1997 (Act 559) section 51 an act committed by a child who is not '*balig*' is not an offence. According to section 2(1) of the same Act the word '*balig*' denotes the age of puberty according to Islamic law. Section 2(1) of the Act provides that an offender means a person above the age of 10 and below the age of 16 years.[135]

In Malaysia, before the Shariat Court, the criminal responsibility of a child is ascertained according to Islamic law. Criminal responsibility starts at age seven and the children have to be treated as minors unless they have reached to the age of puberty. There are two main opinions as to the signs or age of puberty, which set it at 15 or 18 years. Further, the Sharia Criminal Procedure (Federal Territories) Act 1984, defines a 'youthful offender' as a person who is above 10 and below the age of 16 years of age.[136] However, when sentencing, the objectives before the Court seem to be reform and deterrence for the best interest of child/offender. Further, the sentence procedure has to be rehabilitative, so that once the offender has completed his sentence, his reputation and name should not be in a list of 'dangerous or hardened criminals'.[137] The reformation and rehabilitation is of paramount concern to the State. Therefore, to ensure the well-being of children involved, the Shariat Court treats child offenders differently from mature adult criminals. [138]

V. THE DEATH PENALTY AND CHILD OFFENDERS

In Islamic law the death penalty is prescribed for crimes such as murder, adultery, apostasy and armed/highway robbery.[139] According to Islamic

---

[134] Hussin (n 109) 4–5. [135] ibid 10.
[136] ibid 18. [137] ibid 18–19. [138] Hussin (n 109) 19.
[139] Al-Jareema Wal Aquba fi Fiq Al Islami, 134–137; Imam Allaudin Abi-Baqar Bin Masood, Badai-us-Sanaiy, educational press Karachi, Egypt 1910 vol 7, 135,339; Ibn-i-Quddama, Al Mughni, Alazher (Egypt), 1965) vol 4, 143.

jurists and scholars, the manner and circumstances of the offences committed are vital in assessing whether to impose the death penalty. The argument
of the Muslim jurists and scholars is that the manner and circumstances in
which the stated offences are committed must be very serious. For example,
for the crime of murder, Sharia prescribes the death penalty under the principle 'a life for a life.'[140] The source of the prescribed death penalty in
certain offences under Sharia is the Quran. Therefore, challenging the legality of the death penalty, according to Islamic jurists and scholars, should
not be left to human authority.[141]

In considering the crime of murder, Islamic jurists often cite the Quranic
verse which says: 'In the law of *qisas* (retribution) there is (saving of) life for
you, O people of understanding; that you may restrain yourself'.[142] When
an offender infringes the right to life of any other member of the society, his
own right to life becomes conditional and is dependant on the amnesty
offered by the aggrieved party.

The Muslim States where Islamic criminal law is applicable only proce-
durally or commutatively tend to avoid the death penalty in criminal practice, rather than abolish it completely under man-made laws. It is important
to highlight that in order to punish offenders with capital punishment in
Islamic law, irrefutable and strict evidence is required.[143] If the evidence in
a murder case does not meet the evidential requirements according to the
Sharia, it permits, in lieu, payment of *diyah* (blood money) for murder to
the heirs of the victim rather than punishing the offender with the death
penalty and discretionary punishments (*tazeer*) for capital offences under
hudood. In this regard, the *hadith* of the Prophet Muhammed supports the
avoidance of the death penalty.[144] Consequently, Islamic law attempts to
strike a balance between the aggrieved and the aggressor by equalizing the
right of both of the parties to life and then by urging avoidance of the death
penalty as much as possible, through forgiveness by the affected party.

With regard to *qisas* and *diyah*, the Prophet said that 'if a man is
murdered, his heirs have the option to retaliate or agree to accept *diyah*'.[145]
With regard to the amount of blood money, the Prophet stated '*diyah* for
the murdered, is a hundred camels'[146] or money equivalent to their price,[147]

---

[140] Baderin (n 41) 70; Al-Jazari, AR, *Kitab al-Fiqh Ala al-Madhahib al Arba'ah* (1997) vol
5, 281; Al Moqwamat Al Jareema wa Dawafi o-ha, 90.
[141] Baderin ibid.
[142] Q2:179.
[143] Baderin (n 41) 70.
[144] Muhammad bin Ali bin Muhammad Shokani, *Naile al Autar* (Idara tul Quran wa Uloom
Al Islamia, Karachi) vol 7, 118; Baderin ibid 71.
[145] Ash-Shawkani in *Nayl al-Awtar* vol 7, 57, and *Subul-us-Salam* vol 3, 322.
[146] Al Muwatta Imam Malik, 'Chapter 43: Book of Blood-Money' 43 1 (Diwan Press, 1982)
407.
[147] *Tirmazi* (n 59) vol 6, regarding Diyat, 163.

therefore, according to the aforementioned *hadith*, the punishments for wilful murder may be commuted into blood money, provided the heirs of the victim agree on it and accept the amount of blood money.[148] When the heirs of a victim reconcile an offence it results in invalidation of the punishment. The act of reconciliation is effective only up to the extent of *qisas* and *diyah*, and has no bearings on other punishments.[149]

However, in principle the right of *qisas* and the commutation of death penalty in murder cases in lieu of blood money is the right of the victim's heirs. It has been reported in one of the traditions that in cases of *qisas* the Prophet Muhammed recommended pardon.[150] Further, the Quran on this subject emphasizes equity and forgiveness:

> And do not take any human being's life—[the life] which God has willed to be sacred—otherwise than in [the pursuit of] justice. Hence, if anyone has been slain wrongfully, we have empowered the defender of his rights [to exact a just retribution]; but even so, let him not exceed the bounds of equity in [retributive] killing. [And as for him who has been slain wrong-fully-] behold, he is indeed succoured [by God].[151] But [remember that an attempt at] requiting evil may, too, become an evil: hence, whoever pardons [his foe] and makes peace, his rewards rests with God-for verily, he does not love evildoers.[152]

At the international level, the imposition of the death penalty on a juvenile—those under 18—is prohibited under the UNCRC[153] and generally to everyone under the ICCPR,[154] and there is no distinction as to the gravity of the crime. Similarly, based upon the tradition of the Prophet Mohammed, the death penalty cannot be prescribed for a child in Islamic law.[155] The only difference in the UN Conventions and Islamic law is the age of maturity, which is set at 18 years in the former. However, as discussed earlier, the majority of the Islamic jurists fix it at 15 years old corresponding to the age of puberty, whereas the majority of Maliki jurists establish this age at 18 years.[156]

---

[148] *Sunan Abu-Daood, Book Book 39, Number 4491: Chapter: Types of Blood-Wit (Kitab Al-Diyat)* Narrated Abdullah ibn Amr ibn al-'As: The Prophet said: 'A believer will not be killed for an infidel. If anyone kills a man deliberately, he is to be handed over to the relatives of the one who has been killed. If they wish, they may kill, but if they wish, they may accept blood-wit.'

[149] Awdah (n 7) 179; Rad-Al Mukhtar, vol 4 64.

[150] Baderin (n 41) 73; Al-Zuhayli (n 5) vol 5 224–227.

[151] Q17:33.
[152] Q42:40.
[153] Art 37.
[154] Art 1.
[155] Al-Jaziri, Kitab al-Fiqh Ala al- Madahahib al-Arba'ah 1997, Vol 5 269; Baderin (n 41) 74; Bada-Al-Sanai, vol 739.

[156] Awdah (n 7) 334–335.

A. Voluntary ('Semi-wilful' Murder) and Punishment for Child Offenders

The punishment for 'semi-wilful' murder is *diyah (mugalza)*.[157] *Diyah* in Islamic law can be given in place of capital punishment, where the act of murder or injury is not premeditated or otherwise inadvertent. This is a fixed punishment, and the court is not authorized to increase, decrease or waive it. Moreover, it varies according to the nature and extent of an injury or infraction. It is important to note that the *diyah* punishment does not vary on the basis of whether the victim was a child or adult, weak or strong, poor or rich, or ruler or subject.[158]

Islamic scholars and the Sharia diverge from international law on the question of the status of women. According to the majority of the traditional scholars,[159] in the case of murder, the *diyah* for murdering a woman is half the *diyah* of man. In the case of injuries, *diyah* for a female according to Imam Shafi'i and Imam Abu Hanifa is half of that for a male.[160] In contrast, Imam Malik and Imam Ahmed accept it as equal up to the extent of one third; however, if the amount increases, *diyah* becomes half of that of a male.[161] There are a growing number of scholars who are challenging this interpretation, the most prominent being Shaikh Yusuf al-Qaradawi, from Egypt. He has pressed for gender equality on the amount of *diyah* for manslaughter. He argues that 'there is no evidence backing that the compensation paid for mistakenly killing a woman should be half that for a slaughtered man'. Additionally, '[N]o evidence in the Noble *Quran* supports such arguments on discrimination drawn between men and women in that regard.' Stating also 'earlier generations of scholars such as Ibn Alia and Al-Aasam used to pay equal blood money to compensate the families of those killed regardless of their gender.'[162]

In Islamic law murder or homicide is categorized into intentional and quasi-international murder. In cases of intentional murder, the Sharia proscribes *qisas,* whereas in the case of quasi-intentional murder, it

---

[157] Sabiq (n 13) 517–518; AQ Awdah, *Criminal Law of Islam: Volume 1* (International Islamic Publishers, Karachi) 139.

[158] AQ Awdah, *Criminal Law of Islam: Volume 3* (International Islamic Publishers, Karachi) 66.

[159] The Sunni orthodoxy was the culmination of a battleground of ideas in the formative years of Islam in the period following its establishment in the 7th century AD. In this case 'traditional' scholars refers to those Muslim scholars and Imams who follow a strict interpretation of the Quran and the Sharia.

[160] Badai-us-Sanaiy, Imam Allaudin Abi-Baqar Bin Masood (Educational Press Karachi, Egypt, 1910) vol 7 312; Nihayat-ul-Muhtaj, Vol 302; Awdah (n 158) 67.

[161] Sharh-ul-Durdeer, Vol 4, 248; Al Mughni, Vol 9, 523; Awdah ibid 67.

[162] F Al Abbar 'Qaradawi Urges Gender Equality on Blood Money' *Islam Online* http://www.islamonline.net/English/News/2004-12/24/article05.shtml (accessed 20 January 2010). For further details see, Markez Al-darasat Al Arabi-lil Moasir wa Al Mallomat, http://www.amanjordan.org/aman_studies/wmview.php?ArtID=905, accessed 20 January 2010.

proscribes *diyat mugalazah* (heavy *diyah*—blood money). The difference between intentional and quasi-intentional homicide is their difference in punitive measures. The *qisas* punishment is not applicable to quasi-intentional homicide, because for *qisas*, consistency between the criminal act and the punishment is required. In the case of quasi-intentional homicide, there is a lack of *mens rea* for murder and so capital punishment cannot be proscribed. This is the key difference between intentional homicide and quasi-intentional killing.[163] Further, there is a distinction between voluntary and involuntary inadvertent offences; hence *qisas* is the punishment for a voluntary offence, and *diyat mukhafafa* (light *diyah*) is for involuntary offences.[164] However, as far as the case of a child is concerned, their intention is not considered 'valid' due to their inherent weaker understanding. In these cases, *diyat mukhafafa* is payable by child's family.[165]

Qisas punishment is not prescribed for unintentional murder because there is no motive. However, as the offence did occur due to the negligence and carelessness of the offender and he has nonetheless caused a loss to the victim or his legal heirs, pecuniary or materially, (loss of the family breadwinner for example), in this case the Sharia prescribes punishment. Similarly, if someone damages another's property, similar compensatory punishment is awarded. Moreover, this punishment also functions as a warning to others in the community not to act negligently or carelessly.[166] In short, *diyah* is the punishment for intentional offences which do not extend to *qisas*, quasi-intentional offence and involuntary offence. However, the amount of *diyah* differs. *Diyah almukhafafa* (light *diyah)* will be awarded in case of an involuntary offence, whereas heavy *diyah* will apply in the other two cases.[167]

In Sharia, the *diyah* is 100 camels. However, in distinguishing between heavy and light *diyah* the stress is not on numbers, but the kinds and ages of camels.[168] This can be equated to their monetary value in the present day, as white camels are more costly then red, or ordinary camels. Young camels are also more valuable than old camels. Hence, this scale to convert the amount to the form of other material property or currency would be satisfying to the victim or legal heirs.[169]

Regarding the punishment prescribed in the Quran in the case of murder in error:

> The prophet Muhammad said the punishments for wilful murder may be commuted into *diyah,* providing that the heirs of the victim agree on it

[163] Sabiq (n 13) 518; Awdah (n 158) 67.
[164] Nihayat Al Mohtaj, vol 7, 315; Awdah ibid 67.
[165] Al-Zuhayli (n 5) vol 4, 23.   [166] Awdah (n 158) 68–69.
[167] Awdah ibid 69.   [168] Badai Al Sanai, vol 7 383;
[169] Awdah (n 158) 69.

and the amount of blood money will be 30 four-year-old camels, 30 five-year-old camels and 40 pregnant camels, or the monetary equivalent (according to the market value of that time).[170]

Whereas the amount of *diyah* prescribed by Prophet Mohammed for murder by mistake 'is twenty camels four years old, twenty camels five years old, twenty female colts two years old; twenty male colts two year old and as twenty female colts, three years old.'[171] Accordingly, murder in error is unlawful and the punishment for it is light *diyah*.[172] The second caliph, Umar bin al-Khatab, and fourth, Ali bin Abu Talib, believed that if a child is accused of intent to murder, his crime will be considered a mistake because murder by a minor cannot be intentional.[173] However, a child will be punished with the aim of reformation and rehabilitation.[174]

VI. WAYS OF AVOIDING THE DEATH PENALTY FOR JUVENILE OFFENDERS: EXTENTS AND LIMITS

A. *The Relevance of* Ijtihad *and Interpretation of Punishments under Changing Circumstances*

Sharia jurists have formulated three methods of interpretation. The first is literal interpretation, which means that while interpreting a text, the jurist has to remain close to its original meaning in order to understand the original intention. If the text or matter in question needs more clarity, jurists adopt the second mode which is analogy (*qiyas*). In this case, the jurist attempts to extend an original ruling through analogy, indeed some of its forms are close to literal interpretation. [175]

The third mode is *ijtihad* (judicial interpretation)—when several facts have to be decided that are not clearly stated in the texts—without precedent derived from the first or second methods—so the situation appears to be novel. In this case, the interpretation will be based on what is understood as the *purpose* of the law. The basic difference is that in analogy, a legal problem has to be solved by broadening the meaning from a single text. However, while invoking the purpose or the spirit of the law, the jurists interpret by looking at all the text, group of texts collectively. In the third method, the jurist analyses the text on the basis of general principles of law,

---

[170] *Tirmaz* (n 59) vol 6, 'Chapter regarding Diyat' 160.
[171] ibid 157.
[172] Awdah (n 158) 140; *Nihayat Al Mohtaj*, vol 7, 315.
[173] I Khan, *Laws Relating to Children* (Pakistan Law House, Karachi, 2004) 2.
[174] ibid.
[175] Nyazee (n 43) 291.

where they conform to the Sharia.[176] The scope of *ijtihad* remains wide, as where there is no existing provision, a vast base such as *qiyas* or analogy, *urf* (customs) and *muslah murssila* (consideration of common good) are available to reach a verdict. *Ijtihad* would only be resorted to in personal and civil cases and not in matters of crime and punishment (*hudood and qisas*) because clear provisions are required to serve this purpose.[177] Hence, punishments for which clear provisions already exist cannot be changed. Nevertheless, with regard to legislation, two broad approaches are available. In the first, the injunctions ordained in Sharia by commission or by omission have to be followed in letter and spirit and the remaining laws are regarded as permissible, or *mubah*, based on the principle that 'the original rule for all things is permissibility'.[178]

The second legislative approach is to consider everything as prohibited until its permissibility is justified by specific or general principles of the Sharia. This means that every provision of law should be proved valid according to the principles of Sharia. The first approach towards legislation has been followed in Pakistan. In general, the practice is to repeal the laws which contradict the Quran and *sunnah*, and to leave the rest of the laws integral, considering the remaining laws in conformity with the Quran and *sunnah*. For instance, through the promulgation of the Hudood Ordinances, several new provisions have been introduced and some of the provisions of the Penal Code have been repealed while leaving a huge number of the penal laws integral and unaffected; this is also the case with the Criminal Procedural Code. In this case, it has been assumed that the remaining provisions are not contradictory to the text of the Quran and *sunnah*.[179]

In the light of changing circumstances, *ijtihad* among the jurists of the time and the different modes of interpretation and legislation are tools which facilitate the reformation of laws and procedures. In the context of formulation and reformation of laws dealing with juvenile offenders, the possibility of *ijtihad* in evolving and changing circumstances seems to be more relevant and practical for legislation and codification of laws and procedures.

1. Changing societal circumstances and the age of criminal responsibility

An important question is whether changing societal circumstances can be taken into account when setting a threshold age of criminal responsibility, and for achieving compatibility between Islamic law and international law. Ways to bridge the gap in this regard need to be examined, particularly since several Muslim States that practise Sharia at national level have also ratified the UNCRC and other relevant international conventions.

---

[176] ibid.
[178] Nyazee (n 43) 293.
[177] Awdah (n 91) 151.
[179] ibid.

If we look at these questions in the light of the *hadith* of the Prophet relating to the age of puberty and mental maturity, we see they are treated separately.[180] Accordingly, if a person is physically mature, but mentally immature, they cannot be held responsible for their acts. Physical maturity alone is not enough to ensure criminal responsibility, because physical maturity does not always imply mental maturity. The age of puberty and mental maturity may be different from person to person, with various different reasons, including genetic, geographical, cultural, educational, and level of development of a particular country. In the present day, associating the age of criminal liability with puberty can not be done with a reliable, fixed point. Imam Malik sets the age of puberty and accountability at 18 years old. This seems to be more practical as it does not contradict the core principle of equity and sources of Islamic law. This juristic interpretation appears to consider the elements of physical as well as mental maturity, mentioned in the *hadith*, and both of them are equally important for defining criminal accountability and penal majority, as well as being compatible with the UNCRC.

Is *ijtihad* through analogy permitted in deciding matters of crime and punishment? Islamic jurists differ on the question of drawing analogy. Jurists who allow the analogy principle for the determination of crime and punishment derive their argument from an interpretation of the Prophet Mohammed's dialogue with Mu'atdh bin Jabal on the eve of appointing him as the governor of Yemen. When the Prophet asked how he would decide the matter in hand, Mu'adth ibn Jabal said, 'I will first try to decide it in accordance with the *Quran*. If no provision is to be found in the *Quran*, then I will seek guidance from the *Sunnah*. But if no provision is found in the *Sunnah* either, then I will decide the matter at my own discretion'.[181] The Prophet approved this method. Although the statement is general and not related specifically to crime and punishment, it is felt by jurists that Mu'adt ibn Jabal was being sent on an administrative assignment, wherein, as head of the province, law and justice were part of his remit. His observation that he would resort to *ijtihad* (discretionary inference) constitutes a general statement containing no details whatsoever and therefore, the justification for analogy could apply in matters of crime and punishment.[182]

Jurists also resort to the opinion of the Prophet's cousin, companion and fourth Caliph of the Muslims, Ali Ibn Abi Talib, on the punishment of an alcoholic. When the Prophet's companions sought Ali's guidance as to the kind of punishment to be imposed on a drunkard, he observed, 'When a person drinks liquor, he will naturally be intoxicated and will, in a state of

---

[180] Al- Hafiz Abi Essa Mohammed Bin Essa Al-Tirmazi, *Sunnan Tirmazi,* 'Chapter regarding person who are exempted from hudood Punishments' vol 2, 64.
[181] *Sunan Abu Daood,* 'Chapter on Ijtihad' Hadith No 3592.
[182] Awdah (n 7) 220.

delirium, utter nonsense and calumniate the people'. The Prophet's Companions then prescribed the punishment of slander for drinking liquor as well. Analogy was used to extract the ruling for slander to find the appropriate punishment for drinking. However, there are some jurists who do not accept analogy as a way to determine crime and punishment. They argue that the *hudood* and expiations are a priori matters; therefore, assumptions cannot be made about them. On the other hand, the purpose of analogy is to reach out to the root cause of the problem, so for those provisions of which the root cause cannot be understood, analogy is not the best possible route.[183]

Further, they argue that *hudood* are punishments. If the method of analogy were invoked, there would be a chance of error which could create doubt and in case of doubt, a *hudood* punishment is quashed. The punishments of *hudood* and *qisas* cannot be quashed if the offender and the offence fulfil all of the requirements. For cases of doubt, the Prophet said, analogy involves the risk of error, which in its turn involves doubt, which invalidates *hudood*. As the Prophet enjoins that 'the presence of doubts rescinds the *hudood*'.[184] Some punishments, like the death penalty under *hudood* or *qisas,* cannot be changed. They can be avoided if there is some sort of doubt about, or missing part, of the procedure, or in cases of intentional murder if there is an agreement on blood money.[185]

However, jurists in favour of analogy in the matters of crime tend not to support the creation of new crimes and punishments.[186] Their intention seems to be to broaden the scope of the application of existing rules to other, similar matters. This is the reason analogy has acquired a place as a method of law-making in matters of crime and punishment. Further, analogy is a tool used for interpretation, limited only to ascertaining facts which closely resemble the existing provisions. For example, if a provision of the Sharia declares anything specifically unlawful for a particular reason, if analogy is used, it will cover all the similar cases under its ambit, where the reason or cause of its unlawfulness is known. However the intent should be to avoid injustice.[187]

It is clear that Islamic jurists are not opposed to analogical deduction in analytical reasoning in criminal cases. In order to provide a wide scope to assess crime and punishment, the jurists have even acknowledged customary practices or the practices of the companions of the Prophet as sources of law, although they do not accept them as origins of criminal law.[188]

---

[183] ibid.
[185] Awdah (n 7) 221–222.
[187] Awdah (n 7) 221–222.

[184] Al Shokani (n 144) vol 7 118.
[186] ibid 221–222.
[188] ibid 222.

2. Conclusion

The above interpretations and differences of opinion do not have any direct impact on offences committed by children. As mentioned above, children are exempt from *hudood* and *qisas* punishments. Therefore if a child commits an offence, for which the punishment is death, then they have to be exempt from this punishment and that could be converted into light *diyah,* for murder and *tazeer* in cases of other *hudood* crimes. In fact most of the legislation with regard to child offenders is done in the area of *tazeer,* which is quite flexible and where *ijtihad,* under changing circumstances, might play a significant role.

B. Basis for Diyah *and Islamic Law*

Diyah (blood money) is discussed in the following verses of the Quran:

> O you who have attained to faith! Just retribution is ordained for you in cases of killing: the free for the free, and the slave for the slave, and the woman for the woman. And if something (of his guilt] is remitted to a guilty person by his brother, this [remission] shall be adhered to with fairness, and restitution to this fellowman shall be made in a goodly manner. This is an alleviation from your Sustainer, and an act of his grace. And for him who none the less, wilfully transgresses the bounds of what is right there is grievous suffering in store:[189] for, in [the law of] just retribution, O you who are endowed with insight, there is life for you, so that you might remain conscious of God'.[190]

In Islam there is no justification of arbitrary killings. To ensure justice and due process of law, the Quran states: '... take not life which Allah has made sacred, except by way of justice and law. ...' [191]

1. Settlement, reconciliation or compromise

Under Islamic law, another method to avoid the death penalty is settlement or compromise. According to jurists, in cases of intentional murder the heirs of the victim are allowed to make a compromise to release the

---

[189] Q2:178; Asad (n 12) 47–48. As for as the term *qisas* occurring at the beginning of the above passage, it must be pointed out that—according to all the classical commentators—it is almost synonymous with *mussawah*, ie, 'making a thing equal [to another thing]'; in this instance, making the punishment equal (or appropriate) to the crime—a meaning which is best rendered as 'just retribution' and not (as it has been often, and erroneously rendered) as 'retaliation'.

[190] Q2:178.

[191] Q6:151.

offender from *qisas* against any valuable thing agreed upon between the parties.[192] The amount of the valuable thing could be more or less than the amount of *diyah*. The parties are also allowed to pay the amount in lump sum, or in installments.[193] Settlement and compromise has also been encouraged by Islamic law, in all the matters in this regard the Quran says 'and compromise is better'.[194] The difference between *diyah* and compromise is that for *diyah*, the amount and modes of payment are fixed whereas, for compromise, these are decided at the discretion of the parties involved.

As the death penalty under *qisas* and *hudood* cannot be imposed on a child, light *diyah* has to be payable by the child's family.[195] Islamic jurists have differing opinions regarding the imposition of *diyah*. Imam Malik, Abu Hanifa and Ahmed argue that *diyah* is obligatory for a delinquent child. However, the payment of the *diyah* has to be made by the family. In their opinion, even the intentional offence of a child is actually inadvertent and not a premeditated offence, and for this reason the intention will be considered inadvertent. [196]

However, in this regard the Shafi'i school of thought have two opinions. One supports the above opinion, whereas the other believes that the intention of a child will be considered as intention only and *qisas* will not be enforced against a child even if a child commits an intentional homicide. However, in such cases, corrective chastisement is justifiable and the child's intention will be considered as equivalent to that of a sensible adult. Therefore, their property will be subject to the payment of blood money.[197]

2. Justification of the payment of blood money by the family of a juvenile offender

In Sharia, the principle of personal accountability is strictly applied.[198] Therefore, everyone is responsible for his own acts and not for the act of any other person.[199] In this regard the Quran says: 'Who so doeth right, it is for his soul; and whoso doeth wrong it is against it (his soul)'.[200] The Quran states: 'He who doeth wrong will have the recompense thereof'[201] and 'Every soul draws the need of its act on none but itself: no bearer of burden shall bear the burden of another.'[202]

The only exception to this convention is the sharing of the payment of blood money whereby the burden of compensation in case of 'quasi-wilful'

---

[192] Anwarullah (n 39) 98.
[193] The amount or property on which the settlement occurs is called Badal al-Sulh.
[194] Q4:128.   [195] Al-Zuhayli (n 5) vol 4, 23.
[196] Awdah (n 91) 70.   [197] ibid 70.
[198] Khan and Syed (n 8) 132.   [199] Anwarullah (n 39) 28
[200] Q41:46.   [201] Q4:123.
[202] Q6:164.

homicide or homicide committed by error is shared by the members of the offender's family. This exception is based on the principle of pure justice, since, in the case of quasi-wilful murder or murder committed in error, personal punishment appears to be extremely unjust and cruel.[203] However, some Islamic jurists do not treat the imposition of *diyah* on the family members of the offender under the principle of personal punishment as an exception. Their argument is that blood money is not imposed on them because they are held accountable for the act of the offender. In fact, the basic responsibility for the compensation in such a case still lies with the offender, and the family is enjoined to share the burden as a matter of filial sympathy, without incurring accountability for any part of the offender's crime.[204]

3. The amount of blood money paid by the family of child offender

Islamic jurists differ on the amount of payment of blood money that should be paid by the members of a child's family in cases of a semi-intentional and unintentional offence. In the opinion of Imam Ahmed, the offender's family members would pay up to one third or more of the blood money, whereas the offender is liable to pay less than one third of the full *diyah*. According to Imam Abu Hanifa, less than one twentieth of the *diyah* due will be paid by the offender and whatever is in excess of this will be paid by his or her family.[205] However, according to Imam Shafi'i, whatever the amount of *diyah* is, it will be borne by the offender's family in full.[206]

Who is to pay the *diyah* if there is no *aqila* (kinsmen on the father's side)? There are two opinions on what should occur if there is no *aqila*, if the offender is poor, or if his family or community is so small that they are unable to pay the whole amount of *diyah*.. The four schools of *Sunni* Islamic jurisprudence believe that if there is no one to stand as *aqila* or if an offender is poor, the public exchequer or the government will stand as *aqila*. This is the opinion held by the schools of Imam Malik and Imam Shafi'i. The apparent position of the Hanafis and the Hanbalis is the same. The second opinion is that only the offender is liable to pay, and the money has to be recovered from the assets or property of the offender. The burden on the family is only to ease an offender's burden.[207]

---

[203] Khan and Syed (n 8) 132.
[204] ibid.
[205] Awdah (n 91) 70–71.
[206] The term '*aqila*' includes all the kinsmen and relations on the father's side, however remote they may be. However, *diyah* is imposed upon the *aqila* as a help and compassion for the offender and not due to fault of their own'; Awdah ibid 71.
[207] ibid 72–73.

In this manner, the Sharia has allowed the system of payment of *diyah* by the family, as a way of attempting to ensure mercy and justice. However, at present the possibility of establishing a system of relying on an *aqila* is questionable because the system of *aqila* presupposes the continuation of the family system, which has to some extent disintegrated. In this case, the remaining family consists of a number of individuals who have to share the burden of *diyah*. The existence of *aqila* is only possible if people adhere to their paternal tribes and clans. However, in most States, this situation no longer exists. Therefore, one has to accept either of the two alternatives prescribed by the Muslim jurists, that is, that the offender should bear the entire burden of *diyah* or that it will be paid out of the public treasury.[208]

The concept of *aqila* enables the victim and or their next of kin to receive some degree of compensation for their injuries from the family of offenders. The alternative is that the public exchequer pays out the *diyah*. This view appears to be closer to meeting the ends of justice.[209]

The logic behind the act of pardoning the offender has seemed to be to avert feuds and future animosity in communities, as well as giving the offender the opportunity to reform and learn from their actions without punitive measures. Although the compensation cannot equate the harm done to the victim, it offers some sort of remedy. Otherwise, the victim's party would be in a worse situation, particularly if the victim was the sole breadwinner. In such cases, legal heirs should not be left destitute. [210] In an attempt to maintain justice, Sharia law disregards the offender's personality or status in the society if the offence undermines social life, in order to protect the community. However, as far as other crimes are concerned, Sharia gives due consideration to the personality of the offender and, while sentencing, it allows the court or person in authority to take into account the offender's personality, moral character and the circumstances of the case.[211]

4. *The* diyah *debate*

The debate over *diyah* highlights the dual nature of *diyah* within Islamic criminal law and mark out the two functions of *diyah*: as a tortious compensatory claim (monetary compensation as a substitute for *qisas*) and as a penal measure. Therefore, in cases of intentional murder or injury, the legal heirs of the victim may opt for *diyah* or monetary compensation instead of penal measures under *qisas*/retribution, as a compensatory tortious remedy under their sole prerogative as legal heirs. In these cases the

---

[208] ibid 76.
[209] ibid 76–77.
[210] Al- Zuhayli (n 5) 431–446; Khan and Syed (n 8) 343–344.
[211] Awdah (n 158) 4.

State authorities only honour the agreement between the parties and monitor it to ensure there is no injustice.

However, in case of unintentional death or injury, *diyah* stands as a penal measure unless the State orders the offender to pay the *diyah* to the legal heirs and, in case of injury, to the victim. On the other hand, in cases where death or injury is unintentional, *diyah* serves as a primarily penal measure, ordered by the State to be paid to the victim or his heirs. This is more or less a State administrative action for achieving justice for the legal heirs or victim; therefore it does not need to ask the parties for their willingness. Jurists have argued over the *diyah* as a penal as well as tortious provision. However, the nature of *diyah* as a penal measure or a tortious remedy remains deeply contested, which will be illustrated by the following.

The difference between the Islamic concept of *diyah* as compensation or blood money along with optional penal provision from the Western concept of criminal justice is that in the Western system, it is the State that has the right to prosecute and punish the offender for homicide or injury.[212] However, in Islamic criminal jurisprudence the right to opt for *diyah* lies with the legal heirs or victim. Hence, in Islamic criminal justice, homicide or injuries are considered within the jurisdiction of private prosecution under the rubric of the Islamic criminal justice system, that is, State prosecution. This leads to a hypothetical argument with regard to the nature of *diyah,* along with the possible purpose it draws from this arrangement. Some scholars view it as a punishment because the *diyah* amounts are predetermined by the State and not by the victim or their legal heirs.[213] Others see *diyah* as a tortious remedy whose purpose is to ensure equality, in order to preserve justice between the parties. Since the *qisas* attempts to redress and match the injury or method adopted by the offender, and because in most cases it is difficult to know the exact mode or level, *diyah* seems to serve the purpose of justice.[214] However, according to Rudolph Peters, since the *diyah* is liable to be paid by the *aqila* (family) and not by the offender, it is a tortious claim and does not fall under penal law.[215]

The second argument regarding the tortious nature of *diyah* is that the victim is free to opt either to pardon the offender without compensation, or to demand it. Therefore, this action of pardoning or claiming compensation

---

[212] Even within Islamic criminal law, the State retains the right to punish the offender through discretionary punishments (*tazeer*). However, the right to demand *diyah* in place of retaliation rests with the victim and his family.

[213] Lippman, McConville and Yerushalmi (n 14) 82.

[214] A Abd al-Aziz al Alfi, 'Punishment in Islamic Criminal Law' in Cherif Bassiouni (n 5) 230.

[215] R Peters, *Crime and Punishment in Islamic Law* (CUP, Cambridge, 2006) 49; The offenders' solidarity group. For an elaboration of the historical usage of *Aqilah* and its modern understanding, see the lecture delivered by Sayed Sikandar Shah, 'Homicide in Islam: Major Legal Themes' (the International Islamic University, Malaysia, April 1999) 15.

does not seem to resemble punishment, which is more or less of a corporal nature. This reveals that strictly speaking it is a tort and not a crime: 'not strictly punishment, but ... in the nature of compensation, which must be paid to the victim as reparation for the injury.'[216] In short, if the two juristic opinions are put together the purpose of understanding the intended context *diyah* becomes clearer. In the case of intentional homicide and injury, it provides primarily a compensatory option to *qisas*, whereas in unintentional acts, *diyah* stands as a punishment under the authority of the State.

One criticism on the applicability of the law of *diyah* is that there are States where there are no codified provisions regarding *diyah*, such as Saudi Arabia. All the power is with the legal heirs of the victim; therefore, *diyah* law can be used unjustly and at the whim of one party. In some instances it has been observed that some of the conditions or amounts of *diyah* were so high that it was not possible for ordinary families to raise that amount on their own, which is an abuse of authority. [217]

The *diyah* is not just a monetary amount. It is an instrument in Islamic criminal law which provides a criminal as well as civil remedy.[218] It is a punitive measure, but on the other hand it is a civil or tortious remedy in which the payment of damages are transferred to the victim or his legal heirs. As a result, it cannot be defined strictly as either a penal or civil provision. Its function is also to send a message of forgiveness and monetary compensation to victims or their legal heirs. The nature of the *diyah* raises a question about the possibility of Islamic criminal law being compatible or reconcilable with the Western legal system. Schacht answers this question in the affirmative—its application according to him is 'well in line with the trend of contemporary Western legal thought'.[219]

It is important to examine the role of States in acting as mediators between victim and offender families in cases involving child offenders. These State initiatives aim to avoid the death penalty for child offenders by the principle and amount of *diyah*. In Saudi Arabia for example, cases of murder and manslaughter are dealt with under the Islamic right of *qisas*, wherein legal heirs of the victim have the right to decide. Therefore, under the principle of *qisas*, they have been given three options. They can demand execution of the offender, accept *diyah*, or forgive unconditionally. However, in Saudi Arabian culture the *aqila*/family is at liberty to set any condition; for example the legal heirs can demand any amount as *diyah* or

---

[216] A Abd al-Aziz al Alfi (n 214) 230.

[217] ibid fn 10.

[218] R Peters, 'The Islamization of Criminal Law: A Comparative Analysis' (1994) 34 Die Welt des Islams 2.

[219] J Schacht, *Islamic Law in Contemporary States* (1959) B The American Journal of Comparative Law 2, 147.

ask it to be paid within a certain time period. As mentioned above, in the *hadith* the amount is specified, so culture also has an influence on how this right is carried out. The Saudi King, as well as the government and other leaders are involved as goodwill ambassadors to both parties in order to mutually agree on the amount of *diyah*. Therefore, reconciliatory committees work to help the parties to settle their cases. For example, the Makkah Committee[220] dealt with 420 cases and secured 104 pardons in one year.[221] This is one practical initiative of the State in working to avoid death penalty enforcement, where the law provides a way out. However, this does not appear to be a permanent solution. For example, the royal family encouraged a settlement between both families in the case of the 17-year-old Sadiq Ali Abdullah al-Jama, who was sentenced to death for murder. According to Human Rights Watch, the Royal family encouraged the settlement in lieu by *diyah* of a sum of 12 million riyals (US$3.2 million) which was reduced to 5 million riyals (US$1.3 million) after negotiations. In this case the offender remained in prison during the raising of the *diyah* money and until the legal heirs of the victim attained puberty, thus making them legally able to accept the *diyah* as settlement.[222] In Saudi Arabia, children who have reached 'puberty' can receive the death penalty for crimes. Judges can also consider a defendant's physical characteristics when meting punishment, rather than specific ages. Until recent years the age of criminal responsibility in Saudi Arabia was seven years (it was raised to 12 in 2006 but only for boys, and it is applied inconsistently). There is no minimum age of criminal responsibility for girls.

In another case, 17-year-old Abd al Majid bin Mubark al-Anizi was sentenced to death for murder. The legal heirs of the victim agreed not to resort to *qisas*, but put a condition that the amount of 10 million riyals (US$2.68 million) had to be paid as *diyah* within one year of the decision. The family of the offender collected the demanded amount but fell short by about 4 million riyals. According to Human Rights Watch, the balance was raised with the help of the Crown Prince and the Governor of Riyadh region in March 2007, within the time set by the victim's party.[223] Similarly, in another case in April 2005, a boy aged 14, Fawaz Bin Mohamed, was sentenced to death for murdering his classmate. A sum of 3.5 million riyals (US$ 933,300) was demanded by the legal heirs of victim as *diyah*, payable in one year and on the condition that the offender leave the area.[224]

---

[220] Reconciliation Committees in murder cases operating in Mecca.
[221] 'Royal decree OKs Terms of Pardon in Murder Cases' http://arabnews.com/ ?page=1&section=0&article=118966&d=7&m=2&y=2009.
[222] ibid.
[223] http://www.hrw.org/en/node/62308/section/6#_ftn93.
[224] ibid;see also http://www.okaz.com.sa/okaz/osf/20060730/Con2006073035715.htm (HRW report).

Due to the concern and outcry within the State over the unjust abuse of authority, the current ruler, King Abdullah, on recommendations, issued a Royal Decree aiming to regulate the conditions of pardon to those sentenced to death in homicide cases. Further, it also required that committees be set up at local level in order to help the victim's family and offender to reach at just agreement.[225]

In Iran, the judiciary newsletters[226] reported[227] that a juvenile offender on death row for committing a murder was granted amnesty by the victim's family and was spared execution as a result of the Department of Justice's negotiations with both families. The role of the authorities in reaching this deal was confirmed b the Iranian Public prosecutor.[228] On 2 June 2009, the chief of the special court for juveniles in Khuzestan province, in the city of Ahvaz, reported that more than 100 cases reached a compromise between the parties due to the hard work of the judges. [229]

In other Muslim jurisdictions the *diyah* is defined and fixed in the law. The Zamfara Sharia Penal Code of Northern Nigeria, for example, defines *diyah* as 'a fixed amount of money paid to a victim of bodily hurt or to the deceased's agnatic heirs in murder cases, the quantum of which is one thousand dinars, or twelve thousand dirham or 100 camels'.[230]

However, in intentional homicide cases the legal heirs may ask for retaliation (*qisas*) or resort to *diyah* as an alternative, thus forfeiting their right of *qisas*.[231] Hence, if properly enforced this fixation of the amount of *diyah* could lead towards more stability, and could stop exploitation through demands of high amounts, for putting undue pressure on the other party. The objection rose as to the purpose and manner of *qisas,* which is to punish the offender as befits the original crime; this is the strict legal punishment. The alternative to *qisas* is *diyah* and full pardon, which is in line with the ethical or communal ethos of the Islamic legal system, which urges the victim to forgive and reconcile. [232]

It is important that while incorporating the *diyah* into a legal system, that first the aim and intent of this ethical/reconciliatory provision has to be understood. The Islamic mode of compensation and punishment aims to achieve 'justice, general and specific deterrence and reformation and rehabilitation'.[233]

---

[225] ibid 8.
[226] Iranian Judicial Gazette, Maa'va website 30 November 2008.
[227] ibid.
[228] Iranian Judicial Gazette, Maa'va website 30 November 2008.
[230] S 59 Zamfara Sharia Penal Code (hereinafter ZSPC).
[231] S 200 ZSPC.
[232] L Ahmed, *Women and Gender in Islam: Historical Roots of a Modern Debate* (Yale University Press, New Haven, 1993).
[233] Ahmad Abd al-Aziz al Alfi (n 214).

VII. CONCLUSIONS

Under Sharia law a child cannot be liable under criminal law, due to immaturity—they can only be liable for correctional or disciplinary action. Only the ruler or person in authority, according to the circumstances of the case, can decide the suitable punishment.[234] The principle of treating juveniles as distinct from adults is clearly present in Islamic jurisprudence (although in practice in modern States these conventions are not always adhered do). If a minor is guilty of an offence, according to Islamic principles, he or she should not be punished in the same manner as an adult.[235] Imam-Abu-Yusuf believed that a child cannot be sentenced in case there are doubts about their age.[236] Abu Bakr Siddiq, the first caliph[237] after the death of Mohammed, did not mete out punishment when a minor charged with theft appeared before him. Further, as mentioned above, the second caliph, Umar bin al-khatab, and fourth, Ali bin Abu Talib, believed that if a child is accused of intent to murder, his crime will be considered a mistake because murder by a minor cannot be intentional. However, a child will be punished with the aim of reformation and rehabilitation.[238]

Regarding disciplinary punishment, the person in authority is given wide discretion to consider all relevant circumstances according to the best interests of the child. Therefore, a wide range of punishments exist, which may include beating (light beating), admonishing, handing over to a guardian for reformation, or to any institution established for such a purpose. These measures adopted should reform the child and provide an environment away from the one in which they were involved in wrongdoing.[239] Therefore, disciplinary punishment is an opportunity to avoid being labelled a criminal or habitual offender, so that the child might be able to rehabilitate himself and not carry the stigma of criminality into their adult life.[240]

In Sharia law, a close link is found between the age of the offender and criminal accountability. Criminal accountability is closely linked with free choice, full mental awareness, and reaching maturity. If any of these elements are missing, an individual is not liable for the punishment for a specific crime which they have committed. As explored in the sections above, the exemption of children from being punished according to the

---

[234] Awdah (n 7) 337.
[235] I Khan, *Laws Relating to Children* (Pakistan Law House, Karachi, 2004) 2.
[236] ibid.
[237] Head of the Caliphate (the first system of governance established in Islam) a caliph is the political and religious leader of the Ummah (Muslim Community). The word caliph is also used to describe the successors to the Prophet Mohammed.
[238] ibid.
[239] Awdah (n 7) 337.
[240] ibid 338.

more serious measures of *hudood* and *qisas* is rooted in the original *hadiths*, or sayings of the Prophet's life recorded after his death. These *hadiths* have guided life in Muslim States, and provided further explanations in matters of law and jurisprudence (among other spheres of life) to the laws set out in the Quran which form the first source of Islamic law.

Basing upon the *hadith*, Islamic jurists admit that a child would not be liable to the death penalty under *hudood* and *qisas*. However, there are many different opinions among Muslim jurists about when an individual is no longer a child and for attaining criminal responsibility and penal majority; these range from seven to 19. Accordingly, setting the age limit for penal majority regarding the implementation of the death penalty under *hudood* and *qisas,* is an important part of protecting children from receiving these penalties. The non-specification of age in the Quran and *sunnah* provides room and flexibility for setting the age of criminal liability at 18 or even 19. In order to avoid the death penalty, the age threshold needs to rise; this will not only make it compatible with international standards for the protection of children but it will also offer substantive increased protection for children in Muslim States.

A balance must be struck between the victim and the offenders. As children cannot be given the death penalty, in order to compensate the loss to some extent, the punishment can be converted to *diyah*. *Diyah* attempts to provide a solution to the problem. However, in practice States implementing the rules of Islamic criminal law do not follow them as intended. In Islamic law the amount of *diyah* is fixed and clear guidelines have been provided by *sunnah* in this regard, but in practice States are exceeding limits and setting their own standards, sometimes too high, which puts pressure on the vulnerable and renders the payment of blood money almost impossible. Consequently, these acts lead to a situation in which *diyah* becomes a problem in itself, and not the solution. Proper codification of those procedures and law should lead to greater uniformity and more protection.

Some instruments have been developed for the protection of human rights, for the individual generally and also for children particularly. The Universal Islamic Declaration of Human Rights and the Cairo Declaration on Human Rights in Islam include some of the provisions regarding criminal procedure, and no doubt those provisions could also be invoked for the protection of the rights of child offenders. However, these two instruments are declarations and carry little legal obligation. It is hoped that proper implementation at national level of the legally binding Covenant on the Rights of the Child in Islam (2005) could offer more protection for children.

PART II

Introduction

This Chapter presents national laws and case studies of selected Muslim States, and non-Muslim States related to juvenile offenders: reports appear for Afghanistan, Egypt, Iran, Lebanon, Malaysia, Nigeria, Pakistan, Turkey, Spain, the UAE and the UK. The Chapter highlights issues relating to the mechanism of integration of international law into domestic legal systems, and examines the relevant national laws pertaining to the child in criminal matters, such as the legal minimum age of criminal liability, special courts, and court procedures for juvenile offenders. It also explores the laws and court practices related to the death penalty of under-18s in each jurisdiction. It also analyses the extent of considerations of given to Islamic law and the impact and the Convention of the Rights of the Child (UNCRC) on the legal situation of juvenile offenders in Muslim States. Additionally, it focuses on measures adopted by States for the protection of the rights of the juvenile offenders and in cases of the death penalty involving children. Finally, it attempts to identify and analyse different judicial trends on the subject and examines the interpretation of the age of criminal liability by the courts, observing the difference between law and practice.

CHAPTER 4

Criminal Law and Rights of the Child in Afghanistan[*]

I. INTRODUCTION

In Afghanistan the drastically changing political scenario, particularly in the last 30 years, has shaken the basic infrastructure of the judiciary and the various law enforcement agencies.[1] Poor working conditions, including the lack of security provided to judges, and the present state of war, provide little incentive to promote human rights. Corruption in the justice sector, amongst both judges and police, is a further obstacle to the administration of justice.[2]

In the present legal system of the Islamic Republic of Afghanistan, the conduct of the parties in the criminal justice system is mainly regulated by several codes and legal instruments. For trials, investigations and punishment of offences and crimes, a body of codes and laws are applicable along with the specific provisions of the Afghan Constitution (AC) of 2004. This legislation includes the Criminal Procedure Law of 1965 (1344) and its 1974 amendments (CPL), the Interim Criminal Procedure Code for Courts (ICPC) of 2004, the Law on Detection and Investigation of Crimes (LDIC) of 1978, for the punishment of crimes the Afghan Penal Code (PC) of 1976 and its amendments, Offences relating to the Anti-Money Laundering and Proceeds of Crime Law (AML) of 2004, Crimes regarding the Financing of Terrorism Law of 2004, the Counter Narcotics Law (CNL) of 2005, and the Juvenile Code (JC) of 2005.

In an attempt to re-establish the judiciary, in 2001 the United Nations sponsored a conference in Bonn, which was successful in providing agreement[3] calling for the establishment of a Supreme Court.[4] Therefore, the

---

[*] Mohamed Elewa Badar, LLB, LLM, PhD.

[1] Commentary on the Interim Criminal Procedure Code for Courts for the Transitional Islamic State of Afghanistan by Justice Dr Giuseppe di Gennaro (internally circulated within Afghanistan international community) which he drafted whilst heading the Italian Justice Project Office in Kabul. For the full text of the Afghan Interim Criminal Procedure Code for Courts, see the Official Gazette, Extraordinary Issue, Issue No 820, February 25, 2004, available online at http://www.afghanistantranslation.com/, last accessed 28 March, 2009.

[2] Afghanistan profile on Human Rights Watch World Report 2009 available at http://www.hrw.org/en/node/79295, accessed 17 September 2009.

[3] Known as the Bonn 2001 agreement.

[4] 1(2) of the Bonn Agreement.

restablishment of the justice system was one of the significant parts of that process.[5]

II. NATIONAL LEGAL FRAMEWORK

In an effort to rebuild the three branches of the Afghan State after the conflict that began in 2001, the Bonn Conference mandated a new Constitution, adopted on 3 January 2004. The Constitution declares Afghanistan an Islamic Republic. In this spirit, it asserts that 'no law can be contrary to the beliefs and provisions of the sacred religion'.[6] This indicates that the laws of the State should be compatible with the Islamic injunctions.

Also worth noting is article 130, which instructs the judges how to apply the law. The article states that:

> While processing the cases, the courts apply the provisions of this Constitution and other laws. When there is no provision in the Constitution or other laws regarding ruling on an issue, the courts' decisions shall be within the limits of this Constitution in accordance with the Hanafi[7] jurisprudence and in a way to serve justice in the best possible manner.

In fact, article 130 set forth a hierarchy of laws which are to be followed by the Afghan courts. The hierarchy includes: the Afghan Constitution, international instruments and Islamic law (Shariah) in specific cases, and these latter sources should be applied in conformity with the Afghan Constitution. Article 27[8] provides that:

> [N]o deed shall be considered a crime unless ruled by a law promulgated prior to commitment of the offense. No one shall be pursued, arrested, or detained without due process of law. No one shall be punished without the decision of an authoritative court taken in accordance with the provisions of the law, promulgated prior to commitment of the offence.

---

[5] Commentary on the Interim Criminal Procedure Code for Courts for the Transitional Islamic State of Afghanistan by Justice Dr Giuseppe di Gennaro (internally circulated within Afghanistan international community) which he drafted whilst heading the Italian Justice Project Office in Kabul. For the full text of the Afghan Interim Criminal Procedure Code for Courts, see the Official Gazette, Extraordinary Issue, Issue No 820, Feb 25, 2004, available online at http://www.afghanistantranslation.com/, accessed 28 March, 2009.

[6] Art 3, The Constitution of Afghanistan.

[7] Hanafi is one of the four Madhhab (Schools of Law) in jurisprudence within Sunni Islam. It is the oldest of the four, with a reputation for putting greater emphasis on the role of reason and being slightly more liberal than the other three schools.

[8] Reporture for Afghanistan.

A. Protection under Constitutional Law

The Constitution of Afghanistan asserts a dedication to the respect for fundamental rights and freedoms, with reference to the United Nations Charter as well as the Universal Declaration of Human Rights.[9] Discrimination on any grounds is prohibited by article 22, which specifically mentions the equal standing of men and women before the law. Rights protected by the Constitution include: the right to life,[10] right to liberty,[11] right to a fair trial, freedom from torture,[12] right to hold un-armed demonstrations for legitimate peaceful purposes,[13] freedom and confidentiality of correspondence,[14] right to not have residence invaded,[15] the right to education[16] and the right to work.[17]

It is important to note that not all of the above rights are absolute in their protection. Many have limitations as the obligation of the State in upholding the right. To cite an example, the right to not have one's property invaded does not apply where there is evidence of a crime. In this case, the official in charge of the investigation may enter the property and investigate. Other rights can be suspended, though this is subject to there being a state of emergency. Examples of such rights include the right to be pursued, arrested or detained only in accordance with the law,[18] freedom to hold un-armed demonstrations,[19] right to correspond and communicate without state interference[20] and right to not have one's residence invaded.[21]

In an effort to encourage the protection of the rights and freedoms enshrined in the Constitution, article 58 calls for the establishment of an Independent Human Rights Commission. Any individual who has suffered a violation of their fundamental rights is able to file a complaint to the Commission.[22] The Commission is entitled to inform the legal authorities of the violation and provide assistance in defending the complainant's rights.

The provisions of the constitution could be invoked for the protection of children who come in conflict with the laws, since the provisions offer protection to all the citizens of Afghanistan irrespective of age or gender.

1. Right to life

Under article 23, the right to life states that 'no one shall be deprived of this

---

[9] Art 7(1) of the Constitution of the Islamic Republic of Afghanistan (3 January 2004).
[10] ibid art 23.
[11] ibid art 24.
[12] ibid art 29.
[13] ibid art 36.
[14] Art 37, The Constitution of Afghanistan.
[15] ibid art 38.
[16] ibid art 43.
[17] ibid art 48.
[18] ibid art 27.
[19] ibid art 36.
[20] ibid art 37.
[21] ibid art 38.
[22] ibid art 58.

... except by legal provisions'. This clearly makes possible the use of capital punishment, which may be provided for in the case of serious crimes.[23] The Constitution states that 'all specific decisions of the courts shall be enforced, except for capital punishment, which shall require Presidential approval'.[24]

2. *Right to a fair trial*

One of the fundamental elements of the right to fair trial under article 23 of the Afghan Constitution is the presumption of innocence: 'an accused is considered innocent until convicted by a final decision of an authorized court'.[25] Afghan scholars have considered that reference to this principle of law can be found in Islamic principles:[26] 'We never punish until we have sent a messenger'[27] and 'eliminate the prescribed punishments whenever it is possible; and if you manage a dismissal of a Muslim [the accused] do it. It is better for *Iman*[28] to be mistaken in pardon than to be mistaken in penalty'.[29]

Article 27 provides that: 'No deed shall be considered a crime unless ruled by a law promulgated prior to commitment of the offence'. As such the article stipulates the need for legislation in order to prosecute an individual for a crime. Therefore, in order to be punished for a crime, the government must have first adopted a statute criminalizing the act in question. Furthermore, the Constitution states that: 'Crime is a personal act. Investigation, arrest and detention of an accused as well as penalty execution shall not incriminate another person'. This provision encapsulates one of the core principles in Sharia: the offender is the only person who should be held accountable for his crime. No other individual, regardless of his relationship with the defendant, can be punished for the criminal act. With regard to this notion the Quran states: 'No soul benefits except from its own work, and none bears the burden of another'[30]; 'Whoever works righteousness does so for his own good, and whoever works evil does so to his own detriment. Your Lord is never unjust towards the people';[31] 'It is not in accordance with your wishes, or the wishes of the people of the scripture:

---

23 ibid art 24, Afghan Penal Code 1976.
24 Art 129, The Constitution of Afghanistan.
25 ibid art 25.
26 Abd El-Khaleq Ebn Al Mofaddal Ahmaddon, Qa'edat dar'e al hedood bel-Shobehat wa atharoha fi al fiqh al gena'ei al islami (The Rule of Eliminating Penalty on Suspicion Criterion and Its Role in Islamic Penal Jurisdiction) (1995) 7 Contemporary Jurisprudence Research Journal 7–75, 9.
27 Quran, Chapter 17, 'Bani Israel': 15.
28 Islamic term usually translated as 'belief' or 'faith'.
29 Sunan Al Tirmizi, volume 4, 25.
30 Quran, Chapter 6, 'Al-An'am': 164).
31 Quran, Chapter 41, 'Fussilat': 46).

anyone who commits evil pays for it, and will have no helper or supporter against God'.[32]

The right to defence in a trial can be found in article 31 of the Constitution. This is based on the position that, upon granting Ali the governorship of Yemen, the Prophet said: '... people will appeal to you for justice. If two adversaries come to you for arbitration, do not rule for the one, before you have similarly heard from the other. It is more proper for justice to become evident to you and for you to know who is right'.[33] Further components of the right to a fair trial include the right to be informed of the charge against him, to be brought to a court of law within a reasonable time and to correspond and communicate with his advocate in confidence.[34]

3. Prohibition on torture and cruel, inhuman or degrading treatment

Article 29 asserts that 'no person, even for the purpose of discovering the truth, can resort to torture or order the torture of another person who may be under prosecution, arrest, or imprisoned, or convicted to punishment'.

The infliction of torture and other cruel, inhuman and degrading treatment is considered to be strictly prohibited by Islam, as it is incompatible with the religion's central principle that views the individual as the 'prize creation of Allah' who must be treated with justice and dignity.[35] This precept is reflected in the words of the Prophet Mohammed: 'God shall torture on the Day of Recompense those who inflict torture on people.'[36]

Article 30 of the Constitution deems inadmissible evidence, in the form of a statement, testimony or confession, where it has been obtained through compulsion. A confession is only valid if made voluntarily before an authorized court and where the accused is of sound mind.[37] Sharia stipulates a similar requirement: 'A man would not be secure from incriminating himself if you made him hungry, frightened him, or confined him'.[38]

---

[32] Quran, Chapter 4, 'Al-Nisa': 123.

[33] Awad M Awad, 'The Right of the Accused under Islamic Criminal Procedure' in M Cherif Bassiouni, *The Islamic Criminal Justice System* (Oceana Publicaions, London, New York, 1982) 97.

[34] Art 31, Constitution of Afghanistan.

[35] M Cherif Bassiouni, 'Sources of Islamic Law and the Protection of Human Rights in the Criminal Justice System' in Bassiouni (n 34) 19.

[36] Quoted by Osman Abd-el-Malek al-Saleh, 'The Right of the Individual to Personal Security in Islam' in Mahmoud Cherif Bassiouni (ed), The Islamic Criminal Justice System, (Oceana Publications,London, New York, 1982) 72.

[37] Art 30, The Constitution of Afghanistan

[38] Words of Omar ibn el Khattab, quoted by Osman Abd-el-Malek al-Saleh in 'The Right of the Individual to Personal Security in Islam' in M Cherif Bassiouni, *The Islamic Criminal Justice System* by (Oceana Publicaions, London, New York, 1982) 72 with reference to Ya'qub Ibn Ibrahim Abu Youssuf, Kitab Al-Kharaj, (AlMatba'ah al-Salafiyah Cairo, 1933) 115.

III. THE INTERNATIONAL FRAMEWORK

A. *The Place of International Human Rights Law in the Afghan Judicial System*

Under article 7 of the Constitution, Afghanistan has a duty to abide by the UN Charter, international treaties to which it is party, as well as the Universal Declaration of Human Rights. Hence, 'to be able to adjudicate fairly and equitably, a judge shall be knowledgeable of all ... Treaties and Conventions to which Afghanistan is a signatory, and stay committed to their implementation'[39]. In 1994 Afghanistan ratified the UN Convention on the Rights of the Child (UNCRC). Moreover, with the aim of endorsing obligations and commitments under the UNCRC in national law, in 2005 the country passed the Juvenile Code (JC). Since then several efforts have been made with the aim of developing the juvenile justice system. In 2005, under the supervision of the Ministry of Justice and with collaboration of UNODC and UNICEF, the Juvenile Justice Administration Department (JJAD) was established. More than 250 professionals, including judges, prosecutors, police, and social workers have also been trained.[40]

In addition, development offices for the expert juvenile prosecutors' have been established in Balkh, Herat, Kandahar, Kabul and Kunduz. However in practice, because of the lack of legal aid and social support for systems set up for the implementation of juvenile courts, the situation of children who came into conflict with the law has not been changed significantly. In Kabul, Mazar Sharif, and Jalalabad, Juvenile Courts have been established.

Nevertheless, despite the Juvenile Code explicitly requiring that juvenile offenders be tried in specialized juvenile courts, 28 provinces have no formal plans with regard to the juvenile courts. Therefore, the National Justice Sector Strategy 2008 acknowledged that in order to enhance the

---

[39] Art 18, Regulation of Judicial Conduct for Judges of Afghanistan. Afghanistan is a party to several international human rights instruments including: The International Covenant on Civil and Political Rights (ICCPR) was ratified on 24 April 1983. The International Covenant on Economics, Social and Cultural Rights (ICESCR) was ratified on 24 April 1983. The International Convention on the Elimination of all Forms of Racial Discrimination (CERD) was ratified on 5 August 1983. The Convention on the Elimination of all Forms of Discrimination against Women (CEDAW) was ratified on 5 March 2003. The Convention against Torture and Other Cruel, Inhuman and Degrading Treatment or Punishment (CAT) was ratified on 26 June 1987. The UN Convention on the Rights of the Child (UNCRC) was ratified on 27 April 1994. The Optional Protocol of the Convention of the Rights of the Child (CRC-OP-SC) on the sale of children, child prostitution and child pornography was ratified on 19 October 2002. The Optional Protocol to the Convention on the Rights of the Child (CRC-OP-AC) on the involvement of children in armed conflict was ratified on 24 September 2003.

[40] UNICEF, 'Justice for Children: The Situation for Children in Conflict with the Law in Afghanistan' 7, available at http://www.unhcr.org/refworld/category,REFERENCE, AIHRC,,,47fdfae50,0.html, accessed 18 September 2009.

quality of justice and institutional capacity for sustainable justice services, the juvenile justice system needs significant reform. Consequently, their strategy for implementation of reforms concerning juvenile justice by 2010 include: expansion and improvement of juvenile justice facilities and programs at national level, development of regulations, protocols, and manuals for the proper implementation of the Juvenile Justice Code, and international standards regarding juvenile justice.[41]

It is also worth noting that Afghanistan has not ratified the Second Optional Protocol to ICCPR—which calls for the abolition of the death penalty—and is therefore not acting in violation of its international obligations.

IV. THE AFGHAN JUVENILE CODE 2005 AND COMPATIBILITY WITH THE CONVENTION ON THE RIGHTS OF THE CHILD

The compatibility of the Afghan Juvenile Code (JC) of 2005 with the UNCRC will be analysed through the analysis of five major issues relating to rights of the child in Afghanistan: (a) the age of criminal liability, (b) the deprivation of liberty, (c) the conditions of detention, (d) the procedural rights, and finally (e) the death penalty.

The Afghan Penal Code of 1976 ('APC') contains provisions for juvenile justice. Further, in 2005 the Juvenile Code of 2005 ('JC') was passed. This marked an adherence to article 40(3) of the UNCRC which encourages, amongst other things, the adoption of laws specifically applicable to children alleged as having infringed criminal law.

A. Age of Criminal Responsibility

On this matter, the UNCRC simply states that a minimum age should be established. Varying history, culture and morals clearly call for some discretion. However the fact that no absolute minimum standard is stipulated may pose problems, in that a country could justify setting it at too low an age. In the APC, a child between the ages of seven and 12 was considered to be a juvenile. The Juvenile Code (JC) however has increased this age to 12.[42] Under the new legislation, a person under the age of 12 cannot be held criminally responsible.[43]

Although the age limits are compatible with Afghanistan's international obligations, putting the law into practice has proven problematic. As noted by UNICEF,[44] the determination of age is far from simple. Many children

---

41 ibid.
43 Art 5, Juvenile Code 2005.

42 Art 4(4), Juvenile Code 2005.
44 UNICEF (n 41) 5.

are unaware of their birth date and, more importantly, lack the necessary ID cards to prove their age. The absence of an effective birth registration system is largely to blame. It is approximated that a mere 10 per cent of births are registered.[45] The system then is clearly prone to abuse by law enforcement officials or the parties themselves.[46] In an effort to achieve targets, for example for gaining promotion or in order to secure convictions, children may be registered as adults. Sometimes, in order to avoid harsh punishments and to get benefits from the rehabilitation centres they get, the children registered as adults. The juvenile justice system is designed to take into consideration the child's maturity, age and situation. So, by being consigned to the ordinary criminal system, which is largely based on retributive justice, the child may receive a much harsher punishment than would otherwise be the case. Even to be identified as a juvenile, for a child below the age of 12 and therefore immune from criminal responsibility, poses risks; he would have been entitled to special care and protection.

Alternatively, there could be instances where an adult is processed as a child. Justice would not be served as this would inevitably result in a lighter punishment. However given the vulnerability of children, the first scenario is of greater concern. The consequences of being wrongly charged as an adult can be life-changing for the individual. It could result in the child being detained in an adult prison where he would be at risk of physical and sexual exploitation.[47]

Article 6 of the JC states that in cases where the child does not possess an ID card or the physical appearance of the child suggests an age different to that depicted in the card, the opinion of a forensic doctor shall be sought. In the event that the opinion contradicts the background of the case and the child's physical appearance, the issue of determining age shall be referred to a medical team of no fewer than three doctors. This procedure mirrors the one specified in the APC. However, it evidently poses a number of problems. First and foremost, if a child is assigned an age different to what he believes it to be or what the ID card says, it is highly unlikely that the child has legal representation and the necessary resources in order to challenge this. Although the child has a right to legal assistance under the UNCRC[48] and JC,[49] given the problems with legal aid[50] it is highly unlikely that every child without a lawyer wanting to challenge their age, will be able to do so. Furthermore, the tests would require an abundance of forensic doctors. According to one study in Afghanistan, around 53 per cent of the popula-

[45] ibid 18.   [46] ibid 7.

[47] ibid 5.   [48] Art 37, UNCRC.

[49] Art 22, Juvenile Code 2005.

[50] Amnesty International, 'Country Report on Afghanistan 2008' (published 2009) available at http://thereport.amnesty.org/en/regions/asia-pacific/afghanistan, accessed 18 September 2009.

tion is under the age of 18.[51] A more recent study estimated that the number is actually 57 per cent.[52] With a birth registration system that is virtually non-existent, that leaves nearly all of these children in need of forensic doctors. The country is one of the world's poorest, torn by not just the present war, but decades of conflict. It would be naïve to assume that there will be enough of these specific doctors to assist every child that needs their age determined.

Another question as regards the referral to a team of doctors is: If there is disagreement amongst them, who is to decide which opinion is the most credible? A further problem is posed by the age supplied by the doctor or medical team—this will rarely be exact and more likely, an approximate age or a range of ages will be provided. Certainty is clearly important for the child—the maximum sentence for a 15-year-old is a third of the maximum adult sentence, while for a 16-year-old, it is half. An 11-year-old is not criminally responsible but a 12-year-old is. The process ignores the fact that children may be over or under-developed for their age and therefore, there will inevitably be cases where physical maturity does not depict the actual age. No specific tests exist that can determine age with certainty and those assessments which can be used, such as bone density or pubic development, are not conclusive in themselves.

B. Deprivation of Liberty

The UNCRC stipulates that the arrest, detention and imprisonment of a child should be used 'only as a measure of last resort and for the shortest appropriate period of time'.[53] This should be reserved for cases of serious acts of violence or for persistent offenders. In this spirit, article 8 of the JC contains the same requirements: 'Confinement of a child is considered to be the last resort for rehabilitation and re-education of the child. The court shall consider minimum possible duration for confinement.'

A list of available measures can be found in article 40 of the JC, which range from education and training to enrolment in social rehabilitation programs. The courts also have the authority, at the time of issuing a pre-trial detention order, to consider other appropriate alternatives instead of detention. Moreover, it should be noted that a child who has been sentenced to a confinement period of more than two years but less than three, can be granted a suspension of his sentence. If during this period the child does not re-offend the sentence will be removed.[54]

---

[51] Afghan Independent Human Rights Commission, 'A Call for Justice: A National Consultation on Past Human Rights Violations in Afghanistan' Kabul, January 2005.

[52] World Vision UK: http://www.worldvision.org.uk/server.php?show=nav.1897.

[53] Art 37(b), UNCRC.

[54] Art 40(2), Juvenile Code 2005.

With regard to the maximum time of detention, according to Afghan Police Law the time period for keeping a person in custody could be up to 72 hours.[55] This provision clearly contradicts the approach approved by the Human Rights Committee. As in the case of Gabon in 2000, the Committee recommended that it is the responsibility of the State party to implement the 48-hour police custody rule.

C. Conditions of Detention

Under article 37(c) of the UNCRC, Afghanistan has a duty to detain or imprison children in facilities separate to adults. This obligation is mirrored in article 12 of the JC:

> The suspected and arrested child shall be detained in a special temporary location. The detention authority is obliged to provide access for the detained child to social, educational, vocational, and psychological and health services considering the age and gender requirements of the child.

Although the new legislation is compatible with international obligations, a report by the United Nations Assistance Mission in Afghanistan suggests that this has yet to be implemented on the ground.[56] In Kandahar and Jalalabad, the juvenile rehabilitation centre is in a separate wing of the adult prison. However, it seems that such centres are usually only available to male juveniles, whilst female ones are detained in a women's prison. This is a clear breach of article 2 of the UNCRC which states that the rights should be applied without discrimination.

The separation demarcation of adults and children may not be so easy. Reports by the US State Department suggest that children under the age of 12 whose mothers have committed a crime have been imprisoned with their mothers. At one point, Pol-e-Charki[57] prison held 106 female inmates, of which 56 were incarcerated with their children, none of whom had committed any crime.[58] Evidently this rule would be difficult to implement in cases such as these where there is no other guardian or a social service to care for the infants, as is often the case.

It has also been reported that juvenile correction centres that do exist frequently fall below internationally accepted standards. A juvenile centre

---

[55] Arts 15 and 25 of the Police Law.

[56] United Nations Assistance Mission in Afghanistan, 'Afghanistan Justice Sector Overview' (January 2007) 27.

[57] Located in eastern Afghanistan, just east of Kabul.

[58] 2007 Report by the Bureau of Democracy, Human Rights and Labor on events in Afghanistan, published on 11 March 2008, available at http://www.state.gov/g/drl/rls/hrrpt/2007/100611.htm, accessed 18 September 2009.

in Kabul for instance is located in a rented house outside of the adult prison, which suggests that the living conditions may not be adequate. Overcrowding and lack of sanitation for instance, can easily become problems. Incarcerating children in cells of poor condition may breach the UNCRC under article 37(c) which obliges Afghanistan to treat the child with humanity and respect their dignity.

D. Procedural Rights

Even though article 10 of the JC allows for the arrest of a juvenile against whom there is evidence of crime, if the child is under 18, the police are not allowed to use handcuffs. Therefore, the laws take into account the vulnerability of a child upon his or her arrest. However, some exceptions to this rule apply such as if 'there is a risk of flight or if they pose imminent threat to themselves or to others'.[59]

Further, due to the vulnerability of children, cases involving alleged juvenile offenders are not allowed to be heard in open court but behind 'closed doors'.[60] Likewise, disclosing their identity or publishing anything in the media related to case, for example, documents, witness evidence or any expert opinions, is prohibited.[61] Care has to be taken even during the trial, where if the behaviour of the child is not 'normal,' the prosecution has the duty to refer him/her to hospital for 'mental health diagnosis and treatment'.[62]

Below are some of the minimum guarantees relating to a fair trial stipulated by the UNCRC and also present in the JC:

1. To have the matter determined without delay by a competent, independent and impartial authority...in a fair hearing according to law[63]

With regard to issuing an order, the JC contains clear time limits. The juvenile court is given three days in which to study the file and return it to the prosecutor for resolving defects.[64] Upon receipt the prosecutor has one week to send the file to the relevant court,[65] after which the court has 10 days to issue its decision.[66] This is in clear conformity not only with the UNCRC but also the ICCPR standards on the right to a fair trial, both of which require state parties to issue a prompt decision.[67] These are strict requirements and work well in theory but how realistic they are to achieve

---

[59] Art 10, JC.   [60] ibid.   [61] Art 32, JC.
[62] ibid art 38 JC.   [63] Art 40(b)iii, UNCRC.   [64] Art 30(1), JC.
[65] ibid art 30(2).   [66] ibid 30(3).
[67] Art 10(b) ICCPR: 'Accused juvenile persons shall be ... brought speedily as possible for adjudication'.

in practice, given the shortage of judicial personnel and abundance of children, is highly questionable.

2. To have legal or other appropriate assistance in the preparation and presentation of his or her defence[68]

Article 22 of the JC clearly stipulates the right to have an attorney. In the event that the parents or legal representative cannot afford defence counsel, the government shall provide one. This was obviously recognized as a highly ambitious provision, in light of the poverty and thus lack of resources, as indicated by article 65: 'since there are not sufficient defence counsels at present in the country, the suspected or accused child can refer to educated people who have knowledge of legal issues'. An educated person would clearly not possess the same legal expertise as a qualified attorney. Nevertheless, the provision entails realism; it is acknowledging the situation as it is, as opposed to calling for unachievable aspirations.

3. If considered to have infringed penal law, to have this decision and any measures imposed in consequence thereof reviewed by a higher competent, independent and impartial authority ... according to law[69]

As mentioned above, the child has a right to appeal a decision on their case, provided by article 42 of the JC. Again, this may be harder to implement in practice. Given that the physical infrastructure for the judicial system is incomplete, it seems that appealing the decision may prove problematic or impossible. The child and his legal representative may have to travel a long-distance, which likely will not be possible given the war. Even if it were, there may be issues of jurisdiction.

V. CHILD RIGHTS VIOLATIONS AND THE DEATH PENALTY

Like the UNCRC, the JC defines a child as an individual who has not attained 18 years.[70] Accordingly, he or she cannot be imprisoned for life nor can he be subjected to the death penalty.[71] Although Afghanistan has retained the death penalty, the JC is compatible with international obligations as the UNCRC, despite declaring the inherent right to life of all children,[72] defines a child as a person under 18,[73] and therefore allows the

---

[68] Art 40(b)ii, UNCRC.
[70] Art 4, JC.
[72] Art 6(1), UNCRC.
[69] Art 40(b)v, UNCRC.
[71] ibid art 39(1)(c).
[73] ibid art 37(a), UNCRC. This article also states that persons below the age of eighteen may not be subjected to life imprisonment or capital punishment.

imposition of life imprisonment or the death penalty for those who have attained this age.

Article 39 of JC provides that under 18s cannot be sentenced to death or life imprisonment, and that the pre-trial detention period will be treated as time spent under punishment hence will be excluded from the total sentence. Furthermore, the JC requires that children above 12 years but under 16 years can be sentenced up to one third of the sentence given to over-18s for the same crime. Moreover, if the accused child is more than 16 years but less than 18, his sanction would be half of the sentence given in similar case to over-18s.

VI. THE CUSTOMARY LEGAL SYSTEM

The Afghan customary legal justice system has numerous names, for example, tribal judge(s), *qadi(s)*, *jirga* and *shura*. There is no certainty that this traditional system has community involvement or is easily accessible. The concerning issue is that of breach of individual human rights, eg in murder cases, the *jirga* (tribal jury system) can recommend revenge or alternatively, the marriage of a girl or a child from the family of murderer to a near relative of the victim, which is called *bad*.[74] This customary practice is being used in settling murder cases committed by one member of tribe or community against a member of another tribe or community. Hence, this is collective punishment given to the whole family, however, the real victim is the girl,[75] who without committing a crime has been punished. Similarly, in Badal[76] the rivals settle their disputes by agreeing to give a girl in marriage to a person belonging to the other rival family. In the whole customary judicial system the woman or girl has no say. Therefore, the fate of one is attached to the treatment of others. These cultural practices are not only contrary to the national law of Afghanistan but are also a violation of Islamic Sharia and human rights. It is reported in a study that drug traffickers use women and girls as assets, which are as beneficial or have material value similar to that of land. A study of indebted drug traffickers in Badakhshan province shows that women and girls rank next to land in the choice of disposable assets used to settle debts. In the report it was found

[74] See United States Agency for International Development (USAID), 'Afghanistan Rule of Law Project: Field Study of Informal and Customary Justice in Afghanistan and Recommendations on Improving Access to Justice and Relations between Formal Courts and Informal Bodies', June 2005, p 48.

[75] See United States Agency for International Development (USAID), 'Afghanistan Rule of Law Project: Field Study of Informal and Customary Justice in Afghanistan and Recommendations on Improving Access to Justice and Relations between Formal Courts and Informal Bodies', June 2005, p 48.

[76] Badal is located in Southeastern Afghanistan, near the border with Pakistan.

that of the traffickers interviewed, 32 per cent reported selling a female relative, 78 per cent selling daughters, and 22 per cent sisters.[77]

Because of the various abuses of the customary judical system and the other child rights violations, a Task Force was established in June 2006 under the UNCRC in order to Monitor and Report the Child Rights Violations. Previously, in 2004, resolution No 1539, the UNSC demanded the establishment of a comprehensive monitoring mechanism in order to eradicate or decrease child rights violations and assist the Afghan Government in reporting to UNCRC.[78]

VII. CONCLUSION

As mentioned above, at present in Afghanistan the infrastructure of the judiciary and the law enforcement agencies are fragile. Moreover, due to the constant state of war, the protection of human rights is minimal. However, as far as the laws relating to the protection of juvenile offenders are concerned, a significant body of laws including the constitution and the Juvenile Code, do exist for the protection of the rights of juvenile offenders. One major aspect of the violation of children's rights in Afghanistan has sprung up from the discrimination which takes place against women.[79] According to the Afghan Independent Human Rights Commission (AIHRC) several children have been found imprisoned along with their mothers who have committed the crimes.[80] Apart from this, many children are being kept in detention centers which don't meet the international minimum standards.[81]

The United Nations Assistance Mission in Afghanistan (UNAMA) acknowledges that in Afganistan, children as young as 11 years of age may be arrested and imprisoned along with adults, even for what may be considered petty crimes.[82]

The key issue in need of consideration for the purposes of criminal responsibility, is the determination of age. At present, the procedure is flawed. Physical development cannot be used as a sufficient ground upon which to decipher exact age. Such a test should either be done with or

[77] Deniz Kandiyoti, 'Post-Conflict Reconstruction, Islam and Women's Rights', 513.
[78] UN Doc S/Res/1539(2004), adopted by the UN Security Council at its 4948th meeting, on 22 April 2004.
[79] Afghanistan Human Development Report 2007, 'Bridging Modernity and Tradition: Rule of Law and the Search for Justice', Centre for Policy and Human Development, Kabul University, pp 58–59.
[80] United Nations Assistance Mission in Afghanistan, 'Afghanistan Justice Sector Overview' (January 2007) 27.
[81] ibid.
[82] ibid.

instead of assessments which test the cognitive and emotional maturity of the child. After all, it is these elements that will determine whether one commits a crime, not their physical maturity. The difficulties in determining age are rooted in the lack of a birth registration system. Even though Afghanistan has not abolished the death penalty, the JC has exempted the children from the death penalty by defining a child as a person who is under 18 years of age. Therefore, the JC makes the national law compatible with international obligations imposed by as the UNCRC. Nevertheless, within Afghanistan a system of tribalism continues to exist and presents in some of the cases regarding their treatment of women and girls a major cause of concern.

CHAPTER 5

Criminal Law and the Rights of the Child in Egypt[1]

I. INTRODUCTION

According to the Egyptian Constitution, the Republic of Egypt is a democratic, socialist State and Islam is the religion of the State.[2] Although Egyptian laws are not necessarily based on Islamic jurisprudence, Sharia Law is enshrined in the Constitution as the primary source of legislation.[3] Children in Egypt are dealt with by the Juvenile Justice System, which operates with a specific set of rules and procedures intended to reflect the limited responsibility of children. This subsection analyses both the major amendments of the laws regarding children and their implementation.

In order to understand the evolutionary changes pertaining to the treatment of children in criminal justice, it is important to examine the first penal codes. The first criminal legislation was enacted in 1829, accompanied by the gradual elaboration of legal procedures and the establishment of a police force. Throughout the 19th century, the necessities of the 'modern State', together with the emergence of scientific means of investigation, gave birth to a structured system of justice where Sharia and secular jurisprudence were adaptable and complementary. Secular councils (*majalis*) were used alongside the traditional Sharia Courts.[4] In relation to criminal matters, both judicial systems functioned in a complementary fashion to one another. While the Sharia Courts still operated using Sharia law and rules of evidence, their role became confined to settling private claims related to the crime, whether punitive or financial.[5] The case was then also considered by the secular councils that were primarily concerned with public order matters. While the Sharia was still a valid consideration in the

---

[1] This report was researched and written by Magda Boutros, researcher with the Egyptian Initiative for Personal Rights (EIPR). Research and writing assistance was provided by Bahaa Ezzelarab, EIPR legal intern from the University of Toronto Law School. EIPR executive director Hossam Bahgat reviewed the report.

[2] Arts 1 and 2 of the Constitution.

[3] A child or juvenile is defined as anyone under the age of 18 full Gregorian years.

[4] K Fahmy, 'The Anatomy of Justice: Forensic Medicine and Criminal Law in Nineteenth-Century Egypt' (1999) 6 Islamic Law and Society 2, 224–271.

[5] R Peters, 'Islamic and Secular Criminal Law in Nineteenth Century Egypt: The Role and Function of the Qadi' (1997) 4 Islamic Law and Society 1, 70–90.

councils, some of its rules were disregarded for considerations of public order and security.[6]

II. NATIONAL FRAMEWORK

Under the first 1883 comprehensive penal code, which included rules regarding juvenile offenders, children under the age of seven were not subject to criminal sanctions and children under the age of 17 who committed crimes could either be given a social measure or carry out a reduced penalty. The law set a system of graded responses to the criminal behavior of children, with each age group being subject to different measures. For instance, children under 12 could only be sentenced to be handed over to a legal guardian or be placed in a 'reform school'. Children below 15 could be either sentenced to these measures or be given a third of the penalty provided for by the law. No death penalty, imprisonment for life or imprisonment with hard labor could be imposed on anyone under the age of 17.[7]

Children were also dealt with under the Juvenile Vagrancy Law 2/1908 (later replaced by Law 124/1949) which aimed at protecting society, by reforming children who are at risk of becoming unemployed and delinquent. The 1949 Vagrancy Law applied to anyone under the age of 18, with no minimum age limit. This lack of minimum age of responsibility was intentional, and justified by the fact that the behaviours addressed were not considered criminal in nature, and that the measures taken were not punishments.[8] The law defined a juvenile vagrant as anyone under the age of 18 found begging, collecting stubs and other waste, having no fixed abode, mixing with disreputable individuals, exhibiting bad or immoral behavior, or abandoned by parents and relatives.

In 1950, Criminal Procedures Law (Law 150/1950) established for the first time in Egypt a special set of procedures to be followed in juvenile trials. The law established specialized Juvenile Courts, competent in all cases of vagrancy and delinquency for juveniles under 15. These Courts operated differently from regular criminal Courts, as the judges had to take into consideration the social and environmental circumstances of the juvenile before passing a decision. The causes that led to the delinquent act or vagrancy situation were taken into account and the measures taken by the Court were meant to address these causes. The Court was then entrusted with the duty to follow up on the measure taken, to ensure its effectiveness.[9] Further, the law stipulated that juveniles under the age of 12 could

---

[6] Fahmy (n 4).   [7] Penal code 58/1937.
[8] A Al Sharkawi, *Inhiraf al Ahdath* (1986) Anglo-Egyptian Library.
[9] ibid.

not be detained pre-trial and that juvenile trials should not be public, juvenile judges also had the power to modify or terminate measures taken against juveniles at any time.[10] Moreover, in 1957, the Juvenile Police (*shortat al-ahdath*) was created to perform both a security function and a social function. It became responsible for arrests and investigations, but also for coordinating with institutions responsible for the protection of children and for protecting children from potential threats.[11] This Juvenile Police separated, for the first time, juveniles from adults in the pre-trial process. By the first half of the 20th century, laws regarding the criminal treatment of juveniles made a clear difference between juvenile delinquents and adult criminals. Laws concerning juveniles were underpinned by the idea that children are not fully responsible for their actions. Therefore, special procedures and special measures applied to them. Since juveniles had limited responsibility, the parents or guardians were held responsible for their children's behavior. Further, the role of adults in assisting or encouraging deviant acts by children was criminalized. Indeed, the Juvenile Vagrancy Law provided for criminal penalties to be imposed on any adult who encourages, assists or leads a child to be in a state of vagrancy or to commit a crime.[12] Nevertheless, it was still believed that some form of measures should be taken against juveniles who are delinquent or vagrant. These measures were aimed at reforming the children rather than punishing them. The passage from reform for children to retributive punishment for adults was gradual: younger children were only sentenced to reformative measures; however the older the child got, the more likely he was to be given a criminal penalty—albeit reduced—rather than a reformative measure.

The Juvenile Law 31/1974 came to replace the provisions dealing with juvenile offenders in the Penal Code, the Vagrancy Law and the Penal Procedures Law. The aim of the law was therefore to protect society from this danger by controlling the juvenile and seeking to reform him or her. Similarly to the previous laws, control and supervision of the child were entrusted first to the parents or guardians who were consequently held responsible for the actions of the child and could be held criminally liable in case the child was found in a state of liability to deviance again.

Another indicator of the influence of the social defense movement was the debate on the minimum age of criminal responsibility that preceded the drafting of the law. While some advocated for establishing a minimum age

---

[10] ibid.

[11] A Wahdan, 'Dawr Shortat al Ahdath fi Marhalat al Dabt al Qada'i ' in *Al Afaq al Jadida lel Adala al Jina'eya fi Majal al Ahdath*, Fifth conference of the Egyptian Criminal Law Association, Cairo, 18–20 April 1992: Dar al Nahda al Arabiya.

[12] This crime is punishable with imprisonment (three months to one year), with increased penalty if the accused is responsible for the child's care.

of criminal responsibility, the view that prevailed was one concerned primarily with the protection of society.[13] It was claimed that society cannot be indifferent to a criminal act merely because the offender is below a certain age. Hence, article 3 of the Juvenile Law stated: 'a juvenile under 7 years of age is considered to be socially dangerous if he is found to be engaged in any of the acts of delinquency mentioned in the previous article or if he has committed any act considered by the law to be a felony or a misdemeanor'. However, the law stipulated that children below the age of seven years could not be held criminally responsible. Juveniles below the age of 15 years who committed a crime were sentenced to social measures and those above the age of 15 years could be sentenced either to social measures or to reduced penalties. Social measures included reprimands, handing the child over to their parents or guardians, training and qualification, probation or the institutionalization in a social care institution or specialized hospital. In cases of children committing an offence punishable by death or imprisonment, the sentence was reduced and no death penalty, imprisonment for life or imprisonment with hard labour could be imposed on a juvenile. For juveniles found in a state of liability to deviance, the prosecutor first warned the parents or guardians to adequately supervise the child, and if the child was found again in a state of liability to deviance, he or she was referred to the Court that had the discretion to order a social measure.

Egypt was one of the initiators of the first World Summit for Children in 1990 and one of the first signatories of the UN Convention on the Rights of the Child (UNCRC). At the local level, two consecutive decades dedicated to the Egyptian Child (1989–1999 and 2000–2010) placed the rights and welfare of children at the heart of governmental policies. This focus on child welfare issues resulted in the enactment of a unified Child Law, which deals with all matters affecting children: civil status, social, educational and health protection and criminal treatment. The unified law was presented as incorporating all the necessary amendments to conform to the 'letter and spirit' of the UNCRC.[14] However, in relation to criminal treatment, the Child Law 12/1996 mirrored most of the stipulations of its predecessor, the 1974 Juvenile Law, which were not in line with the rights protected by the Convention. Chapter 8 of the Child Law ('Criminal Treatment for Children') followed the same ideology and kept references to social danger and liability to deviance. The provisions applicable to delinquents and juveniles liable to deviance remained unchanged. Moreover, the penalties applicable to juveniles and in particular to those aged 16 to 18 years,

---

[13] I Bibars, 'Street Children In Egypt: From The Home To The Street To Inappropriate Corrective Institutions' (1998) 10 Environment and Urbanization 1, 201–216.

[14] For example: UNICEF, *The Situation of Egyptian Children and Women: A Rights-Based Analysis*, Arab Republic of Egypt and Unicef, Cairo, August 2002.

increased. Indeed the Child Law removed the possibility of sentencing children above the age of 16 to social measures, thus leaving judges with no choice but imposing penal sanctions. Some commentators suggest that this came as a response to the perceived threat caused by the use of juveniles by terrorist groups.[15]

A. *The 2008 Amendments: The Child as a Victim of Circumstance*

Upon reviewing Egypt's periodic report in 2001, the UN Committee on the Rights of the Child (CRC) strongly criticized the Child Law provisions in relation to the criminal treatment of children. It made the following observations.[16]

The age of criminal responsibility in Egypt (seven years) is very low and should be raised. The committee expressed concern that status offences, such as begging and truancy, are in practice criminalized. The CRC recommended that the State conform in the administration of juvenile justice to articles 37, 39 and 40 of the Convention as well as to the standards included in the Beijing Rules and Riyadh Guidelines. The CRC recommended that the State party ensure separation of children from adults in pre-trial detention; establish effective independent complaints mechanisms for child detainees; and develop facilities and programmes for the physical and psychological recovery and social reintegration of juveniles.

A National Strategy for the Rehabilitation and Reintegration of Street Children was launched in 2002. The strategy sought to change prevailing negative attitudes towards street children and to shift the policy from one where they are viewed as criminals to one where they are viewed as victims of their circumstances and in need of protection.[17] In sum, the increased attention to the problem of street children and the pressure on the government to react to the CRC's recommendations were determining factors in the amendments to the Child Law in 2008. Following extensive public debate about the amended provisions, Law 126/2008 brought them into effect.

Concerning children committing crimes, the main development achieved by the 2008 amendments is the raising of the age of criminal responsibility to 12 years, largely a result of pressures from the CRC. Measures applicable to juvenile delinquents remain very similar to the provisions of the 1996

---

[15] I Bibars, 'Street children in Egypt: from the home to the street to inappropriate corrective institutions' (1998) 10 Environment and Urbanization 1, 201–216.

[16] Egypt's Third and Fourth Periodic Report to the International Committee on the Rights of the Child, period 2001–2008, December 2008.

[17] N Ammar, 'The Relationship Between Street Children and the Justice System in Egypt' in International Journal of Offender Therapy and Comparative Criminology, OnlineFirst, published on July 29, 2008.

law. Social measures and reduced penalties form the basis of the Court's response to juvenile delinquency.

In relation to children liable to deviance and children exposed to danger, the new law brought about a complete shift in policy. The legalistic and criminalizing provisions were replaced by a system of social protection outside of the criminal justice system.

III. INTERNATIONAL FRAMEWORK: THE UNCRC AND THE OTHER INTERNATIONAL HUMAN RIGHTS INSTRUMENTS AND THE EGYPTIAN LAW

A. Introduction

The Egyptian Constitution, enacted in 1971, guarantees fundamental rights and freedoms to all citizens without discrimination (part three of the Constitution). These include the right to be free from arbitrary arrest and detention,[18] the right to be treated with respect for one's dignity, the right of arrested and detained persons to be free from moral or physical harm and the inadmissibility of confession obtained under duress.[19] Moreover, it grants the right to every individual whose rights or liberties have been violated to seek redress in criminal or civil Courts, without prescription.[20] The Supreme Constitutional Court can judge on the unconstitutionality of legal provisions when they are incompatible with rights guaranteed by the Constitution.

Egypt has also ratified a large number of International Conventions protecting children, in addition to the UNCRC, namely: the International Covenant on Civil and Political Rights (ICCPR), the Convention on the Elimination of All Forms of Discrimination against Women (CEDAW), the Convention against Torture and Other Cruel, Inhuman or Degrading Treatment or Punishment (CAT), and the Convention on the Rights of Persons with Disabilities (CRPD).

Despite these constitutional guarantees and international obligations, an important exception applies. Since 1981, a state of emergency allows State officials to derogate from human rights standards when justified by necessities of national security. These powers have a serious detrimental effect on the constitutional guarantees granted to arrestees, suspects and criminals. Human rights violations such as arbitrary arrest and detention, *incommunicado* detention, preventive detention and the trial of civilians in military tribunals are routine and officially allowed under the state of emergency.

International human rights instruments, once they are signed and ratified by the State of Egypt, have force of law.[21] Therefore, the rights guaranteed

---

[18] Art 71 of the Constitution.
[20] Art 57 of the Constitution.

[19] Art 42 of the Constitution.
[21] Art 151 of the Constitution.

under international human rights charters are considered equal to domestic legal provisions and can be invoked directly in any judicial claim. The General Comment No 10 issued by the CRC in 2007 stated:

> A comprehensive policy for juvenile justice must deal with the following core elements: the prevention of juvenile delinquency; interventions without resorting to judicial proceedings and interventions in the context of judicial proceedings; the minimum age of criminal responsibility and the upper age limits for juvenile justice; the guarantees for a fair trial; and deprivation of liberty including pre-trial detention and post-trial incarceration.

The UNCRC requires that the best interest of the child be a primary consideration 'in all actions concerning children, whether undertaken by public or private social welfare institutions, Courts of law, administrative authorities or legislative bodies', and that the child be heard in all proceedings affecting him or her. Although article 3 of the Child Law stipulates the right of children to be heard in all matters affecting them and provides that the best interest of the child shall assume priority in all procedures concerning children, the reality on the ground is far removed from these principles. Indeed, as we will see in greater detail below, police, prosecutors, judges and social workers fail to consider the well-being of children and to ensure decisions are taken based on the child's best interests. Further, the structure of the proceedings does not allow the child's views to be heard or taken into consideration.

The new provisions of the Child Law represent a shift in policy, with a new focus on prevention. For the first time, children at risk of delinquency are not treated as delinquents but as children in need of support. However, the preventive system does not always comply with the Riyadh Guidelines on the Prevention of Juvenile Delinquency.[22]

According to the Riyadh Guidelines, prevention of juvenile delinquency should be an integral part of any juvenile justice system. The Child Law purports to establish a comprehensive system aimed at ensuring the welfare of the child. The law highlights the necessity of creating a healthy environment for the development of children[23] and guarantees to every child the right to family life, the right to be free from violence and exploitation, and the right to be protected against all forms of discrimination. Moreover, children are granted the right to social and health care services,[24] free immunization[25] and free public schooling.[26] Still, violations of these rights are

---

[22] United Nations Guidelines for the Prevention of Juvenile Delinquency (The Riyadh Guidelines). Adopted and proclaimed by General Assembly resolution 45/112 of 14 December 1990.

[23] Art 1 of the Child Law.   [24] Art 7bis(a) of the Child Law.

[25] Art 25 of the Child Law.   [26] Art 54 of the Child Law.

widespread and policies still fall short of guaranteeing the full enjoyment of child rights to all children.[27]

In line with recommendations of the Riyadh Guidelines, the law focuses on the role of the family as the primary caregiver, with the State playing a supplementary role where the family is unable to provide for the child. The law also stresses the primary role of the state in areas of health care, nutrition and education.[28] Moreover, the 2008 amendments to the Child Law saw the creation of the General Department for Child Rescue, which works as an ombudsman office responsible for receiving and dealing with complaints of violence, risk or negligence,[29] in line with recommendation 57 of the Riyadh Guidelines.

The Child Law institutes a system of social response to children at risk (children exposed to danger) through a multi-agency response. Children in vulnerable circumstances, who were previously criminalized, will now be dealt with by Childhood Protection Committees, through an array of social care measures. However, these committees can, if they see fit, refer the child to the public prosecutor to take one of the measures applicable to children committing crimes. Hence, the distinction becomes blurred between children at risk and juvenile delinquents, and social measures aimed at preventing children from entering the criminal justice system can result in actually fast-tracking those children within the system.

B. From Arrest to Trial: Procedural Safeguards

Article 40 of the UNCRC imposes a duty on States Parties to 'recognize the right of every child alleged as, accused of, or recognized as having infringed the penal law to be treated in a manner consistent with the promotion of the child's sense of dignity and worth'. In Egypt, the law protects—in theory—most of the procedural safeguards of a fair trial. Rights such as the presumption of innocence,[30] the right to be notified of the charges (for child and parent),[31] the right to legal counsel[32] and the right to appeal[33] are explicitly protected by the law. Moreover, juvenile offenders can—in theory—take comfort in the fact that the law has provided them with specialized institutions dealing exclusively with juveniles. From the moment of arrest by the Juvenile Police, throughout the period of investigation by

---

[27] See the latest figures for child rights indicators in Egypt at http://www.unicef.org/infobycountry/egypt_statistics.html

[28] In line with the Riyadh Guidelines, recommendations 21 and 45.

[29] Art 97 of the Child Law.

[30] Art 67 of the Constitution, not reiterated in the Child Law or Penal Code.

[31] Art 113 of the Child Law.

[32] Art 125 of the Child Law.

[33] Arts 94 and 121 of the Child Law. Note however that art 130 provides that measures shall be enforceable, even if appealable.

the Juvenile Prosecution and reaching the stage of trial in the Child Court, children in conflict with the law are dealt with by specialized institutions.

The State guarantees child protection and implementation of the Convention through three different mechanisms: criminal sentences applicable to adults placing a child at risk of harm, social measures for children at risk, and training and accountability mechanisms for those working in contact with vulnerable children.

C. Criminal Sentences

The Child Law contains penal provisions aimed at protecting children from harm. The law criminalizes the neglect of a child by his or her legal guardian,[34] punishes an adult assisting or encouraging a juvenile to commit a crime[35] and provides for aggravated penalties in cases of crimes committed against children.[36] Moreover, it provides for criminal sanctions against public officials 'detaining, jailing or imprisoning a child with one or more adults in the same place'.[37] This last provision is an important tool to ensure effective implementation of the law. However, it remains to be seen how this provision will be applied in practice.

D. Monitoring Mechanisms: Sketchy and Inefficient

In order to ensure the law's provisions are implemented in practice, monitoring and accountability mechanisms should be set up. Yet, these mechanisms in Egypt are patchy and inefficient. Two examples below demonstrate the inefficiency of monitoring mechanisms to adequately protect children within the juvenile justice system.

1. Monitoring of conditions of arrest and detention

There is no mechanism responsible for monitoring the conditions of arrest and detention of children. According to Human Rights Watch,[38] the Ministry of Interior does not investigate or keep statistics on police abuse of children and there is no procedure for children to make complaints about police ill-treatment. Moreover, despite the legal requirement to do so, juveniles prosecutors do not conduct adequate investigations of the circumstances of children's arrest and detention.[39]

---

[34] Art 113 and 114 of the Child Law. [35] Art 116 of the Child Law.
[36] Art 116 bis(a) of the Child Law. [37] Art 112 of the Child Law.
[38] Human Rights Watch, 'Charged With Being Children: Egyptian Police Abuse of Children in Need of Protection' (Human Rights Watch, New York, 2003).
[39] Interviews with lawyer and NCCM project manager.

2. Monitoring of places of rehabilitation and detention

Article 134 of the Child Law stipulates that:

> The head of juvenile Court or his authorized expert shall visit observation institutions, vocational training centers, children's social care institutions, vocational qualification institutes, specialized hospitals and other authorities that cooperate with the juvenile Court of spatial jurisdiction, at least once every three months.

This power has a double function: first, it allows the juvenile judge to ensure that the measures that are taken against juveniles do fulfil their rehabilitative function; second, it allows for a monitoring of these places, as the judge can send visit reports to the General Childhood Protection Committee to take appropriate action. However, our interviews revealed that these powers are not used and that no regular investigations of places of detention take place. The judges complained of a heavy workload and lack of resources that affect their ability to carry out these visits.[40]

IV. LAWS PERTAINING TO THE CHILD IN CRIMINAL MATTERS:
GAPS AND CHALLENGES

This section looks at the state of the law as it stands today in relation to the criminal treatment of juveniles. It will be demonstrated that the legal provisions comply, to a large extent, with the UNCRC and other international human rights instruments. Many of the amended legal provisions are reproduced, almost verbatim, from the international conventions. While this section briefly presents the current legislative position, the next section will explore in detail the gaps in the law, and more importantly, in the implementation of the law, and the resulting human rights violations.

A. Special Courts/Court Procedures for Juvenile Offenders

Juvenile delinquents are tried in special Courts with special procedures, which, on paper, comply with most of the requirements stipulated in the UNCRC. Children committing offences are tried in Juvenile Courts, which, since the 2008 amendments are renamed 'Child Courts'.[41] While the Court's composition and procedures have not changed much with the 2008

---

[40] Interviews with judges, NCCM.   [41] Art 122 of the Child Law.

amendments, the name change was intended to avoid the negative connotations associated with the word 'juvenile' *('hadath')* in Arabic.[42]

The Child Law stipulates that each governorate should have at least one Child Court,[43] composed of three judges assisted by two specialized experts, of whom at least one is a woman.[44] The two experts investigate and review the child's circumstances in all respects and submit a report to the Court before the judgment. Article 94 gives the Child Court exclusive jurisdiction over any child accused of committing a felony or misdemeanour, with the exception of cases where adults are party to the offence and the child is older than 15 years, in which case the juvenile may be tried, together with the adult(s), in the Criminal Court or the Supreme State Security Court.[45] In this case, the authorized Court is also under a duty to investigate the child's circumstances before making a judgment. Nonetheless, the Court of Cassation has narrowed this exception and strongly emphasized that the Child Court is the 'natural adjudicator' for children in conflict with the law.[46]

Special procedures apply in juvenile trials, in line with the requirements of the Beijing Rules.[47] The Child Law provides that the trial shall be attended solely by the child's relatives, witnesses, lawyers, social controllers and persons admitted by special permission.[48] These social controllers are in charge of presenting the Court with a social report for each child charged with an offence. This report contains a complete investigation of the child's educational, psychological, mental, physical and social condition.[49] Prior to taking a decision on the case, the Court discusses the report and can request additional information to be provided by the social controllers.[50] If the Court is of the opinion that the physical, mental or psychological conditions of the child require further examination prior to reaching a decision, it may order the child to be put to observation at an adequate place for the duration deemed necessary.[51] The proceedings are suspended until this examination is completed. Children are also granted the right to legal counsel,[52] with the prosecution or the Court being required to appoint a defence lawyer in case the child is charged with an offence punishable with imprisonment.[53] Since the 2008 amendments, this right is granted in felony and misdemeanour cases.

---

[42] Interview with Judge, NCCM.   [43] Art 120 of the Child Law.
[44] Art 121 of the Child Law.   [45] Art 122 of the Child Law.
[46] Appeal 17320, JY 67 (2005); Court of Cassation.
[47] United Nations Standard Minimum Rules for the Administration of Juvenile Justice ('The Beijing Rules'). Adopted by General Assembly resolution 40/33 of 29 November 1985.
[48] This is in line with Beijing Rule No 15.2 guaranteeing the right of parents to attend the trial.
[49] This is in line with Beijing Rule No 16.   [50] Art 127 of the Child Law.
[51] Art128 of the Child Law.   [52] This is in line with Beijing Rule No. 15
[53] Art 125 of the Child Law.

Judgments issued by the Child Court may be appealed, except for judgments imposing a reprimand or a handover of the child to his or her legal guardian. These latter decisions may only be appealed on grounds of incorrect application of the law or nullity of judgment or procedures.[54] Appeals are heard by a Court of Appeal formed within each Court of first instance, consisting of three judges, at least two of whom are of the rank of head of Court.[55] The composition of the Court of Appeal is subject to the same requirements as the composition of the Child Court.[56] In addition to the possibility of appeal, the Court may, at any time, review the reports submitted to it and reconsider the measure taken against the juvenile, upon request by the public prosecutor, the child, his guardian or the person to whom the child has been handed over, and except in cases where the Court has given the juvenile a reprimand. If the Court accepts the request, the measure may be terminated, amended or replaced with another measure.[57] If the request is rejected, no similar request can be made within the three months following the refusal. The decision taken by the Court in such cases cannot be appealed.

The Child Law therefore provides for special Court procedures for juvenile trials. In principle, the Child Court's composition and procedures guarantee that decisions will be based on the child's best interests. However, the practical implementation of these special procedures fall short of giving the child the protection intended.

B. The Legal Minimum Age of Criminal Liability

In line with the CRC's recommendation,[58] article 94 of the Child Law stipulates that the age of criminal responsibility is 12. Full penal responsibility starts at age 18, so children between the ages of 12 and 18 are subject to special penalties. However, if a child between the ages of seven and 12 commits a criminal offence, the Child Court can consider his or her case and take a limited number of measures.[59] The problems resulting from this approach will be elaborated upon below.

The penal measures stipulated in the Child Law are different from those applicable to adult offenders. The Court of Cassation has stated that the procedures and measures applicable to children are aimed at reforming offenders and preventing them from re-offending, not at punishing them.[60]

---

[54] Art 132 of the Child Law.   [55] Art 121 of the Child Law.
[56] ibid.
[57] Art 137 of the Child Law.
[58] Committee on the Rights of the Child, *General Comment No 10 (2007): Children's Rights in Juvenile Justice*, Forty-fourth session. Geneva, 15 January–2 February 2007.
[59] Art 94 of the Child Law.
[60] Appeal 1730, JY 67 (2005); Court of Cassation.

Offenders who are under 18 at the time of the offence cannot be sentenced to the death penalty, imprisonment for life or imprisonment with hard labour.[61] Moreover, children may not be detained with adults in the same place.[62]

The Child Law makes a difference between children below 15 and children above 15. As a general rule, offenders between the ages of 12 and 15 years are sentenced to social measures, while offenders between 15 and 18 are subject to reduced penalties. The availability of a range of social measures which provide judges with alternatives to detention is in line with the Beijing Rules.[63]

1. Offenders under the age of 15

Children below the age of 15 years committing criminal offences can be subject to one of the following measures:[64]

- a reprimand
- handing the child over to his or her parents, legal guardians or to another responsible person
- training and qualification in a centre or factory allocated for this purpose
- ordering the child to comply with certain obligations, such as prohibitions to be in certain places or duty to present oneself to meetings
- probation
- community service[65]
- placement in a specialized hospital
- placement in a social care institution

Institutionalization can only be used as a last resort and for the shortest possible duration.[66] Community service can only be imposed on a child if it does not damage his or her physical and mental well-being. Similarly, training and qualification cannot be imposed if it impairs the child's basic education.[67] Any social measure taken against a juvenile offender is automatically terminated when the offender reaches the age of 21 years (except in the case of placement in a specialized hospital). However, upon termination of the measure, the Court may, at the request of the public prosecutor and after consultations with the social controller, place the offender under probation for a period not exceeding two years.[68]

---

[61] Art 111 of the Child Law.
[63] Beijing Rules, recommendation 18.
[65] This measure was added by the 2008 amendments.
[66] Art 107 of the Child Law.
[68] Art 110 of the Child Law.

[62] Art 112 of the Child Law.
[64] Art 101 of the Child Law.

[67] Art 106 of the Child Law.

2. *Offenders over the age of 15 years*

Children over the age of 15 years committing criminal offences are sentenced to reduced penalties. The Child Law stipulates: 'If the child commits a felony punishable with death penalty, imprisonment for life or imprisonment with hard labour, he or she shall be sentenced to imprisonment. If the child commits a felony punishable with imprisonment, he or she shall be detained for a period no less than three months'.[69] The Court also has the discretion to order the child's placement in a specialized hospital.

If the child commits a misdemeanor punishable with detention, the Court may order, in lieu of detention, the placement of the child under probation, in community service or the institutionalization in a specialized hospital.[70]

All international conventions on child rights require State Parties to set a minimum age below which children are presumed not to have the capacity to infringe the penal law.[71] This means that children who commit an offence at a younger age cannot be formally charged or held responsible in a penal law procedure.[72] Special protective measures can be taken if necessary in the best interest of the child. The General Comment No 10 by the CRC also recommends that the minimum age should not be below 12 years.

In Egypt, the law sets the minimum age of criminal responsibility at 12 years. Yet, article 94 of the Child Law goes on to stipulate that children between the ages of seven and 12 who commit crimes shall have their case considered by the Child Court. The Court can take any of the following measures: reprimand, handing the child over to the parents or guardians, placement in a social care institution or specialized hospital. Hence, although the age of criminal responsibility is stated as 12 in the law, children can be tried and institutionalized starting at age seven. The possibility of referring the child to a Court that will consider the case from a criminal law perspective and that will decide on a measure based on the offence committed, is basically lowering the age of criminal responsibility to seven. This is a violation of Egypt's international obligations. Indeed, the CRC 'strongly recommends that States Parties set a minimum age of criminal responsibility that does not allow, by way of exception, the use of a lower age'.[73] Hence, several important gaps—in the law and in the facts—deserve further attention. These points concern the minimum age of criminal

---

[69] Art 111 of the Child Law.
[70] ibid.
[71] Art 40.3(a) of the UNCRC; art 4 of the Beijing Rules.
[72] Committee on the Rights of the Child, (44th Session) 'General Comment No. 10 (2007): Children's rights in Juvenile Justice' (15 January–2 February 2007).
[73] ibid.

responsibility, the treatment of children by law enforcement personnel, the rules on pre-trial detention and the functioning of the judicial trial.

C. Treatment by Law Enforcement Officials: Violence, Sexual Abuse and Humiliation

1. Arrest, transport and police lock-ups: systematic abuse

Members of the NCCM conceded that the arrest phase and the subsequent treatment by the police are the 'worst' phases of the juvenile justice system in terms of human rights abuses.[74] While it is hard to correctly estimate the nature of the problem, the overwhelming consensus is that there is police brutality towards children in conflict with the law, especially street children. It is a systematic problem and not one of individual incidents.[75] One of the most comprehensive studies on the treatment of children by the police was carried out by Human Rights Watch (HRW) in 2003.[76] The study shows that the police routinely and systematically use violence—physical, sexual and psychological—on children in vulnerable situations.

At the time of the HRW study, the law allowed police officers to arrest juveniles when they were found in a state of liability to delinquency, which gave the police very broad powers to arrest any child found loitering or sleeping on the street. While the 2008 amendments theoretically remove this, the change has not been implemented yet. In these cases, the police often arrest children, keep them in detention for one or two days and then let them go without recording their arrest.[77] This is in violation of the law, but nevertheless often happens, especially when the child is young. This practice is meant as a form of mild disciplining by the police. Worse, despite the legal prohibition to keep children in custody for more than 24 hours without charge, most of the detained children interviewed in a 2005 study reported being kept in custody for longer periods of time, which extended to two months in some cases.[78] Despite the amended provisions, such practices might continue, unless the newly instituted protection committees play a real monitoring role of the police.

Transport, from the place of arrest to the police station, takes place in unsafe conditions, and children are often mixed with adult detainees during transportation.[79]

---

[74] Interviews with judges and project managers at the NCCM.   [75] Ammar (n 17).

[76] Human Rights Watch (n 38).   [77] ibid; Interview with lawyer, NGO.

[78] S Mehanna, and M Al-Sharmani *Participatory Assessment Research on Violence against Street Children—A UNICEF Report* (Social Research Center, the American University in Cairo, 2005).

[79] Human Rights Watch (n 38); S Mehanna and M Al-Sharmani, (2005) Participatory Assessment Research on Violence against Street Children; A UNICEF Report (Social Research Center, American University in Cairo, 2005).

The most dangerous of [the vehicles used for transport], large metal trucks used to transport prisoners, lack seating and adequate ventilation. Children told us police often transported them in these vehicles with adult criminal detainees who verbally abused them and sometimes physically assaulted them; one girl reported being sexually abused by a police guard during transport.[80]

When children are not transported in these vehicles, they are often humiliated in public. 'Police bind children together with ropes or handcuffs, sometimes in large groups, and force them to walk several blocks or to ride public transportation while bound or handcuffed'.[81]

The police then transfer the juvenile to the Juveniles Care Administration (*Idarat Ri'ayat al Ahdath*). Abuse goes on at the police station, where children are also denied their basic rights, such as the right to inform someone of their detention[82] and the right to access adequate food, medical care and bedding.[83] Violence in the police station is systematic: 'All of the children reported being beaten or subjected to obscene and degrading language while in police custody'.[84] Moreover, it is during police custody that most cases of torture occur.[85] The lawyer interviewed told us the story of a boy who got electrocuted by the officers while in their custody.

Abuse can also take other forms, such as verbal insults and humiliation, or the confiscation of the child's belongings or of his or her identification document, without returning them at the time of release.[86] Children are sometimes denied access to food or bathrooms as a form of punishment.[87] Exploitation of the children, who are often asked to perform cleaning or other chores, is also commonplace.[88] In addition, police officers often use the threat of violence or arrest to extort money or sexual favors from children:[89]

Both girls and boys told Human Rights Watch that police frequently extorted money in exchange for avoiding arrest, securing early release from detention, or gaining access to food during detention. Girls said they sometimes agreed to sex with low-level police in exchange for police protection from sexual violence by other men and boys.[90]

---

[80] Human Rights Watch (n 38).   [81] ibid.
[82] Organisation Mondiale Contre la Torture, *The Rights of the Child in Egypt* (Geneva, 2001).
[83] Human Rights Watch (n 38).   [84] ibid 4.
[85] See (n 82).
[86] Interview with lawyer, NGO.
[87] Mehanna and Al-Sharmani (n 79).
[88] Human Rights Watch (n 38) 37; Interview with lawyer, NGO.
[89] Human Rights Watch (n 38).
[90] Human Rights Watch ibid 18.

The violence directed at children from the arrest to the police lock-up is compounded by the fact that, despite the legal prohibition, children are regularly mixed with adult detainees.[91] Human Rights Watch reported that:

> [F]ifteen of the thirty-five children interviewed who had been arrested had been detained with adult criminal detainees at least once. These children reported being held with unrelated adults in adult police lockups for periods averaging from one to three days, and sometimes lasting as long as two weeks.[92]

Our interviews also revealed that, despite the recent legal amendments, this practice was still ongoing in police stations.[93]

Police treatment of children in conflict with the law constitutes a violation of the State's obligation under the UNCRC to protect children from 'all forms of physical or mental violence, injury or abuse, neglect or negligent treatment, maltreatment or exploitation, including sexual abuse, while in the care of parent(s), legal guardian(s) or any other person who has the care of the child'.[94] Moreover, some of the documented cases of police abuse amount to cruel, degrading or inhumane treatment and in some cases can be defined as torture, in violation of the Convention, the International Covenant on Civil and Political Rights and the Convention against Torture.[95]

The situation has not changed with the 2008 amendments to the Child Law,[96] partly because most changes have not been implemented yet, but also and more significantly because police violence towards children stems from an entrenched police culture that will take more than a legislative amendment to change. This culture is one where police officers view children, in particular street children, as undeserving criminals who only understand the language of violence and ill-treatment.[97] While not every police officer thinks this way, the lack of adequate training and effective accountability mechanisms for police officers working in the juveniles department, allows for this culture to go on unaddressed.[98] The result is that treatment of children by police officers largely depends on the individual managing the police station.

---

[91] Ammar (n 17).
[92] Human Rights Watch (n 38) 28.
[93] Interview with lawyer, NGO.
[94] Human Rights Watch (n 38).
[95] Organisation Mondiale Contre la Torture. (2001). *The rights of the child in Egypt.* Geneva, Switzerland: Author; Human Rights Watch (n 38).
[96] Interview with lawyer, NGO.
[97] Human Rights Watch. (n 38); Interview with social researchers, AUC.
[98] See question 16 below on police training.

For example the person in charge of the juveniles department can be someone with understanding for the issue, with feelings for the children, someone who tries to help them. But once this person gets re-located or promoted, the whole situation changes. Everything depends on the new person to come.[99]

This culture is not exclusive to police officers, though. As one of the interviewed judges pointed out, the culture of the whole society stigmatizes street children, and police officers cannot be singled out as the only problem.[100] Moreover, as we have seen, the juvenile justice procedure does not give the child a chance to make a complaint about ill-treatment by the police and neither prosecutors nor juvenile judges investigate the circumstances of children's arrest and detention.[101]

D. Pre-Trial Detention: Excessive Use of the Judges' Broad Powers

The Beijing Rules stipulate that

> detention pending trial shall be used only as a measure of last resort and for the shortest possible period of time. Whenever possible, detention pending trial shall be replaced by alternative measures such as close supervision, intensive care or placement with a family or in an educational setting or home.[102]

In violation of these international standards, the Egyptian law grants large powers to judges and prosecutors to keep a child in pre-trail detention.

The Child Law states that no child under 15 years may be detained on remand.[103] However, the public prosecutor may, if it is deemed necessary, order the placement of the child in an observation institution, for a period not exceeding one week. This detention can be extended for one or more periods, as per the rules of criminal procedures. Children over the age of 15 years are subject to the regular (adult) rules of pre-trail detention.

The UN Rules for the Protection of Juveniles Deprived of their Liberty provide that 'detention before trial shall be avoided to the extent possible and limited to exceptional circumstances'. Moreover, the Riyadh Guidelines indicate that the institutionalization of children for preventive purposes should be strictly limited by a set of defined criteria.[104] Yet, Egyptian law

---

[99] Interview with lawyer, NGO.
[100] Phone interview with judge.
[101] Human Rights Watch (n 38).
[102] Beijing Rules, recommendation 13.1.
[103] Art 119 of the Child Law.
[104] (a) where the child or young person has suffered harm that has been inflicted by the

does not contain any criteria determining under what circumstances a child may be deprived of his or her liberty. The decision is left to the discretion of the judge and practice reveals that pre-trial detention is the norm rather than the exception. Judges explained that pre-trial detention was the only way to protect both the child and ensure the collection of evidence.[105] Neither the Child Law nor the Criminal Procedures Code contains safeguards guaranteeing that preventive detention will only be used in exceptional circumstances. Judicial discretion is only limited in the Criminal Procedures Code, by the requirement that the offence with which the suspect has been charged carry a minimum punishment of three months.[106] In addition, when the suspect has no stable place of residence, remand detention becomes automatic.[107] This provision is very dangerous as it results in the pre-trial detention of the most vulnerable juveniles for what are often minor offences. Indeed, official statistics show that pre-trail detention rates are far higher than the rates of those sentenced to detention,[108] which suggests that pre-trial detention is used extensively for minor offences which, at the conviction stage, do not justify a detention sentence.

Further, the UN Rules stipulate that 'when preventive detention is nevertheless used, juvenile Courts and investigative bodies shall give the highest priority to the most expeditious processing of such cases to ensure the shortest possible duration of detention'. Children younger than 15 years old are detained in observation institutions and those over 15 years old detained in social care institutions, both are subject to the regular rules of criminal procedure. These rules, far from guaranteeing the shortest possible duration of detention, grant the instruction judge and the public prosecutor wide powers to extend the duration with little guarantees of expediency. While the judge and prosecutor can extend the duration of preventive detention to up to 45 days, the criminal Court of appeal can extend it to six months and more if deemed necessary for the purposes of the investigation.[109]

---

parents or guardians; (b) where the child or young person has been sexually, physically or emotionally abused by the parents or guardians; (c) where the child or young person has been neglected, abandoned or exploited by the parents or guardians; (d) where the child or young person is threatened by physical or moral danger due to the behaviour of the parents or guardians; and (e) where a serious physical or psychological danger to the child or young person has manifested itself in his or her own behaviour and neither the parents, the guardians, the juvenile himself or herself nor non-residential community services can meet the danger by means other than institutionalization.

[105] Interviews with judges, NCCM.
[106] Art 134 of the Criminal Procedures Code 150/1950.
[107] ibid.
[108] Egypt's Third and Fourth Periodic Report to the International Committee on the Rights of the Child, period 2001–2008, December 2008.
[109] Art 143 of the Criminal Procedures Code.

Not only are the legal powers granted to the judiciary extensive, these rules are sometimes violated, such as when children are arrested and detained without any record of the arrest or the detention.[110]

E. The Judicial Trial: Lack of Implementation of the Procedural Safeguards

The rationale for having a specialized Child Court was explained by the Court of Cassation in a 2005 judgment[111] that pointed out that the legislators' creation of guarantees for the protection of child offenders, such as having specialized judges and increasing their number from one to three judges, proved that the Child Court was meant to instil a sense of trust and calm in the child. The Court of Cassation compared the judge in the Child Court to a father who acts according to the 'established fact' that the child doesn't choose a criminal path because of inherent qualities, but is rather a victim of the surrounding social and economic circumstances. Thus, the Court went on, measures are rehabilitative and preventive, and not punitive.

In reality however, the Court's process is far from complying with this paternalistic ideology. Interviews with key people revealed that Court proceedings are in practice unsophisticated and the outcome depends mostly on the judges' pre-conceived ideas about youth and delinquency.

While the law might include provisions for a specialized Court, in reality only two of Egypt's governorates, Cairo and Alexandria, possess a stand-alone Juvenile Court[112] (now renamed Child Court). In the remaining 28 governorates, makeshift juvenile Courts are held on a periodic basis, and their judges are not trained to deal with juvenile cases.[113] It is also notable that while an important rationale for having a specialized Court is to build specialized judicial expertise, the position of Juvenile Judge is not a specialization in Egypt. Judges work in many different areas of judiciary during their career, and may be appointed to sit in Child Courts without having received any specialized training.[114] Even if a judge has enrolled onto a special juvenile justice training courses and gains a strong understanding of the complex issues of juvenile delinquency, the high rate of turnover makes it impossible to guarantee that every judge sitting in the Child Court will have the required specialization.[115] Human Rights Watch also point to the fact that judges are often recruited from the ranks of prosecu-

---

[110] Interview with lawyer, NGO.
[111] Appeal 17320, JY 67 (2005); Court of Cassation.
[112] Ammar (n 17).
[113] ibid.
[114] The Human Rights Association for the Assistance of Prisoners (HRAAP), *Detention and Detainees in Egypt 2004*, Conditions of Detainees and Detention Centers in Egypt. The Seventh Annual Report: HRAAP.
[115] Interview with social researchers, AUC.

tors, who in turn are recruited from police academy graduates, casting doubts on their ability to provide independent oversight on police abuse.[116]

Another problem is the lack of qualified assistance by the experts or social controllers. The Court of Cassation has stressed the importance of the Child Court's social function. In a 1995 decision, the Court held that the absence of the two social experts invalidates the Court's decision. The Court stressed that the presence of the experts 'guides the judge in his decision, so as to achieve the social function of the Juvenile Court. Otherwise, the decision is invalid'.[117] Further, the Court of Cassation emphasized the importance of the social controller's reports and role in the juvenile trial as a 'fundamental procedure' both in Child Courts and in any other Court hearing the case of a juvenile.[118] Yet, there is a consensus amongst stakeholders that the level of qualification of social experts and social controllers is very low. The social reports mostly contain brief and superficial information.[119] For instance, a study looking at the social controller reports for street children found that reports did not provide information on the causes and factors which drove the child to live on the street.[120] Moreover, judges rarely took these reports into account, due in the most part because of their low quality. However the fact that these reports are seen to be irrelevant to the adjudication process creates disincentive for controllers to improve them, perpetuating this state of affairs.[121] One lawyer also explained that, despite the legal requirement, many judicial decisions are taken in the absence of any social report being presented to the Court.[122] One judge, while recognizing that this was the case, assured us that once the 2008 amendments come into force, this requirement will be implemented.[123]

Theoretically, legal representation is afforded to every child, however the interviewed lawyer informed us that, in practice, judges pick and choose which cases are important enough to merit legal representation.[124] This was confirmed by the government's own report to the CRC, which states that in 2006, 12,224 juveniles in conflict with the law were not provided with any legal assistance, because legal assistance was deemed unnecessary.[125] When they are granted legal counsel, lawyers are also not always present at the

---

[116] Human Rights Watch (n 38).
[117] Appeal 50556, JY 59 (1995); Court of Cassation.
[118] Appeal 25243, JY 67 (1998); Court of Cassation.
[119] Social Research Center (submitting to NGO Coalition on Child Rights), *The Inclusion of the Excluded: A Rights-based Approach to Child Protection Policies in Egypt* (American University Press, Cairo, 2007).
[120] ibid.
[121] Interview with NCCM project manager.
[122] Interview with lawyer, NGO.
[123] Phone interview with judge.
[124] Interview with lawyer, NGO.
[125] Egypt's Third and Fourth Periodic Report to the International Committee on the Rights of the Child, period 2001–2008, December 2008.

trial, and when they are, it is generally the first time they meet the child.[126] Legal assistance thus falls short of the quality needed to be of any use.

F. Lack of Available and Effective Community Sentences

When a juvenile is convicted of a crime, judges can take, at their discretion, a number of measures, including educational and rehabilitative measures within the community. However, available statistics indicate that the Child Courts hardly ever sentence children to these measures.[127] The main measures taken against children liable to deviance or committing crimes are probation, handing the child over to their guardians, or institutionalization.[128] The Beijing Rules stipulate that deprivation of personal liberty shall only be imposed as a measure of last resort, and not unless the juvenile is adjudicated of a serious act involving violence against another person or of persistence in committing other serious offences. These requirements are not transposed into Egyptian law and placement in detention is allowed in cases of exposure to danger as well as in cases of misdemeanors.[129] Institutionalization is the outcome in 42 per cent of cases.[130]

The excessive use of detention seems to be a result of the absence of alternatives, both in terms of social support networks for children who should be handed over to their guardians, and in terms of the availability of alternative community measures. A study found that most juveniles found in institutions have no social support network, ie have unstable home environments or no stable place of residence.[131] This study contains the example of a nine-year-old child who was arrested because he was found walking the streets late at night. The child's mother said she did not want to take care of the child as she could not afford it, so he was sentenced to five years in a reform institution. While this example dates back to the 1980s, our interviews suggest that the same still happens today. The social and economic conditions therefore play a major role in the decision to institutionalize a child, which is often justified by pragmatism rather than by the nature of the offence. This is especially true considering that the conditions in social care institutions can be better than in some homes. The lawyer we interviewed conceded:

---

[126] Interview with lawyer, NGO.
[127] *A Rights-based Analysis of Child Protection in Egypt: Final Report*, Report commissioned by Save the Children UK, Cairo, Egypt, 2007; NGO Coalition on the Rights of the Child, 2002.
[128] Community and Institutional Development (CID), ibid.
[129] Arts 99bis(a) and 101 of the Child Law.
[130] Community and Institutional Development (CID) (n 127).
[131] S Mehanna, 'Social Change, Legal Transformation and State Intervention: Youth Justice in the Arab Republic of Egypt' in J Hudson and B Galaway (eds), *Children and Youth: Dealing with Young Persons.* (Dordrecht, The Netherlands, 1990).

In some cases, I let the judge pass a sentence of institutionalization because this will be better for the child than returning home. I had this case of a young girl who was being sexually abused by her father, it was better for her to stay in the social care institution rather than go back to her father.

Judges confirmed this view, explaining that when faced with a child who may have committed a minor offence but would be in grave danger if released in the community, they prefer to send the child to a social care institution.[132]

The second reason behind the high rate of institutionalization is the lack of availability of the alternative measures provided for in the law. While the law contains a range of measures that judges can choose from when deciding on the sentence, in reality, the necessary resources for social community measures are non-existent (in violation of the Beijing Rules). For instance, there are no training and vocational centers, responsible for taking on juvenile delinquents in Egypt.[133] Judges are therefore often left with a choice between handing the children over to his guardians and institutionalizing them. Many judges also use probation as an intermediate measure between hand-over and institutionalization. Although the probation system is not functional and supervision is irregular and often ineffective, this measure is seen as providing the child and his family with the necessary warning, without going as far as detaining him.[134] Yet, this sentence might place the child at risk of further abuse by the police officer in charge of the supervision.

In addition, the sentences contain no element of supervision. When the child is released from detention or probation, there is no appropriate follow-up with the child after the end of the sentence to ensure his or her smooth reintegration within society. This is especially problematic in case of release from detention, as children released from detention need to be provided with the basic social services that will allow their full reintegration (housing, health, education, etc).

Although these problems point to the failure of the State to make community sentences available in sufficient quantity and quality, the government seems oblivious of its responsibility and places the blame on others.[135] Families are blamed for their failure to raise children appropriately, while the State's role in socio-economic development and family support is ignored. The community is blamed for refusing to accept juvenile delinquents within foster families and training centers, while neither the law

---

[132] Interview with judges, NCCM.
[133] Interview with NCCM project manager; Interview with lawyer.
[134] Interview with judges, NCCM; Interview with NCCM project manager.
[135] This view is confirmed by the various government reports, namely the CRC Egypt report, 2008.

nor its executive regulations impose a duty on the State to ensure such measures are available. Finally, the State's proposed solutions are disproportionately based on the provision of services by NGOs,[136] with the associated problems of lack of accountability and lack of sustainability of NGO projects.

The Beijing Rules provide that sentences given to juveniles 'shall always be in proportion not only to the circumstances and the gravity of the offence but also to the circumstances and the needs of the juvenile as well as to the needs of the society'. All three aspects should therefore be taken into consideration to achieve proportionality in the penal response. Even when taking social measures against juveniles, proportionality should be respected. In relation to the social measures applicable to juveniles, the proportionality principle is not always respected. For some penalties, such as the placement under training and qualification, the judge decides on the duration of the placement. However, for most of the measures, the judge does not decide on the duration of the placement. Placement under probation, in community service or under certain obligations has a legal maximum duration (three years), but the actual duration of stay cannot be decided upon by the Child Court. Similarly, the Child Court is not allowed to determine the duration of stay in a social care or health institution.[137] This is justified, the Court of Cassation explained, by the fact that the duration of the measure should not be proportional to the severity of the offence but rather to the offender's dangerousness.[138] This constitutes a direct violation of section 2 of the UN Rules for the Protection Deprived of their Liberty which states: 'the length of the sanction should be determined by the judicial authority'.

In relation to deprivation of liberty, the Egyptian law stipulates that, once the child has been institutionalized, the institution should send the Court periodic reports on the situation of the child. Upon consideration of these reports, the Court decides whether to uphold the order, terminate it or replace it with another measure. This decision is taken solely on the basis of the child's 'progress' in rehabilitation, without taking into consideration the seriousness of the offence. In the case of placement in a social care institution, the law contains a legal maximum duration (10 years for felonies and five years for misdemeanors), but for placement in a hospital, there is no maximum duration and the juvenile can stay in the hospital even after reaching the age of 21 (provided he or she is placed in an adult hospital then). The measure bears therefore no proportionality to the circumstances of the offence, and its duration is decided upon according to the circum-

---

[136] Egypt's Third and Fourth Periodic Report to the International Committee on the Rights of the Child, period 2001–2008, December 2008; Interview with NCCM project manager.
[137] Appeal 7767, JY 63 (1998) and Appeal 1292, JY 67 (2005); Court of Cassation.
[138] Appeal 5926, JY 60 (1997); Court of Cassation.

stances of the child alone, without reference to the nature and severity of the offence. Moreover, while the law specifies that placement in a social care institution should be a measure of last resort and for the shortest duration possible,[139] the evidence shows that some children are institutionalized for very long periods of time. This is often due to the child having no stable living arrangement to go back to, rather than to a need to keep the child institutionalized for retributive or rehabilitative purposes.

1. Deprivation of liberty and conditions of detention

Rule 11(b) of the UN Rules defines deprivation of liberty as 'any form of detention or imprisonment or the placement of a person in a public or private custodial setting, from which this person is not permitted to leave at will, by order of any judicial, administrative or other public authority'. The UN Rules therefore apply to pre-trail detention as well as institutionalization and imprisonment. In Egypt, there are 26 custodial institutions for juveniles. Children below 15 years old and those detained pending trial are detained in social care institutions, some of which are open or semi-open. Children above 15 years old sentenced to custody are detained in juvenile corrective institutions. Official statistics show that, in 2006, a total of 7455 juveniles were deprived of their liberty.[140]

Juveniles deprived of their liberty and grounds for detention, 2006

Reason for deprivation of liberty	Number of juveniles
Acting contrary to societal rules or laws, when these acts constitute misdemeanors or liability to delinquency	2081
Committed a crime (felony)	923 (15+ years)
Children liable to delinquency, according to the Child Law	1220
Awaiting trial in an observation institution	2553
Detained provisionally	678

Source: Social Defense Unit 2006, from the Egypt CRC country report 2008

These numbers, especially the high number of juveniles detained pre-trial, show clearly the violation of UN Rules, which provide that depriva-

---

[139] Art 107 of the Child Law.
[140] Egypt's Third and Fourth Periodic Report to the International Committee on the Rights of the Child, period 2001–2008, December 2008.

tion of liberty occur as a last resort. This rule is applicable even when detention is carried out in social care institutions as opposed to prison facilities. Moreover, the conditions in places of detention are far from complying with the minimum standards applicable in international law. The Beijing Rules stipulate: 'While in custody, juveniles shall receive care, protection and all necessary individual assistance—social, educational, vocational, psychological, medical and physical—that they may require in view of their age, sex and personality'. Yet, the available evidence reveals that institutionalized juveniles suffer violence at the hands of workers and inmates, receive inadequate food, bedding, clothing and medical services and are not offered the required educational or rehabilitative programs.[141]

The architectural design of institutions reflects an enclosed and restrictive atmosphere, rather than a healthy living environment. A study by Abdel Satar[142] revealed that the sleeping quarters were cramped; children lacked space where they could carry out daily activities such as watching TV, studying, painting or reading, and tended to get into fights because of the closed structure of the place.

Several studies show that the institutions are severely under-staffed and that the staff is insufficiently trained. This problem is partly due to the employment of a large proportion of staff employed on a contractual basis, which increases the rate of unskilled workers and reduces accountability.[143] Juveniles are subject to physical, psychological and sexual violence by professionals working in the institutions.[144] For instance, a study carried out by Bibars on the Girls Social Care Institute in Agouza, showed that beating was a common form of punishment. 'If a girl is renowned for recurrent escaping and "mischievous conduct", she would be beaten in front of the others and, in some cases, her hair and eyebrows shaved for further humiliation'.[145] A grave problem in Egyptian social care institutions is that the same institutions serve as shelters for children who have no legal guardians willing to take care of them, as a care centre for children at risk of harm and as a corrective institution for juvenile delinquents. All children

---

[141] Human Rights Watch (n 38); Human Rights Association for the Assistance of Prisoners (HRAAP), *Detention and Detainees in Egypt 2004*, Conditions of Detainees and Detention Centers in Egypt. The Seventh Annual Report: HRAAP.

[142] M Abdel Satar, *The Human Dimension in Designing Social Care Institutions for Children at Risk of Delinquency* (2005) A study conducted under the auspices of the PDR project. (Social Research Center, the American University in Cairo).

[143] Interview with Wafaa Al Mistikawi, Director General of the Social Defense Administration *Al Ahram*, (9 June 2007) Interview with Wafaa Al Mistikawi, Director General of the Social Defense Administration.

[144] Human Rights Watch (n 38); Abdel Satar (n 142); A Badran, *Evaluation of the Role and Impact of Social Care Institutions for Juvenile Delinquents*. (2005) A study conducted under the auspices of the PDR Project. Social Research Center, the American University in Cairo.

[145] I Bibars, 'Street children in Egypt: from the home to the street to inappropriate corrective institutions', *Environment and Urbanization*, Vol 10, No 1, April 1998, pp 201–216.

are institutionalized in the same setting, and although they are supposed to be kept separate according to the reason for institutionalization, studies show that children are not properly classified into different categories inside the social care institutions.[146] Moreover, children at risk in social care institutions are only separated from delinquent children at night, with the activities and meal times gathering them all together.[147] This situation impacts negatively on the most vulnerable children, who, when they come in contact with older, more experienced children, can come out of the institution more damaged than when they entered.

Healthcare services are also very insufficient. A study of six juvenile institutions showed that none had psychiatrists or separate rooms where the children could receive psychological care.[148] Moreover, in those institutions that do have psychologists, their numbers and qualifications are insufficient.[149] Medical care specialists are also absent from juvenile institutions, thus severely affecting the well-being of inmates, in particular those affected by disabilities or diseases.[150]

In terms of educational and rehabilitative services, the institutions are staffed with inexperienced and ineffective staff, who are unable to provide children with the necessary rehabilitative programs.[151] According to Badran,[152] 'the production and training programs inside these institutions failed to absorb the workforce and energies of the delinquents [and] the literacy programs offered in these institutions were not compulsory and effective'.

G. Case Law: Death Penalty

It is important to note that first instance and Appeal Court judgments concerning juveniles are not available for consultation and only Court of Cassation decisions are made public. Yet, few juvenile cases are considered by the Court of Cassation, as defendants are mostly from poor backgrounds and do not have the means to go through appeal and cassation procedures. Moreover, some sentences cannot be appealed (reprimand and

---

[146] A Badran, *Evaluation of the Role and Impact of Social Care Institutions for Juvenile Delinquents*. A study conducted under the auspices of the PDR Project (Social Research Center, American University in Cairo, 2005).

[147] Interview with Wafaa Al Mistikawi, Director General of the Social Defense Administration *Al Ahram* (9/6/2007) Interview with Wafaa Al Mistikawi, Director General of the Social Defense Administration.

[148] Abdel Satar (n 142).

[149] Human Rights Association for the Assistance of Prisoners (HRAAP), *Detention and Detainees in Egypt 2004*, Conditions of Detainees and Detention Centers in Egypt. The Seventh Annual Report: HRAAP.

[150] ibid.

[151] Human Rights Watch (n 38).

[152] Badran (n 146).

hand-over to the guardians) and other sentences are often seen as not 'worth' an appeal. Besides, Court of Cassation judgments only contain rulings on points of law, rather than a full consideration of the facts of the case. Therefore, the analysis of the few Court of Cassation judgments available was useful in highlighting how the highest Court interpreted certain legal provisions; however, it could not constitute the basis for a case law analysis that takes into account the circumstances of the crime or the background of offenders and victims.

The case known as 'El Torbini' captivated the media and the Egyptian public for over two years (2007–2009) and helped to bring the issue of street children and juvenile delinquency to the fore of public debates. This infamous story concerned a series of crimes against street children, which involved the kidnapping, sexual abuse and killing of possibly more than 30 children. A group of young people was charged with these crimes, with the gang leader allegedly being a 26-year-old nicknamed 'El Torbini' (the fast train) who operated with a group of seven young men, some of whom were under the age of 18 years. All of the alleged 'gang' members, like their victims, had been living on the streets since their childhood and some of them had been sentenced to detention previously.

The Criminal Court sentenced two of the gang members, including 'El Torbini', to the death penalty, and the other members to long prison sentences or life sentences. One of the accused juveniles was referred to the Juvenile Court and two others (16- and 17-year-olds) were judged together with the rest of the accused in the Criminal Court and given prison sentences. The sentences were upheld by Court of Cassation. Although the case did not concern juvenile delinquents only, the Court of Cassation judgment issued in January 2009 contains several interesting points that are relevant to the situation of juvenile delinquents and children in need of protection.

While the Court of Cassation decided to uphold the sentences imposed on the young men, it emphasized the failure of Egyptian society and institutions to adequately protect street children. All the accused, the Court said,[153] are street children who had been abandoned by their families, by the governmental and by civil society institutions. Living on the streets exposed these youths to many negative influences which in turn led them to a life of crime and delinquency, 'despite the constitutional guarantee for the protection of childhood, care for youth and the provision of appropriate conditions for their development'. The Court went on to affirm that 'it is the Court's duty to remind all those responsible, in the state and the civil society institutions, of their duties under the Constitution and the Child

---

[153] 'The merits of the case of El Torbini and his associates: the suspects committed the crimes of murder associated with sexual abuse' *Al Dostour* (18 June 2009).

Law'. Describing the legal and constitutional protection as mere 'ink on paper', the Court of Cassation took the opportunity of this high profile case to call on 'those responsible' to render these normative protections a reality on the ground.

This judgment is of importance as it illustrates the complexity of juvenile crime and judicial decision-making in Egypt. The Court rightly pointed out that victims and offenders alike were both victims of an institutional and social system that completely failed to address their most basic needs. While this case was an especially serious crime, the same applies to most juvenile crimes, as they are mostly committed by disadvantaged children to other disadvantaged children. The Court also rightly observed that, on paper protections exist for children in the form of constitutional guarantees and legal provisions. However, without adequate implementation of these provisions, street children as well as society at large will remain unprotected. A third and most important point stands out from the Court of Cassation judgment, despite recognizing that these crimes were triggered by the failure of the State to protect its most vulnerable children, the Court maintained the death and prison sentences imposed on the accused. This was justified by the fact that the evidence convinced the Court beyond reasonable doubt that the crimes had been committed with premeditation. This decision shows the reluctance of the judicial body to go further than verbal criticism of the child rights situation the State has allowed to go on for many years. It also shows the complexity of judicial decision-making in a context of deteriorating socio-economic conditions and increasing social exclusion. Indeed, the young people accused have been exposed to so many violations of their rights to basic protection that it is difficult to hold them fully responsible for their actions. Yet, they have also been proved to have committed crimes with premeditation and with full mental capacity.

The 'El Torbini' case illustrates how strongly juvenile delinquency is intertwined with the level of protection afforded to children by the State, in terms of the protection of their family life, basic social care, education, health and freedom from violence. The link between lack of protection and delinquency is starting to be recognized at a policy level, but, as our study has shown, on the ground, practitioners still struggle to take sufficient account of the circumstances of juveniles in conflict with the law. The amended Child Law seeks to give more weight to the protection of children and to the prevention of delinquency through measures directed at 'at risk' children. However, by failing to revise the procedures and measures applicable to juveniles breaching the law to ensure their social and protective function, the Child Law might have missed one of the key reforms in the field of youth justice.

V. CONCLUSION

The Egyptian Juvenile Justice System is currently at a crossroads. In 2008, major legislative amendments were introduced to the Child Law, modifying various provisions relating to juvenile delinquents and the protection of children 'at risk'. These changes, which, by and large, represented a positive step forward in guaranteeing child rights and in putting the Egyptian legislation in line with the UNCRC, have not been fully implemented yet. Concerns around the lack of available resources for the police and for the judiciary in terms of training and availabilities of specialized expertise compromise the process of putting the 'best interest of the child' into practice. Therefore, the impact of the amendments is yet to be seen, especially since the new executive regulations of the law have not been issued yet.

CHAPTER 6

Part I:
*Criminal Law and the Rights of the Child in Iran**

I. INTRODUCTION

Iran became a constitutional Islamic Republic in 1979, when the monarchy was overthrown and religious clerics assumed political control under the supreme leader, Ayatollah Khomenei. The Iranian revolution put an end to the rule of the Shah, who had alienated powerful religious and political forces with a programme of modernization and Westernization.[1] It is important to mention two important figures of the Islamic Republic: the Supreme Leader and the President. The Supreme Leader of Iran is responsible for the delineation and supervision of 'the general policies of the Islamic Republic of Iran.' He is commander-in-chief of the armed forces and controls the Islamic Republic's intelligence and security operations; he alone can declare war. He has the power to appoint and dismiss the leaders of the judiciary, the State radio and television networks, and the supreme commander of the Islamic Revolutionary Guard Corps. He also appoints six of the 12 members of the Council of Guardians. He, or the council of religious leaders, are elected by the Assembly of Experts, on the basis of their qualifications and the high popular esteem in which they are held. After the office of Leadership, the President of Iran is the highest official in the country. His is the responsibility for implementing the Constitution and acting as the head of the executive, except in matters directly concerned with (the office of) the Leadership.[2]

Though most people in the Islamic Republic of Iran enjoy an average quality of life, many challenges exist. These include high unemployment, disparities in income, and inequality of opportunity. Approximately 20 per cent of the population lives below the poverty line and serious regional disparities exist. Populations in rural areas suffer the most, with lower

---

* Prepared and Compiled by Behrooz Javanmard, PhD student in Penal Law and Criminology, Shahid Beheshti University, First-Class Attorney at Law.
  [1] http://news.bbc.co.uk/1/hi/world/europe/country_profiles/790877.stm, accessed 12 March 2010.
  [2] http://www.nyulawglobal.org/globalex/iran.htm#_System_of_Government, accessed 12 March 2010.

household incomes, higher unemployment rates, lower literacy rates and fewer available services.[3]

Several recent studies in Iran have reported that child abuse and exploitation is common around the country. One survey showed that more than one in five children between the ages of six to 11 was physically punished by caregivers in the previous week. Corporal punishment in schools and remand homes is also common.[4] This led the authorities to reform the laws, in order to adhere to more modern criminological standards. Nevertheless, the laws regarding juvenile offenders still have considerable gaps.

II. INTERNATIONAL FRAMEWORK

In order to discuss the international framework within Iran, it is imperative to first understand that the basic human rights definitions, as established by various international treaties and conventions, do not necessarily converge with that of Iran's national legislation. Whilst Iran has signed and ratified many international treaties, it is primarily an Islamic Republic with its own set of codified laws governed by Sharia law. Therefore, any international treaty which is in direct contravention with such laws will not be applicable within the Republic.

An international treaty will only acquire legal status once it has been (i) signed by the representative of Iran, (ii) approved by Parliament[5] (iii) confirmed by the Guardian Council.[6] If, despite Parliament's approval, it is rejected by the Guardian Council, it may be confirmed by the Expediency Discernment Council. Once it has been published in the Official Gazette, it has force of law. It should be kept in mind that when ratifying an international treaty, article 4 of the Constitution, stating that all provisions should be consistent with Islamic standards, plays a crucial role. If provisions of the treaty contradict Islamic legal standards, reservations will have to be made before the treaty can be signed. Accordingly, in the Act of Accession of the Government of Iran to the UNCRC of 9 February 1994 (1/12/1372), it is stated that:

---

[3] http://www.unicef.org/infobycountry/iran_2142.html, accessed 12 March 2010.

[4] ibid 3.

[5] Art 77 of the Iranian Constitution: 'International treaties, pacts, contracts and agreements should be ratified by the National Consultative Assembly', available at: http://www.irol.com/iran/iran-info/Government/constitution-6-2.html, accessed 9/03/2010. The text of the Constitution is available at: http://www.irol.com/iran/iran-info/Government/constitution.html, accessed 9 March 2010.

[6] Art 94 of the Iranian Constitution: 'All legislations of the Assembly should be delivered to the Council of Guardians to be verified according to Article 4 for compatibility of these legislations with Islamic regulations', available at: http://www.irol.com/iran/iran-info/Government/constitution-6-2.html, accessed 9 March 2010.

The Convention on the Rights of the Child, including a preamble and 54 articles, is ratified as follows and the accession of the Government of the Islamic Republic of Iran to it is authorised, on the condition that if its provisions in any case and at any time are in conflict with the internal laws and Islamic standards, they shall not be binding for the Government of the Islamic Republic of Iran.[7]

Thus, it is understood that Islamic law has precedence over any other non-Islamic jurisprudence so that the legal system recognizes international human rights standards and principles so long as they are not incompatible with Sharia law.

The concept of human rights in the Islamic Republic of Iran is therefore different from the concept commonly accepted by the international community. This lack of unity between national and international approaches to human rights has caused some tension between Iran and the international community. Indeed, Western States often accuse the government of Iran of violating the basic rights of its citizens, while the Iranian government accuses Western ones of using human rights as a pretext to interfere with its internal affairs.

A. The Convention on the Rights of the Child

When the members of the Islamic Consultative Assembly ratified the Bill for Accession to the UN Convention on the Rights of the Child (hereinafter referred to as the UNCRC) in 1993 by a majority vote, it made certain reservations. These reservations were mostly limited to situations where incompatibilities arose between the treaty and domestic legislation. The Bill was then dispatched to the Council of Guardians for further verification, but was objected to on the following grounds:

- Article 12(1) on the right of the child to freely express his views
- Article 13(2) on possible restrictions on the exercise of the right to freedom of expression
- Article 14(1) on freedom of thought, conscience and religion
- Article 14(3) on possible limitations to such rights
- Article 15(2) on restrictions to the right to freedom of association
- Article 16(1) on arbitrary interferences with a child's privacy, family and correspondence.
- Article 29(1) on the purpose of education of the child.[8]

---

[7] http://www.schrr.net/spip.php?page=sarticle&id_article=2531, accessed 11 March 2010 (in Farsi).

[8] http://hright.iran-emrooz.net/index.php?/hright/more/16474/, accessed 9 March 2010 (in Farsi).

Interestingly, the Council did not object to the prohibition of capital punishment and life imprisonment for youths aged 18 and under. After further negotiations and verification processes, Iran ratified the UNCRC on 13 July 1994, with one broad reservation: 'The Government of the Islamic Republic of Iran reserves the right not to apply any provisions or articles of the Convention that are incompatible with Islamic Laws and the international legislation in effect.'[9] The Committee on the Rights of the Child (CRC) responded to this reservation by stating that 'the broad and imprecise nature of the State party's general reservation potentially negates many of the Convention's provisions and raises concern as to its compatibility with the object and purpose of the Convention'.[10] Such a position in effect violates the overarching principles of the UNCRC, but more specifically, those enshrined within articles 37(a) and 40(3).[11] The CRC's objections to such broad reservations were an attempt to highlight Iran's obligations upon ratification.

Although Iran has made efforts to incorporate the UNCRC into domestic legislation, it still refuses to alter some of the more controversial provisions in domestic law, namely those regarding the minimum age of criminal responsibility and the treatment of convicted juvenile offenders. This has resulted in various calls for reform by human rights organizations and other signatory States. Due to the lengthy verification process, many of the Bills that were drafted to implement the UNCRC are only now being integrated into the legal framework. One of these is the Bill for Protection of Children and Young Adults, approved in 2002, which had three goals. The first was the unification of domestic law and regulations with the principles of the UNCRC. The second was the amendment of incomplete legislation in order to make it more coherent. The third was a commitment to prevent child abuse, thus creating a supportive environment of mental and physical well-being.

In light of the fact that the Republic of Iran is an Islamic State and the Council of Guardians reserves the right to veto any law incompatible with the principles of Sharia law, a very cautious approach to the signing and ratification of international treaties has been adopted thus making reservations various international instruments. However, where incompatibilities between domestic legislation and international obligations emerge, Iran has

---

[9] http://treaties.un.org/Pages/ViewDetails.aspx?src=TREATY&mtdsg_no=IV-11&chapter=4&lang=en, accessed 09/03/2010.

[10] Committee on the Rights of the Child (24th Session), Consideration of Reports Submitted by State Parties under art 44 of the Convention, Concluding Observations, Islamic Republic of Iran, 2, available at http://daccess-dds-ny.un.org/doc/UNDOC/GEN/G00/429/91/PDF/G0042991.pdf?OpenElement, accessed 11 March 2010.

[11] Available at: http://www2.ohchr.org/english/law/crc.htm, accessed 9 March 2010.

created a system open to adaptation. Legislation makes it possible to amend incompatibilities in the law in two ways: i) by referral to the Expediency Council, an external body that examines differing opinions between the Parliament and Council of Guardians; or ii) by issuance of governmental decrees of the Supreme Leader, who is a fully qualified Islamic jurist also known as *faqih*, after consulting with other religious authorities (*marja'*).

III. DOMESTIC LEGISLATION ON THE PROTECTION OF THE RIGHTS OF THE CHILD IN CRIMINAL LAW

A. Procedural Rights

1. Courts and procedure

Since there is no specific law governing the Youth Court in Iran, the trial of minors is conducted in public courts. However, articles 219–230 of the Iranian Code of Criminal Procedure (hereinafter referred to as the CCP) are concerned with the special legal procedures for minors. For example, article 219 states that in each jurisdiction, one division of the public court should be used for court proceedings involving minors, even in cases where the minor has committed a crime alongside an adult. Where no such facilities are available, the general courts are to hear youth offenders.[12] In terms of procedure, the CCP stipulates that when a minor appears in court, the judge is required to inform his or her natural legal guardian and to appoint legal representation. Where the guardian does not appoint a lawyer, the court must do so instead.

2. Proceedings

Children are notified of the preliminary hearings via their legal guardians, but in cases where the legal guardian does not attend, the offenders are summoned themselves. After the preliminary hearings have taken place, the courts must determine whether it is necessary to detain the child. According to the CCP,[13] there are two ways in which a child can avoid detention: (i) through a pledge made by the guardian to bring the juvenile offender before the courts whenever he is requested to do along with a security payment or (ii) through bail made on behalf of the offender by the guardian. However, article 224 of the CCP states[14] that:

---

[12] Ch 5 CCP.
[13] Art 2 of the CCP.
[14] http://www.iranbar.org/pmm191.php, accessed 9 March 2010 (in Farsi).

[I]f it is necessary to detain the child in order to perform investigations or to prevent conspiracy due to the importance of the crime, or if the child does not have a custodian or legal guardian, if the custodian or guardian does not agree to give a pledge or pay bail, and there is no one else as mentioned above to pledge or pay bail, the accused will be temporarily kept in the Centre for Correction and Training.

In the circumstances where no such centre is available, the CCP dictates that the offender be held in 'another appropriate place,' most often a detention centre for adults.

3. Safeguards

There are certain safeguards for the protection of children during proceedings. The trial itself is not held in public and the only individuals present are the legal guardian, the offender and his lawyer, the witnesses, a representative of the Centre for Correction and Training (where applicable) and other individuals whose presence is deemed necessary. If the best interests of the child so require, he may be excused from trial.[15] The publication of any details of the trial and the identities of the accused is illegal and is subject to prosecution.[16] However, the sentence may be pronounced in public. All sentences of the juvenile court may be appealed to the Province Court of Appeal, an adult court.[17] The juvenile court can revise its previous decision, perhaps reducing the sentence, based on the reports received from the Centre for Correction and Training.

Occasionally, the National Supreme Court issues procedural statements relating to matters which have legal implications on the hearing of cases.[18] There are also procedural statements which have a bearing on the process of juvenile justice. For example, procedural statement No 651 issued on 24 October 2000 stated that: 'All charges against persons under 18 years of age, including drug-related crimes should be tried in the juvenile court.'

B. The Long-Awaited Bills

1. The Bill for the establishment of the Courts of Children and Young Adults

The Bill for Establishment of the Courts of Children and Young Adults was

---

[15] http://www.ghazavat.com/ghazavat.com/ghezavat19/Selection.htm, accessed 9 March 2010 (in Farsi).

[16] Art 648 of the Islamic Penal Code (on disclosure of information) and art 648 CPP.

[17] http://hoghoogh.online.fr/article.php3?id_article=375, accessed 09 March 2010 (in Farsi).

[18] http://hoghoogh.online.fr/article.php3?id_article=375.

presented to Parliament in 2003 but has not yet been approved by Parliament and the Guardian Council.

2. The Bill for Proceedings of the Crimes of Children and Young Adults

On 22 October 2008, the Speaker of the Judiciary announced the approval of the Bill on Proceedings of Crimes of Children and Young Adults by Parliament, after five years of waiting. In this Bill, a child is defined as a person under 18 years of age.[19] Minors are divided into three different age groups: nine to 12, 12 to 15, and 15 to 18. For children aged nine to 12, the penalties are mostly training, referral of the child and his parents to a social worker, admonition by the judge, and so on. For children aged 12 to 15, punishments are applicable. For children aged 15 to 18 reduced punishments apply. Perhaps the most innovative feature of this Bill is the possibility to convert punitive sentences into vocational ones, aimed at future rehabilitation. Despite these efforts, the Bill has some shortcomings as it does not adequately guarantee the protection of children and their rights. For example, where discretionary sanctions are applicable, they do not differ between adults and children.[20] Moreover, it introduces some draconian controls such as the establishment of a special police force solely for children, which contravenes many of the principles enshrined in the Act of the Fourth Economic, Social, and Cultural Development Plan of the Islamic Republic of Iran.

3. Summary of content

a) the term 'law-breaking children' is used instead of 'child offenders' to avoid stigmatization.

b) Article 1 of this Bill states that all children under 18 years of age who are in Iran and are considered at risk will benefit from the protection offered by this bill. There is no discrimination in this regard, whether female or male, Iranian or non-Iranian. High-risk children include: (i) children who do not have a guardian or who have irresponsible and uncaring parents, (ii) children whose parents have personality disorders or are drug of alcohol addicts, (iii) children whose parents are involved in prostitution and corrupt centres, (iv) children who suffer from domestic violence, (v) children who are deprived of education or drop out of school, (vi) children of divorced parents, (vi) children with sexual ambiguity or physical and mental disability, (vii) children who are

---

[19] http://www.siasatrooz.ir/CNewsRDetail.aspx?QSCNDId=10544&QSDNId=235, accessed 11 March 2010 (in Farsi).

[20] http://www.magiran.com/npview.asp?ID=1724043, accessed 09/03/2010 (in Farsi).

involved in beggary and smuggling and (viii) children who are exploited at school and in the workplace. [21]

c)   public prosecutors are required to start prompt action when they are informed of the presence of high-risk children.[22]

d)   juvenile courts composed of a judge, a number of counsellors (if the offender is a girl, at least one female counsellor must be present) and a representative of the Centre for Correction and Training are to be established.

e)   proceedings are to focus on the child and the offence committed, taking into consideration the child's level of growth and development, in order to find the appropriate sanction

f)   proceedings involving minors who have committed serious crimes cannot be brought if the former do not have legal representation.

g)   the Public Prosecutor's Office may suspend a youth offender's prosecution for minor offences and where the child has already been convicted, he may suspend his/her sentence.

h)   if the child is not aware of his actions or the consequences of his doings, or if there is hesitation and uncertainty about his maturity, majority and sanity, and this is confirmed upon medical examination, capital punishment is revoked and converted to another sentence.[23]

i)   the various implementing institutions, namely the Ministry of Education, the police, the municipalities and the Welfare Organization, are to cooperate under a newly structured framework.

j)   IRIB (Islamic Republic of Iran Broadcasting) is required to broadcast advertisements related to children while the Welfare Organization is in charge of creating a computer and communication systems for collection and processing of information.

k)   social workers now have a role similar to police officers. They may forcibly remove exploited children from their environment. They are required to submit reports on the condition of the child to the court and judges should take them into consideration.

l)   failure to register a child's birth or the interference with the registration of the child aimed at exploiting the child for smuggling or sexual abuse have been penalized. Those who encourage children to leave school, or who do not permit children to go to school, will be penalized.

m)   heavy sanctions are applicable to those who encourage children to commit suicide, for crimes against disabled children or children under 12 years of age and for organized crimes committed against minors.

---

[21] http://www.humanrightsiran.com/FA/Print.aspx?ID=3355, accessed 11/03/2010 (in Farsi).

[22] http://www.siasatrooz.ir/CNewsRDetail.aspx?QSCNDId=10544&QSDNId=235, accessed 11 March 2010 (in Farsi).

[23] ibid 22, art 35 of the Bill.

4. The Bill on Investigation of Crimes of Children and Juveniles

In February 2005, the Judiciary submitted the Bill on Investigation of Crimes of Juveniles to the government. The Bill was ratified by the government and submitted to Parliament. It was passed in its first reading in August 2006 and then submitted to a parliamentary committee where it still remains. It is said that one of the reasons for the delay is Guardian Council's comments on the Bill, regarding the incompatibility of some provisions with Islamic law.

5.The Bill on the Protection of Juveniles

In October 2008 the Iranian Judiciary verified a draft Bill 'on the protection of the juvenile'. The Bill was completed by the Judiciary and is now awaiting government approval. Once this is given, it will be sent to Parliament for final ratification. This Bill contains provisions (i) for the protection of vulnerable children and adolescents and their families (ii) for the protection of the physical, mental and social well-being of children and young adults and (iii) for the establishment of a system whereby relationships between the judiciary and educational, social, governmental and non-governmental organizations are maintained.[24]

C. The Age of Criminal Liability

In the legal system of Iran, the age of criminal responsibility has not been specifically defined but there has always been a 'common sense' and legal synonymy between the religious and legal age of maturity and the minimum age of criminal responsibility.

According to Islamic jurisprudence, the minimum age of criminal responsibility is attained once a child reaches puberty. Once that age has been attained, a child offender will have to face the criminal justice system in the same way as adults. It is interesting to note that there is disagreement among Islamic jurists when it comes to determining that age.

According to the Constitution, the age of maturity is based on the Islamic definition of sexual maturity:[25] 15 years for boys and nine years for girls. Age is determined by a birth certificate but in cases where it is disputed, the judicial authority has an obligation to seek an expert opinion to determine the age of the accused. Many States argue that age is subjective and based on various factors, including mental capacity. Iran's

---

[24] http://www.humanrightsiran.com/FA/Print.aspx?ID=3355, accessed 11 March 2010 (in Farsi).
[25] http://hoghough85.blogfa.com/post-1630.aspx, accessed 9 March 2010 (in Farsi).

determination of age is far less subjective and is based upon perceived sexual characteristics.[26]

According to the Islamic Penal Code[27] (hereinafter referred to as the IPC) the age of legal maturity is the minimum age of criminal responsibility. Since there is no specific definition of that age, the authorities rely on the definition provided by the Civil Code: nine years for girls and 15 years for boys.[28] Article 1210, note 2 of the Civil Code[29] stipulates that a child can only handle his own finances and inherit property when his maturity is proven. Attaining maturity is thus imperative to handle matters such as finances, and the same applies to those who have committed crimes. In practice however, maturity is not always a prerequisite and it is often the case that children receive sentences comparable to those applicable to adults.

Article 49 of the IPC exonerates child offenders from penal responsibility. Article 49, note 1 sets the Sharia adult age as the criteria to distinguish a child from an adult. Article 49, note 2 allows physical punishment of child offenders to the extent thought necessary and in their interests.[30]

A number of issues emerge. According to the legislator, a child must be at least 18 years old before he or she can apply for a passport,[31] enrol for military service,[32] operate a vehicle or obtain employment (see the Government Employment Act). According to article 1043 of the Civil Code, the marriage of a female must be consented to by her father or paternal grandfather even if she has reached the full age of majority.[33] And finally, in order to vote, one must be at least 15 years old. Thus, from the legislator's point of view, children under 18 years of age do not have the requisite level of physical, mental and rational capacity to perform some of the above-mentioned activities. In contrast, the law stipulates that 'mature' children, such as nine-year-old girls and 15-year-old boys, are old enough to be criminally responsible and endure religious and conventional penalties such as *qisas*, execution, stoning, flogging, and imprisonment.

Furthermore, there seems to be some discrepancy and incongruity in the civil process of attainment of the age of majority and of its consequences in the Civil Code, especially when comparing article 1210 with article 1210,

---

[26] http://hoghough85.blogfa.com/post-1630.aspx, accessed 9 March 2010 (in Farsi).
[27] Art 49 Note 1 IPC.
[28] Arti 1210 Note 1, available at: http://www.alaviandassociates.com/documents/civilcode.pdf, accessed 9 March 2010.
[29] http://www.alaviandassociates.com/documents/civilcode.pdf, accessed 09/03/2010.
[30] A Abghari, *Introduction to the Iranian Legal System and the Protection of Human Rights in Iran* (British Institute of International and Comparative Law, London, 2008) 147.
[31] http://vekalat88.com/post-19.aspx, accessed 09/03/2010 (in Farsi).
[32] Art 2 of the Public Military Service Act 1984.
[33] http://pnu-8g.mihanblog.com/post/7, accessed 9 March 2010 (in Farsi). See also: http://www.alaviandassociates.com/documents/civilcode.pdf, accessed 09 March 2010.

note 2. Article 1210 of the Civil Code, provides that 'No one can be considered incapacitate on the pretext of immaturity or insanity after the age of puberty, except if his immaturity or insanity is proved.' This acknowledges reciprocity between puberty and maturity, whereas article 1210, note 2 provides that attaining puberty does not always correspond to maturity, except cases when puberty has been proved.[34] Hence the comparison of these two parts unveils that, according to article 1210 the mere appearance of the signs of physical puberty can be considered as evidence of maturity while according to article 1210, note 2, appearance of these signs are not sufficient evidence for maturity. Maturity or mental aptitude is not proven until the following two are present i) corporal development and ii) mental and psychological development. If both apply, then the individual concerned is no longer considered a minor. It seems that there are essential differences between the concept of puberty, which is physically evident, and the concept of maturity, which is dependent upon other conditions like wisdom, the power of understanding, and the development of mental and rational capabilities.

D. Discrimination

There is no gender discrimination in access to justice. Rather, gender discrimination relates to the age of criminal liability. For example, a 9-year-old girl who commits an offence is treated like an 18-year-old adult while boys, who are not considered minors but rather young adults, only become criminally liable at 15. It is worth mentioning that there is no difference between young adults and adults when it comes to determining the types and terms of sanctions applicable. Another area where gender plays an important role is that of 'blood money', also known as *diyah*.

1. Diyah

Sexual discrimination begins with conception. Indeed, article 487 of the IPC provides that *diyah* for an aborted foetus is payable in full for a boy, in half for a girl and in three quarters if the sex is undetermined.[35] According to Sharia law, *diyah*, or blood money, is an acceptable form of retribution paid by the offender's family to the victim's family. However, article 300 of the IPC provides that the amount of *diyah* payable for female victims shall be half of what is payable when the same offence is carried out against a

---

[34] https://www.aftab.ir/articles/social/law/c4c1210848179_children_rights_p1.php.
[35] Art 487 IPC available in English at: http://learningpartnership.org/en/resources/legislation/nationallaw/iran, accessed 11 March 2010.

man.[36] This highlights the fundamentally discriminatory laws that exist in Iran in relation to women and the decisions taken by the court in light of this law. Spatz highlights that the half-*diyah* rule and the resulting discrimination against women is outside of the ambit of Islamic principles and is rooted simply in cultural beliefs.[37]

According to the IPC, *diyah* is applicable to all forms of killing including voluntary murder and manslaughter.[38] It applies to cases where the offender acted in self-defence and this resulted in the victim's death. It also applies to cases where the requirements of retaliation, referred to as *qisas*, are not met. The IPC determines the extent, amount, and conditions of *qisas* and the payments of *diyah* in relation to the harming of various parts of the human body. However, it does not distinguish between penal and tortious *diyah*, so that it draws no distinction between intentional and unintentional wrongs. Due to the inherently civil law nature of *diyah*, academics remain divided on whether *diyah* should be classified as a 'punishment' or a tortious remedy. The IPC lays down the law and firmly identifies *diyah* as a punishment, not accounting or highlighting any tortious aspect.

2. Diyah: *discrimination and the affordability of justice*

The Leila Fathi case highlights the discriminatory nature of *diyah* laws in Iran and the ways in which these laws have made justice unaffordable for many. The victim in this case was an 11-year-old girl who was raped and murdered. One of the three suspects confessed and subsequently committed suicide while in prison. The remaining two were tried in court and after a series of appeals, were found guilty by the Supreme Court. The injustice of this decision came when the court ordered the heirs of the victim to pay *diyah* to the offenders so that the *qisas* punishment (death sentence in this case) may be carried out. The legal basis for this is article 209 of the IPC[39] which provides that, 'if a Muslim man commits first-degree murder against a Muslim woman, the penalty of retribution shall apply. The victim's next of kin, however, shall pay to the culprit half of his blood money before the act of retribution is carried out'. Thus, compensation is payable by the victim's family in order to execute the murderers. This shows the utter injustice caused by differential *diyah* amounts in relation to men and women. The *diyah* payable by Leila's family to her two offenders amounted to approximately US$18,000. In order to raise the necessary funds, the

---

[36] For an overview of Iranian *diyah* laws relating to women, see http://www.learningpartnership.org/resources/legislation/nationallaw/iran, accessed 9 March 2010.

[37] M Spatz; 'A Lesser Crime: A Comparative Study of Legal Defences for Men Who Kill Their Wives' (1991) 24 Columbia Journal of Law and Social Problems, 638.

[38] Arts 15, 300, & 301 IPC.

[39] ibid 35.

victim's parents had to sell their property and possessions. Still short, the father and brother of the victim attempted to sell their kidneys in desperation. The doctor refused and approached the courts to highlight the helplessness of the family.[40] The case received wide media coverage, placing Iran's human rights incompatibilities under the limelight. As a result of the growing international pressure and following a request from the victim's family, the judiciary ultimately decided that the State would pay one third of the sum required. However, on appeal, this offer of financial assistance was revoked and Leila's family appealed yet again. After 12 years and four trials, the State agreed to pay part of the *diyah*. Even though this eased the family's financial burden, it is considered as a one-off decision. It has been widely criticized and causes a great deal of concern, especially since there has been no amendment to the law.

This case has shed light on the discriminatory effect of *diyah* laws. Religious scholars are now beginning to emphasize the fact that Iranian *diyah* laws are against Sharia principles and Islamic law, in that the value of *diyah* is discriminatory between men and women. Lawyers and scholars have also attempted to draw attention to this injustice in recent times.[41] However, the Guardian Council has recently vetoed the parliamentary approval of the UN Convention on the Elimination of All Forms of Discrimination against Women (CEDAW). Thus, there still remains hesitation to allow equal rights for men and women namely because the authorities consider this to be contradictory to Sharia principles. Indeed, according to Iranian clerics, the Islamic inspiration for this discriminatory treatment lies in the conventional reading of the Shi'ite jurisprudence. The latter provides that a women's testimony in court is given half the weight of a man's and women inherit half of what men inherit. By analogy therefore, compensation paid to the family of a female murder victim ought to be half of what a man's family would receive.

The case of Afsaneh Nowrouzi is also relevant. Nowrouzi was sentenced to death for killing a police officer who tried to rape her. The court rejected her self-defence plea and sentenced her to death in 2001. The flagrant injustice of this decision provoked many women activist groups and gathered wide attention from international media and human rights organizations. As a consequence, judiciary chief Ayatollah Mahmoud Hashemi Shahroudi ordered a stay of the verdict. After seven years of imprisonment and following an agreement by the victim's heirs to receive US$62,500 as *diyah*,

---

[40] N Fathi, 'Shirin Ebadi And Iran's Women: In the Vanguard Of Change' (30 October 2003) available at http://www.opendemocracy.net/people-irandemocracy/article_1557.jsp, accessed 9 March 2010. S Kamali Dehghan, 'The Gag Is Tightened' *The Observer* (6 January 2008) available at http://www.codir.net/books/index.html, accessed 9 March 2010.

[41] One prominent lawyer raising awareness on this particular case is Nobel Prize winner Shirin Ebadi: http://www.womensenews.org/article.cfm/dyn/aid/1619/context/archive.

Nowrouzi's death sentence was put aside. This was deemed to be a victory for Nowrouzi, whose lawyer commented: 'the victim's family members did a good thing signing documents not calling for Nowrouzi's death, despite my client's refusal to request clemency'.[42]

The *diyah* sum in this case was a disproportionately high amount of money that Nowrouzi's family was expected to pay in order to have her death sentence overturned. It highlights the dual role of *diyah*. On the one hand, it serves a positive function by offering a route for offenders to escape the death penalty and it is often used by lawyers as a tool to ensure that death sentences are not issued. On the other hand, the amount of *diyah* is often so unreasonably large that it actually results in an impossible burden on the offender's family, thus making justice a commodity available to those who can afford it. This results in the exclusion of the less privileged, unable to 'buy justice'. A paradox emerges, namely in cases where child offenders are saved from execution as a result of *diyah*.

3. Risk factors

According to 2008 data, children under 18 represent more than 30 per cent of Iran's population.[43] This triggers poverty. *Diyah* can thus be very effective in solving financial problems of deprived families. Consider a family with six children, in which the father is unemployed or retired and the children are students in school or university. Now, imagine a 17-year-old male child in this family is killed in a street fight and the sentence for retribution is issued by the court. The family of the offender, whose single child is incidentally the same age as the victim,[44] tries to acquire the consent of the victim's family to avoid the death penalty. Here, even though the government specifies the official amount of *diyah* (in 2009, the blood money for a Muslim man was determined 40 million Tomans, equivalent to £25,000) Iranian law authorizes the two parties to settle on a different amount, higher or lower to rescue the offender from execution. The financial abilities of the offender's family is thus very important. If they are able to afford the *diyah* irrespective of the amount, then there is no problem. The problem arises when the offender's family is not well off. Financial problems may also be relevant when it comes to the victim's family. If a victim comes from a wealthy family, acquiring consent to pay *diyah* to avoid execution of the offender can be difficult, as money would not be beneficial to the family. In contrast, a less advantaged family is more akin to accept the

---

[42] 'Blood money saves Iranian woman who killed attacker' available at: http://www.freerepublic.com/focus/f-news/1319798/posts, accessed 9 March 2010.
[43] http://www.unicef.org/infobycountry/iran_statistics.html, accessed 11 March 2010.
[44] Reporter.

money. Furthermore, if the offender is a man and the victim is a girl, then the victim's family should pay half the blood money of a man to the offender's family for the execution of the murderer (as in the Leila Fathi case).[45] If the victim's family do not consent to waiving the sentence or they cannot raise the amount required, the offender is imprisoned for the crime in the interest of the public and is released from prison following a specified period of time. In other words, the court does not wait for the family of the victim to raise the sufficient funds. It is here that discrimination between boys and girls is evident.[46]

Another important factor is the sense of retaliation and animosity which is prevalent in Iranian culture. This might dissuade some families from accepting money as compensation for a relative's death. The type of crime carried out is also significant. If the victim's family believes that the murder was unfair and undignified, they may decide to request retribution. If it is established that the victim provoked the offender, the judges might not sentence the latter to retribution. Finally, marital and moral issues such as jealousy, referred to as 'ardour' or *gheyrat,* also play a role in insisting on the execution of the murderer. For instance, in Western and Southern parts of Iran, 'ardent and marital murders' still occur. This is a situation where a man kills his sister, his niece or his sister-in-law if she becomes pregnant out of wedlock or if he suspects that she is committing adultery. In some cases, after proving that the suspicion was true, the victim's family members surprisingly give their consent not to execute the murderer. The latter is however imprisoned in the interest of the public. In cases where it is shown that the killer acted under groundless suspicions, the victim's family can insist on retribution, even though the offender might be one of their relatives.[47]

E. The Death Penalty

There are two international documents regarding capital punishment for children under 18 years of age that have been approved by Iran. One of them is the International Covenant on Civil and Political Rights (hereinafter referred to as ICCPR), to which Iran acceded in 1975,[48] and the other is the UNCRC.

Upon signing and ratifying the ICCPR, Iran agreed to be bound by certain principles regarding the welfare of prisoners. Article 6(2) of the

[45] http://www.hawzah.net/Hawzah/Magazines/MagArt.aspx?id=41507, accessed 11 March 2010 (in Farsi).
[46] Reporter.
[47] Reporter.
[48] http://treaties.un.org/Pages/ViewDetails.aspx?src=TREATY&mtdsg_no=IV-4&chapter=4&lang=en, accessed 11 March 2010.

ICCPR dictates that 'in countries which have not abolished the death penalty, sentence of death may be imposed only for the most serious crimes in accordance with the law in force at the time of the commission of the crime'[49]. The Human Rights Committee suggested that this phrase, although ambiguous in its interpretation, should be read so as to mean 'quite an exceptional measure'.[50] In 1984, the Office of the United Nations High Commissioner on Human Rights adopted a document entitled Safeguards Guaranteeing the Protection of the Rights of Those Facing the Death Penalty. According to section 2, 'capital punishment may be imposed only for the most serious crimes, it being understood that their scope should not go beyond intentional crimes which are lethal or other extremely grave consequences'.[51] In defining intention, the United Nations Special Rapporteur on Extrajudicial, Summary and Arbitrary Executions considers that 'the term intentional should be equated to premeditation and should be understood as deliberate intention to kill'.[52] From these comments, one can conclude that the death penalty should be applicable to children only in the most extreme circumstances, which is not the case in Iran.

Two articles of the UNCRC are worth highlighting here. Article 1[53] which states that, 'for the purposes of the present Convention, a child means every human being below the age of 18 years *unless under the law applicable to the child, majority is attained earlier*' (emphasis added) and article 37(a) which provides that[54] 'no child shall be subjected to torture or other cruel, inhuman or degrading treatment or punishment. Neither capital punishment nor life imprisonment without possibility of release shall be imposed for offences committed by persons below 18 years of age'.

The noteworthy point is that this last paragraph has not been rejected by the Guardian Council. In theory therefore, cases where a child is sentenced to the death penalty are contrary to Sharia law. Unfortunately, some jurists and most of the judges deem this article to be inconsistent with the IPC. Thus, juveniles are being subjected to the death penalty and to heavy penalties such as flogging and long-term imprisonment. This clearly violates the

[49] http://www2.ohchr.org/english/law/ccpr.htm, accessed 11 March 2010.
[50] CCPR General Comment No 6: The Right To Life, Sixteenth Session, 1982, para 7, available at: http://www.unhchr.ch/tbs/doc.nsf/0/84ab9690ccd81fc7c12563ed0046fae3, accessed 11 March 2010.
[51] http://www2.ohchr.org/english/law/protection.htm, accessed 11 March 2010.
[52] N Afshini-Jan and T Danesh, *From Cradle to Coffin: A Report on Child Execution In Iran* (Foreign Policy Centre, London, 2009). See also: Report of the Special Rapporteur on Extra-Judicial, Summary Or Arbitrary Executions On His Mission tot USA, UN Doc E/CN.4/1998/68/Add.3, (22 January 1998) para 21, available at http://daccess-dds-ny.un.org/doc/UNDOC/GEN/G98/102/37/PDF/G9810237.pdf?OpenElement, accessed 11 March 2010.
[53] Available at: http://www2.ohchr.org/english/law/crc.htm, accessed 11 March 2010.
[54] http://www.hawzah.net/Per/Magazine/fs/016/Copy%20of%20FS01612.ASP, accessed 11 March 2010 (in Farsi).

UNCRC's position which 'consider[s] the prohibition against executing children to be part of international customary law, and thus not open to reservation'.[55] Finally, it can be argued that the Convention, by providing that majority can be attained before 18, has opened what seems to be an escape route allowing some heavy sanctions, including the death penalty, to be imposed to minors.

1. Case law

Even though Iran has ratified both the ICCPR and the UNCRC, in practice, it executes more individuals per capita compared to any other nation in the world. In the last five years, there have been 33 child executions in Iran and as of June 2009, there were at least 160 youth offenders on death row.[56]

In November 2003, Delara Darabi's boyfriend was suspected to have killed a female relative of Delara. At the time of the offence Delara was 17 and her boyfriend 19. The boyfriend, who convinced Delara that because of her age she would not be tried as an adult and would therefore be spared execution, persuaded her to confess to the crime. She later retracted the confession, unsuccessfully. As a result she was charged and sentenced to the death penalty. Her case was publicized in domestic as well as international press. During her period of incarceration, she was subjected to physical abuse and inhumane practices. As a result, she attempted to commit suicide. On 19 April 2009, after numerous appeals had been heard and dismissed, a two month stay on her execution was issued in order to allow negotiations between both families. However, nothing came of these negotiations. In theory, the offender's family is entitled to a 48-hour notice period before the execution. In spite of this and the fact that a decree had been issued to prevent her execution, Delara was hung on 1 May 2009 and her parents were informed by telephone only a few seconds before. Her boyfriend was sentenced to 10 years imprisonment.[57]

The case of Sina Paymard provides another example. Paymard was 15 years old when he received a death sentence from the Tehran Penal Court in 2004, which was later confirmed by the Supreme Court. Sina Paymard was pardoned by the victim's family on the day of his hanging in exchange of *diyah*.[58] What is concerning is that the *diyah* sum was reported to be US$160,000. It was raised by his family and made possible through the help of private donors. This is clearly an extremely large sum, impossible for many middle-class families to raise, as illustrated by the Leila Fathi case. This often means that families are devastated by their inability to cope with

---

[55] See (n 53).   [56] ibid.   [57] ibid.
[58] Human Rights Watch, Letter on Juvenile Death Penalty in Iran, (21 September 2006) available at http://www.hrw.org/en/news/2006/09/21/human-rights-watch-letter-juvenile-death-penalty-iran, accessed 11 March 2010.

the extreme financial burden that is placed upon them. As in the case of other countries with codified *diyah* laws, questions of the affordability of justice begin to re-emerge.[59]

Similarly, in the case of Ali Alijan, the offender was convicted of murder when he was less than 18 years of age. His sentence was awarded by the Tehran Penal Court and confirmed by the Supreme Court. As with Sina Paymard, Alijan was also pardoned by the victim's family in exchange for *diyah*.[60] However, as is often the case, the *diyah* amount remains undisclosed. It is reported that the offender's family had to mortgage their home and borrow large sums of money at high interest rates in order to pay off the required sum.[61]

Nazanin Fatehi's case received immense publicity. Nazanin was sentenced to death for murder after she killed a man who attempted to rape her and her 15-year-old niece. Nazanin was 17 at the time and thus below the minimum age of criminal responsibility. Activists angered by the case managed to involve Amnesty International, Canadian Members of Parliament, the European Union and the UN to put pressure on Iranian officials to spare her life. Following considerable international press, pressure from various non-governmental organizations and the efforts of the defence lawyers, a stay of execution was ordered and a retrial was called for by the Head of the Judiciary.[62] The retrial established the case as one that concerned self-defence and Nazanin was required to pay *diyah*. However, she came from an extremely poor family and was unable to meet the *diyah* requirements. As a result of online-donation-petitions and other donations, the required amount was raised, she was released and the charges against her were dropped.

This case again sheds light on the inconsistent role that *diyah* has come to play in Iran. Although it helped the accused escape the death penalty, the amount requested was so large that the family would have been unable to bear the burden had it not been for the help of private donors.[63] Thus, the attempts made by the settlement unit of the Public Prosecutor's Office which is the department responsible for the execution of the sentence, by independent lawyers active in the field of juvenile justice and by some approved NGOs along with the publicity of some murder cases involving juvenile offenders have in some cases led to the actual consent of the victim's family to prevent the execution of the offender.

---

[59] Etemad E Mali Newspaper (22 October 2006) 14; http://www.stopchildexecutions.com/minors/14_30_6_1385.pdf, accessed 11 March 2010 (in Farsi).

[60] ibid 58.

[61] http://www.stopchildexecutions.com/Saved_Prisoners.aspx.

[62] See (n 53).

[63] http://www.stopchildexecutions.com/Saved_Prisoners.aspx.

IV. CONCLUSION

The current legal framework does not adequately protect the rights of children in Iran. One important reason for this is the belief that the religious laws in place should not be changed although in 2007, the Supreme Leader of Iran stated 'some issues in Islamic jurisprudence like the issues of women and children are not final; it is possible that a skilful jurist who is adept in the bases and methods of jurisprudence (*fiqahat*) might work out new points'.[64]

However, when three fully-qualified male Islamic scholars, known as *mujtahids*, were asked about their opinion regarding the increase of the age of criminal responsibility, they all rejected the proposition.[65] And when, in 2003, the Guardian Council rejected Iranian accession to CEDAW it referred to a speech by Imam Khomeini: '[...]the position of Islam in regard to those who believe in the equality of the rights of men and women in inheritance, divorce, etc, is clear'. The Guardian Council declared: 'This statute [the CEDAW] conflicts with some obvious principles in Islam, such as inheritance, retribution (*qisas*), blood money (*diyah*), attestation, age of maturity, intimacy (*mahramiyyat*), veil (*hijab*), polygamy, etc.'[66] It is unfortunate that Islamic jurists who believe in modern interpretations of Islamic laws are not in the decision-making layer of government.

Another important problem is the lack of implementation of the Constitution and of national and international instruments.[67] Even in those cases where there has been partial implementation, some issues still exist, especially with regard to human and financial resources. Furthermore, the lack of effective NGOs for the protection of children, the triviality of the rights of children in the mind of some politicians, the disregard of the best interests of children and the preference given to short-term over long-term comprehensive projects are factors that influence the inadequate protection in place.

The third, and perhaps most important, problem is the concept of *diyah*. Although Iran insists upon the Islamic legitimacy of *diyah* laws, there is no denying that the practical consequences of their codification has been detrimental, in that it has promoted a culture of violence and hatred towards certain classes of society. Arshadi notes this when she states that:

Islamic punishments have encouraged a culture of violence against women, especially within the family [...] The fact that men receive a

---

[64] http://www.sign4change.info/spip.php?article785, accessed 12 March 2010 (in Farsi).

[65] http://norooznews.ir/news/9938.php, accessed 12 March 2010 (in Farsi).

[66] http://www.women.gov.ir/pages/?cid=352, accessed 12 March 2010 (in Farsi).

[67] See arts 3 and 21 of the Constitution which lay down laudable principles that are completely absent in practice.

lighter punishment if they commit violence against women undoubtedly encourages such violence [...] Newspapers are full of accounts of wives, sisters, daughters, and children murdered and its inevitable corollary: the killing of the husband. The family has become an institution of violence. The psychological effects of these laws, reflecting as they do in the legal world the constant degradation women have to face in government offices, courts, streets etc, that is wherever they come face to face with officialdom, is profound though immeasurable.[68]

---

[68] Z Arshadi, 'Islamic Republic of Iran and Penal Codes: Restructuring Society on the Basis of Violence And Sexual Apartheid' available at http://www.iran-bulletin.org/political_islam/punishmnt.html, accessed 11 March 2010.

CHAPTER 6

Part II:
Focus on the Death Penalty for Persons under the Age of 18 in the Legal System of Iran: Approaches and Methods *

I. DEALING WITH CHILDREN CRIMES IN IRAN'S LEGAL SYSTEM AND THE DEATH PENALTY

Iran has come under criticism and condemnation on the world stage because of imposing death sentences on persons under the age of 18. The Special Rapporteur on extrajudicial, summary or arbitrary executions issued a statement on 28 March 2007 protesting at the execution of child offenders in Iran.

Even though Philip Alston's[1] information about the number of death sentences for persons under the age of 18 was not up-to-date, Iran's legal system was accused of having imposed the highest number of death sentences on persons under the age of 18.

At this time, Iran is a State party of the International Covenant on Civil and Political Rights (ICCPR) and by clause 6 of article 5, execution of persons under the age of 18 is banned. In addition, Iran has been a State party to the UN Convention on the Rights of Child (UNCRC) since 1994. According to the text of article 1 and meanings of article 37 of this Convention, the term 'child' means all persons under the age of 18, and the State parties are obligated not to impose or carry out the death penalty against persons who commit a crime while under the age of 18.

According to article 9 of Iran's Civil Code, international conventions and treaties (ratified by) the Iranian Government have the force of internal law, and accordingly the UNCRC and ICCPR carry the force of internal laws of Iran.

The history of the first penal code specific to children goes back to the 'Formation of the Child Offenders Court Act' of 27 Aban 1338 (19 November 1959). According to this law:

---

* Ardeshir Amir Arjmand Saber Niavarani
[1] UN Special Rapporteur on Extrajudicial, Summary or Arbitrary Killings.

For crimes which carry the penalty of death or life imprisonment, the child shall be detained in the provisional detention section of the Correction and Rehabilitation Centre. The details of the detention will be specified in the bylaw of the Justice Ministry.

It can be seen that prior to the 1979 revolution, too, the possibility of imposing death sentences against children existed in the law, even though in practice it was rare that such a sentence was imposed or carried out, and incidents of this were not found in the research.

After the 1979 revolution, this law was abandoned too and children were tried in general courts, until the note to article 220 of the Procedures of Penal Prosecution Act of 1378 (1999–2000) granted the competence for hearing child offences to the Special Courts of Children. Meanwhile, according to article 230 of the Prosecution Procedures of the General and Revolutionary Courts, the Children Court has the competence to hear all child offenses. Article 219 of the Prosecution Procedures of the General and Revolutionary Courts Act too has provisioned assignment of a branch or branches of the general courts for hearing child offences. It is interesting that the same law has assigned the competence for hearings for persons considered adults in jurisprudence, but that are still under the age of 18, to the child courts. Following the difficulties in the interpretation and implementation of the laws on prosecution procedures, the Supreme Court issued the Unifying Procedure Verdict 687 on 2/3/1385 (23 May 2006), in which it declared under the note to article 220 of the Procedures of Penal Prosecution Act of 22/1/1378 [11 April 1999], that all offences by persons under the age of 18 are dealt with in the child courts under the general rules.

Further, according to note 1 of the Reform Act, of 21/7/1381 of the Establishment of General and Revolutionary Courts Act, the hearing of crimes punishable by *qisas* (retribution) of limb or *qisas* of life, death, stoning, crucifixion or life imprisonment, as well as press and political offences, are dealt with in the appeal court of the province—named as the penal court of the province. According to this note, preliminary hearings mentioned in this law, considering their importance in terms of the severity of punishment and the necessity of taking extra care with regards to social effects, are excluded from the general and overall competence of child courts (with a single judge) and their competence are assigned exclusively to the penal court of the province (which is often set up with five judges).

II. THE AGES OF MATURITY, ADULTHOOD AND PENAL RESPONSIBILITY

The Islamic Penal Code regards children who have not reached the Sharia adulthood age as lacking penal responsibility. According to the notes to articles 295 and 306 of the law, intentional crimes of children are regarded as an absolute mistake and the *aqilah* (guardian) is responsible for paying their *diyah* (blood money).

Article 49 of the Islamic Penal Code, the experimental implementation of which was approved by the Islamic Assembly in 1370 (1991–1992), also stipulates that children lack penal responsibility when committing a crime, and their rehabilitation, by the court's decision, shall be assigned to their guardian or, if appropriate, to the Correction and Rehabilitation Centre. This is despite in the fact that in determining the notion of 'child', note 1 to the latter-mentioned article has not specified a certain age, and regarded the Sharia age of adulthood as the boundary between childhood and adulthood.

The Sharia adulthood age in the Islamic jurisprudence is the threshold of persons becoming duty-bound or able to observe the Sharia 'dos and don'ts,' and in the well-known view of the *faqihs* (Shia scholars), it is also the basis of penal responsibility. The threshold of adulthood age is also a point of contention between the *faqihs*.

Although the majority of *faqihs* regard the full nine lunar years for girls and full 15 lunar years for boys as the age of their Sharia adulthood, some *faqihs*,[2] using the rule of inference, have declared full 13 lunar years or the same full 15 lunar years as the age of adulthood for girls.[3] And all these, against the background of firstly in the Quranic verses and early *hadiths* (traditions of the Prophet and 12 Imams) determination of this age is based on the signs of physical maturity in human beings. On this theme, it is acknowledged that the signs of physical maturity vary from region to region and evidence is found in the Islamic jurisprudence that refers the determination of the age of criminal responsibility to geographical and climatic circumstances.[4]

III. IRAN'S LEGAL SYSTEM AND PROTECTION OF CHILDREN

On 16 December 2002, the Islamic Assembly approved the nine articles of the Protection of Children and Juveniles Act, which was ratified by the Guardian Council on 1 January 2003.

It is noteworthy that according to article 1 of this Act, 'All persons who have not reached the full 18 solar years of age shall benefit from the legal

---

[2] Including Ayatollah Sanei.

[3] Ayatollah Makarem Shirazi.

[4] Emad-od-din Baghi, in the book *The Right to Life (2): the Question of Execution of under 18s in Iran: the Roots, and Cultural and Jurisprudential Remedies* outlines 18 jurisprudential arguments.

protections contained in this law.' This is the first time that the Islamic legislator has officially recognized the right of persons under the age of 18 to benefit from children's rights, and based on the *a fortiori* rule and notion of consent, the text of this article confirms that the person's age of criminal responsibility is 18. However, the provisions of this law apply only to cases of abuse, physical and mental harm, trafficking or exploitation and/or use of children in crimes and offences, torture, injury or mental abuse, and depriving them of education.

The terms used in this law, on the one hand, confirm the awareness of the legislator of the necessity of multiple protections of children in society, changing the penal policy of the legal system in regards to the necessity of protection of persons under the age of 18; and on the other, is a confirmation of the threshold for 'childhood' set out in article 1 of the Act. But since in practice, the interpretation of laws and regulations in Iran's legal system are not carried out methodically, many judges are reluctant to accept that this law has changed the age of maturity, and that age 18 should be the basis of both legal protection and criminal responsibility. Because of this, even after the passage of this law, there have been incidents of death and *qisas* sentences being handed to persons under the age of 18, even though in practice, carrying out the death sentence is delayed until the person reaches the age of 18.

In any case, in the next step we are witnessing that in 2003–2004, Mr Shahroodi, then Head of the Judiciary, issued a directive asking all judges to stop imposing death sentences on under-18s. It was then argued that directives have no force of law, nevertheless, to some extent, imposing death sentences and carrying them out were reduced in that period. Mr Sharoodi issued another directive in 2008–2009 aimed at stopping death sentences for children, which was also not fully and unanimously applied by the judiciary.

Finally, in early February 2005, the Hearing of Offences by Children and Juveniles Bill was handed to the government by the judiciary, and submitted to the Seventh Assembly. In spite of its very high importance, debating the bill was stalled in the Assembly until August 2006, when its generality was approved. The approval of the generality of the bill attracted widespread positive responses. However, the bill was referred to the relevant Commission, and after extensive consultation with the Guardian Council, it is at present still at the discussion stage. Because of the existing duality in the penal policy, and the supremacy of religious *fatwas* over the absolute social necessities in Iran's legislative system, this bill too is fraught with duality and contradictions.

In its early draft, according to article 2 of the bill, children had no criminal responsibility, and in clause 3 of article 33, imposing *qisas* sentences against persons under the age of 18 committing murder had been banned, but in the present draft, no mention is made of abolishing the death sentence for children.

In any case, according to article 1 of this bill 'all persons who have not reached the full solar age of 18 are entitled to the protections contained in this law'. But the bill has no specific provision on banning death and *qisas* sentences for persons under the age of 18, so it seems unlikely that any change will happen in practice, and the death penalty and *qisas* sentences will most likely continue to be imposed on persons under the age of 18.

It is noteworthy that there are also other laws in Iran's legal system which specify that the age of civil and social responsibility is 18. For instance, the following laws can be highlighted:

1. According to Note 3 of article 10 of the Issuing Passports Act (amended 1999) and article 18 of the same Act, only persons who have reached the full age of 18 can independently apply for a passport;
2. According to article 57 of the National Documents and Properties Registration Act, only persons who have reached the full age of 18 can carry out a transaction in their own names;
3. According to article 1043 of the Civil Code, marriage of a virgin girl even after reaching the adulthood age is conditional upon consent by her father or paternal grandfather,
4. According to article 2 of the National Service Act of 1363 (1984–1985), conscription of male persons is conditional on them reaching the full 18 years of age and entering the age of 19;
5. Clause 2 of article 27 of the Election Act has declared the age of adulthood for taking part in elections as being 15 for both girls and boys;
6. The Driving and Traffic Act too has set the minimum age for acquiring driving license to be full 18 years;
7. The National Banking Affairs Act has declared the opening of account and independently withdrawing money from any account conditional upon the person having reached the full 18 years.

In the Penal Code of 1304 (1925–1926) the age of penal responsibility had been set at 18, and this process continued in the later Act except for homicide happening between the ages of 15 and 18 in which case the convict was subject to severe punishment.

The question is, how is it that the legislator has conditioned entitlement to normal citizenship rights, such as the right to conduct transactions or acquire a driving license, or carry out important social duties such as the national service, to reaching the full 18 years (of age) and mental and physical adulthood, while at the time according to the current law and the interpretations given, a nine-year-old girl or 15-year boy who causes the loss of life of somebody or for any reason commits major crimes, could be subjected to *qisas* or death sentences?

IV. IRAN'S HUMAN RIGHTS OBLIGATIONS UNDER INTERNATIONAL TREATIES

As mentioned above, Iran is a State party to the International Covenant on Civil and Political Rights (ICCPR) and the UN Convention on the Rights of Child (UNCRC). In addition to clause 5 of article 6 of the ICCPR, which deals with the strict obligation of Member States to refrain from imposing and carrying out the death penalty on persons under the age of 18, the UNCRC specifically stipulates in article 37 that:

> States Parties shall ensure that:
> A—No child shall be subjected to torture or other cruel, inhuman or degrading treatment or punishment. Neither capital punishment nor life imprisonment without possibility of release shall be imposed for offences committed by persons below eighteen years of age.

On this basis, the State parties to the Convention are not only obliged not to impose death sentences, but to remove life imprisonment without possibility of release from their list of punishments for children. The only issue that merits being raised in this context is that Iran's reservations have prevented implementation of these rules.

Based on the established norm in international law, recognized in article 19 of the 1969 Vienna Convention on the Law of Treaties, governments have the right to make reservations to human rights treaties, and in this way, they escape from some of the provisions of a treaty. The UNCRC, even though in clause 1 of article 51 has sanctioned making reservations to this human rights treaty, in clause 2 it has ruled out reservations that are incompatible with the aim and subject of the Convention.

Some States, including the Islamic Republic of Iran, have made general reservations when they join human rights conventions, the extent of which has always been the subject of questions raised by the Committee on the Rights of the Child (CRC). The CRC, after going through the Periodic Reviews of Iran and some other countries that have made such reservations, has always asked them to clarify their effects in an exact and transparent manner, together with details of the provisions to which the reservations apply.

Such reservations not only are incompatible with the aim and subject of the Convention, but have also provided a channel for discrediting any reliance on these reservations and, as the CRC, protection agencies and experts believe, these reservations per se have no effect on the international obligations of the government towards treaty undertakings and would not make void the government's obligations. The UN Human Rights Committee's case-law confirms that these reservations should not be interpreted in ways that are incompatible with the aim and subject of the

Convention, and considering the clear and undisputed text of article 37 of the UNCRC, it should be said that whatever the effects of the general reservations of Iran on the UNCRC, it can in no way remove its obligations contained in article 37. The ban on executing persons under the age of 18 is one of the lynchpins of the UNCRC, and a reservation on this should have no credibility.

V. STATISTICS OF DEATH SENTENCES FOR UNDER-18S

Over the last 30 years, it seems Iran has frequently executed child offenders. Based on the data gathered from the press, which do not necessarily reflect the true numbers, during the years of 1998 to 2009, the courts in the Islamic Republic of Iran have passed at least 180 death sentences on children, and at present 114 persons are on death row.

VI. JURISPRUDENTIAL ARGUMENTS AGAINST CAPITAL PUNISHMENT

A. General Arguments against Capital Punishment in Islamic Jurisprudence[5]

According to what some *faqihs* such as Allameh Helli, Mohaqqeq Helli, Ayatollah Khansari and others believe, carrying out *hudood* (fixed punishments specified in Sharia for certain actions) and *qisas,* is restricted to the time of the rule of the Infallible Imam[6] and he has the sole authority to so impose these. Even though *hudood* and *qisas* are ordained by God, in the eyes of the Shia, in the absence of the Infallible Imam, their implementation is prohibited. As a result, resolutions of such enmities are left to human beings, subject to the requirements of the time and common sense.

According to the views of Ayatollah Khomeini, the Sharia government can put a moratorium on religious dictates and primary edicts on the

---

[5] Points summarized here from points in E Baghi, *The Right to Life*—an investigation into the possibility of abolishing the death penalty in the Islamic Sharia and Iranian laws, and a report on execution in Iran, from the website of *anjoman-e pasdaran-e haqq-e hayat* (the Society of Guardians of the Right to Life). Baghi is an Iranian human rights activist, investigative journalist, and founder of the Committee for the Defense of Prisoners' Rights and the Society of Right to Life Guardians. He has written 20 books, six of which have been banned in Iran. Baghi was imprisoned in connection with his writings and Amnesty International has highlighted his work. In *The Right to Life* (banned in Iran) he argues for the abolition of the death penalty using Islamic texts and jurisprudence.

[6] Adherents of the Shia faith believe that the 12 Infallible Imams are the only true Caliphs (religious and political leaders of the Muslim Community)—who are all descended from the Prophet Mohammed. The first of these was Imam Ali Ibin Abe Taleb, the nephew of the Prophet Mohammed.

grounds of expediency. A priori, this can be applied to those edicts that, though mentioned in Quran, are not regarded as religious 'pillars'. Many examples may be advanced, such as banning *Hajj* (the pilgrimage to Mecca) on the order of Mr Khomeini in 1987–1988, or laws passed by the Assembly which were declared contrary to Sharia by the Guardian Council. Principally, the Expediency Council is the objective and external symbol of the possibility of putting moratoriums on Islamic edicts on the grounds of the expediency of the Islamic system. We have many instances of this, such as the repeated rulings by the Guardian Council on the incompatibility with Sharia of receiving rented property premiums, which were in compliance with the views of Mr Khomeini in the book he wrote as a guide for Muslims. It was finally ruled as acceptable by the Expediency Council on 15 January 1991, on the grounds that current realities of the society and interests of the day demanded it.

On the basis of *tazahom* (when two rules conflict) and the dependence of Sharia edicts on costs and benefits, if in the present time, carrying out capital punishment is somehow detrimental to the religion, it is obligatory to put an end to it.

In countries that have joined international treaties and signed the Universal Decoration of Human Rights and the twin Conventions (ICCPR and ICESCR), by the Quranic inferences of the necessity of fulfilling obligations, the international law on human rights (which are subject of the international obligations of Muslims or their representative government) take precedence over domestic laws, and they must change their internal laws to abolish capital punishment except for the most serious crimes. However, in the case of capital punishment for children, considering the text of the UNCRC, article 32 and sub-clause 5 of article of the ICCPR, any imposition and carrying out death sentences against persons under the age of 18 is contrary to the international obligations of Member States of the UNCRC.

VII. LIST OF LEGAL PROVSIONS IN IRANIAN LAW RELATED TO THE DEATH
PENALTY FOR PERSONS UNDER THE AGE OF 18

A. *Internal Law*

1. *The Islamic Penal Code*

Articles 166 and 176:—the punishment for drinking alcohol in normal situations and when the perpetrator is conscious, adult, willing and sane, is *hudood* (a fixed punishment specified in Sharia—meaning that the offense is always punished as set out in the Quran).

Article 167—'if a person, for reasons of preventing death or as a remedy for a serious illness, is compelled to drink wine to the extent necessary, they will not be sentenced to *hudood*.'

Article 174—The punishment for drinking intoxicants is 80 lashes for both men and women.

Article 179—A person who drinks intoxicants repeatedly, and is subjected to *hudood* on each occasion, will be killed in the fourth instance.

2. Qisas Book One—Life retribution (qisas)

a) Chapter One—Intentional murder

Article 204—Homicide is of three types: intentional, quasi-intentional and by mistake.

Article 205—Intentional homicide is subject to *qisas* as specified in this chapter, and *vali-e dams* have the right, with the sanction of the State Ruler, to take *qisas* against the killer according to the provisions laid out in the next chapters, and the State Ruler may pass this authority to the Head of Judiciary or someone else.

Article 206—Homicide in the following cases will be regarded as intentional:
    i) Cases where the killer, by an action, aims to kill a particular person or some non-particular person or persons amongst a group, whether or not the action is normally fatal but one that causes death in practice.
    ii) Cases where the killer intentionally does something that is usually fatal, even without intending to kill someone.
    iii) Cases where the killer has no intention of killing, and the action of the killer is not usually fatal, but is usually fatal when used against a person who is frail, sick, old or minor, and the killer is aware of that.

Article 207—Whenever a Muslim is killed, the killer is subject to *qisas*, and the killer accomplice will be sentenced to between three and 15 years imprisonment.

Article 208—Whoever commits intentional killing and has no plaintiff or the plaintiff waives their right to *qisas*, and the killer's action causes disorder or apprehension in the society or insolence of the perpetrator or others, shall be sentenced to between three to 10 years imprisonment. Note, in this case, complicity to murder shall result in one to five years imprisonment.

Article 209—If a Muslim man intentionally kills a Muslim woman, the penalty of *qisas* shall apply; however, the victim's family shall pay to the culprit half of his *diyah* [blood money] before the act of *qisas* is carried out.

Article 210—If a *zemmi kafer* (a follower of a recognized non-Islamic religion) commits intentional murder against another, *qisas* shall apply even if they profess to two different religions. And if the victim is a *zemmi* woman her family shall pay the offender half of a *zemmi diyah* before *qisas* is carried out.

b) Chapter Two—Killing under duress

Article 211—Duress, or being ordered to kill, are no justification for murder. Therefore, if someone is made or ordered to kill a person, the killer shall be subjected to *qisas*, and the person who ordered the killing or made the killer to do so shall be sentenced to life imprisonment. Note 1—If the person acting under duress is a non-discriminatory child or mentally retarded, then the guardian shall be subject to *qisas*.

c) Chapter Three—Conditions of *qisas*

Article 219—A person sentenced to *qisas* should be killed with the consent of *vali-e dam*. Therefore, if they were killed without the *vali-e dam's* consent, it would amount to murder, which implies *qisas*.

Article 220—A father or paternal grandfather who kills their offspring will not be subject to *qisas*, but shall be sentenced to *tazeer* (sentences not specified by Sharia) and to pay *diyah* to the victim's inheritors.

Article 221—If a mentally handicapped person or a non-adult intentionally kills someone, the killing shall be regarded as being by mistake and the killer shall not be the subject of *qisas*, but their *aqilah* (adult guardian) shall pay *diyah* to the victim's inheritors. Note—In crimes of homicide or dismembering, if the crime is intentional and the culprit is a minor or mentally handicapped, and the victim dies as a result after the culprit's adulthood or becoming of sound mind, they shall not be subject to *qisas*.

Article 222—If a person of sound mind kills a mentally retarded person, they shall not be subject to *qisas* but shall pay *diyah* to the victim's family, and if their action causes disorder or apprehension in the society, or insolence of the perpetrator or others, they shall be subject to *ta'eziri* sentence of between three to 10 years imprisonment.

Article 223—If an adult kills a non-adult, they shall be subject to *qisas*.

Article 224—Killing while under the influence of alcohol shall be subject to *qisas*, unless it can be proven that, the offender had been so intoxicated that they had totally lost their control, and had not drunk with the aim of carrying out the killing. If their action causes disorder in the society they shall be subject to *ta'eziri* sentence of between three to 10 years imprisonment.

Article 225—If a person kills someone while in sleep or unconscious, they will not be subject to *qisas*, and shall only be sentenced to pay *diyah* to the victim's family.

Article 226—Homicide is only subject to *qisas* if the victim is not liable to be killed according to the Sharia, in which case the killer must prove the victim's deservedness through the court procedures.

Article 257—Intentional killing is subject to *qisas*, but with the consent of *vali-e dam* (the victim's family) and the killer, it can be replaced by an amount equal to complete *diyah* or higher or lower than that.

Article 258—If a man murders a woman, the woman's *vali-e dam* may ask for *qisas* if they pay the murderer half of his *diyah*, or in case of consent, the murderer may agree to a settlement equal to complete *diyah* or higher or lower amount.

Article 259—If the person who has committed a killing of the type requiring *qisas* dies, both *qisas* and *diyah* is quashed.

Article 261—*Vali-e dams* who have the power of asking for *qisas* or *diyah* are the same as inheritors of the victim, except for husband or wife who shall have no say in either *qisas*, pardon or carrying out the punishment.

Article 262—*Qisas* shall not be carried out against a pregnant woman before giving birth, and after the birth, if *qisas* would endanger the newborn's survival it shall be delayed until such time that the child's life is no longer in danger.

Article 263—Carrying out *qisas* by using a blunt and non-sharp instrument, that would cause suffering to the culprit, is banned.

Article 264—When there are a number of *vali-e dams*, the consent of all of them shall be necessary for *qisas*, and if all ask for *qisas*, it shall be carried out, and if some ask for *qisas* and some for *diyah,* the first group can carry the *qisas* provided that they pay the share of *diyah* for the other *vali-e dams*, and if some opted to pardon the killer, those seeking *qisas* can do so after they pay to the killer the share of *diyah* of the those who forgave.

Article 265—After the sentence of *qisas* is imposed, with the sanction of the State Ruler, *vali-e dam* has the right to carry out the *qisas* personally or assign it to a representative.

Article 266—If the victim has no *vali-e dam*, or they are not known, or are not accessible, the Muslim State Ruler becomes *vali-e dam*, and the Head of Judiciary, with the consent of the State Ruler and by giving authority to the relevant prosecutors, shall act to prosecute the culprit and ask for *qisas* or *diyah* as the case may require.

Article 267—If a person or persons help a person sentenced to *qisas* to escape, they shall be duty bound to deliver the convict, and if the hearing judge decides that they are failing in their duty and that their imprisonment would help return the offender, they shall be sentenced to imprisonment until the convict is returned. If the killer dies before being delivered, or otherwise cannot be delivered, the person helping their escape shall be liable to pay *diyah* to the victim.

Article 268—If, before dying, the victim absolves the culprit from life *qisas*, the right to *qisas* shall be dropped, and *vali-e dams* cannot demand *qisas* after the victim's death.

Article 300—The *diyah* for killing a Muslim woman, whether intentional or otherwise, is half of that of a Muslim man.

Article 489—If a woman aborts her foetus at any stage of pregnancy she shall pay its *diyah* and no share of the *diyah* shall go to her.

Article 492—The *diyah* for the aborted foetus in intentional and quasi-intentional cases shall be paid by the culprit, if it was a mistake, by their *aqeleh*, (guardian) no matter if the foetus has acquired spirit or not.

d) Other crimes punishable by the death penalty:

Article 513—Any person who disrespects Islamic sanctities or any of the great prophets or untainted Imams ... if this amounts to insulting the Prophet Muhammad, they shall be executed.

Article 578—Any official or personnel working in the judiciary or non-judiciary services using physical abuse and mistreatment against a suspect in order to force them into confession, in addition to *qisas* or paying *diyah*, as the case may be, shall be sentenced to between six months to three years imprisonment, and if someone has ordered this to be carried out, only they shall be punished by the said imprisonment, and if the suspect dies as a result of torture, the perpetrator will be punished as a murderer and the person issuing the order as ordering a murder.

Article 622—Any person who, by beating or abuse and mistreatment of a pregnant woman, intentionally and knowingly causes the abortion of her child shall be convicted and in addition to *qisas* or paying the *diyah* as the case may require shall be sentenced to between one to three years imprisonment.

Article 624—If a physician or midwife or chemist or persons who act as medics or midwives or surgeons or drug dispensers provide means of aborting a foetus or get involved in doing so, they shall be sentenced to between two to five years imprisonment, and judgement in respect of the *diyah* shall be as the rules apply.

Article 625—Homicide, beating and injuries accruing in the course of defending one's life, honour or property, or that of somebody else's—where the defender is in charge of protecting their property—while respecting legal requirements, shall not result in the perpetrator being punished, provided that the defence is proportional to the danger that threatened the perpetrator.

Article 629—Specifies cases where intentional killing is regarded as self defense and not liable for punishment.

Article 630— If a man sees his wife having sex with a strange man and is aware that the woman has consented, he can kill them on the spot, and if the woman has been forced, only the man can be killed. The judgement on beating and injuries in this case is similar to that of killing.

3. *The method of carrying out* hudood

Article 98—If a person is sentenced to a number of *hudoods*, they should be carried out in the order that none eliminates the grounds for the other. Therefore, if a person is sentenced to lashes and stoning, first the lashing should be carried out and then the stoning.

Article 102—The stoning shall be carried out with the person placed in a hole and covered with soil, the man up to his waist and the woman to near her breasts.

Article 103—If a person sentenced to stoning escapes from the hole they have been put in, if the adultery had been proved by witnesses, they shall be returned for the *hudood* to be carried out, but if it was based on their confession, they shall not be returned.

4. Hudood *for sodomy*

Article 110—The *hudood* for sodomy, in case of penetration, is death, and the way of carrying it out shall be at the discretion of the judge.

Article 111—Sodomy is punishable by death when both parties are adults, of sound mind and willing.

Article 112—If an adult man commits sodomy on a non-adult, he shall be killed and the non-adult shall be lashed 74 times if the sodomy was not forced on them.

5. *Lesbian acts*

Article 131—If the act of lesbianism has been repeated three times and punishment has been carried out each time, on the fourth occasion the death penalty shall apply.

6. Hudood *of moharebeh* ('waging war against God and/or the State') *and efsad fi al-Arz* ('the spread of Corruption on Earth').

Article 190—The *hudood* (fixed punishment) of *moharebeh* and *efsad fi al-Arz* is killing, hanging, cutting the right hand first and then the left foot, or banishment.

Article 191—It is at the discretion of the judge to select any of the above four punishments, whether the *mohareb* has killed or injured somebody or taken their property.

Article 192—The *hudood* for *moharebeh* and *efsad fi al-Arz* will not be dropped by waiver from the victim.

Article 195—Crucifixion of *mofsed* and *mohareb* shall be carried out as follows:

    i) The way of tying should not cause death.

    ii) Should not stay on the cross for more than three days, but if they die during this period, they may be brought down.

    iii) If they stay alive after three days, they shall not be killed.

Article 196—Cutting off the *mohareb's* right hand and left foot shall be carried out in the same manner as the *hudood* for theft.

7. Hudood *for theft*

Article 201—*Hudood* for theft is as follows:

In the first instance, four fingers of the right hand are cut in a way that thumb and palm are left intact. In the second instance, the thief's left foot is cut below the arch in a way that half of the feet and part of the area for *mas-h* (where the wet hand rubs the foot during the ablutions for prayer) are left intact. In the third instance, it shall be life imprisonment. In the fourth instance, it shall be execution even if the theft is committed in jail.

B. The Protection of Children and Juveniles Act

Article 1—All persons who have not reached the full 18 years of age shall benefit from protections mentioned in this law.

Article 2 —Any form of abuse and mistreatment of children and juveniles that result in physical, mental or moral harm to them and endanger their physical or mental health are prohibited.

Article 3—Any trafficking, exploitation and the use of children to commit unlawful acts such as smuggling are prohibited and, in addition to making good the damages, the offender shall be punished by six months imprisonment or/and cash fine of 10 million Rials (about £700) to 20 million Rials (about £1400).

Article 4—Any physical or mental harm, abuse, mistreatment and torture of children and intentional neglect of their health and physical or mental well-being, and preventing them from schooling, are prohibited, and the perpetrator shall be sentenced to between three months and one day to six months imprisonment or/and a cash fine of up to 10 million Rials (£700).

Article 5—Abuse of children is a public crime and does not require a private plaintiff.

Article 6—All individuals, institutions and centres that in some way have the responsibility of protection and guardianship of children are duty bound to report immediately any child abuse to the competent judicial authorities for legal action and appropriate decision. Failure of this duty shall result in up to six months imprisonment or cash fine of up to five million Rials (£350).

Article 7—Training measures in the framework of the Islamic Penal Code of 7/9/1370 (28 November 1391) and article 1179 of the Civil Code of 19/1/1314 (9 April 1935) are excluded from provisions of this law.

Article 8—If offences covered by this law are governed by other legal headings, or in other laws heavier *hudood* or punishment are prescribed for them, depending on the case, the heavier Sharia *hudood* or punishment shall apply.

Article 9—From the time this law is enacted all regulations at variance with it shall become ineffective.

This law containing nine articles was passed in the public session of the Islamic Assembly on Monday 25th of Azar-month of 1389 (16 December 2002) and confirmed by the Guardian Council (1 January 2003).

C. Articles Related to the Right to Life in Iran's Legal Principles and Regulations, by Subject

1. Iran's international commitments over the ban on imposing or carrying out the death penalty for criminal acts of persons under the age of 18

1) Article 3 of the Universal Declaration of Human Rights

2) Article 6 of the ICCPR:
i) Every human being has the inherent right to life. This right shall be protected by law. No one shall be arbitrarily deprived of his life.
ii) In countries which have not abolished the death penalty, sentence of death may be imposed only for the most serious crimes in accordance

with the law in force at the time of the commission of the crime and not contrary to the provisions of the present Covenant and to the Convention on the Prevention and Punishment of the Crime of Genocide. This penalty can only be carried out pursuant to a final judgement rendered by a competent court.

iii) When deprivation of life constitutes the crime of genocide, it is understood that nothing in this article shall authorize any State Party to the present Covenant to derogate in any way from any obligation assumed under the provisions of the Convention on the Prevention and Punishment of the Crime of Genocide.

iv) Anyone sentenced to death shall have the right to seek pardon or commutation of the sentence. Amnesty, pardon or commutation of the sentence of death may be granted in all cases.

v) Sentence of death shall not be imposed for crimes committed by persons below eighteen years of age and shall not be carried out on pregnant women.

vi) Nothing in this article shall be invoked to delay or to prevent the abolition of capital punishment by any State Party to the present Covenant.

3) UN Convention on the Rights of Child, Clause 1 of article 6 and article 37:

States Parties shall ensure that:

i) No child shall be subjected to torture or other cruel, inhuman or degrading treatment or punishment. Neither capital punishment nor life imprisonment without possibility of release shall be imposed for offences committed by persons below eighteen years of age;

ii) No child shall be deprived of his or her liberty unlawfully or arbitrarily. The arrest, detention or imprisonment of a child shall be in conformity with the law and shall be used only as a measure of last resort and for the shortest appropriate period of time;

iii) Every child deprived of liberty shall be treated with humanity and respect for the inherent dignity of the human person, and in a manner which takes into account the needs of persons of his or her age. In particular, every child deprived of liberty shall be separated from adults unless it is considered in the child's best interest not to do so and shall have the right to maintain contact with his or her family through correspondence and visits, save in exceptional circumstances;

iv) Every child deprived of his or her liberty shall have the right to prompt access to legal and other appropriate assistance, as well as the right to challenge the legality of the deprivation of his or her liberty before a court or other competent, independent and impartial authority, and to a prompt decision on any such action.

4) Safeguards guaranteeing protection of the rights of those facing the death penalty—Approved by Economic and Social Council resolution 1984/50 of 25 May 1984.

i) In States which have not abolished the death penalty, capital punishment may be imposed only for the most serious crimes, it being understood that their scope should not go beyond intentional crimes with lethal or other extremely grave consequences.

ii) Capital punishment may be imposed only for a crime for which the death penalty is prescribed by law at the time of its commission, it being understood that if, subsequent to the commission of the crime, provision is made by law for the imposition of a lighter penalty, the offender shall benefit thereby.

iii) Persons below 18 years of age at the time of the commission of the crime shall not be sentenced to death, nor shall the death sentence be carried out on pregnant women, or on new mothers, or on persons who have become insane.

CHAPTER 7

*Criminal Law and the Rights of the Child in a Multi-Confessional State: The Case of Lebanon**

I. INTRODUCTION

Lebanon is a parliamentary democracy, which implements a special system known as confessionalism. This system is intended to deter sectarian conflict and attempts to fairly represent the demographic distribution of the 18 recognized religious denominations in government.[1] The Constitution recognizes equal rights to the 18 denominations that may each adjudicate on personal status issues through their own courts and personal status laws. Although they form part of the national legal system of Lebanon, personal status (religious) laws are a particular set of norms very much linked to the pluralized political system of the country. The competence of religious tribunals is not uniform as its scope varies from one community to another[2] and depends on each community's customs and traditions. It is not an absolute competence because it remains subjected to the State's *ordre public* whereby civil courts can reverse any religious court decision that was taken beyond its competence or that contradicts the State's *ordre public*. Thus, a dual judicial system (one civil and one religious) exists in Lebanon, and is the source of various problems in practice.

Following close collaboration between the Ministry of Justice, the Ministry of Social Affairs and UNODC,[3] a separate piece of legislation concerning children in conflict with the law and those at risk was enacted in 2002.[4] This law was particularly necessary since the phenomenon of juvenile delinquency was previously poorly understood by the authorities, as shown by the measures of imprisonment, the length of preventive detention and the generally coercive regime in prisons. The main focus of the

---

[*] Georges J Assaf, Ph.D, August 2009.
[1] http://en.wikipedia.org/wiki/Lebanon#French_mandate_and_independence, accessed 3 March 2010.
[2] For example, since 1959, succession matters are within the scope of the civil law for non-Muslim (Christian and Jewish) communities.
[3] Projects on 'Strengthening legislative and institutional capacity for juvenile justice' and on 'Support to the juvenile justice system in Lebanon'.
[4] Law No 422 of 6 June 2002.

reform was thus on ensuring better conditions of detention and treatment of young offenders, attempting to prevent delinquency, ensuring educational assistance to young people in danger and protecting young victims.[5]

A. National Legal Framework

1. The Lebanese Constitution

The first constitution[6] of the modern State of Lebanon was adopted in 1926 and has continued to regulate political life since. It underwent two major amendments: one in 1943 upon Lebanon's formal accession to independence, and one in 1990 marking the end of the war. It is a liberal constitution modelled on France's Third Republic Constitution. It provides for a consensus between ethnic and religious communities (including Christian, Muslim and Jewish communities), described as 'historical communities' for their active role in creating the modern State of Lebanon.

As in the previous system which regulated political life under the Ottoman rule, the 1926 Constitution and the laws that supplemented it under the French mandate[7] shaped a power-sharing system between the various ethnic/religious communities. Thus, powers were to be shared in Parliament and in the major political and administrative executive positions in what resembled an early expression of 'affirmative action', while preserving the secular principles of democracy whereby every citizen is entitled to benefit from the same rights without reference to religion, colour or race.[8] It also defined the contours of the competencies left to these communities in applying their personal status laws. It gave individuals the option to be governed by the civil law if they preferred not to be subjected to their own (religious) personal status law. This law was opposed by the Sunni Muslim religious leadership and its implementation has been suspended since 1936.

The Constitution does not refer to any religion as a State religion nor does it refer to any religion as a source or the main source of law. It does however mention respect to the Almighty and to all religions. Legislative Decision No 60 LR of 13 March 1936 issued by the French mandatory

---

[5] http://www.unodc.org/pdf/crime/forum/forum3_note2.pdf, accessed 3 March 2010.

[6] The original text of the Constitution was in French.

[7] In 1920, the League of Nations gave France mandatory power over Lebanon and Syria with the objective of helping them acquire independence.

[8] The principle of affirmative action as regards legislative elections was challenged before the administrative court, which rejected the claim of discrimination that an Armenian candidate to legislative elections in the capital, Beirut, put before the court because his candidature was not accepted. Conseil d' Etat No. 239 of 10 February 1994, Journal of Administrative Jurisprudence, 1995, TI, 278. It was likewise unsuccessfully challenged by a civil servant. Conseil d'Etat No 130 of 29 November 1993, Journal of Administrative Jurisprudence (1995) TI, 116.

power recognized[9] the various religious communities as distinctive entities, which have the right to determine their own personal status rules and to establish their own tribunals with regard to personal status matters, ie exclusively family law matters (marriage, divorce, custody of children, filiation, adoption where applicable,[10] eventually succession).[11] This is now enshrined in article 9 of the Constitution.

2. The Lebanese judicial system and human rights

Dual jurisdiction in Lebanon (civil and religious court systems) reflects the dual layer on which the Constitution rests, ie one layer organizing the liberal parliamentary democracy and another layer guaranteeing the respect of communal particularities, well-rooted in the religious bedrock of the Lebanese historical communities.

Article 20 of the Constitution provides for an independent judiciary, guaranteeing to render justice neutrally. It lays down the principle of non-removability of judges and that of the independence of the judiciary. Judges are appointed by the Executive upon suggestion of the Higher Council of the Judiciary, the membership of which is reserved to high ranking judges appointed by the Executive and to judges elected by their peers.

The constitutional law of 21 September 1990 defines Lebanon as a 'free homeland' and a member of the United Nations Organization thus bound by its Charter, the Universal Declaration of Human Rights and other UN Conventions, with an express obligation to integrate international standards in all aspects of the legal field. Lebanese case-law reflects this idea through the courts' application of general principles of law which amount to international human rights standards.[12] In one of its early decisions, the Constitutional Council held that the Preamble of the Constitution, which incorporates the UN Charter and other international human rights conventions, has constitutional value. In one of its Plenary Assembly decisions, which are binding in principle, the Court of Cassation explicitly referred to the application by the judiciary of general principles of law and further, to the precedence of international standards as provided for by international human rights conventions[13] over national legislation.

---

[9] Since 1905, the State in France does not recognize any 'cult'.

[10] Adoption is not allowed by Sharia law.

[11] A civil law regulating succession was enacted in 1959 to be applicable only to non-Muslim communities, since the various Muslim communities expressed their opposition to it as contrary to Sharia law. Consequently, discrimination against women in the field of succession continues to exist for Muslim citizens, especially for Sunni women who only inherit half of what a man would be entitled to.

[12] For example, the principle of non-discrimination.

[13] Court of Cassation Plenary Assembly Decision No of 2000.

B. The Integration of International Human Rights Standards in the National Legal System

Uniform reception of international law takes the form of ratification of international treaties by the legislature, with either a complementary procedure of formal legislative integration or a direct self-executing effect. The latter form is enforced in Lebanon. Direct application of international human rights standards, which take precedence over national legislation, by national courts raises the issue of application of those standards by religious courts when ruling on various aspects of family law, such as marriage, divorce, custody of children, and, for Muslims only, succession matters. In this context, the contradiction between constitutional norms incorporating the UDHR and UN human rights conventions on the one hand and personal status (religious) laws as applied by religious tribunals on the other hand, is undoubtedly detrimental to the rights of individuals in general and those of the child in particular. An urgent reform of the system, which would unify personal status laws and narrow the competence of religious courts, is thus required in order to uphold the rights of the child, specially in the criminal law field. Another option would be for all the courts to apply international human rights conventions. In practice however, many obstacles would obstruct this course of action.

In contrast with other treaties, international human rights conventions govern the relationship between the State and its citizens and resident aliens. They create obligations towards the latter and towards the international community.[14] Consequently, provisions of international human rights conventions, which express customary international law, may not be subject to reservations by the ratifying or acceding State.

1. Ratification of treaties

Following the amendment of article 52 of the Constitution in 1990, the ratification or accession of the State to an international convention involves a complex system. The process is initiated by the President of the Republic who negotiates international treaties in coordination with the Prime Minister. However, in order to ratify a treaty, prior approval of the Council of Ministers and the consent of Parliament are necessary. Promulgation of the decree of ratification followed by publication in the *Journal Officiel*

---

[14] General comment No 24 on 'Issues relating to reservations made upon ratification or accession to the Covenant' adopted by the ICCPR Committee at its 52nd session in 1994, available at: http://www.unhchr.ch/tbs/doc.nsf/%28Symbol%29/69c55b086f72957ec12563 ed004ecf7a?Opendocument, accessed 1 March 2010. It highlights the difference between treaties that express mere exchange of obligations between States and international human rights conventions which benefit individuals under the jurisdiction of those States bound by such conventions.

(Official Gazette) render the convention self-executing and thus effectively applicable before national tribunals in conformity with article 2 of the Code of Civil Procedure. The jurisprudence of Lebanese courts, though very strict with regard to publication of laws and decrees in the *Journal Officiel* (Official Gazette), has a long-standing liberal position on this and has held that the publication of an international treaty, through whatever means of publication, is enough to incorporate it in the national body of legislation[15] and therefore to make it enforceable in the national legal system so long as the ratification law is published in the *Journal Officiel*.[16]

2. Hierarchy

When invoked before a tribunal, provisions of an international convention have precedence over domestic law whether or not the latter contradicts international norms.[17] However, this will not affect the validity of the national legislation which will continue to be in force until harmonization with international standards takes place through an amendment approved by Parliament.[18] This is the case whether the national law in question was enacted before or after the ratification of the international instrument. On the other hand, the Constitutional Council has held, albeit implicitly, that international standards also have precedence over constitutional provisions when the former overlap with general legal principles.[19]

3. Interpretation

When it comes to the interpretation of international conventions, legal doctrine[20] and case-law in Lebanon are inspired by French doctrine and jurisprudence expressed by the locution *ejus est interpretari, cujus est condere*. This places the power to interpret treaties and international conventions in the hands of the government with regards to public international law matters, especially when the case under consideration relates to international relations. Tribunals retain full competency to interpret international conventions when it comes to individual liberties and freedoms.

---

[15] Most of the ILO conventions ratified by Lebanon were only published in 1997 in a special issue of the *Journal Officiel*.

[16] Judicial Journal (An Nashra Al Qada'iyya) 1950 50:650; IDREL Index of Jurisprudence (Fahras Al Ijtihad) 2379, Beirut.

[17] Court of Cassation, No 59, 9 December 1973. AA 1974, 277; Beirut Court of Appeal, No 121, 26 April 1988. Judicial Journal (1988) 692.

[18] E Rabbath, *Treatise of Constitutional Law* vol II, 336 (Arabic: dar al 'ilm lil malayine 1972).

[19] Constitutional Council Decision No 2/95 of 25 February 1995 and 395 of 18 September 1995 published in *L' Orient-Le Jour* newspaper of 22 September 1995.

[20] M Augi, *Principles of Civil Law* (Bahsoun Publishers, Beirut, 1992) 148–150.

This jurisprudence has remained unchanged for more than 50 years. The Court of Cassation has held that when an individual interest is at stake, only national tribunals have the competence to interpret provisions of international conventions because the latter are considered part of national legislation.[21] The jurisprudence of the administrative court (*Conseil d'Etat*) in this field is identical[22] to that of the civil courts. The Labour Court (*Commission arbitrale du travail*) jurisprudence in applying International Labour Organisation (ILO) conventions, is also in conformity with the above-mentioned case-law, notably in cases relating to discrimination against women and children.[23]

The Juvenile Courts extensively refer to the UN Convention on the Rights of the Child (hereinafter referred to as the UNCRC), which was ratified by Lebanon without reservations,[24] when interpreting national legislation namely to ensure that it is UNCRC-compliant. This does not only occur when national legislation is in contradiction with the UNCRC but also, in certain instances, when Sharia law, as applied by religious courts in their decisions, violates provisions of the UNCRC, which goes against the principle of the best interest of the child.[25]

4. *The application of international human rights conventions in the context of the dual civil and religious judicial system*

The application of international human rights conventions in the Lebanese context is polarized between civil and religious courts, more so with respect to Muslim religious courts.[26]

Two basic ideas permeate the problems that the judiciary has to face when applying the UNCRC in family law matters. The first idea revolves around the principles of universality and indivisibility of human rights that civil courts integrate into their jurisprudence, even in cases where religious concepts are invoked by the parties. In this respect, the judiciary often applies international conventions relating to gender equality. This is contrary to Sharia law, which recognizes the pre-eminence of men in conducting family affairs, which may have adverse effects on the protection

---

[21] Civil Court of Cassation, Decision of 5 March 1974. Judicial Journal 74:166. Compendium Baz, No 18, 2377.

[22] Council of State Decision of 3 March 1971, 71:630, ibid IDREL Index of Jurisprudence, 2378.

[23] Beirut Labour Court (Conseil arbitral du travail), Decision No 46/95 of 19 December 1995, ASSAF *v National Social Security Fund*. Unpublished.

[24] See (n 28).

[25] Beirut Juvenile Court, Decision No 313/2008 of 14 July 2008.

[26] Each Lebanese citizen is subject to the personal status laws and courts of one of the 18 historical communities regulating matters pertaining to family law. In addition, Muslim *Sunni*, *Shi'a* and *Druze* courts regulate issues of inheritance.

of children.[27] However, the Court of Cassation has held that discrimination against women based on religious law goes against international standards binding on the State and unwritten general principles of law that express fundamental rights. In that same case, the denial by the National Social Security Fund of the right of a separated woman to family allowances for her children, by invoking religious law which exclusively considers the husband to be the head of the family, was rejected.[28] Likewise, the judiciary considers that the protection of children from their own parents is a matter distinct from custody, which remains within the competence of religious tribunals. In such situations, it has been held that a child should benefit from temporary protection measures in accordance with the principle of the best interests of the child, regardless of the decision to grant custody to one of his parents by the religious court.[29]

The second idea contradicts the axiomatic approach expressed by the first one and can be summarized as follows: international human rights concepts and values are detrimental to family values in as much as they favour individual rights at the expense of cultural specificities and contribute to the disintegration of the traditional family cell. Indeed, the ideology of human rights was initially totally alien to family law whereas today it is at the heart of it and has become, since the enactment of the Universal Declaration of Human Rights (UDHR), the main protecting shield of the family.[30] The UNCRC[31] and the Convention on Elimination of All Forms of discrimination Against Women (CEDAW)[32] gave those rights proclaimed by the UDHR a much larger scope and made their implementation possible at the national level through ratification by the legislature, despite the fact that

---

[27] The CEDAW Committee in its Concluding Comments on the Lebanese government's national report of 22 July 2005 expressed strong concerns '*about the pervasiveness of patriarchal attitudes and deep-rooted traditional and cultural stereotypes regarding the roles and responsibilities of women and men in the family, in the workplace and in society, thus constituting serious obstacles to women's enjoyment of their human rights and impeding the full implementation of the Convention*'. (emphasis added). Available at: http://www.un.org/womenwatch/daw/cedaw/cedaw33/conclude/lebanon/0545048E.pdf, para 29, accessed 1 March 2010.

[28] Court of Cassation, Plenary Assembly, Decision No of 2002.

[29] Beirut Court of First Instance (Chamber of Juvenile Justice), Decision dated 7 November 2007. Al ADL (2008) TI, 429.

[30] See arts 12, 16, 23(3), 25(2) and 26 UDHR available at: http://www.un.org/en/documents/udhr/index.shtml#a12, last visited 01/03/2010.

[31] Ratified by Lebanon on 14 May 1991, see: http://treaties.un.org/Pages/ViewDetails.aspx?src=TREATY&mtdsg_no=IV-11&chapter=4&lang=en, accessed 1 March 2010.

[32] Ratified by Lebanon on 16 April 1997 with important reservations on arts 9, 16 and 29 pertaining to family law. For details see: http://www.un.org/womenwatch/daw/cedaw/reservations-country.htm#N36, accessed 1 March 2010. In its concluding comments, the Committee on CEDAW considered these reservations contrary to the object and purpose of the Convention. See Concluding Comments of the Committee on CEDAW, Lebanon, 22 July 2005, para 77–126, available at http://www1.umn.edu/humanrts/cedaw/cedaw-lebanon 2005.html, accessed 1 March 2010.

there are many provisions, especially in the UNCRC, that lack sufficient clarity, making their application by the judiciary uncertain.

The problem of 'intrusion' of universal values and international standards into the sphere of family law, be it civil or religious law, poses a problem to the judiciary when it is faced by parties invoking international human rights conventions. Indeed, in a case involving family law issues, such as gender equality in the married couple, equality of children regardless of their birth status (illegitimate or born out of wedlock), freedom of conscience of the members of the family including children, protection of women from their husbands, protection of children from their parents, the courts have to make a choice as to which law to apply. The jurisprudence on this shows a cautious approach undertaken by the courts when addressing issues regarded as intimately linked to the cultural order, so as to avoid destabilizing the traditional Judeo-Christian and Muslim family concepts. In fact, the judiciary appears to be consistently conservative in this regard in the sense that it does not challenge the absolute prohibition of recognizing an equal status between children born in and out of wedlock.[33] At the same time however, it shows some flexibility with regards to the recognition of patrimonial rights of children born out of wedlock, based on international human rights standards and the UNCRC.[34]

The Court of Cassation has avoided discussing arguments drawn from the Committees on CEDAW and the UNCRC which challenge the discriminatory approach of religious laws to the rights of the child born out of wedlock. In a case brought by the legitimate children of a Lebanese citizen who had lived abroad and had a child out of wedlock, whom he officially recognized, the Court decided that the decision issued by the foreign court, granting the child the right to conduct an inventory of the elements of the succession, was applicable in Lebanon and that religious courts had no competence to rule on granting exequatur of the foreign judicial decision. It also held that civil law concerning inheritance rights of a child born outside marriage applies outside Lebanon but religious law which excludes children born outside marriage from benefiting from inheritance is valid only in Lebanon.[35]

C. Domestic Legislation on the Protection of the Rights of the Child in Criminal Law

Despite having ratified the UNCRC without any reservations, a special

---

[33] Beirut Court of Appeals, Decision dated 27 May 2005, Proche-Orient Etudes Juridiques, 2005, 22.

[34] Mount-Lebanon Court of First Instance, Decision dated 8 February 2007, Al Adl Law Journal 2007, T3, 1358.

[35] Court of Cassation, Decision No 79 of 31 May 2007, AL ADL 2007, T3, 286.

effort must be made by Lebanon to harmonize its criminal laws affecting children. This is an on-going concern that has been expressed by the Committee on the Rights of the Child (the CRC).

1. *The minimum age of criminal liability*

The minimum legal age of criminal liability is seven years of age and was kept as such by Law No 422 of 2002 (hereinafter referred to as Law 422/2002) on the Protection of Children in Conflict with the Law and Children at Risk.[36] However, in its article 4, the law nuanced the criminal liability of the child through the establishment of a special procedure reducing the sanctions in the Penal Code by listing three categories of juvenile offenders (according to age).

2. *Measures applicable against a juvenile offender*

Sanctions[37] applicable to juvenile offenders range from very light sanctions, such as blame, to deprivation of liberty measures.

Non liberty-depriving measures entail:

1. Blame
2. Probation
3. Protection measures
4. Freedom on parole
5. Community work

Liberty-depriving measures include:

1. Rehabilitation measures
2. Correctional measures
3. Reduced prison sentences

Three classes of juvenile offenders are described in article 6 of Law 422/2002. The first class of offenders includes children aged between seven and 12 to whom all the measures apply, short of correctional measures and reduced sanctions. The second category includes juvenile offenders between 12 and 15 years of age. They are subject to all the measures provided for in the above scale, except reduced prison sentences. Finally, child offenders between 15 and 18 years of age are subject to all the measures provided for in the scale. Thus, they can be sentenced to any kind of liberty depriving measures although these differ depending on the offence. If they commit

---

[36] Art 3.   [37] Art 5 Law 422/2002.

contraventions or misdemeanours, the sanction provided for in the Penal Code can be reduced by half. In a case of homicide where the sanction is capital punishment or life imprisonment with forced labour, the sentence will be reduced to a minimum of five or a maximum of 15 years imprisonment as capital punishment for children is proscribed by law. Blood money and financial compensation are irrelevant issues in this context. For all other crimes, the sanction may be reduced to half the minimum and maximum periods of time in prison or to reduced sanctions. It is up to the juvenile judge to decide whether the sentence will be purged by reclusion in a correctional centre or in a prison for juveniles.

3. Risk factors

The social, economic and cultural background of juvenile offenders is a major determinant of juvenile criminality. In this respect the family situation plays an important role. A sizeable number of juvenile offenders come from poor environments, dislocated families, blended families that leave children without care, families who do not send their children to school but rather send them to work at an early age, especially in rural areas, despite the presence of legal provisions making education compulsory until 14 years of age. Often, school drop-outs join street gangs in poor neighbourhoods that offer them relative protection, thus encouraging the development of criminal activities in the surrounding areas. These poor neighbourhoods, along with refugee camps and squatted urban areas, are not policed which means that juveniles are left at the mercy of organized crime.

In addition, the use of children by adult members of their extended family to commit crimes of honour is not uncommon. This is because honour crimes are punishable by the death penalty when committed by an adult, although the sanction may be reduced.[38] The CRC has repeatedly urged the Lebanese government to amend the Penal Code so as to eliminate the provisions allowing reduced sentences for adult perpetrators of such crimes but has not raised the issue of the use of children to perpetrate honour crimes.

Proliferation of small firearms is also a cause of juvenile criminality. Highway banditry is still a phenomenon that is alive and well in remote

---

[38] Extenuating circumstances are provided for in the Penal Code for so-called passion crimes including honour crimes (art 192). An amendment to the Penal Code by Legislative Decree No 112/83 (art 10) to narrow the concept of 'honour' that is acceptable for applying extenuating circumstances gave the judiciary added competence to strictly sanction such crimes. The power to assess if the criminal is motivated by the concept of honour is left to the court (Criminal Court of North Lebanon Decision No 11/98 of 8 January 1998). In some recent examples of the use of children to commit such murders, the instigators have been held fully responsible of the crime.

areas of the country, where arms and drug smuggling did not come to an end after the war. This issue has not been tackled at all by the CRC.

Since the death penalty is not applicable to children, blood money can, on occasion, be a way of solving the problem for the family of the offender in the sense that it will prevent 'vendetta', a phenomenon of the clan society that subsists in remote parts of Lebanon, mainly the North.

4. *Lebanon and the UNCRC*

Lebanon ratified the UNCRC and submitted three reports respectively in 1995, 2000 and 2005.[39] Three sets of Concluding Observations were made by the CRC respectively in 1996, 2002 and 2006.[40] Lebanon has signed but has not yet ratified the first Optional protocol to the UNCRC regarding the Involvement of Children in Armed conflict.[41] The Second Optional Protocol on the Sale of Children, Child Prostitution and Child Pornography was ratified in 2004.[42]

The first set of observations issued upon examination of Lebanon's initial report included an important recommendation urging a comprehensive reform of the juvenile justice system in light of the Convention, in particular its articles 37, 39 and 40, as well as other relevant UN instruments, such as the Beijing Rules, the Riyadh guidelines and the UN Rules for the Protection of Children deprived of their Liberty. Particular attention was to be given to the consideration of deprivation of liberty as a measure of last resort and for the shortest period of time, to the protection of children deprived of their liberty, to due process of law and to the full independence and impartiality of the judiciary.[43] This is because in practice, the process of prosecution is often marred by inexcusable delays; the great majority of juvenile offenders are arrested pending trial for periods that sometimes extend over several months and the trial period itself suffers from greater delays, sometimes as long as three years.

The second set of comments relating to the second periodic report insisted on raising the minimum age of criminal responsibility and other minimum age requirements while ensuring that they were gender neutral

---

[39] http://tb.ohchr.org/default.aspx?country=lb, accessed 3 March 2010.

[40] ibid 37.

[41] http://treaties.un.org/Pages/ViewDetails.aspx?src=TREATY&mtdsg_no=IV-11-b& chapter=4&lang=en, accessed 2 March 2010.

[42] http://treaties.un.org/Pages/ViewDetails.aspx?src=TREATY&mtdsg_no=IV-11-c& chapter=4&lang=en, accessed 2 March 2010.

[43] UN Committee on the Rights of the Child: Concluding Observations: Lebanon, 7 June 1996, CRC/C/15/Add.54, para 44, available at: http://www.unhcr.org/refworld/docid/3ae6af5b28.html, accessed 2 March 2010.

and enforced by law.[44] At the same time, the CRC expressed some concern regarding national legislation, and its failure to implement the principle of the best interests of the child, and domestic policies concerning institutionalization and imprisonment.[45] Furthermore, the CRC recommended that Lebanon (i) review its legislation, namely article 562 of the Penal Code, with a view to eliminating all provisions allowing sentences to be reduced when a crime is committed by an adult in the name of honour. (ii) amend it so that it complies with international standards and provides for prompt and thorough investigations and prosecutions to be carried out and (iii) undertake awareness raising activities to make sure that such practices are socially and morally unacceptable.[46] Finally, it noted the negative impact of past armed conflict on children and of past practices of recruitment of children by armed groups during the civil war.[47] Thus, it reiterated its previous recommendation to establish a juvenile justice system that would comply with the UNCRC and other UN standards.

The third set of observations issued after examining the third periodic report welcomed the establishment of (i) a new residential institution for girls in conflict with the law at Dahr El Bashek governmental hospital and (ii) a specialized police unit for minors, responsible for questioning delinquent minors and taking statements from young victims.[48] It noted with concern that Law 422/2002 was still not fully compliant with the UNCRC, especially with regard to the minimum age of criminal responsibility.[49] It recommended that the latter be raised to 12 years of age as a matter of priority.[50] It also noted that juveniles could still undergo the same penal trial procedures as adults.[51] It recommended that community service orders and interventions in restorative justice be developed and that suspended sentences and early release be effectively implemented.[52] It also urged the State to ensure that persons under 18 years of age have access to legal aid and to an independent and effective complaints mechanism.[53]

---

[44] UN Committee on the Rights of the Child: Concluding Observations: Lebanon, 21 March 2002, CRC/C/15/Add.169, para 22(b), available at: http://www.unhcr.org/refworld/docid/3df5887b4.html, accessed 2 March 2010.

[45] ibid paras 26–27.

[46] ibid paras 28–29.

[47] ibid para 50.

[48] UN Committee on the Rights of the Child: Concluding Observations, Lebanon, 8 June 2006, CRC/C/LBN/CO/3, para 84, available at: http://www.unhcr.org/refworld/docid/45377ee70.html, accessed 2 March 2010.

[49] ibid para 84(a).

[50] ibid para para 85(a).

[51] ibid para 84(b).

[52] ibid para 85(b).

[53] ibid para 85(f).

5. The juvenile justice system: Law 422/2002

In the criminal justice context, there is no room for the application of Sharia law or any other kind of religious law.[54] As already noted, Law 422/2002 regulates all the issues concerning children in conflict with the law. This law was the result of a multi-faceted cooperation ('Strengthening legislative and institutional capacity for juvenile justice' and 'Support to the juvenile justice system in Lebanon') between the Ministry of Justice and UNODC. It is however marked by serious drawbacks with regards to the age of criminal liability and the imprisonment of juvenile offenders, having little regard to the principle of deprivation of liberty as a measure of last resort and for the shortest appropriate period of time as stipulated by article 37(B) of the UNCRC.

Protection issues have been a continuing concern for the legislator since 2000. In this respect the provisions of the UNCRC were adopted as guidelines for law reform. Law 422/2002 is currently the only framework that provides for protection measures. It is systematically applied by juvenile courts in accordance with the UNCRC provisions as can be noted in practically all judgments that expressly invoke the principle of the best interests of the child when applying numerous articles of the said convention. Moreover, these courts interpret very extensively the articles of Law 422/2002 taking as a base line the provisions of the UNCRC. Reference to articles 16, 19, 32, 33, 34, 35, 36, 41 of the UNCRC in the reasoning of one single judgment issued by the Juvenile Court of Beirut[55] has been identified. Such a line of reasoning has become very frequent in most decisions of juvenile courts.

The inadequate protection provided by Law 422/2002 has been recognized by the State, which is slow in providing judges with means to apply its policy of upholding the rights of the child and providing a protection shield for the more vulnerable among children including juvenile offenders. Indeed, the lack of an effective mechanism for follow-up is a crucial issue. Better strategies for improving the situation of juvenile offenders have been expressed in the form of recommendations by the UNCRC upon review of the second periodic report of Lebanon. Many of these strategies rely on prevention measures such as legal provisions to prevent in-family violence and abuse, the establishment of mechanisms for receiving, investigating and following up on complaints, making sure that the judicial procedure is respectful of the vulnerability of the child offender, legal aid and advice for

---

[54] No customary law is currently enforced in Lebanon, except for residual matters related to land property under the Ottoman rule (ex: the use of water resources for irrigation in Mount Lebanon).

[55] Juvenile Courts Jurisprudence IDREL Jurisprudence. Data Base Vol I p 344–346. Updated 25 January 2009.

juvenile offenders for reintegration into society, a special hotline for children to use for urgent calls. The strategy that judges prefer is a two-pronged strategy implicating parallel tracks, one of which is the creation of a special curriculum at the Institute of Judicial Studies for judges who opt for a career in juvenile justice, and the second, legal reform in line with international legal instruments.

Furthermore, the recommendations issued by the CRC upon examining the Third National Periodic Report presented by the government have initiated a process of reform, although it is still in its early stages. A Draft Law on the Protection of Children from All Forms of Ill-treatment, Neglect and Abuse, which is intended to supplement the current law, is ready for discussion with stakeholders. It includes a series of measures to ensure enhanced protection of juveniles, among these, juvenile offenders. It goes beyond the issue of protection to that of prevention and encompasses children at risk. However, it does not tackle the minimum age of criminality.

This draft law proposal, based on the principle of the best interests of the child, is perceived as a cornerstone for the development of a national strategy for the protection of children. It includes:

- a section on legal sanctions that are taken outside the scope of juvenile justice,
- a section on penal sanctions pronounced by juvenile courts,
- a section on mechanisms of protection (including the creation of a specialized unit at the Ministry of Justice with a mandate to provide for social measures, the creation of a special police corps within the general framework of the Internal Security Forces and the creation of an independent children's ombudsman) and
- a section establishing specialized juvenile courts that apply a special code of procedure when faced with children in conflict with the law. Psychologists and sociologists, nominated by the Ministry of Social Affairs, would also be present in these cases.

In addition, a five-year program is being implemented by the Higher Council for Childhood (an assembly of NGOs specialized in children's rights) to incorporate the provisions of the UNCRC in the national legislation.

Given the inadequate protection currently offered by the government, such as insufficient activities for prevention and awareness raising programs for juveniles and very limited facilities for the education of juvenile offenders, non-governmental organizations continue to bear the burden of offering remedies to eradicate the adverse effects of the current inadequate framework. They are very active in providing care for children deprived of their liberty and implementing programs aimed at the reintegration of juvenile offenders into society by providing them with vocational training and ensuring that they find a job upon release from jail. Furthermore, social workers commissioned by the NGO Union Pour la Protection de l'Enfance, which has been accredited by the Ministry of Justice for the past 50 years to assist juvenile offenders, often play the role of official mediators between the victim and the offender's families.

Finally, support from international organizations will contribute to keeping the momentum started by the cooperation program between the UN (principally UNODC) and the Ministry of Justice, as well as the Ministry of Social Affairs. These organizations can also provide capacity-building programmes to the NGO sector working in the field of criminal justice and the rights of the child.

6. Rights of minors in detention

Male minors are incarcerated in a special wing of the Roumieh central penitentiary while female juvenile offenders are incarcerated in a rather small facility attached to Dahr El Bashek governmental hospital. Training of law enforcement agents who man these prison facilities takes place sporadically without ensuring that they will continue in their functions. This poses a problem as they may not be aware of the vulnerabilities and needs of children in detention. The provision aimed at creating a Juvenile Police Corps within the Internal Security Forces framework would solve this problem.

Minors in detention enjoy some rights as prisoners. They have the right to meet with their families and lawyers without any interference. No discrimination is made in the law between boys and girls, who enjoy equal right of access to justice.

7. Juvenile justice and judicial activism

According to Law 422/2002, special juvenile courts apply the Penal Code and the Criminal Procedure Code when the case concerns a juvenile offender. They have absolute jurisdiction in applying the principle of the best interests of the child. Their competence emanates *ab initio* to take appropriate measures to that end.[56] In practice, the rather slow progress in establishing a comprehensive juvenile justice system seems to be offset by emerging judicial activism, based on the direct application of provisions of the UNCRC even if they contradict national legislation. However, such activism still needs to gain momentum.

Judges have gained more interest in the field of juvenile justice due to better awareness of international human rights conventions, which are of

---

[56] See (n 67).

assistance when reasoning their case. There are activists among them who initiate new solutions based on the UNCRC. This has narrowed discrepancy between law and practice.

D. Case Law: The Duality between Civil And Religious Courts

Serious difficulties appear with regard to the application of international human rights conventions in family law proceedings, as family law is enforced by autonomous religious tribunals. Indeed, civil courts do not have exclusive jurisdiction over personal status laws since these are of a residual nature, state civil law being the common law of Lebanon.[57] In this regard, the CRC remains concerned about the inconsistencies between national legislation and the Convention, particularly regarding the different confessional justice systems. Although the latter have no jurisdiction with regard to criminal justice, the application of religious law in personal status proceedings often disregards the best interests of the child. This may result in putting the children at risk, thus inducing juvenile criminality.

Based on article 95(4) and article 738(3) of the new Code of Civil Procedure, [58] the Court of Cassation, in its Plenary Assembly, has set public policy principles which cannot be ignored by religious courts. The violation of these principles is sanctioned by the invalidation of the religious court's decisions using arguments such as illegal composition of the religious tribunal[59] or the violation of the right of defence.[60] In the same line of jurisprudence, the Court of Cassation has held that the competence of religious tribunals is of a residual nature, civil law being the common law of the nation. It added that Law No 2 of 1951 on the competence of religious courts is of a specific nature and does not cover matters that are not expressly stipulated in it, be it matters related to family law.[61]

The Beirut Juvenile Court has likewise upheld such principles by suspending indefinitely a Muslim Sunni court decision and applying the UNCRC principle of the best interest of the child.[62] This was publicly challenged by the Sunni religious authorities but the Ministry of Justice rejected the challenge. A later appeal against this decision was rejected by the court, based on the principle that religious law and the competence of religious tribunals is residual and that Sharia law cannot be considered as positive law in Lebanon.[63]

---

[57] Court of Cassation Decision No 56, 1968, Baz Compendium of Jurisprudence, 1968.

[58] Décret-loi n° 83/90 du 16.09.1983.

[59] Decision No 7/85; Decision No 25/96. IDREL Jurisprudence Data Base, Vol 1, 344–346 updated 25 January 2009.

[60] Decision No 9/91, Decision No 5/97 IDREL Jurisprudence Data Base, Vol 1, 344–346 updated 25 January 2009.

[61] Decision dated 23 April 2007 in Al Adl Law Journal 3/2009, 487.

[62] Beirut Juvenile Court Decision No 31 of 24.10.2007 Al Adl Law Journal, 1/2008.

[63] Al Nahar Beirut Daily, 27.10.2007.

The Higher Criminal Court has held that it is not competent to judge a person who, at the time of committing a crime, was under 18 years of age and that only the juvenile court has jurisdiction over such a case.[64] In other cases involving uncertainty regarding the exact age of the offender, the Higher Criminal Court shows some liberalism with respect to proof of juvenile age.[65] Juvenile courts have developed a similar jurisprudence.[66] Criminal Courts in general show the same trend in matters put to their consideration.[67] Their jurisprudence is strict in applying reduced sentences for juvenile offenders as per the provisions of Law No 422.[68]

In the last few years, the jurisprudence of the Juvenile courts reflects systematic recourse to the UNCRC when interpreting of national legislation relating to children.[69] This renders child protection an issue of public concern.[70]

E. Conclusion

Following the ratification of the UNCRC, Lebanon has made some significant improvements in terms of child protection, namely through the enactment of Law 422/2002 which deals with children in conflict with the law and those at risk. It provides for specific sanctions to be applied to juvenile offenders by special juvenile courts. Furthermore, in the last few years, the jurisprudence of the juvenile courts reflects systematic recourse to the UNCRC when interpreting national legislation relating to children.[71] This renders child protection an issue of public concern.[72]

However, a number of problems continue to exist, the most important being the very low age of criminal liability, currently seven years. This has been criticized on several occasions by the CRC and Lebanon has repeatedly been urged to attend to this matter. Another issue concerns the existence of two judicial systems, one civil and one religious. This is problematic because each apply their own laws, the latter often being in

---

[64] Decision No 96/167, 10 July 1996; Decision 2001/1, 9 January 2001; Decision No 281/2001, 19 December 2001. IDREL Jurisprudence Data Base, Vol 1, 344–346 updated 25 January 2009.

[65] Decision No 98/69, 24 March 1998. IDREL Jurisprudence Data Base, Vol 1, 344–346 updated 25 January 2009.

[66] Juvenile Court of Beirut, Decision dated 12 August 2008 published in Al Adl Law Journal 2009/1, 377.

[67] Criminal Court of Mount Lebanon . Decision No 547/2003, 13 November 2003 IDREL Jurisprudence Data Base, Vol 1, p 344–346 updated 25 January 2009.

[68] ibid.

[69] Juvenile Court of Beirut Decision dated 28 August 2008, Al Adl Law Journal 3/2009.

[70] Juvenile Court of Beirut Decision dated 19 November 2008, in Adl Law Journal 3/2009, 491.

[71] Juvenile Court of Beirut Decision ibid.

[72] ibid.

contradiction with international standards. Thus, in the absence of any legal reform of the gender bias personal status laws, especially those of Muslim communities, a more structured mechanism for child protection will continue to be inexistent and ineffective. It is thought that this obstacle can only be overcome by judicial activism since legislative amendments will undoubtedly be challenged by the religious authorities, particularly Muslim clerics.

CHAPTER 8

Criminal Law and the Rights of the Child in Malaysia[1]

I. INTRODUCTION

Malaysia is a multi-religious society where freedom of worship is protected by the Federal Constitution. However, since Muslims[2] represent 65.9 per cent of the total population,[3] the Constitution declares Islam as the official State religion.[4] The federal make-up of the State implies that are three kinds of laws applicable in Malaysia including, (1) federal laws that apply throughout Malaysia; (2) laws that apply to any or each of the three major components of Malaysia, ie, West Malaysia, Sabah and Sarawak, and (3) Laws that apply to any or each of the 13 states of Malaysia. A system of legal pluralism is thus prevalent. On the one hand, there are laws, such as the Penal Code and the Evidence Act, that are generally applicable to everyone, irrespective of their creed or race. The courts can enforce these laws on everyone, including Muslims, even when their provisions go against the precepts of Islamic law.[5]

---

[1] Dr Farah Nini Dusuki, Senior Lecturer, Law Faculty, University of Malaya, (farah-dusuki@yahoo.co.uk).

[2] Amongst the Muslims, the majority are Shafii with Hanafi minorities.

[3] Department of Statistics, 2005.

[4] See art 3 of the Malaysian Constitution available at confinder.richmond.edu/admin/docs/Malaysia.pdf accessed 7 February 2010.

[5] This assertion is debatable depending on the perception of the problem. For instance, in *Che Omar Che Soh v Public Prosecutor* [1988] 2 MLJ 55, it was argued before the Supreme Court of Malaysia that capital punishment for drug trafficking was unconstitutional. The basis of this argument was that it is against the precepts of Islam, which under art 3 of the Federal Constitution is the 'religion of the Federation'. It was held that the term 'Islam' or 'Islamic religion', in art 3 only includes acts relating to rituals and ceremonies. There are interesting deliberations contained in the judgement of Salleh Abas LP with respect to the British colonial attitude towards Islam and also the current position of Islam in the Malaysian society. He notes, inter alia, 'If the religion of Islam in the context means only such acts as relate to rituals and ceremonies, the argument has no basis whatsoever; On the other hand, if the religion of Islam or Islam itself is an all-embracing concept, as is normally understood, which consists not only the ritualistic aspect but also a comprehensive system of life, including its jurisprudence and moral standard, then the submission has a great implication in that every law has to be tested according to this yardstick.' It is interesting to note that the *Che Omar* decision was not followed by the High Court in *Meor Atiqulrahman Ishak v Fatimah bte Sihi* [2000] 5 MLJ 375. Instead it held that Islam is *ad-deen*—a way of life. Therefore it was held that regulations violating art 3 can be invalidated.

Child protection[6] and domestic violence[7] laws are also among those laws that have general applicability.[8] On the other hand, Muslims have a prerogative to be governed by their own personal status laws when it comes to marriage, divorce, guardianship[9] and adoption[10] of children, although these laws apply equally to non-Muslims. This prerogative dates back to the pre-colonial era.[11] Even during British rule, 'each (the Malay) ruler was bound to accept British advice on all matters except Mohammedan[12] religion and Malay custom'.[13]

The court system[14] is divided into superior and subordinate courts. The superior courts are the High Court, Court of Appeal, and the Federal Court, which is the highest court in Malaysia, while the Magistrate's Courts and the Sessions Courts are classified as subordinate courts. Article 121 of the Constitution provides for two High Courts of coordinate jurisdiction, the High Court in Malaya, and the High Court in Sabah and Sarawak. The highest position in the judiciary of Malaysia is Chief Justice of the Federal Court of Malaysia (also known as Chief Justice of Malaysia), followed by President of the Court of Appeal, Chief Judge of Malaya and Chief Judge of Sabah and Sarawak. In addition to the civil courts, there is a parallel system of State Syariah[15] Courts. The Constitution has vested the power to

---

[6] See Child Act 2001 (Act 511) available at www.parlimen.gov.my/actindexbi/pdf/ACT-611.pdf accessed 7 February 2010.

[7] See Domestic Violence Act 1994 (Act 521) available at www.parlimen.gov.my/actindexbi/pdf/ACT-521.pdf accessed 7 February 2010.

[8] There are no provisions in both Acts that limit their application to Muslims.

[9] As per s 1(2) of the Guardianship of Infants Act, 1961, 'Nothing in this Act shall apply in any State to persons professing the religion of Islam until this Act has been adopted by law made by the Legislature of that State.' available at www.agc.gov.my/agc/Akta/Vol.%208/Act%20351.pdf accessed 7 February 2010. It is worth noting that the Act has been adopted with some modifications in the States in Peninsular Malaysia. However, recently it was provided that the Act shall not apply to the Federal Territories—see Act A902 (After amendment the relevant section will be s 1(3).)

[10] The Adoption Act 1952 does not apply to Muslims. See *Tang Kong Meng v Zainon* [1995] 5 MLJ 408.

[11] Prior to the advent of the British, Islamic law was the law of the land. In *Shaik Abdul Latif and others v Shaik Elias Bux* (1915) 1 FMSLR 204 at 214, Edmonds JC said '*Before the first treaties the population of these states consisted almost solely of Mohammedan Malays with a large industrial and mining community in their midst. The only law at that time applicable to Malays was Mohammedan law modified by local customs.*' In *Ramah v Laton* (1927) 6 FMSLR 128, the Court of Appeal held that Islamic law is not foreign but local law and is in fact the law of the land. See also MJ Rutter, 'The Applicable law in Singapore and Malaysia' [1989] Malayan Law Journal, 443–447.

[12] Mohammed is the name of the 'final messenger' and 'Mohammedan law' refers to 'Islamic Law'.

[13] British Government Paper, 'Malaya: Statement of Policy for the Future Constitution of the Malayan Union and the Colony of Singapore' January 1946.

[14] Part IX of the Malaysian Constitution provides for the establishment of the judiciary, see FN3 for reference.

[15] Islamic law is known as Sharia law, and in Malaysia it is known as *Syariah*. The court is

enact laws relating to the constitution, organization and procedure of the Syariah courts[16] in the states, except with regards to the Federal Territories. These Syariah courts have limited jurisdiction over matters of Islamic (Sharia) law so that they only have jurisdiction over matters involving Muslims. They can generally only pass sentences for terms not exceeding two years imprisonment or a fine of up to RM 3,000. Any offence that carries a sentence exceeding three years imprisonment, a fine exceeding RM 5,000 or lashes exceeding six strokes or any combination thereof is outside their jurisdiction.[17]

As far as children are concerned, general public law is applicable to those in conflict with the law, irrespective of their religion or race. Child offenders will not be subjected to Sharia law unless the offence in question is recognized within the Sharia state enactments. These are limited to offences such as consumption of alcoholic beverages or not fasting during the month of Ramadan.

II. NATIONAL FRAMEWORK ON THE RIGHTS OF THE CHILD IN CRIMINAL MATTERS

Historically, the driving force behind the introduction of child laws is linked to a perceived[18] increase in the rate of social problems involving children. The enactment of the first law relating to juvenile delinquents in Malaysia is a case in point. The Japanese occupation of Malaya (as Malaysia was then known) resulted in the emergence of a number of social problems such as the break-up of homes, school closures and the removal of parental control. One of the significant repercussions of this was an abrupt rise in juvenile delinquency.[19] Consequently, the Juvenile Delinquency and Juvenile Welfare Committee was appointed on 18 November 1946 with the purpose of advising the government on the necessary measures needed to combat this issue and recommending any actions required in the interest of

known as the *Syariah Court*, see http://en.wikipedia.org/wiki/Syariah_Court accessed 7 February 2010.

[16] See List II of the Ninth Schedule of the Federal Constitution available at http://www.commonlii.org/my/legis/const/1957/24.html accessed 07/02/2010.

[17] http://en.wikipedia.org/wiki/Courts_of_Malaysia#Syariah_Courts accessed 07/02/2010.

[18] The use of the term 'perceived' is due to the absence of any study conducted on the actual extent of social problems, such as child abuse, domestic violence and so on, affecting children. Statistics provided by the Royal Malaysian Police, the Social Welfare Department and hospitals only represent the total number of cases that come to their attention and therefore do not provide a real picture of the actual extent of the problem nationwide.

[19] *Report of the Juvenile Delinquency and Juvenile Welfare Committee*, No 18, February 1947, c 289 at c 291–291, MU 3484/47.

juvenile welfare in the Malayan Union.[20] The Committee produced a laudable report, which indicated that the total absence of legislation dealing with juvenile delinquency had already put the Presiding Officers of the Courts in the Malaya Union in serious trouble.[21] This work constituted the foundation of the first ever law on juveniles, the Juvenile Courts Ordinance, 1947.

The most essential features of this Act were the establishment of a Juvenile Court for the trial of children and young persons and the introduction of a proper probation system.[22] These new courts had jurisdiction over all offences with the exception of those that carried the death penalty.[23] Part III[24] of the Juvenile Courts Act contained provisions with regard to places of detention. It provided for remand homes to which those juvenile offenders who were refused bail could be sent to instead of sending them to regular prisons. Part IV[25] of the Act provided for a proper probation system and appointment of a probation officer. Section 23 contained the duties of a probation officer and included the duty to visit and receive reports from the child or young person placed on probation, a duty to report to the Juvenile Court regarding the probationer's behaviour, to

[20] The Report comprises very useful information on the background of the problem and the underlying principle behind the establishment of various mechanisms to curb and regulate the problem.

[21] See c300 of the Report. The only legal provisions even remotely dealing with juvenile delinquents were the following: The Reformatory Schools Enactment (Cap 37) by virtue of which delinquents of the Federated Malayan states could be sent to the Reformatory in Singapore after having obtained the consent of the Government of Singapore; s 173A of the Colonial Procedure Code which refers to probation and s 293 and 293A which gave certain powers over young offenders. Besides the aforesaid provisions, the law was practically silent on juvenile delinquents.

[22] S 2 defined children as persons below the age of 14 and young persons as persons between 14 and 17 years of age. However, in the Child Act of 2001 (The Child Act consolidated the Juvenile Courts Act 1947, the Women and Young Girls' Protection Act 1973 and the Child Protection Act 1991) the distinction between children and young persons was removed and a child was defined as a person who is below 18 years of age.

[23] In contrast, the Child Act 2001 has provided for the establishment of Courts for Children. This Act does not impose any restrictions on the offences that are admissible. S 11 of the Act reads, inter alia, 'Courts constituted in accordance with this Act and sitting for the purpose of—(a) hearing, determining or disposing of any charge against a child.' Even though a Court for Children can try an offence that carries the death penalty, it does not have the power to impose capital punishment if at the time the crime was committed, the offender was a child. S 97(1) prohibits the death penalty for a child offender while s 97(2), provides for imprisonment as the penalty in substitution of the death sentence. It is up to the King to decide on the period and conditions of detention, and whether to release or detain the offender upon review.

[24] In the Child Act of 2001, these provisions are contained in Part IX. Besides differences in division of sections, there is no significant distinction between these two parts of the respective Acts.

[25] The 2001 Act contains the probation procedures in Part X, Chapter 4. See ss 98–104 for the situations where a probation order may be given, effects of the order and breach thereof and the procedures to be complied with.

advise, assist and take care of the probationer, and also to find an appropriate employment when necessary.[26] Part V[27] provided for 'approved' schools that the children would be sent to for a period of three years or until they reached 14 years of age (whichever was longer). For children between 14–16 years of age, advanced approved schools were provided for.[28] These schools were similar to erstwhile Borstals in the United Kingdom.[29] However, the main purpose behind the establishment of these schools was reformatory and educational rather than penal. Despite this, the discipline of those schools was stricter than that of the approved schools meant for juvenile delinquents.[30] Besides sending children to approved schools, the Juvenile Court also had the option of placing them in the care of a fit person. The parent or guardian of the child could be ordered to share the cost of the child's maintenance in such a case.[31] This system was also borrowed from England and Wales.[32]

Malaysia's most elaborate legislation protecting children from parental or guardian misconduct was the now repealed Child Protection Act 1991.[33] Seemingly, Parliament would not have dealt with this problem as swiftly if it had not been for the public outrage incited by the *Balasundram* case.[34]

---

[26] Unlike the 1947 Act, the 2001 Act does not emphasize the duties of the Probation Officer but instead stresses on the ensuing responsibilities of the probationer.

[27] In the 2001 Act, Part VII, Chapter 4 contains the provisions on 'approved schools'. See ss 65–72. The current statute has adopted a relatively more lenient stance by limiting the maximum period of detention of a child to three years. This can be extended to another period not exceeding six months in case the child needs further care and training or if he cannot be placed in appropriate employment without such care and training. However, this period should not extend beyond the date the child attains 18 years of age. See s 69 of the 2001 Act.

[28] See Part VIII of the 1947 Act. There is no equivalent provision in the 2001 Act as the approved schools are meant to cater to all children between 10–18 years of age. See ss 66 and 69.

[29] The Prevention of Crime Act 1908 established a system of borstal institutions in England and Wales. The principal objective behind this system was to provide specialized treatment to young offenders instead of detaining them with the adult offenders. According to Professor Bevan, it began as an extension of the reformatory principle to young offenders, ie persons no longer juveniles but still under the age of 21. This system was ultimately abolished by the Criminal Justice Act, 1982, s 1(3). See Bevan, Child Law, para 13.75–13.76.

[30] See the Council debate on the Juvenile Courts Bill, 1947 at B169.

[31] See part VI of the 1947 Act. In the 2001 Act, comparable provisions can be found in Part XI, ss 105–107. Part XII, s 108 contains provisions relating to orders for contribution.

[32] See the Council debate at B169. The report of the debate stated that while the 'fit person order' provided the most effective means of reforming juvenile delinquents, in practice such orders were limited as people could not be forced to accommodate juvenile delinquents into their homes. Of the approximately 30,000 juvenile delinquents that were convicted in 1938 in England, only 211 were subjected to the 'fit person order'.

[33] Act 468 available at www.parlimen.gov.my/pdf/a468.pdf accessed 7 February 2010, 43 onwards, c.i.f. West Malaysia & Federal Territoty of Labuan 1.3. 1992-PU(B) 77/92; Sarawak: 30.9.1993-PU(B) 450/93 and Sabah 27.1.1995- PU(B) 34/95. See also the accompanying legislations.

[34] Although, the *Balasundaram* case was not the first case of child abuse in Malaysia, it certainly was the first one that resulted in wide scale public outrage. Balasundram was an 18-

Alongside the Social Welfare Department, which deserves credit for its groundwork related to the 1991 Act, the Suspected Child Abuse and Neglect team also deserve to be mentioned for playing an important role in transforming child abuse into an issue of national concern.[35] The Child Protection Act 1991 had a novel approach to tackling the problem of child abuse. It recognized all the different forms of child abuse as specific offences and provided for instant involvement. At the policy-making level, it placed emphasis on inter-agency collaboration by setting up a Coordinating Council for Child Protection that had to compulsorily meet four times a year. It further encouraged this collaboration by providing the necessary mechanisms to carry out the essential inter-agency plan. A Central Registrar and a register of children in need of protection were to be created.[36] In order to promote identification and referral of cases, reporting of suspected child abuse cases was made compulsory on medical practitioners. According to physicians and social workers, the maintenance of a nationwide central registry of reported information in child abuse cases is an essential feature of a program aiming to tackle the problem of child abuse. A Child Protection Team, a multi-disciplinary medium whose function it was to help the Department in carrying out its protection plans and aiding families with children, was also to be created at every district level. Despite the introduction of an advanced system to prevent abuse and neglect cases by the 1991 Act, it was never wholeheartedly enforced[37] and suffered from ineffective implementation. But putting the entire blame on the Social Welfare Department would be unfair as the body also has to deal with other aspects of welfare such as the disabled, the elderly and single parents, while suffering from a dearth of resources. It could however be argued that children's issues need to be given preference so as to ensure that they receive adequate protection.

With a view to consolidating the law on child protection, namely the Child Protection Act 1991, the Women and Girl's Protection Act 1973,[38]

---

month-old child who was left to die in the lavatory of the General Hospital of Kuala Lumpur in 1992. Post-mortem reports provided evidence of physical abuse as well as sodomy. For further details see F Nini Dusuki, 'What Malaysia can Learn from the Experience of England and Wales to Protect Victims of Child Abuse and Neglect' unpublished PhD thesis, Cardiff University, 2002, ch 2 and 3.

[35] It is important to note that upon being questioned, a Social Welfare Department officer rejected this deduction and instead claimed that the new Act was well under way when the *Balasundaram* incident took place. However, the sequence of events that led to the enactment of the 1991 law clearly indicate that despite the previous attempts made by the Social Welfare Department and expedited by the SCAN Team's work in drafting an alternative bill, it was the *Balasundram* incident that provoked the Government to replace the outdated Children and Young Persons Act, 1947.

[36] Ss 4 and 5 Child Protection Act 1991.

[37] See Dusuki (n 34) ch 4 and 5 generally.

[38] Act 106. cif West Malaysia 19.9.1973-PU(B) 381/73; Sabah 1.7.1981-PU(B) 347/81;

and the Juvenile Courts Act 1947, the Government of Malaysia announced that a new law was being drafted in late 1997.[39] The Government was well aware of the impending need to explore the most appropriate measures to effectively tackle social problems related to children and to ensure that children do not come under the influence of harmful elements.[40] The chief drawback of the earlier laws was that they did not adequately consider the developmental aspects of children and also ignored the role of parents in that regard. The commitment was further strengthened when, in 1985, the country ratified the UN Convention on Rights of the Child (UNCRC). In the past, issues of child welfare had been under the jurisdiction of the Ministry of National Unity and Community Development. However, under the Act it has now been transferred to the Ministry of Education. This was followed by the establishment of a Working Committee on the Study and Enactment of Legislation Regulating Social Problems under the chairmanship of the Education Minister, Dato' Seri Najib. The preliminary draft of the law was prepared by a team of consultants from the University of Malaya under the guidance of Dato' Dr Mimi Kamariah Majid[41] and submitted to the Ministry of National Unity and Community Development. Three months later, a workshop was organized by the Malaysian Prevention of Crime Foundation with the principal aim of obtaining feedback from non-governmental organizations (NGOs) on the legal changes suggested by the Committee.[42] Initially, the Committee was considering four Acts that were related to child welfare. However, it later discovered that the Child Care Centres Act 1984 was only regulatory in character and was therefore kept outside the ambit of amendment and consolidation.[43] The presence of overlapping provisions in the three Acts led to the idea of consolidating them into a single piece of comprehensive legislation. Therefore, the Child Act 2001 consolidates and repeals the three erstwhile

---

Sarawak 1.3.1983-PU(B) 482/82. The preamble states: 'An act to amend and consolidate the law relating to the protection of women and girls and to provide for matters incidental thereto.' This Act was not discussed previously as its main concern was the protection of women and girls from prostitution, which is in itself a complex problem and beyond the scope of this research (although dealing with sexual abuse of children, does not extend to prostitution). Moreover, 'girls' here refers to those who are under 21 years of age (See Part III of the Act), whereas the main concern of this research are children under 18 years of age.

[39] See Dusuki (n 34) ch 3 generally. See also NB bt Ariffin, 'The Child Act, 2001: How far is it fairing?' paper presented at the 11th Malaysian Law Conference, 2001, Kuala Lampur, 8–10 November, 2001.

[40] bt Ariffin ibid.

[41] Former Dean and Professor at the Faculty of Law, University of Malaya.

[42] The change that was most fervently challenged was the lowering of age of criminal responsibility from 10 to seven. The participants contested that this move would neither reduce crimes nor serve the well-being of the child. See proposed features of the new bill in M Kamariah Majid, Legislation on Social Ills, Auditorium Perdanasiswa, University of Malaya, 17 November, 1997.

[43] See Kamariah Majid ibid 1.

Acts that dealt with children. These Acts were the Child Protection Act 1991[44] (An Act protecting children in need of care and protection), the Juvenile Courts Act 1947[45] (An Act that vehemently established the Juvenile Court and regulated proceedings affecting juvenile offenders), and the Women and Girls Protection Act 1973[46] (An Act to protect women and girls exposed to sexual vices).

At present, the law that is applicable to children who come into conflict with the law is the Child Act 2001. It is a comprehensive piece of legislation that covers the areas of care, protection and rehabilitation of children. Even though the Act has retained several important features of the previous three Acts it repealed, it nevertheless made significant additions with regard to proper care, security, support, rehabilitation and development in a bid to provide more protection to children.

III. INTERNATIONAL HUMAN RIGHTS FRAMEWORK

Malaysia ratified the UNCRC on 17 February 1995 and submitted its first Report to the UNCRC Committee (the CRC) on 25 January 2007.[47] In the beginning, Malaysia made reservations to 12 different articles of the UNCRC on various grounds such as contradiction with the Country's Constitution, national laws and policies and religious and cultural practices.[48] Consequently, four reservations were withdrawn. Responding to Malaysia's first report, the CRC recommended that Malaysia persist in its attempts to ensure the complete implementation of juvenile justice standards as protected by articles 37, 39 and 40 of the Convention and other relevant international standards.[49] As stated earlier, the Child Act 2001(Act

---

[44] Act 468.

[45] Act 90.

[46] Act 106.

[47] There were some concerns raised by the CRC upon Malaysia's submission of the first report, notably on Malaysia's current reservations of the UNCRC.

[48] The reservation states: 'The Government of Malaysia accepts the provisions of the Convention on the Rights of the Child but expresses reservations with respect to articles 1, 2.7, 13, 14, 15, [...], 28, [para 1 (a)] 37, [...] of the Convention and declares that the said provisions shall be applicable only if they are in conformity with the Constitution, national laws and national policies of the Government of Malaysia.' 23 March 1999, available at http://treaties.un.org/doc/publication/mtdsg/volumel/chapteriv/iv-11.en.pdf, accessed 7 February 2010.

[49] Concluding Observations by the Committee on the Rights of the Child (44th Session) 'Consideration of Reports submitted by State Parties under Article 44 of the Convention' CRC/C/MYS/CO/1 25 available at http://daccess-ods.un.org/TMP/3784512.57944107.html accessed 7 February 2010. These include: the United Nations Standard Minimum rules for the Administration of Juvenile Justice (the 'Beijing Rules'); the United Nations Guidelines for the Prevention of Juvenile Delinquency (the 'Riyadh Guidelines') and the United Nations Rules for the Protection of Juveniles Deprived of Their Liberty (the 'Havana Rules').

611) basically incorporates the principles of the UNCRC and aims to provide care, protection, and psychosocial assistance. Additionally, other laws were enacted to protect and promote children's rights. Subsequent to the pledge made during the World Summit on Children in 1990, Malaysia devised a National Plan of Action for Children's Survival, Protection and Development. The plan was developed owing to the determined and harmonized efforts of various government agencies, NGOs and international organizations, namely UNICEF and the World Health Organisation.[50] This Plan is now superseded by the relatively recently passed National Child Policy and National Child Protection Policy, and their respective Pans of Action which were sanctioned by the Cabinet in July 2009.[51]

Malaysia drafted the Child Act 2001,[52] a comprehensive Act for the protection of children, in order to comply with and respect its obligations under the UNCRC. The Act reveals the Malaysian government's commitment towards meeting the requirements of the UNCRC. It also regulates the various issues relating to children who come into conflict with the law.[53] The *Preamble* to the 2001 Act explicitly reflects several provisions of the UNCRC. It states: 'An Act to consolidate and amend the laws relating to the care, protection and rehabilitation of children and to provide for matters connected therewith and incidental thereto.'[54]

The Act considers that a child is a 'crucial component' of society and the 'key to its survival, development and prosperity'. It acknowledges that due to his 'physical, mental and emotional immaturity', a child needs special care and assistance, so that he can be able to 'participate in and contribute positively towards the attainment of the ideals of a civil Malaysian society'. Moreover, it considers that 'every child is entitled to protection and assistance in all circumstances without regard to distinctions of any kind, such as race, colour, sex, language, religion, social origin or physical, mental or emotional disabilities or any other status'. The family is seen as the provider of a 'natural environment for the growth, support and well-being of all' more specifically of children, so that they would be able to develop in an environment of 'peace, happiness, love, understanding'.[55]

---

[50] Ministry of Women, Family and Community Development, 'Malaysia's First Country Report on the Implementation of the Convention of the Rights of the Child, 2007' 52 available at http://daccess-ods.un.org/TMP/3995074.03373718.html, accessed 7 February 2010.

[51] Ministry of Women, Family and Community Development, *National Policy and Plan of Action for Children* and *National Policy and Plan of Action for the Protection of Children* (2009).

[52] Hereafter will be referred to as the '2001 Act' available at www.parlimen.gov.my/actindexbi/pdfACT-611.pdf accessed 7 February 2010.

[53] 2001 Act.

[54] ibid.

[55] ibid.

IV. DOMESTIC LEGISLATION ON THE PROTECTION OF THE RIGHTS OF
THE CHILD IN CRIMINAL LAW

A. *The Age of Criminal Liability*

Age is an important factor in order to ascertain whether a child can be criminally liable. Therefore, there is a mandatory system of registration of births in Malaysia that is used to obtain proof of age.[56] The same provisions also grant the child a right to a name. This registration, accompanied by a birth certificate, becomes an essential legal document proving the identity of the child and may also be used for other purposes. In the country's legal history, the single local case that looked at the presumption of maturity of juveniles between 10 to 12 years of age, under section 83, was the High Court's decision in *PP v Lim Ah Leng*.[57]

In Malaysia, criminal liability of children can be divided into three different categories. First, complete immunity is available to a child below 10 years of age.[58] Second, partial immunity applies to children between 10 to 12 years of age.[59] Lastly, the criminal liability of children above 12 years of age is the same as that of adults irrespective of the kind of crime they have committed. However, a different criminal procedure[60] and different court disposals apply to them.[61] Despite the fact that their liability is the same as that of adults, the sentence applicable may vary. For example, children may not be sentenced to death, although an adult committing the same offence would be. Instead, and depending on the state in which the crime was committed, the child will serve a prison sentence and the period of detention will be determined by the Ruler.[62] This is illustrated by the case of *Koh Wah Koon v PP*.[63] In this case, an 11-year-old boy was convicted of murdering his tutor's 11-year-old daughter. Since the crime took place in Wilayah Persekutuan, he was sentenced to imprisonment at the Kajang Prison at the pleasure of the Yang Dipertuan Agung.[64] Another example is

---

[56] The Births and Deaths Registration Act 1957(Act 299), Registration of Birth and Death Ordinance of Sabah (Chapter 123) and Registration of Birth and Death Ordinance of Sarawak (Chapter 10) make it mandatory for every birth in the country to be registered with the National Registration Department. Upon registration, the child is given a name.

[57] [1967] 1 MLJ 284.

[58] S 82 Penal Code (Act 574) available at www.agc.gov.my/agc/Akta/Vol.%2012/Act%20574.pdf. accessed 07/02/2010.

[59] S 83 Penal Code.

[60] See generally Child Act 2001, particularly Part X and XIII on criminal procedure for children.

[61] 2001 Act, Part X, Chapter 3, ss 91–97. See also Chapter 4 on probation, Part XI for orders placing the child in the care of a fit and proper person and Part XII for the duty of parents/guardians to make contributions.

[62] S 97 Child Act 2001.

[63] [2004] 5 MLJ 193.

[64] Although it was disputed that sending the boy to prison was not the best available option,

the murder case of Muhammad Farid who was killed by eight fellow students, all aged 17, at a religious school in Seremban.[65] The Court made a similar decision and sentenced the juveniles to prison instead of the death penalty.[66] However, this rule is far from being absolute as is illustrated by the case of *Lim Hang Seoh v PP*[67] where the High Court sentenced a 14-year-old boy to death for possessing firearms in violation of section 57 of the Internal Security Act of 1960. The Federal Court upheld his conviction on appeal. However, in his last appeal to Ruler Yang Dipertuan Agung, his death sentence was altered to detention at the Henry Gurney School until the age of 21. It is important to note that the offence committed is categorized as a security offence under Regulation 2 of Essential (Security Cases) Regulations 1975 (ESCAR). Regulation 3(3) specifically provides that the now repealed Juvenile Courts Act 1947 was inapplicable to juveniles charged with security offences. Although the possibility of replacing the death sentence with indefinite detention is provided for in Child Act 2001, there is no explicit exclusion of Regulation 3(3) of ESCAR in the 2001 Act. Thus, the possibility of a double jurisdiction can be criticized as it provides little protection to the juvenile offenders.

1. Sharia Penal Code

In Sharia law, criminal liability only accrues when a person reaches the age of *balig* (becomes an adult), is of sound mind and has free will. Thus, under Islamic criminal law a child is only liable once he has attained the age of puberty.[68] Male puberty is attained upon the ejaculation of sperm and female puberty begins when a girl first menstruates. When such signs are absent, puberty is determined according to the age of the child concerned. The opinion of Muslim scholars on determining the age of puberty is varied. However, Malaysia follows the Shafi School of Islamic jurisprudence and its authoritative principles in the administration of the Islamic religion, particularly in matters of *ibadah* (religious rituals). Therefore, there is no set minimum age of criminal liability according to Sharia law.

the Judge was bound by the terms *'detained in prison'* in s 97 of the Child Act 2001 as opposed to merely *'detained'* as it was in the repealed Juvenile Courts Act 1947. The boy was however isolated from the older inmates and was given regular classes in preparation for his impending government examination (PMR) the following year.

[65] See *Mohd Haikal bin Mohd Khatib Saddaly & Ors v PP* [2009] 4 MLJ 305.

[66] This case was highly publicized by the media in late December 2003. These boys have since been released upon successful appeal to the Federal Court in February 2010.

[67] [1978] 1 MLJ 68.

[68] Syariah Criminal Offences (Federal Territories) Act 1997 (Act 559) available at www.mylawyer.com.my/pdf/Syariah_Criminal_Offences_Federal_Territories_Act.pdf, accessed 07/02/2010 and the respective State legislations pertaining to Syariah criminal offences, which provide that 'nothing is an offence which is done by a child who is not *baligh*'.

Rather, liability is dependent on attaining puberty, so that the age of the offender may vary between cases.

In contrast with the Child Act 2001, section 2 of the Sharia Criminal Procedure (Federal Territory) Act 1997[69] defines a child offender as 'an offender above the age of ten and below the age of sixteen years.' The rationale behind this provision is that any Muslim child who is above the age of 10 would be in a position to fathom the nature of the act committed but he would still lack an understanding of its legal implications, rendering him undeserving of a prison sentence. When dealing with child offenders, the Court may order their discharge after admonition or send him back to his parents or guardian, with or without executing a bond with a surety that they will be accountable for his conduct. If they fail to comply, they may be fined up to RM 200 (about £40).[70]

Upon reviewing Malaysia's first report, the CRC suggested that Malaysia should immediately increase the minimum age of criminal liability from 10 to 12 and continue to increase it (to the level required by international standards ie 18 years).[71] It also pointed out inconsistencies between the minimum age standards in the Penal Code, the interpretation of Muslim jurists in the Syariah court and the Syariah Criminal Procedure (Federal Territories) Act 1984. Thus, a situation of legal uncertainty prevails where children of the same age may be subjected to different standards. To answer this criticism, Malaysia clarified that not all criminal offences are dealt with in Sharia courts, the latter only try those that are of a religious nature.

B. Special Courts and Procedures for Child Offenders

Special courts and procedures for child offenders exist in Malaysia. In a bid to provide a friendlier name, the former Juvenile Court was renamed the Court For Children.[72] It can try any case under its criminal jurisdiction except offences punishable with the death sentence.[73] However, the jurisdiction of the Court For Children may be ousted in four circumstances which are: (1) cases where the child is charged with an offence after attaining the age of 18,[74] (2) cases where an adult offender is jointly charged with a child, in this case the adult court will assume jurisdiction,[75] (3) cases where the charge against the child is punishable with death,[76] and finally (4) where the charge against the child is under the ESCAR, the Firearms

---

[69] Act 560, available at www.agc.gov.my/agc/Akta/Vol.%2012/Act%20560.pdf.
[70] S 128(1) and (2) Act 560.
[71] Concluding Observations by the Committee on the Rights of the Child (44th Session) 'Consideration of Reports submitted by State Parties under art 44 of the Convention' CRC/C/MYS/CO/1 25, see fn 49.
[72] S 11 2001 Act.   [73] S 11(5) 2001 Act.
[74] S 83(3) 2001 Act.   [75] S 83(4)(b) 2001 Act.
[76] S 11(4) 2001 Act.

(Increased Penalties) Act 1971 (FIPA) or the Dangerous Drugs Act 1952 (DDA). All these laws contain similar provisions that oust the jurisdiction of the Court For Children 'notwithstanding any other written law to the contrary.'[77] The only obligation that is retained in these circumstances is giving due consideration to the probation report and the courts are not even legally bound to follow the composition of the Court For Children, which requires a Magistrate and two court advisers for assistance, one of whom has to be a woman.[78] This was held in *Buri Hemna v PP*[79] where the Court held that '... there is no compulsion for the High Court to be assisted by two advisers when trying juveniles'. Even though this decision was based on relevant provisions contained in the now repealed Juvenile Courts Act 1947, the same rule was applied under the 2001 Act in *Koh Wah Koon v PP* where the High Court heard the case without two advisors.[80] What is more, the High Court is explicitly authorized to impose punishments without paying any heed to the relatively more reformative sanctions provided by section 91 of the 2001 Act.[81] This wide discretion afforded to the Court will obviously result in lesser protection of child offenders.

With regard to court procedures under the Child Act 2001, they are similar to the ones that were available under the Juvenile Act 1947. An important development however is that the 2001 Act incorporates the principles of article 40 of the UNCRC. A further improvement is that proceedings are to be held in camera.[82] The intention of the Malaysian government is demonstrated by the efforts it made in separating child offenders from adults, to avoid the former being stigmatized. Indeed, section 12 of the 2001 Act holds that child offender cases will be heard in separate buildings or rooms and when this is not administratively possible, the hearings should be arranged on a different day.[83] However, it is worth noting that the police have been making efforts to separate, as much as possible, child offenders from adult ones.[84]

In practice, the general rights of the child offender are not adequately respected before the courts. For example, the representation of a child by a

---

[77] For example, s 10 of FIPA states: 'Notwithstanding any other written law to the contrary, a Sessions Court shall have jurisdiction to try all offences under this Act, except offences under s 3 or 3A, and to impose for any offence so tried the full punishment of penalty provided for that offence by this Act, except the penalty of death.'

[78] S 11(2) and (3) of the 2001 Act.

[79] [1998] 5 MLJ 813. See also M Kamariah Majid, *Criminal Procedure in Malaysia* (3rd edn, University of Malaya Press, Malaya, 1999) 30–31.

[80] See SUHAKAM, *Report of the Forum on Malaysia's Reservations to the Convention on the Rights of the Child*, 2008, 53 available at http://www.suhakam.org.my.

[81] Reporter

[82] S 12(3) 2001 Act.   [83] S 12(1) 2001 Act.

[84] Information obtained during roundtable discussions among the various agencies involved in child protection in the Workshop on the Taskforce on Child Law, Quality Hotel, Kuala Lumpur, August 2008.

legal counsel is largely contingent on the provision of one by the family. Even in cases where a parent or guardian is not present at the proceedings, the court may pass any order without paying heed to the needs of the child. This situation directly infringes article 12 UNCRC, which grant the child a right to be heard. Thus, emphasis is being placed on training Court Advisors to better understand the Children Act 2001.

Legal action can be taken against parents who are reluctant to pursue a legal remedy for a child offender. However there is no precedent in which this provision has been invoked.[85] Despite the fact that there are legal restrictions on reporting and publishing information about the child offender in the media, examples of inadequate protection of a child's privacy can be found. Even though direct names have not been revealed, other particulars/hints make the juvenile identifiable and exposed to shame within his community.[86] Nonetheless, as has been seen in the reported cases quoted in this chapter, actual names are usually revealed in the law reports.

C. Deprivation of Liberty

1. Consideration given to the age of the child

Restrictions on the age of entry into the various institutions of reformation offer safeguards for children. For example, a child below 10 years of age cannot, under any circumstances, be sent to a probation hostel or an approved school within the meaning of the Act.[87] A child below 14 years of age shall not be sent to the Henry Gurney School (an advanced approved school run by the Prisons Department).[88] Likewise, a child below 14 must not be committed to prison for any offence or in default of payment of a fine, compensation or costs.[89] Even juveniles who are 14 or above should not be imprisoned for an offence if their case could be better dealt with by probation, a fine, keeping them in a detention centre or an approved school or other suitable measures provided by law.[90] If the Court is uncertain about the age of the offender at the time of the commission of the offence, the court will presume that the offender was below 18 years of age. This principle has been in practice since 1963.[91]

---

[85] S 88 2001 Act.   [86] S 15 2001 Act.
[87] S 66 2001 Act.   [88] S 74 2001 Act.
[89] S 96 2001 Act.   [90] S 96(2) 2001 Act.
[91] See for instance, *Deng Anak Ekom v Regina* [1963] 1 MLJ 343 where the death sentence was quashed as the court was uncertain of the accused's age. In *PP v Nur Hassan b Salib* [1993] MLJU 241; *PP v Ben Ismail* [1993] MLJU 25 and *PP v Boy bin Islais* [1993] MLJU 25, the offenders were detained under the pleasure of the Ruler under section 16 of the Juvenile Courts Act 1947 when they were found guilty of the offence of drug trafficking although this offence is normally punishable with death under section 39B (1) and (2) DDA 1952.

Although the Shafi school of jurisprudence is generally applicable, Islamic law has no direct bearing on the age of criminal responsibility. The reason for this is that criminal responsibility of children comes under the ambit of the Constitution. Therefore, penal law is administered by the Federal law, which applies the civil law.

2. Pre-trial arrest and detention

The main reason behind the insufficient protection afforded to children is the absence of detailed provisions in the law about specific procedures to be applied upon apprehension of a juvenile. For example, when a child comes into conflict with the law, there are many procedural deficiencies, eg how should the police deal with a child in the first 24 hours after his apprehension? According to section 87 of the 2001 Act, the police officer is bound by law to inform the parents or guardian and the probation officer.[92] However, there is no mention of the modalities of arrest of the child or the means of investigation to be followed. As a consequence, the police officer has no alternative but to apply the normal procedure code applicable to adult offenders. Due to difficulties in locating the probation officer in most of the cases, the police often only manage to contact the parents/guardian. The protection offered by section 87 thus becomes ineffective. However, while considering the position of children, the police have guidelines in the form of Administrative Orders, although these have no binding legal force. Thus, proper protection cannot be guaranteed unless a special procedure is put in place, bearing in mind the best interests of the child and the aim of reintegrating him into the society. This special procedure should not allow the police to resort to the general Criminal Procedure meant for adult criminals. Section 83 of the Child Act 2001 provides that the general provisions of the Act regarding arrest, detention and trial are applicable to those children who come into conflict with the law. However, the details of a special procedure have not yet been fully provided. For example, the maximum time limit on the period of remand is not provided by the Act. Consequently, the provisions of the Criminal Procedure Code are applicable. This was held in *Public Prosecutor v N (A Child)*[93] wherein the absence of a specific remand period under section 84(2) of the Child Act 2001 led to the application of section 117 of Criminal Procedure Code to the juvenile who was detained for four days in police custody.[94]

It should be noted that juvenile offenders are not kept with adult offenders while in police custody. However, important facilities like the provision

---

[92] This information was obtained from consultations with police and social welfare officers.
[93] [2004] 2 MLJ 299.
[94] ibid.

of books, magazines etc, appropriate to their age are lacking. An important issue that requires immediate attention is that of children who have committed minor offences, such as the inability to provide an identity card, who are kept in prison for a significant period while awaiting their trials.[95]

3. Access to justice

Concerns over children in conflict with the law can be explained by the neglect of their legal rights, such as the right to legal counsel, the right to be released from custody as soon as possible and resorting to detention as the last option, during remand and pre-trial periods. Therefore, the officer who deals with the children needs to be aware of, and specialized in, the rights provided in articles 37 and 40 so that the dignity and self-respect of a juvenile offender, as a human being, is not undermined.[96] The law does not explicitly provide for compulsory legal assistance in cases involving children. This results in the child not being informed and advised about his rights, which means he cannot effectively express his wishes, a prerequisite of article 12 of the UNCRC.[97]

4. Separation of detainees

Under the Child Act 2001, the Prison Act 1995[98] and the Prison Regulations 2000,[99] if a child is ordered to be held in prison,[100] the Acts specifically call for the separation of child prisoners from the adult offenders.[101] However, complaints were received by SUHAKAM (Human Rights

---

[95] SUHAKAM, *Report on the Roundtable Consultation*, 2004.

[96] Reporter.

[97] See F Nini Dusuki, 'Implementation of Article 12 of the CRC within Juvenile Justice System in Malaysia' for UNICEF Malaysia, 11–21 July 2006. Input to the Day of General Discussion in Geneva, 15 September 2006 on the theme 'Speak, Participate & Decide—The Child's Right to be Heard' organized by the United Nation's Committee on the Rights of the Child available at www.crin.org/docs/GDD_2006_UNICEF_Malaysia2.doc.

[98] S 49(3) 2001 Act provides that 'A young prisoner shall, so far as local conditions permit, be kept apart from adults under detention.' S 2 defines a 'young prisoner' as one who is below the age of 21 years old.

[99] Rule 6 states: '(1) Prisoners appearing to the Officer in Charge to be a young prisoner, whether male or female, shall be kept apart from adults. (2) A prisoner who declares himself to be more than twenty one years of age but who, in the opinion of the Officer-in-Charge and the Medical Officer, should not, having regard to his character, constitution and antecedents, be classed with adult prisoners, shall be treated as a young prisoner.'

[100] S 91(h) permits a child above the age of 14 to be sentenced to imprisonment for any term which could be awarded by the Sessions Court. S 96 clearly prohibits a child under the age of 14 from being imprisoned for any offence or even be committed to prison in default of payment of a fine, compensation or costs. Further, a child under the age of 14 shall not be sentenced to prison if he can suitably be dealt with in any other way whether by probation, a fine or being sent to a place of detention or an approved school.

[101] S 96(3) 2001 Act.

Commission of Malaysia) claiming that in practice, this requirement is not being strictly followed, as there have been incidents where juveniles are being kept with adult offenders.[102]

Although separate facilities are provided to juveniles for educational purposes, they have to join the adult's facility upon final completion of their education, at a time when they are still vulnerable.

5. Sentences available and the death penalty

If a juvenile is found guilty of an offence that is not punishable by the death penalty, then according to the Child Act 2001, the Magistrate is obliged to refer to any of the disposal orders provided by section 91.[103]

The 2001 Act provides for an indeterminate sentence (which has been applied in a number of cases) for child offenders who are found guilty of offences punishable by the death penalty.[104] This intermediate punishment is not in line with article 37 as a child's fate then remains undecided and uncertain provoking feelings of fear and anxiety. The situation can become even more dangerous if upon reaching the age of 18, he is transferred to an adult offenders detention centre, where inmates are nevertheless under 21. If he has not been released after attaining the age of 21, he then has to join adult offenders. This is even more serious because after this age there are no special seclusions.

6. Procedural matters

Usually, the provision that is often disregarded is the one that requires the parent(s) or guardian to attend court proceedings where a juvenile is involved.[105] Due to the responsibility element, the Act provides that, irrespective of the nature of the offence, the Child Court shall require the parent or guardian to attend proceedings of the court at all stages of the

---

[102] See SUHAKAM, *Report of the Forum on Malaysia's Reservations to the Convention on the Rights of the Child* (2008) 53 available at http://www.suhakam.org.my.

[103] The Court has the power to: admonish and discharge the child; discharge the child upon his executing a bond to be of good behaviour and to comply with such conditions as may be imposed by the Court; order the child to be placed in the care of a relative or other fit and proper person for such period to be specified by the Court and with such conditions as may be imposed by the Court; order the child to pay a fine, compensation or costs; make a probation order under section 98; order the child to be sent to an approved school or a Henry Gurney School; order the child, if a male, to be whipped with not more than 10 strokes of a light cane-(i)within the Court premises and (ii)in the presence, if he desires to be present, of the parent or guardian of the child; impose on the child, if he is aged fourteen years and above and the offence is punishable with imprisonment and subject to subsection 96(2), any term of imprisonment which could be awarded by a Sessions Court.

[104] S 97 2001 Act.

[105] S 88(1) 2001 Act.

case. If they fail to attend they commit an offence and if convicted are liable to a fine of up to RM 5,000 (about £5000) or a period not exceeding two years imprisonment or both.[106] Where the Court finds their attendance unwarranted, this provision is not applied. Thus, it seems that this attendance requirement is subject to exceptions. According to one of the Magistrates in practice, this requirement has too often not been enforced due to the financial situation of the parents. In some cases, the parents were found uninterested because they were of the view that their child deserved punishment for committing an offence. Perhaps the intention behind section 88 is that irresponsible parents share the responsibility of the offence committed by their child, thus encouraging them to become responsible parents, not only as a right (of the child) but also as a duty towards their children.[107]

Under normal circumstances, the prosecution takes between six months to one year. During this trial period, no support is officially offered by any of the State agencies. However, some legal aid has been provided on the defendant's personal initiatives or through the help of some of the NGOs. Similarly, there is no support at the State level for the offender's family. Also, there is no effort of mediation between the victims' family and that of the offenders. One might say a culture of mediation is lacking and therefore mediation is not really provided for by law. Even though child offenders are kept detached from adult offenders and placed in separate cells, prison wardens do at times subject them to brutal and degrading punishments for the smallest faults on their part.[108]

Visits by family and lawyers are allowed without any kind of control. For example, in the above-mentioned 11 murder cases in which the young offenders are prisoners at the pleasure of the ruler, the families are permitted to have routine fortnightly visits.

Judges in Malaysia are of the opinion that the main reasons behind this are the hindrances in the system such as financial problems and the poor implementation of legislation by the State agencies. Strategies for enhancing the rights of juvenile offenders could include educating and training all relevant officers, especially judges who deal with juvenile offenders. International organizations also play an important role in child protection by providing resources and assistance. UNICEF has always been at the forefront by helping and supporting the improvement of the quality of training by providing resources for the publication of manuals and supporting essential research projects. A specific Child Division was set up in 2005 in the Department of Social Welfare in order to deal with child related

---

[106] S 88(2) 2001 Act.
[107] Feedback from Magistrates obtained from roundtable discussions, during the Workshop on Taskforce on Child Law, August 2008.
[108] Reporter.

matters. In order to fulfil the aims of the Child Act 2001 a Coordinating Council for child protection was established. Its responsibilities include advising the Minister of Women, Family and Community Development regarding child protection and coordinating the resources of Government departments working for child protection.[109]

It is important to note at this point that reviewing the effectiveness of the law and identifying the lacunas therein is the responsibility of State agencies and Parliament has virtually no involvement in this procedure.[110]

According to information given by nine juvenile offenders detained in Kajang Prison for the charge of murder, one since 2003 and the others since 2004, the Board of Visiting Justices has only come to visit them twice in the last five and six years respectively.[111] This factual situation is a clear violation of the law, which requires reviewing each case at least once annually. In such circumstances, a request may be made to the Yang Di-Pertuan Agung or the Ruler or the Yang Di-Pertua Negeri asking for the early release or further detention of the child to protect him from the worst case scenario.[112] However, where there is no regular review of the child offender's case, there is no chance that he will be released.

D. Risk Factors

The Malaysian Crime Prevention Foundation conducted a study in 2001 on the reasons and factors that bring a child into conflict with the law.[113] Since then, no up-to-date research study has been carried out on the issue. The factors that were pointed out in 2001 were: psychological and personal reasons (low self-esteem); poor reading skills; lack of religious awareness, and this despite the fact that all religious faiths are free to practice.[114] Strict disciplinary rules implemented by the families at home are also one of the contributory factors along with poverty and poor family and parental relations, lack of cohesion and adaptability. The societal factor also plays a role: experience at school where there is lack of encouragement; influence by peers; the media's impact through films, television series etc and the overall effect of living in neighbourhoods where crime is almost is part of daily life.[115] It can be argued that national laws sufficiently protect children who are in conflict with the law. However, the problem seems to be grounded in insufficient details in the law along with a lack of understanding of its

---

[109] Reporter.   [110] Reporter.

[111] The Rapporteur interviewed the boys in Kajang Prison on 19 June 2009. They were the nine out of 11 boys currently detained at the pleasure of the Ruler.

[112] S 97(4) 2001 Act.

[113] K Kassim, T Hsien Jin, L Gaik Suan and Z Azmi, *Juvenile Delinquency: A Study Report*, (Malaysian Crime Prevention Foundation, 2001).

[114] ibid.   [115] ibid.

rationale and spirit, which means that proper enforcement and implementation has yet to be achieved.[116]

Existing institutions that deal with children who come in conflict with the law generally do not appear child-friendly. The people working in such institutions are not properly trained and are neither sensitive nor responsive to the special needs of children. A natural consequence that follows is an adverse effect on their health, mental, spiritual, moral and overall development. However, some encouraging efforts are being made by some of the organizations such as SUHAKAM who are working to help children generally and child offenders specifically. In order to raise awareness among the community, the Faculty of Law of the University of Malaya has started a course called 'Community Outreach Programme', whereby the students have to develop lesson plans for children in prisons and meet them on a regular basis. Furthermore, in 2006, prisons for children were declared 'Integrated Schools' thus allowing regular teachers teach in them daily. [117]

At present, the Child Protection Unit of the Royal Malaysian Police holds periodical multi-disciplinary trainings on child protection. However, these trainings are not comprehensive as they only target the rights of children, as victims and offenders, but do not consider mental health issues. In addition, there are some prevention and awareness-raising programs regarding juveniles and aimed at educating juvenile offenders, but they are not organized on a national scale because of the limited coordination between the various government departments.[118]

1. Motives of crimes

Using the available data, it was found that in 11 cases of murder at Kajang Prison, the motive of the murders was as follows. In the first case, a Chinese boy murdered the victim on sudden provocation by the latter. The boy carried out multiple stabbings in the kitchen of the victim's house; both were 13 years old. In the second case, eight Malay boys, aged 17, caused the death of one victim in a dormitory fight that went out of control. They used excessive physical assaults as a group whereas the victim was alone and defenceless. In the third case, two Chinese boys killed their victim, with the influence of their girlfriends, by stabbing him to death.

2. Reservations

The primary reason why Malaysia has made a reservation to article 37 of the UNCRC is the presence of the terms 'torture or other cruel, inhuman or degrading treatment or punishment' including that of capital punishment.

---

[116] Reporter.   [117] Reporter.   [118] Reporter.

However, section 91(g) of the 2001 Act provides for the possibility of a child to be given the order of 'whipping with a light cane'. Even though this provision has not often been invoked in practice, its existence in statutory form does not sit well with the clear bar in article 37. It should be pointed out that Malaysia is considering amending the Child Act 2001 with a view to making it consistent with the UNCRC, an amendment urged by the CRC.

V. CONCLUSION

It would be unfair to say that Malaysia offers no protection to child offenders. A recent development in this regard has been made, namely the enactment of the Child Act 2001, a comprehensive piece of legislation that consolidated all the previous laws relating to children and inserted various principles of the UNCRC. The Act replaced the former Juvenile Courts with Courts for Children that have specific jurisdiction over all matters involving children. It also clearly enshrined the principle of separation of child offenders from adult offenders and listed their authorized places of detention according to their age. Finally, it prohibited the application of the death penalty to children and substituted it with a prison sentence.

However, a significant number of problems remain, the most significant being the low age of criminal responsibility (10) coupled with legal uncertainty. This is because Sharia law, which is sometimes applied in criminal matters, does not specify a minimum age of responsibility but rather makes criminal liability contingent on attaining puberty. An important challenge related to a low age of criminal responsibility is that the child may not have attained an adequate level of maturity.[119] Undoubtedly, increasing the age of criminal liability of children would ensure that they are in a better position to understand the implications of their actions. In addition, the lack of specialized and trained personnel dealing with children (police officers, judges, institutional workers) renders the protection of children even less effective. In terms of procedures regarding child offenders, a number of shortcomings exist, the most significant being the absence of compulsory legal assistance to children. Finally, and perhaps most importantly, it should be noted that the best interest principle is not always given primary consideration by the courts, which is in clear violation of the UNCRC.

A study undertaken by the international consultancy firm Child Frontiers regarding the State of Juvenile Justice in Malaysia is underway under the supervision of the Ministry of Women, Family and Community Development. It is hoped that the conclusions of this research will be helpful in

---

[119] Reporter.

safeguarding the rights of juvenile offenders who come into conflict with the law. Furthermore, the Amendment Bill to the Child Act 2001, expected to be enacted soon by Parliament, will hopefully adequately address the legal flaws in the Child Act 2001. Other alternatives that are being explored to deal with children include adopting non-punitive measures such as diversion and restorative justice.[120] These non-punitive measures will enable the child offender to easily rehabilitate and re-integrate into society, and are in line with the child's best interest principle provided for by the UNCRC.

---

[120] Reporter.

CHAPTER 9

*Criminal Law and the Rights of the Child in Northern Nigeria**

I. INTRODUCTION

The Federal Republic of Nigeria is a federal constitutional republic composed of 36 states. The constitutional make-up of Nigeria is complex; it is the most populous nation in Africa and long-standing religious and ethnic tensions are pervasive.[1] Nevertheless, Nigeria has ratified the UN Convention on the Rights of the Child (hereinafter referred to as UNCRC)[2] and the African Charter on the Rights and Welfare of the Child (hereinafter referred to as ACRWC).[3] Moreover, in 2003, Nigeria enacted a law enshrining the key principles of the above Conventions, namely, the Child Rights Act of 2003.[4] This was in addition to the existing Children and Young Persons Law (CYPL) first enacted in 1943.[5] Northern Nigeria consists of 19 states, of which 12 have penal laws enacted under the aegis of Sharia, viz: Bauchi, Borno, Gombe, Jigawa, Kaduna, Kano, Katsina, Kebbi, Niger, Sokoto, Yobe and Zamfara State.

Statistical data on juvenile crimes in Northern Nigeria appears to be lacking. However, as is the case in many contexts, most of the children that come into conflict with the law do so through 'status offences' ranging from lack of parental control, truancy, street trading (particularly for girls), etc. Offences like petty theft and political activity are also common. From the above examples of offences it is almost certain that the underlying factors

* Musa Usman Abubakar Ph.D Candidate, School of Law, University of Warwick. The author wishes to acknowledge the invaluable assistance received from Hayatu Sani of Ministry of Justice for the procurement of unreported cases of the High Court of Zamfara State and also thanks the Registry Staff for their fullest co-operation.
[1] The World Factbook https://www.cia.gov/library/publications/the-world-factbook/geos/ni.html.
[2] Ratified by Nigeria on 19 April 1991. See United Nations Treaty Collections at http://treaties.un.org/Pages/ViewDetails.aspx?src=TREATY&mtdsg_no=IV-11&chapter=4&lang=en accessed 24 June 2009.
[3] Ratified by Nigeria on 23 July 2001, available at http://www.africa-union.org/Official_documents/Treaties_%20Conventions_%20Protocols/List/African%20Charter%20on%20the%20Rights%20and%20Welfare%20of%20the%20Child.pdf, accessed 18 June 2009.
[4] Child's Rights Act 2003 is available at http://www.unicef.org/nigeria/ng_publications_CRA.pdf accessed 5 June 2010.
[5] The CYPL, Cap 22 Laws of Sokoto State of Nigeria 1996 (applicable in Zamfara State) is used as the basis of this research since the law in other states is in *pari materia* with it, although slight variations may exist.'

responsible for these include poverty, influence of peer groups, parental irresponsibility, broken homes, and bullying in schools.[6] It is commonplace to find children roaming the street hawking for their parents while school is in session. Such children easily fall prey to the law enforcement agents in states where law prohibiting street hawking exist, like Kano state.[7] On a judicial visit to a remand home in 2008,[8] it was observed that the vast majority of the inmates were surrendered to the authority by their parents as a result of their being uncontrollable. Some of them avoided school only to join a gang of adult burglars.

Poverty seems to be the main contributing factor to juvenile delinquency. Political activity is another chief means of earning a living for children of poor backgrounds. They are used by politicians in political campaigns and as cheap tools for political thuggery and hooliganism. Many states in Northern Nigeria have prohibited participation of children in political activities, but such laws are observed more in breach than in compliance.[9] Influence of peer group is easily discerned in offences like armed robbery as in the case of *Commissioner of Police V Sulaiman A Shanono and Others.*[10]

II. NATIONAL LEGAL FRAMEWORK

Nigeria is a conglomeration of the Northern and Southern Protectorates created in 1914 through obtaining independence from Britain in 1960. It is a federal State and as a result there exists both federal and State legislation. Due to the differences among states and varying degrees of their independence, politically, culturally and economically, different laws and circumstances apply to different states, causing a great degree of disparity.

With regard to legislation concerning juvenile offenders specifically, every Nigerian state has a Children and Young Persons Law (CYPL) applicable within its jurisdiction. The law was first enacted in 1943 by the then British Colonial Authority and made applicable throughout Nigeria as the major legislation relating to children in 1958.[11] In most Northern states,

---

[6] Nigeria: 3rd and 4th Periodic Reports available at http://www2.ohchr.org/english/bodies/crc/crcs54.htm accessed 2 May 2010.

[7] Kano State Petty Trading (Prohibition of Female Juveniles) Edict, Cap.109, Laws of Kano State, 1991 (hereinafter referred to as Kano Petty Trading Law).

[8] The Chief Judge of Zamfara State, Hon Justice Kulu Aliyu went on routine prison visits including remands homes and approved institutions throughout the state and the author was on the entourage.

[9] See generally Part VIII CYPL of Sokoto State.

[10] (2002) NNLR 574 (This was an armed robbery case in which all the four accused were juveniles below the age of 16 years).

[11] I Okagbue, 'Children in Conflict with the Law: The Nigerian Experience' Cap.21 Laws of Northern Nigeria 1963 at http://www.unicef-irc.org/portfolios/documents/487_nigeria.htm accessed 18 June 2009.

the last amendment to the CYPL was in 1991.[12] It is important to note that the CYPL primarily deals with procedures and it aims to be 'a law to make provision for the welfare of juveniles and the treatment of young offenders and to prohibit the participation by juveniles in political activities.' It is important to note that the rights of children enshrined in the CYPL are not couched in mandatory terms. For example, section 5 of the CYPL reads, 'It shall be the duty of all police officers and prison officers to make arrangements for preventing, *so far as practicable* (emphasis added), a juvenile while in custody from associating with an adult charged with or convicted of an offence.' Indeed, this limits the strength of the law itself. The Penal Codes of the Northern States, both secular and religious, contain the substantive provisions applicable to juvenile offenders.

More recently, in 2003 the Nigerian Child's Rights Act (CRA 2003) was passed into law by the National Assembly and Child's Rights Laws were subsequently passed in 18 out of 36 states assemblies.[13]

The CRA may be seen as an agglomeration of many international conventions and appears to try to amend and consolidate all Nigerian legislation relating to children in terms of their rights[14] and corresponding duties of obedience and respect by the state and the public necessary for their protection.[15]

Where a juvenile comes into conflict with law specifically, the Act lays down procedures for dealing with child offenders from the point of arrest and investigation, to adjudication.[16] The Act has been the most recent and significant reform to juvenile protection in Nigeria. However, it faces many challenges, including questions over compatibility with local cultures and religious beliefs. It combines both personal and public law issues which cast doubt to the constitutionality of some of its provisions, particularly those relating to personal laws. There also remain questions over the jurisdiction of family courts as the Act ousted the constitutional jurisdiction of Customary and Sharia Courts of Appeal and vested it in family courts established under the Act.[17] These jurisdictional inconsistencies call into question the true applicability of the Act and the strength of its enforcement within the legal system.

---

[12] See for instance Cap. 22 Laws of Sokoto State of Nigeria 1996 applicable in Zamfara State.

[13] The states are Ogun, Imo, Ebonyi, Anambra, Ekiti, Rivers, Taraba, Plateau, Nassarawa, Jigawa, Kwara, Edo, Bayelsa, Lagos, Oyo, Osun, Ondo and Abia States, see Nigeria (2010):3rd and 4th Periodic Reports p 128 available at http://www2.ohchr.org/english/bodies/crc/crcs54.htm accessed 2 May 2010.

[14] Ss 3–18 of the CRA.   [15] ibid s 19.

[16] ibid Part XX (s 204–246).

[17] MU Abubakar, 'Child's Rights Act: Critical Analysis from the Islamic Perspective'a paper presented at the 7th Annual National Scientific Conference of Islamic Medical Association of Nigeria at Mambayya House, Kano Nigeria, 8–10 July 2005, available at www.gamji.com.

III. THE INTERNATIONAL FRAMEWORK

As stated earlier above, Nigeria is a signatory to a number of important international conventions affecting the rights of the child, including the UNCRC and the ACRWC. The ACRWC is important in reinforcing the protection of juveniles. For example, it completely prohibits the press and public from attending any trial proceedings involving children.[18] It also discourages the imprisonment of expectant or suckling mothers and provides that non-custodial measures should always be prioritized.[19]

Where an international convention is ratified by the Federal government, Section 12 of the 1999 Constitution of the Federal Republic of Nigeria provides for the domestication procedures of international treaties which largely requires enactment into law by the National Assembly, State Assemblies and in exceptional cases, the National Assembly alone.[20]

IV. DOMESTIC LEGISLATION ON THE PROTECTION OF THE RIGHTS OF THE CHILD IN CRIMINAL LAW

A. The Age of Criminal Liability: the Minimum and the Upper Age Limit

Currently, the age of criminal liability in the Northern states of Nigeria largely depends on which Code the juvenile is being prosecuted under—that is either the Penal Code[21] (PC) or the Sharia Penal Code (SPC).[22]

1. Penal Code

Section 50 of the Penal Code sets the minimum age of criminal liability at seven years.[23] For a child between the age of seven and 12 years, criminal liability applies if it is proved that he has attained sufficient maturity of understanding the nature and consequences of the act in question.[24] Juveniles who have attained the age of 12 years but are below the age of 18

---

[18] ACRWC art 17(2)(d).

[19] ibid art 30.

[20] MU Abubakar, 'Unravelling the Knotty Areas in the Child's Rights Act 2003' paper presented at a One-Day Interactive Session on Child's Rights Act 2003, organized by Zamfara State Ministry of Justice, Gusau, 12 May 2005 available at www.gamji.com.

[21] The Penal Code of Sokoto State Cap. 104 Laws of Sokoto State of Nigeria, 1996 (applicable in Zamfara State).

[22] Zamfara State Sharia Penal Code Law No 5 of 2005 (also known as Harmonised Sharia Penal Code) is used in this research. This is because it is accessible via internet at http://www.sharia-in-africa.net/media/publications/sharia-implementation-in-northern-nigeria/vol_4_4_chapter_4_part_III.pdf?wb_session_id=233572382b1bd517663d60f1428d7 05c accessed 27 June 2009.

[23] ibid s 72(a).

[24] ibid.

years are fully responsible for criminal acts and omissions. However such a child will not be processed within the conventional criminal justice but under the juvenile justice procedure provided in the Children and Young Persons Law (CYPL). The CYPL defines a child as person below the age of 14 years, and young person as one who has attained 14 years of age but below 18 years.[25]

2. Sharia Penal Code

Section 72 of the Sharia Penal Code also maintains seven years as the lower limit of child's criminal liability, while the upper limit is the biological age of puberty *(takleef)*.[26]

However in cases of *hudood* and *qisas*, only a child who attains puberty is liable.[27] In other words, a child of seven years but below the age of *takleef* may be held liable for simple offences punishable with *tazeer*.

The combined effects of the decisions of the Nigerian Supreme Court in *Modupe v the State*[28] and *State V Nwabueze*[29] demonstrate that a child of seven is not criminally responsible for any act. A person under the age of 12 years is equally not criminally responsible unless it is proved that at the time of the doing the act or omission he had the capacity to know he ought not to do the act or make the omission in question. As may be observed from the foregoing, although the apex court had given judicial certification to the provisions of the respective penal codes, there is still a problem with the law in that it does not cover a person aged 14, or aged 17 and below 18 years. Such a person may still be imprisoned.

In applying and interpreting age of criminal responsibility, courts in Northern Nigeria are guided by the provisions of the procedural codes governing their proceedings. To that end, sections 9 CYPL, 243A Criminal Procedure Code (CPC) and 210 Sharia Criminal Procedure Code are applicable.

These laws give trial courts wider latitude to use different methods in the determination of age of a juvenile. It may take the form of physical assessment by a presiding judge; calling an expert witness like a medical doctor or even a non-expert. In the case of *R v Oladimeji* [30] the West African Court of Appeal had ruled that where the age of an accused person is at issue, the court may allow the production of birth certificates or a certificate signed by a government medical officer.

Although the UNCRC does not provide the minimum age of criminal responsibility, the United Nations Committee on the Rights of the Child

---

[25] CYPLs 2.
[26] SPC s 64 (1).
[27] ibid s 72 (b).
[28] (1988) 4 NWLR part 130.
[29] (1980) 1 NCR 41.
[30] *R v Oladimeji* (1964) NMLR 31.

(CRC) considered seven years as too low a minimum age and recommended 12 years with the upper limit being 18 years.[31] In view of this recommendation, both the Penal Code and Sharia Penal Code can be said to be in violation of the UNCRC, since in both Codes seven years in the age of criminal responsibility. Similarly, the CRA 2003, a consolidating and harmonizing legislation, is only partly compliant for it pegs the age of majority at 18 but is silent on the minimum age.[32] The issue of minimum age should not have escaped the scrutiny of the drafters. Notably, it is argued that the non-prescription of minimum age is equally a violation of the UNCRC.[33] It is therefore suggested that for better protection of juveniles, a minimum age be enhanced.

B. Deprivation of Liberty

One common feature of the applicable laws in Northern Nigeria is that they all frowned upon the incarceration of children, even though the protection does not apply against all categories of children. Regard is always given to the nature of the offence a juvenile is alleged to have committed and the age of the child. Furthermore, the laws are devoid of uniformity in that respect. For instance, the CYPL provides that any person below the age of 14 is not to be imprisoned.[34] Where a juvenile offender is aged 14 and older, he may only be imprisoned if no other methods would be effective in dealing with him.[35] His detention is only to be ordered when the offence is of serious nature like capital cases, in which case he is to be detained in a remand home.[36] Similarly, under the Sharia Penal Code, the cover extends to the children below the age of 15 years.[37] Indeed, these provisions appear to be strictly followed, as evidenced in the case of *State V Shehu Mohammed*.[38] In this case the convicted juvenile aged 12 was brought under the Penal Code. The trial judge sentenced him to a fine of 10,000 Naira (about US$66) instead of a prison term for homicide. In the judgement, Hon Justice M L Garba, the Chief Judge of Zamfara State (as he then was) stated that he took into consideration the age of the offender, the fact that it as a

---

[31] See General comment no 10 (Children's Rights in Juvenile Justice) of the Committee on CRC released February 2007, available at http://www2.ohchr.org/english/bodies/crc/docs/CRC.C.GC.10.pdf, accessed 11 August 2009.

[32] CRA s 227.

[33] GO Odongo, 'The Impact of International law on Children's Rights on Juvenile Justice Law Reform in the African Context' in J Sloth-Neilsen (ed), *Children's Rights in Africa: A Legal Perspective* (Ashgate Publishing Limited, England, 2008) 150.

[34] CYPL s 12(1).

[35] ibid s 12(3).

[36] ibid s 13.

[37] SPC s 94.

[38] ZMS/GS/3c/2000 (unreported).

first offence, and the circumstances that led to the murder, which was a sudden fight. However, while the judge's consideration of the age of the juvenile offender is important, his decision demonstrates a lack of perhaps more effective measures which could be used in such circumstances to both rehabilitate and reform the juvenile offender whilst ensuring justice and public safety.

Despite the above, the CYPL does provide a number of measures available to a High Court, Magistrate, or Sharia Court judge in cases involving a juvenile. Under these alternative measures a judge may:

(a) dismiss the charge;
(b) discharge the offender upon his entering into a recognizance;
(c) proceed under the provisions of the Probation of Offenders Law;
(d) commit the offender by mandate to the care of a fit person;
(e) commit the offender by mandate to an approved institution;
(f) order the offender to be caned;
(g) proceed under the provision of section 11;
(h) commit the offender to custody in a place of detention provided under this Law for a period not exceeding six months;
(i) if the offender is a young person, order him to be imprisoned, subject nevertheless to the provisions of subsections (2) and (3) of section 12;
(j) deal with the matter in any other manner in which it may be legally dealt with.[39]

Another important provision under the applicable laws is the substitution of capital punishment in favour of detention for the convicted juveniles. Under the secular-based Penal Code, the death sentence is not to be passed on a person under the age of 17.[40] Instead, the offender is to be detained at the Governor's pleasure in any place the Governor may direct.[41] Unfortunately, as juvenile cases are not regularly reviewed, it is possible that he may remain in detention for longer than necessary or beneficial. Section 13 of the CYPL lends support to the above provisions. It provides thus:

Notwithstanding anything to the contrary in this Law or in any other law, where a juvenile is found guilty of an attempt to murder or of manslaughter, or of wounding with intent to do grievous bodily harm the court may order the offender to be detained for such period as may be specified in the order, and where such an order is made the juvenile shall during that period be liable to be detained in such a place and in such a condition as the Commissioner may direct, and whilst so detained shall be deemed to be in legal custody.

[39] ZMS/GS/3c/2000 (unreported).   [40] CPC s 270.   [41] ibid ss 272(1) and 303.

That being the case, by necessary implication, a child of seven and above, if found guilty of any such offences, may be detained at the Governor's pleasure since the term 'juvenile' under the CYPL includes children and 'young persons.'[42]

Conversely, the SCPC allows a presiding Sharia judge to use other alternative measures provided in section 11 of the CYPL itemised above.[43] It may be argued that the Sharia Codes appear to be more child-friendly, considering the wide discretion they give to a judge. It is however one thing to have such protection in a black letter law, and quite another to see it in practice.

The combined effect of sections 64(1), 72(a), 94 and 95 of the Sharia Penal Code and Section 238 and 239 of the Sharia Criminal Procedure Code (SCPC) is that a person below the age of 18 years is not to be imprisoned. Perhaps the fact that a Sharia Court judge has wider latitude to deal with a juvenile either under the CYPL or the Sharia Codes that allow payment of *diyah* and other costs in monetary terms explains why not a single child was detained in prison on the orders of the Sharia Court judge as per the 2005–2006 and 2007 reports of the National Human Rights Commission of Nigeria.[44]

It is interesting to note that during the 2007 prison audit exercise conducted by the National Human Rights Commission, it was discovered that in all the Northern states of Nigeria only one child inmate was found in Maiduguri Prison of Borno State although details of his case were not provided.[45] About six other children were found with their mothers in various prisons across the region.[46] There appears to be improvement in child protection given that in a similar exercise conducted before the Commission recorded more children detained in prisons for less serious crimes like wandering and petty theft.[47]

1. *Pre-trial arrest and detention*

Under the CYPL, any juvenile who is under 16 years is entitled to pre-trial

---

[42] CYPLs.2.

[43] SCPC s239.

[44] National Human Rights Commission (2007) The State of Human Rights in Nigeria 2005–2006 Report, ch 4, available at http://nigeriarights.gov.ng/images/articles/States%20of%20Human%20Rights%20Report%20in%20Nigeria%202005-2006.pdf and A report on the State of Human Rights in Nigeria 2007, Chapter 4 available at http://nigeriarights.gov.ng/images/articles/State%20of%20Human%20Rights%20Report%20in%20Nigeria%202007.pdf, accessed 30 April 2010.

[45] See National Human Rights Commission Nigeria, 2007 NHRC Prison Report at www.nigeriarights.gov.ng 132, accessed25/06/2009.

[46] ibid.

[47] NRHC (2007) State of Human Rights in Nigeria 2005–2006, National Human Rights Commission, Abuja Nigeria available at www.nigeriarights.org.ng accessed 14 July 2009.

bail at the point of arrest by the police, if he cannot be taken to court immediately. The pre-trial bail could be granted with or without a guarantee.[48] The juvenile's right to personal liberty is only curtailed where he is charged with homicide or other grave crimes like armed robbery, or if it is feared that the juvenile's release is not in his best interest or that it would defeat the ends of justice.[49]

A juvenile not granted bail will be entitled to be detained in a remand home by the police officer before he is taken to court.[50] The juvenile will only be treated otherwise where it is impracticable to do so; or he is of unruly or depraved behaviour; or his mental or physical state suggest that it is not advisable to detain him in a remand home.[51] In this case he may be detained in an approved institution, prison, police station or any other suitable place or under the care of any person.[52] The same applies in cases where there is no remand home.[53]

C. The Conditions of Detention

1. Juvenile detention centres

The laws establishing juvenile detention centres are meant to prepare juveniles for future reintegration in their respective communities. As an example, Regulation 4 made under section 4 of the Borstal Institutions and Remand Centres Act of 1962 (BIRCA)[54] provides that the objective of 'borstal training shall be to bring to bear every good influence, which may establish in the inmates the will to lead a good and useful life on release, and fit them to do so by the fullest possible development of their character, capacities and sense of personal responsibility.' However, in reality, the centres are marred by poor management, overpopulation and inadequate facilities.[55] For example, the Kaduna Borstal institution was originally established to house 200 juveniles and young persons but is now housing over 600 inmates.[56] This scenario is not conducive for training and rehabilitation. Moreover, at present, there are only three borstal institutions servicing the whole Nigerian Federation in Abeokuta, Ilorin and Kaduna state and of these only the Borstal Institution at Kakuri,

---

[48] CYPL s 3.
[49] ibid.
[50] ibid ss 4(1) and 14(3).
[51] ibid s 4(1)a-c.
[52] ibid ss 7(1) (ii) and 14(4).
[53] ibid.
[54] (BIRCA—Cap. B 11 LFN, 2004).
[55] CRC(2005a) Concluding Observations: Nigeria, p 22 available at http://www.unhchr.ch/tbs/doc.nsf/898586b1dc7b4043c1256a450044f331/b06804b33ec4eadbc1257018002c82db/$FILE/G0541053.pdf accessed 4 May 2010.
[56] F Moneke (2008) 'Juvenile Justice in Nigeria Dilemma of a Criminal Justice System' available at www.thenationonlineng.com/dynamicpage.asp?id=70910.

Kaduna state is fully functional,[57] and they are managed by the Nigerian Prisons Service.[58]

It is perhaps because of the lack of political will to provide institutional facilities at the federal level that Katsina state established a reformative centre to rehabilitate juveniles engaged in drug use and other anti-social acts. In 2007, a visit was paid to the centre as part of the training workshop organized by League of Democratic Women (LEAD) in collaboration with UNICEF Kaduna Zone for stakeholders in juvenile justice. The centre was running fully operational religion classes as well as providing vocational training in trades like woodwork/carpentry, metal work, sewing and embroidery, etc. The centre was well-staffed and facilities relatively suffi-cient for the number of inmates present then. However, as a state institu-tion it only caters for the juveniles within Katsina state. Notwithstanding this the centre is the first of its kind in Northern Nigeria, and it is hoped that other states provide similar facilities for better rehabilitation and rein-tegration of juveniles.

Lending credence to the above, in an interactive meeting with the members of the CRC in 2005, the Nigerian delegation had, in response to the question whether any programme was designed to reduce the estimated 6000 children in detention centres across the country, decried the inade-quate number of detention centres and absence of facilities. However, the delegation have noted some positive features of the current system:

[C]hildren in conflict with the law were separated from children in need of care and assistance, who were not regarded as offenders. Imprisonment of children was discouraged and was only a last resort. Children were incarcerated in states that had no juvenile detention facil-ities. A plan of action for juvenile justice and administration recom-mended that every state government should open at least one remand centre for children. Since prisons were already overcrowded, it was important to ensure that children were not incarcerated. A child could be transferred from a state that had no juvenile detention facility to one that did. Another problem was that information on the age of incarcerated children was often incorrect. Sometimes a remand warrant stated that a detainee was 18 or 19 years of age, while in reality the person in ques-tion was only 16. In order to address that problem, prison superinten-dents had been encouraged to request a court investigation if they had doubts about a child's age. That had been done in a number of cases, and the children had subsequently been released.[59]

---

[57] ibid, accessed 28 July 2009.   [58] ibid.
[59] CRC (2005b) Summary Record of the 1022nd Meeting: Nigeria, available at http://www.unhchr.ch/tbs/doc.nsf/(Symbol)/CRC.C.SR.1022.En?OpenDocument, accessed 4 May 2010.

In yet another forum, the Working Group on Universal Periodic Review of Human Rights Council reviewed the Nigerian report on human rights in general on 9 February 2009. It was noted that congestion in the Nigerian prison system was one of the greatest obstacles to the required conditions of detention. Indeed, the delegation acknowledged the inadequacy of juvenile detention centres and expressed the government determination to increase the number of institutions.[60]

2. *Separation of Detainees*

The CYPL mandates police officers and prison officers to ensure separation between juvenile and adult offenders.[61] This is also required where juveniles below the age of 16 years are transported to and from the court, and while awaiting hearing and even after hearing.[62] Such a juvenile may only be allowed to be in contact with adult offenders if he is charged together with them.[63] However, this provision does not apply to juvenile offenders who are aged 16 and over and this is problematic in the context of the UNCRC and other international instruments. Another major weakness of the current system is the lack of separation between juveniles guilty of 'status' offences and those imprisoned for violent criminal activity.[64]

3. *Access to family*

The law does not provide the right to maintain contact with families. However, from the interviews conducted with some stakeholders, it is clear that juveniles do have contact with their lawyers and relatives but not on a regular basis. Families and lawyers are allowed to visit their clients or wards while in prisons and other detention centres particularly at the initial stage of the child's arrest.[65] Lack of regular family visits to a detained juvenile will no doubt hamper his smooth re-integration into the wider society. Little wonder the CRA 2003 creates such a right and even mandates the state to defray the expenses incurred by a parent in the course of such visit.[66] It is therefore submitted that it is high time such provision is enacted in the

---

[60] See Report of the Working Group on the Universal Periodic Review on Nigeria at http://www2.ohchr.org/english/bodies/hrcouncil/11session/reports.htm, accessed 4 May 2010.
[61] CYPL s 5.   [62] ibid s 6 (1).   [63] ibid.
[64] Our visit to remand home reveals that, in the absence of other rehabilitation centres, juveniles charged with serious crimes co-existed with other children surrendered to the social welfare department owing to the uncontrollability by their parents, etc.
[65] Amnesty International, 'Killing at Will: Extrajudicial Execution and other Unlawful Killings by the Police in Nigeria' (2009) 21 available at http://www.amnesty.org/en/library/asset/AFR44/038/2009/en/f09b1c15-77b4-40aa-a608-b3b01bde0fc5/afr440382009en.pdf accessed 4 May 2010.
[66] CRA s 56 and item 15 and 16 of the Seventh Schedule to the CRA.

Northern states entitling a juvenile to family visits at least once in a month as that would facilitate his rehabilitation and reintegration. It would also reduce the rate of children being surrendered by the parents on grounds of their being uncontrollable, since some parents do so to simply distance themselves from the child's care and rely on the state to deal with them.

4. Generally applicable prisoner rights

Prisons Act, Cap 366, LFN 1990 governs the rights of prisoners and rights accorded by the Act apply equally to juveniles who are imprisoned although the latter have additional rights in view of their vulnerability and maturity. These rights are practically difficult to enforce as reports by international organizations demonstrate that in reality, prisoners and juveniles live in very terrible conditions. Apart from the inadequate food and water supply, they lack good medical care, bedding, etc. It is indeed not only the denial of such basic necessities, but other abuses like verbal and physical assaults which are routinely meted out to inmates, juveniles included.[67]

V. PROCEDURAL RIGHTS

A. Length of Prosecution Process

The prosecution process depends largely on the enormity of the case and availability of resources. In many areas where there is no specially designated juvenile court, a high court judge will hear the case in a conventional court and as a result, juvenile cases last longer than they ought to. As an example, the case of *State V Adamu Musa*[68] was filed in 2004, prosecution started on 1 March 2005 and judgement delivered on 9 August 2006. Shockingly, the juvenile had been in detention since 2001.

B. Fair Trial

Fair trial is a constitutional right guaranteed under the Nigerian constitution. Section 36 states:

In the determination of his civil rights and obligations, including any question or determination by or against any government or authority, a

---

[67] Amnesty International 'Nigeria: Prisoners' Rights Systematically Flouted' (2008) at http://www.amnesty.org/en/library/asset/AFR44/001/2008/en/4bd14275-e494-11dc-aaf9-5f04e2143f64/afr440012008eng.pdf, accessed 31 July 2009.
[68] ZMS/GS/1c/2004 (unreported).

person shall be entitled to a fair hearing within a reasonable time by a court or other tribunal established by law and constituted in such manner as to secure its independence and impartiality.

The Constitution further empowers the exclusion of public from trial of a person who is under the age of 18 years for their welfare.[69] A juvenile offender is entitled to the presumption of innocence, to defend himself in person or by a legal practitioner of his own choice. He must be informed of the nature of the charge against him in the language he understands, together with free right to an interpreter.[70] The non-observance of the above provisions entitles a juvenile to appeal against a verdict of conviction as it is a fundamental and non-derogable right.

C. Access to Justice

To ensure access to justice, a right to legal representation is available to everybody including children.[71] The Constitution does not however provide for free legal services to juveniles, and it is therefore not uncommon to find children helplessly defending themselves in person with no legal representation.[72]

It is noteworthy that the Criminal Procedure Code of Northern Nigeria mandates the court to assign counsel to represent persons accused of a capital offence.[73] For non-capital cases, an accused may either proceed with it personally or employ the services of a lawyer. More recently, the CRA specified that juveniles are entitled to free legal services, [74] but the right may not be as effective in practice it seems difficult to afford such services to juveniles given the lack of sufficient manpower under the Legal Aid Council.

D. Special Courts and Procedures

1. Nigerian Child's Rights Act

As a pacesetting legislation, the CRA 2003 provides a number of provisions regarding the procedural rights of alleged juvenile offenders.[75] The Act proscribes imposition or even recording a sentence of death penalty against a child who is below the age of 18.[76] He shall not be imprisoned or be subjected to corporal punishment.[77] A child is not to be subjected to the conventional criminal justice system, but to a special procedure of child

---

[69] Nigerian Constitution s 36(4) (a).   [70] ibid.
[71] ibid s 36(6).
[72] NHRC (2007) State of Human Rights in Nigeria 2005–2006 Report 47.
[73] CPC s 319.   [74] CRA s 155.
[75] ibid Part XX (S 204–246).   [76] ibid s 221(1) (a).
[77] ibid s 221(1) (b).

justice administration under the Act.[78] The Act establishes the special Family Courts at Magistrate and High Court levels[79] granting exclusive jurisdiction in any matter relating to children as specified in the Act.[80] It also further empowers Magistrate Courts to impose the maximum fine or imprisonment for offences covered by part III of the Act.[81]

At all levels the court has three members, including the judge and two other members, at least one of whom having been trained in child psychology.[82] At the magistrate level, a further requirement of a woman is provided.[83] The presence of a woman may provide the necessary atmosphere for the juvenile to feel at ease. Provision is to be made for the judicial officers and other court personnel to have professional training in areas like sociology and behavioural sciences through in-service, refresher courses and other modes of education.[84]

To complement the institutional framework at the juridical level, a Specialised Children Police Unit is also established[85] to be manned by highly trained police officers in the prevention, control, apprehension and investigation of child offences.[86] It empowers the police to employ a series of diversion methods at the point of apprehension of a child without recourse to formal trial. They are also to encourage amicable resolution of non-serious cases. The police investigation and court proceedings shall only be used as a last resort.[87]

The downside of the CRA 2003 as far as child justice regime is concerned lies in its lack of a prescription for the minimum age of criminal liability. The implication of this serious lapse is enormous, in that it gives the impression that a child of any age can be criminal responsible. This apparently leaves children in a more difficult situation. In this way, the pre-existing laws offer better protection in that at least for declaring children below seven years as *doli incapax,* although by the standard set by the CRC, seven years is below the international threshold of 12 years.

2. Children and Young Persons Law (CYPL)

Special procedure as contained in the Children and Young Persons Law (CYPL) exist for dealing with juveniles in conflict with the law in all the Northern States of Nigeria. However the CYPL of most states do not provide for juvenile courts.[88]

---

[78] ibid s 204.   [79] ibid s 149.   [80] ibid s 162.
[81] ibid s 39.   [82] ibid s 152 and 153.   [83] ibid s 153(3) (b).
[84] ibid ss 154 and 206.   [85] ibid s 207.   [86] ibid.
[87] ibid s 209.
[88] See for example The Children and Young Persons Law, Cap.22 Laws of Sokoto State of Nigeria 1996.

The CYPL among other things empowers a presiding judge to restrict the public from accessing the court. Only selected individuals including legal representatives, members and officers of the court, person concerned with the case (complainant, parent and guardian) and selected members of the press are allowed.[89] Despite this, it is an offence punishable by fine to expose the identity of a juvenile in a way that he can easily be identifiable without the leave of the court.[90] However, it may be argued that this penalty of 100 Naira (40 pence)[91] is insufficient in ensuring the adequate protection of the juvenile's privacy. Moreover, only a juvenile below the age of 16 years enjoys these rights.[92] The identity of any person of 16 years can be disclosed and his case opened to the general public even though by the CYPL, he is to be processed through a special procedure. It is difficult to reconcile the meaning of a juvenile given under this law covering persons below the age of 18 years and the sub-classes created under it privileging one class and denying the other.

3. The Kano state Juvenile Court

The state of Kano is one of the few known states to have established a Juvenile Court. The Juvenile Court is composed of five members including a Magistrate not below the rank of Magistrate Grade One, a Retired Police Officer not below the rank of Assistant Superintendent of Police, a Senior Social Welfare Officer, an Islamic Scholar and an elderly woman.[93] In the absence of a special court, the situation becomes less consistent. The presiding judge of a High court, Magistrate or Sharia Court simply doubles as a juvenile court judge. A juvenile is processed in the same court room as adults, albeit under a special procedure as provided in the CYPL.

4. Discrimination between boys and girls

There appears to be no discrimination on grounds of sex in determining the age of criminal responsibility. Sections 50 of the Penal Code and Section 2 of the Children and Young Persons Law all employ an age-based criterion. Section 64 of the Sharia Penal Code on the other hand attaches more weight to biological age (*takleef*) than chronogical age. Careful analysis reveals that female juveniles are more likely to be caught in the web of the Sharia Penal Code than their male counterparts since they reach the age of puberty earlier.[94] There are also instances where laws are

---

[89] CYPL s 6(2).   [90] ibid s 6(3).   [91] ibid s 6(4).
[92] ibid s 6(2).   [93] See Kano State Juvenile Court Edict, 1987.
[94] Family Doctor, 'Puberty: What to Expect When your Child goes through Puberty' http://familydoctor.org/online/famdocen/home/children/parents/parents-teens/445.html accessed 5 May 2010.

created specifically targeting a single gender, for instance, the Kano State Petty Trading (Prohibition of Female Juveniles) Edict which only prohibits female juveniles under the age of 16 years from hawking goods, setting up stalls, table, or kiosks for the display of goods.[95] A cursory look at this law may reveal that it was meant to protect the girls against abuses by adults, as they are more vulnerable than boys.

VI. THE DEATH PENALTY

Under the laws operational in Northern Nigeria, the death penalty is not imposed upon any person below the age of 17 years under the Criminal Procedure Code.[96] By necessary implication, a person who is 17 years old at the time of commission of a capital crime is liable for the death penalty as he is outside the protected categories. Similarly, the Sharia Criminal Procedure Code does not allow the imposition of *hudood* and *qisas* on a person below the age of puberty *(takleef)*.[97] *Takleef* is a stage in life characterized by biological changes on a person called a *mukallaf*—that is, a person who is both pubescent and sane thus is accountable for all his deeds. A person who has attained this status is able and required to perform all Islamic religious duties. The problematic nature of this biologically-based criteria lies in the fact that a person may fall foul of the law even though, in chronological terms, they are below the age of 18. In this way, a death sentence may be imposed on them notwithstanding the fact that he is still a child according to the international standards. Perhaps, the Sharia Penal Code sought to address this anomaly when it allowed a court a discretion to exclude persons below the age of 18 from the death penalty by employing other alternative sentences outside those provided for the offence.[98] Cross-reference is made in the Code directing a presiding Sharia judge to treat the child as provided under the section 11 of CYPL, although the victims may claim *diyah* (blood money) in the case of *qisas*.[99] Reference to section 11 of the CYPL means that the Sharia law favours a non-custodial sentence, since the section allows the imposition of fines, damages, costs and giving security for the good behaviour of the juvenile.

What is not clear is whether such discretion is exercisable where the person convicted of a *hudood* or *qisas* offence attained the age of *takleef* but is still under 18. Unfortunately there is no judicial pronouncement on the issue, owing to a number of factors including the tendency for most

---

[95] Cap109 Laws of Kano State of Nigeria, 1991.
[96] CPC s 270.
[97] SCPC s 238.
[98] SPC s 95.
[99] ibid s 239 (1).

capital offences to be channelled through the secular courts,[100] the age and operation of the new Sharia System which recommenced in 1999, and the constitutional problem in relation to criminal case flow from the lower Sharia Court through the Sharia Court of Appeal to the Court of Appeal at the national level. Although criminal appeal jurisdiction is conferred on the Sharia Court of Appeal at the state level, there is no corresponding provision in the Constitution that allows the Court of Appeal to entertain a criminal appeal from the Sharia Court of Appeal.[101]

Most crimes carrying the death penalty such as armed robbery, culpable homicide and rape are mostly processed in the High Court because of its unlimited jurisdiction.[102] Besides, some legislation such as the Robbery and Firearms (Special Provisions) Act confers jurisdiction exclusively to the High Court.[103] The Act being national legislation does not recognize Sharia or customary courts and supersedes state laws. Of course, the Upper Sharia Court has concurrent jurisdiction with the High Court in cases carrying death penalty under the Sharia dispensation such as adultery, homicide, rape, etc.[104] In all these instances however, the death penalty may not be meted on a child.

In determining the sentence to be imposed, it is the age at the time of the commission of the offence that is relevant. In the case of *Modupe v the State*[105] the Supreme Court held that it was wrong of the trial court to sentence a juvenile to death or even to pronounce the sentence once it appears on the record that at the time of the commission of the murder the juvenile was under 17.

The above assessment applies under the Sharia Penal system since the Sharia Procedure Code also mandates a Sharia Court judge to take into consideration the time of commission of the offence and not the time of conviction.[106] Notwithstanding the problem posed by age of *takleef*, it seems that considerable discretion has been given to a judge under section 95(1) of the Sharia Penal Code to substitute any sentence provided where the accused in question is under 18 with either 'confinement in a reformatory home for a period not exceeding one year,' or 'caning which may

---

[100] See for example the recent case of culpable homicide involving a juvenile accused Case No. Gs/201c/09 *Police v Abdulkadir Bello* is instructive. The accused was arraigned before the Chief Magistrate Court, Gusau by the Police where the applicable law is the secular Penal Code.

[101] MU Abubakar, 'Gender and Islamic Criminal Law in Northern Nigeria' (2004) LLM Dissertation submitted to the School of Law, University of Warwick, United Kingdom in partial fulfilment of the requirement for the award of Degree of Master of Laws in Law in Development, 30.

[102] Nigerian Constitution s 272 (1).

[103] S 9 Cap R11, Laws of the Federeation of Nigeria, 2004.

[104] SPC ss 198, 126 and 128 respectively.

[105] (1988) 4 NWLR part 130

[106] SPC s 239.

extend to twenty lashes, or with fine or with both.' The provision of section of section 95 is far reaching enough to extend to persons under the age of 18. This is in contradiction to the 17 years provided under the Criminal Procedure Code. It also demonstrates that the protection provided for children under the Sharia penal system conforms to the UNCRC at least on this point, as observed in the Second Country Periodic Report 2005 of Nigeria.[107]

VII. APPLICABLE LAWS

In light of the above, one must questions whether or not the applicable laws in Northern Nigeria offer adequate protection to the children who come in conflict with the law and how the inadequate protection violates provisions of the UNCRC and the other human rights conventions. In answering these questions the relevant provisions of the UNCRC and other international instruments will have to be juxtaposed with the CYPL and other relevant legislation:

1. Under the UNCRC, a child is a person who has not attained the age of 18 years unless otherwise provided under the child's national law. The CYPL creates two classes of juveniles viz; children as persons under the age of 14 years and young persons as those who attained the age of 14 but below 18 years.

2. The Criminal Procedure Code permits the application of the death penalty on a juvenile who attains the age of 17 years at the time of commission of the offence against the provisions of the UNCRC which frowns upon it. Conversely, the Sharia Criminal Procedure Code adopts the international threshold allowing death penalty to be imposed only on person who attains 18 years.

3. Associating juveniles with adult offenders is outlawed by all the international instruments. The CYPL equally frowns at this though it does not provide protection to all children below 18 years as it uses the phrase 'a young person ... shall not be allowed *so far as practicable* to associate with adult prisoners.'

4. The UNCRC only allows the use of arrest, detention and imprisonment when employed as a last resort. The same is not the case under the CYPL, as a child can be apprehended at the initial stage by the police and the child will be processed through the juvenile justice system.

---

[107] Federal Minstry of Women Affairs (2004) Nigeria: Convention on the Rights of the Child: Second Country Periodic Report available at http://www2.ohchr.org/english/bodies/crc/docs/AdvanceVersions/CRC.C.70.Add.24.Rev.2.pdf accessed 16 July 2009.

5.   Diversion methods are encouraged to be employed by the police and prosecutors under the UNCRC without necessarily taking a child through the formal trial system. This is for non-serious offences that can be amicably settled through payment of compensation, damages or cost. The CYPL falls short of providing such diversion methods. A child must necessarily pass through the formal process. A presiding judge may then decide whether to employ the available disposition methods provided under the CYPL.

6.   The custodial institutions needed to be created under the UNCRC for children in conflict with law shall be those that ensure their rehabilitation and reintegration into the wider society. They shall be those that will take into account their age and those that will not put their educational development in jeopardy. The CYPL creates custodial institutions like the remand homes and approved institutions. However, in reality they generally lack qualified and sufficient personnel for providing training and welfare for the children.

7.   Professionalized personnel with sufficient knowledge in child psychology and development are required under the UNCRC to take charge of the all units and institutions that deal with children in conflict with the law, from the police state, the court and detention centres. However, under the CYPL, although special procedures exist for dealing with juveniles in conflict with the law, the law is silent on the provision of a special court with professionals having special training in dealing children. Presiding judge of a High court, Magistrate or Sharia Court simply doubles as a juvenile court judge whenever a juvenile is charged alone before his court. A juvenile is processed in the same court room as any adult with strict formalities observed in a regular court.

8.   The CYPL emphasizes more on the custodial disposition methods than non-custodial methods, leaving less room for rehabilitation and reintegration of the juvenile.

9.   Publicizing the identity of a juvenile under the international instruments are aimed at reducing social stigma a child is likely to face as a result of his being prosecuted. Similar protection is available to persons under 16 yeas of age. Even in that case, the protection is given with one hand and taken with another in that a small penalty of one hundred Naira (about 40 pence) is stipulated for any person who violates the provision by exposing the identity of a juvenile.

10. Children being nursed by their mothers are being imprisoned with their mothers and this phenomenon is contrary to article 30 of the African Charter for the Rights and Welfare of a Child, a regional instrument ratified by the Nigerian government.

While the CRA 2003 is demonstrative of the government's willingness to reform the current state of affairs, it too has its weaknesses as described above. Much more is required to improve the situation of juvenile who come into conflict with the law. In some instances, individuals such as the Inspector General of Police has taken the initiative by not only establishing at every divisional level a Juvenile/Old People/Women Welfare Office and also Human Rights Office but made it part of the police restructuring process to train and retrain officers in specialized field both within and outside Nigeria.[108] Much as this is an expression of zeal and enthusiasm to observe international norms, the happenings at the police stations raise concern over the observance of such norms as reported by many national international observers.

Apart from the official training provided in various police institutions as the speech of the Inspector General suggests, other human rights-focused NGOs in collaboration with UNICEF are providing training not only to the police but to all other stakeholders in juvenile justice administration. Associations such as LEAD Nigeria, LEDAP, etc, have been active in this endeavour.[109] As a former prosecutor (State Counsel) the author had attended many of these courses from 2001 and in 2007, he was invited as a resource person at a workshop on diversion in juvenile justice at Katsina in Katsina state where police, prison officers, Sharia court judges, prosecutors and practising lawyers among others participated.[110] However, more support and investment is required at the institutional level and extensive legal reform is required if Nigerian laws are to comply with the international conventions it has ratified, most notably the UNCRC.

VIII. CONCLUSION

The last report of the Nigerian delegation on the Rights of the Child was presented on 26 January 2005 at the 38th Session of the CRC.[111] Some of

---

[108] MM Okiro, 'Strategies For Re-Organisation and Re-Orientation of the Police' Paper presented at the Police Service Commission Retreat in Osogbo, Osun State 18–20 August 2008 available at http://www.nigeriapolice.org/news-mainmenu-2/igp/53-the-strategies-for-re-organisation-and-re-orientation-of-the-police-.html accessed 27 July 2009.

[109] For instance Training Workshop for key players in the Juvenile Justice Administration organised by League of Democratic Women (LEADS) at Gusau Hotel, Gusau Zamfara State, December 2006;

[110] See MU Abubakar, 'Accommodating Diversion in the Nigerian Juvenile Justice Regime' a paper presented at a two-day interactive session with Juvenile Justice Administrators organised by LEADS in collaboration with Unicef Zone 'C'at Katsina Motel, Katsina State Nigeria, 21–22 November 2007.

[111] Federal Minisrty of Women Affairs (2004) Nigeria-Convention on the Rights of the Child: Second Country Report available at http://www2.ohchr.org/english/bodies/crc/docs/AdvanceVersions/CRC.C.70.Add.24.Rev.2.pdf, accessed 2 May 2010.

the relevant issues raised by the the CRC include that despite Nigeria's claim that there are no discrepancies between the provisions of the Convention and the Sharia laws with regard to the rights of children and its juvenile justice system in particular, the Sharia court system does not conform to international norms and standards.[112] The CRC particularly questioned the execution of a 17-year-old in 1997 when Nigeria had already ratified the UNCRC.[113] Indeed, the CRC emphatically maintained that article 12 of the Child and Young Persons Act and article 319 (2) of the Criminal Code, as well as the Sharia Penal Codes in 12 northern states all allow for imposition of death penalty on persons below 18. [114]

Having acknowledged the Nigerian government's efforts in establishing a National Working Group on Juvenile Justice Administration and the reforms so far, the CRC noted that wide disparities remain in the minimum age of criminal responsibility across the country, some of which being too low by international standards. The CRC also noted that juvenile offenders are frequently subjected to physical assaults by the police and custodial officers; that persons below 18 years of age are held in the same detention and prison facilities with adults; that lengths of prosecution and detention are excessive and there are instances where persons below 18 years of age are tried in adult courts and moreover, they are often not legally represented during their trials. Furthermore, the CRC found that juveniles are often detained for 'status offences' such as vagrancy, truancy or wandering, or at the request of parents for 'stubbornness or for being beyond parental control.' Finally, the CRC found serious overcrowding and the poor conditions of homes and juvenile centres for persons below 18 in conflict with the law, and the prisons in which they are placed in lack trained professionals and there is an absence of assistance towards the rehabilitation and reintegration of persons below 18 following judicial proceedings.[115]

The insistence by the CRC that the death penalty was being imposed on children in Northern Nigeria and particularly under the Sharia dispensation is, to say the least, unfounded. There was not a decided case to that effect and even the 1997 case the CRC referred to, was held before 1999 when a democratic system was reinstated, which in turn gave birth to the Sharia. Meanwhile substantial improvements have been recorded since the last report, as can be observed from the overdue 3rd and 4th period reports

---

[112] CRC(2005a) Concluding Observations: Nigeria, p 21 available at http://www.unhchr. ch/tbs/doc.nsf/898586b1dc7b4043c1256a450044f331/b06804b33ec4eadbc1257018002c82d b/$FILE/G0541053.pdf, accessed 2 May 2010.

[113] CRC (2005b) Summary Record of the 1022nd Meeting: Nigeria, available at http://www.unhchr.ch/tbs/doc.nsf/(Symbol)/CRC.C.SR.1022.En?OpenDocument, accessed 2 May 2010.

[114] CRC(2005a) ibid 22.

[115] ibid 21–22.

submitted to the CRC, and presented during its 54th Session from 25 May to 11 June 2010.[116] Interestingly, in the latest report the Nigerian government still maintains its earlier declaration on the protection enjoyed by children under the Sharia dispensation.[117]

---

[116] See Nigeria (2010):3rd and 4th Periodic Reports.
[117] ibid 20.

CHAPTER 10

Criminal Law and the Rights of the Child in Pakistan[1]

I. INTRODUCTION

The Islamic Republic of Pakistan is located in South Asia.[2] Islam is the State religion, and the Constitution requires that laws be consistent with Islam. Official figures on religious demography based on the most recent census taken in 1998, show that approximately 97 per cent of the population is Muslim. The majority of Muslims in the country are Sunni, with a Shia minority ranging between 10 to 20 per cent.[3] The legal system of Pakistan is based on English common law with provisions to accommodate Pakistan's status as an Islamic State.[4] The Penal law, the Criminal Procedure Code and the laws of evidence, apart from changes brought under Islamic law, are based on 19th century British laws. However there has been an incremental Islamization of the laws over the last 30 years, more specifically from 1977 to 1988.[5]

The judicial system of Pakistan consists of a hierarchy of courts exercising both civil and criminal jurisdiction. While the Supreme Court and High Courts have been established under the Constitution, there are several other Courts in Pakistan which are established by or under the Acts of the Parliament or Acts of Provincial Assemblies.[6] The Supreme Court is the apex Court of the State, exercising original, appellate and advisory jurisdiction. It

---

[1] Dr Farkhanda Zia Mansoor.
[2] F Muhammed Burfat and A Razzak Ahmed, 'The Juvenile Justice System in Pakistan' in PC Friday and X Reng (eds), *Delinquency and Juvenile Justice Systems in the Non-Western World* (Criminal Justice Press, USA, 2006) 164. <http://books.google.co.uk/books?id=fkpE1Zra_awC&pg=PA169&lpg=PA169&dq=sind+children+act&source=bl&ots=jfKntOgS0b&sig=H9BkWP_X0FKWQqMb-ZR3Cgep6pU&hl=en&ei=77LVSpXPINWFsAa3s43WCw&sa=X&oi=book_result&ct=result&resnum=10&ved=0CCAQ6AEwCTgK#v=onepage&q=&f=false, accessed 15 October 2009.
[3] Pakistan Legal System, http://www.globalsecurity.org/military/world/pakistan/legal-system.htm.
[4] Crime and Society, http://www-rohan.sdsu.edu/faculty/rwinslow/asia_pacific/pakistan.html, accessed 15 October 2009.
[5] Human Rights Commission of Pakistan, 'Slow March to the Gallows: Death Penalty in Pakistan' (January 2007).
[6] See Dr Faqir Hussain, the Judicial system of Pakistan, http://pklegal.org/resources/JUDICIAL_SYSTEM_OF_PAKISTAN-FAQIR_HUSSAIN.doc; See also, Pakistan Judicial Law and Government, available at, http://www.lawresearch.com/v2/global/zpkj.htm.

is the Court of ultimate appeal and therefore final arbiter of law and the Constitution. Its decisions are binding on all other courts. The next in the hierarchy of courts is the Provincial High Court. Each province has its own High Court. High courts have original and appellate jurisdiction.[7]

In every district of a Province, there is a Court of District Judge which is the principal court of original jurisdiction in civil matters. Besides the Court of District Judge in every district, there is a Court of Sessions Judge and Courts of Magistrates. Criminal cases punishable by death and cases arising out of the enforcement of laws relating to *hudood* are tried by Sessions Judges. The Court of a Sessions Judge is competent to pass any sentence authorized by law. Offences not punishable by death are tried by Magistrates. Among the Magistrates there are Magistrates of 1st Class, 2nd Class and 3rd Class. An appeal against the sentence passed by a Sessions Judge lies to the High Court and against the sentence passed by a Magistrate to the Sessions Judge if the term of sentence is up to four years, otherwise to the High Court.[8]

A new legal Ordinance for Pakistan based on Islamic law was promulgated in February 1979, and established the Federal Shariat Court which exercises dual jurisdiction. Under its original jurisdiction, this Court, on its own motion or through petition by a citizen or a government (Federal or provincial), may examine and determine whether or not a certain provision of law is incompatible with the injunctions of Islam.[9] Appeal against its decision lies with the Shariat Appellate Bench of the Supreme Court, consisting of three Muslim Judges of the Supreme Court and not more than two *ulemas,* (Muslim legal scholars) appointed by the President.[10] If a certain provision of law is declared to conflict with the injunctions of Islam, the Government is required to take necessary steps to amend the law so as to make it conform with the injunctions of Islam. The Court also exercises appellate revisional jurisdiction over the criminal courts, deciding *hudood* cases.[11] The decisions of the Court are binding on the High Courts as well as subordinate judiciary.[12] It lies within the discretion of the court of first instance to decide whether to try a case under civil or Sharia law. If the latter, then the appeals process goes to the Federal Shariat Court, rather than to the high courts, the Court consists of eight Muslim Judges, three of whom are required to be *ulemas.*[13]

---

[7] ibid.
[10] Art 203-F.
[13] ibid.

[8] ibid.
[11] Art 203-D.

[9] Art 203-D.
[12] Art 203-G.

II. NATIONAL LAWS PERTAINING TO JUVENILE OFFENDERS IN PAKISTAN

This section explores the past and present juvenile laws and their applicability in different parts of Pakistan. Before the promulgation of the Juvenile Justice System Ordinance (JJSO), laws pertaining to juvenile offenders were in existence in only two provinces of Pakistan, namely, Punjab and Sindh. These were the Punjab Youthful Offenders Ordinance and the Sindh Children's Act respectively. The provinces of NWFP and Balochistan there did not have any laws for the protection of rights of children. Even though the JJSO legally over-rides all the provincial juvenile laws, the Punjab Youthful Offenders Ordinance and the Sindh Children's Act will be studied because they continue to be applied by magistrates in Punjab and Sindh provinces due to their unfamiliarity with the JJSO. The most recent juvenile law in Pakistan is the JJSO of July 2000.[14] It is a federal law and applicable to the whole of Pakistan, with the exception of the tribal areas. Besides these, Hudood Law (Islamic law) will also be examined because of its serious impact upon female child detainees. Also, laws regarding the age of criminal responsibility in Pakistan as well as death penalty for juvenile offenders will be examined.[15]

A. The Sindh Children's Act of 1955

The Sindh Children Act of 1955 'is a consolidated statute relating to the law for the custody, protection, treatment and rehabilitation of children and youthful offenders, and for trial of youthful offenders in the Province of Sindh'.[16] Though it was enacted in 1955, for it to come into force, a notification had to be issued in the Official Gazette. However, in 1955, Sindh was merged into the Province of West Pakistan and no such notification was issued. Consequently, the Act remained virtually unenforced for about 20 years, even after its enactment. However, following Sindh's reconstitution as a province, in 1974, notifications were issued which extended the Act to the divisions of Hyderabad and Sukkur. Two years later, it was also extended to Karachi.[17]

Some of the significant features of this Act include:[18]

---

[14] Amnesty International, 'Denial of Basic Rights for Child Prisoners' http://www.amnesty.org/en/library/asset/ASA33/011/2003/en/4fb4b9fc-d698-11dd-ab95-a13b602c0642/asa330112003en.html accessed 15 October 2009.

[15] ibid.

[16] Kashif Nadeem alias *Pappi v State*: 1992 P Cr L J 1799.

[17] See I Khan, *Laws Relating to Children* (Pakistan Law House, Karachi, 2004) 6–7.

[18] Amnesty International (n 14).

1. It allows the provincial government to establish one or more juvenile courts for any local areas.[19] In areas where such juvenile courts were absent, it empowered the District Magistrate, a Sub-divisional Magistrate and a Magistrate of the First Class to try juvenile cases.[20] Therefore, only juvenile courts had the exclusive jurisdiction to try cases of children in the area. If a juvenile court did not exist, other courts were given the power to try a case of a child.

2. The Act also provided that a youthful offender defined as a person below 16 years of age at the time of commission of the offence, may not be sentenced to death, transportation or imprisonment.[21]

3. It prohibited joint trials of adults and children.[22]

4. The Act provided for several child-friendly measures during trial. For instance, there were provisions relating to in camera proceedings, removal of persons when the child was being examined as a witness and presence of parents or guardians wherever practicable.[23]

5. The Act also empowered a police officer to release a child arrested on charge of a 'non-bailable' offence provided that releasing the child would not place him/her in any danger or bring him in contact with adult criminals.[24] Hence, a child who is accused of an offence punishable with death or imprisonment for life may also be released on bail.[25]

The Orders given by the Sindh High Court led to the establishment of a juvenile Court in Sindh in 1993.[26]

B. *The Punjab Youthful Offenders Ordinance 1983*

The Provincial Legislature of Punjab had passed the Punjab Youthful Offenders Act as early as 1952, but they failed to bring it into force. Later in 1983, The Punjab Youthful Offenders Ordinance was passed and it repealed the old law. The 1983 Ordinance was largely derived from the Sindh Children Act as almost all its provisions were a replica of the provisions of the Sindh Act, though, with two significant exceptions.[27] First, the Punjab Ordinance only covers children who were under 15 years of

---

[19] Sindh Children Act, 1955, s 5.   [20] ibid s 5, 8.
[21] ibid s 68.   [22] ibid s 10.
[23] ibid ss 15, 18 , 19.
[24] ibid s 64. Amnesty International (n 14).   [25] Khan (n 17) 47.
[26] V Parekh, *Prison Bound: The Denial of Juvenile Justice In Pakistan* (Human Rights Watch, New York, 1999) 91. <http://books.google.co.uk/books?id=Ej3oZB3XypUC&pg=PA69&dq=juvenile+delinquency+in+pakistan&lr=&as_brr=3&ei=3rPESpfxKZbWyAT_9ID7Aw#v=onepage&q=juvenile%20delinquency%20in%20pakistan&f=false> accessed 15 October 2009.
[27] Parekh (n 26) 18–19.

age,[28] when the offence in question was committed, while the Sindh Children Act applies to those who were below the age of 16.[29] Second, the ordinance requires police officers to release children on bail when they are arrested in connection with a non-bailable offence and cannot promptly be brought before a court. Under the same circumstances, the Sindh Children Act merely grants police discretion to release children on bail.[30]

Although promulgated in 1983, the ordinance remained inoperative until 1994, when the provincial government enforced it in the district of Sahiwal as part of an experiment in juvenile justice administration. The experiment remained unrealized, however, as the government failed to allocate the resources necessary for the law's enforcement.[31]

The aforesaid laws were legally superseded by the JJSO in July 2000 but continue to be applied by the judiciary due to lack awareness of the JJSO.[32]

C. *The* Hudood *Laws of 1979*

Islamic criminal legislation was introduced in Pakistan in 1979, when five presidential decrees were enacted under the guidance of General Zia ul Haq.[33] These initial presidential decrees incorporated crimes relating to *hudood* and the penalty of flogging. The Federal Shariat Court (FSC) was also established as part of this legal Islamization and fixed punishments were allowed execution only after cases had been tried on appeal by the FSC.[34]

The *hudood* laws of 1979 cover various offences such as armed robbery, theft, rape, fornication, false accusation of fornication, drinking and drug-taking, and replace corresponding sections of the Penal Code. It prescribes

---

[28] According to its s 5 'for the purpose of the Ordinance a person shall be deemed to be a child if at the time of the institution of any proceedings against him under the ordinance, such person has not attained the age of fifteen years...'. Punjab Children Ordinance 1983.

[29] Its s 5 provides that 'for the purpose of this Act, a person is deemed to be a child, if at the time of initiation of any proceedings against him under this Act, or at the time of his arrest in connection with which any proceedings are initiated against him under this Act the person is under the age of sixteen years...) Sindh Children Act 1955.

[30] Parekh (n 26) 18–19.

[31] 'Juvenile Justice in Punjab'<http://www.albarrtrust.com/DesktopDefault.aspx?tabid=70> accessed 15 October 2009.

[32] Amnesty International (n 14).

[33] General Muhammad Zia ul Haq; the president and military ruler of Pakistan (1977–1988).

[34] Art 203-D, Constitution of the Islamic Republic of Pakistan; The FSC originated with the 1978 'Superior Courts Shariat Benches Order', in pursuance of which five Shariat Benches were constituted; four in each High Court and the remaining in the Supreme Court of Pakistan, knows as the Shariat Appellate Bench of the Supreme Court. These Shariat Benches were empowered to strike down all existing or future laws that were found to be incompatible with Islamic principles. In 1980, the four Shariat Benches of the High Court were replaced by the establishment of the Federal Shariat Court in their place.

two sets of punishments: *hudood* and *tazeer*. The *hudood* punishment requires very specific evidence based either on the confession of the accused or the testimony of a specified number of eyewitnesses. *Hudood* punishments also include stoning to death for fornication, judicial amputation for theft and armed robbery and flogging for consumption of intoxicants. Therefore, *hudood* or fixed punishment for specific offences is provided only if certain strict evidentiary requirements are fulfilled.[35]

Though the applicability of *hudood* laws is not dependent on the defendant's age, the punishments meted out give special consideration to children as the harsher *hudood* punishments are not to be imposed on individuals who were children at the time they committed the crimes. However, the *hudood* laws define children differently from the other laws in Pakistan. Under the *hudood* laws, a child is a person who has not attained puberty. The *hudood* law relating to fornication differentiates between the genders of the offenders:[36] According to section 2 (a) 'Adult' means a person who has attained, being a male, the age of eighteen years or, being a female, the age of sixteen years, or has attained puberty'.[37] The definition needs more clarity since in the first part of the definition a male is adult at the age of 18 while a female is considered adult for the purposes of the law at the age of 16. The second part of the definition which states 'or has attained puberty' could be interpreted with conjunction to the rest of the clause that male and female both could be termed as adult if they attained puberty before the age of 18, however, if read with the second part which relates to the female, it only seems to define her and here it leaves a grey area. Thus a girl of 12 years who has attained puberty is legally adult and could be sentenced to the *hudood* punishments outlined above. Though there are no reports of children being sentenced to stoning or judicial amputation, or to public flogging, but there are valid concerns that according to this interpretation girls in particular can be subjected to these punishments at an earlier age as compared to boys, under these laws.[38] However, as fully explained in Chapter Three, under Islamic law, criminal punishments could only be inflicted on a person who has attained physical (*balig*) as well as mental (*aqil*) maturity. Further, this interpretation appears to consider only the element of physical maturity and ignores the mental element of a crime. Obviously, the level of mental maturity of a girl of 12 who has attained puberty could not be same to that of a boy of 18. Similarly, it is also questionable that several boys also attain physical maturity earlier than 18. Hence, while interpreting equal consideration should be given to both of the elements.

---

[35] A Jahangir, 'Women's Commission And Hudood Ordinances' http://www.peacewomen. org/news/Pakistan/newsarchive03/Zina.html, accessed 15 October 2009.
[36] Amnesty International (n 14).
[37] Offence of Zina (Enforcement of Hudood Ordinance, 1979) Ordinance VII of 1979.
[38] Amnesty International (n 14).

There has been a consistent demand for repeal of these laws by various commissions and committees over the years. For example, in 1997, the Commission of Inquiry for Women proposed the repeal of the Hudood Ordinances and re-enactment of the erstwhile repealed provisions of the Pakistan Penal Code 1860. The Special Committee to Review the (Enforcement of Hudood) Ordinances, 1979 under the aegis of the National Commission on the Status of Women also recommended repeal of the Hudood Ordinances on the basis that 'the Hudood Ordinances as enforced, are full of lacunae and anomalies and the enforcement of these has brought about injustice rather than justice, which should be the main purpose of the enforcement of Islamic law.'[39]

Around the same time and in pursuance of the same objectives, the Qisas and Diyah Ordinance was promulgated in 1990.

D. The Qisas and Diyah Ordinance, 1990

1. Historical background of the Ordinance

The Qisas and Diyah Ordinance came as a result of the objections raised over the then law of homicide and assault in Pakistan. In *Federation of Pakistan through Secretary Ministry of Law & Other v Gul Hasan Khan,*[40] the Shariat Appellate Bench of the Supreme Court held that the existing sections of the Pakistan Penal Code (PPC) relating to crimes of homicide and offences against the body were incompatible with the injunctions of Islam as they failed to provide for *qisas, diyah* and other related Islamic provisions. Furthermore, the objections noted that the PPC did not provide for exemptions from the sentence of death in cases of homicide for children not yet having attained puberty.

In the wake of *Gul Hasan*, two Ordinances were promulgated; Criminal Law (Amendment) Ordinance 1990[41] and Criminal Law (Second Amendment) Ordinance 1990.[42] These are jointly and popularly referred to as the Qisas and Diyah Ordinance (hereafter: the Ordinance). By virtue of these, those provisions of the PPC that the Shariat Appellate Bench had declared repugnant to Islam were revised and subsequently replaced with provisions conforming to Islamic criminal injunctions. Commentators have noted that the Islamization of penal measures in Pakistan has been of symbolic value in most areas of enactment. However, the law of homicide and wounding is considered one of the few areas that has been affected

---

[39] D Zuberi, 'Pakistan: Will the NCSW's latest recommendation to repeal the Hudood Ordinances finally put an end to the dreaded law?' 4/11/2003, :http://www.wluml.org/english/newsfulltxt.shtml?cmd[157]=x-157-27267 accessed 3 March 2010.
[40] PLD 1989, SC 633.
[41] Also known as Ordinance IV of 1990.
[42] Also known as Ordinance VII of 1990.

fairly significantly in both theory and practice.[43] The following section analyses the amendment brought about to the law of homicide and wounding.

E. The Effect of Islamic Criminal Laws in Pakistan

When the practice of Ordinances started in the courts, cases were decided in the light of them. Due to the shortcomings of the legislation, courts had to build on the gaps by engaging in *ijtihad* (making a legal decision by independent interpretation). Martin Lau opines that a survey of the Islamization process in Pakistan reveals that it was largely 'judge-led'.[44] Taking this point further, Wasti points out that the judges are to act as *mujtahids* (scientific jurists), they had no training whatsoever in Islamic jurisprudence.[45] These judges who had so far been trained in, and developed expertise relating to, the secular Western legal principles, were now expected to apply Islamic legal thought and implement *ijtihad*. Additionally, these ill-equipped judges, who had little or no knowledge of the Arabic language, were not allowed access to secondary sources, and instead were required to derive judgments from the Quran and *sunnah* alone. This situation wreaked havoc on the implementation of Islamic criminal justice, which was merely grafted onto the pre-existing and largely secular British-drafted Penal Code from 1860.[46] In fact, for the proper interpretation of laws, well-equipped judges and jurists who have command of the language and know the aim of the basic sources and the law, is necessary. Further, for the proper and significant implementation of any sort of the criminal justice system, including Islamic criminal justice system its clarity, suitability with the situation on the ground and complete awareness of pros and cons of the system are extremely important. Furthermore, the implementation should be started from the protection of rights and not from the imposition of punishments. Directly jumping toward the imposition of punishments while sidelining the basic rights of the individuals, and without strengthening the enforcement mechanism, does not seems a logical approach. Furthermore, the amalgamation of different sets of laws into one could lead towards more confusion.

---

[43] See R Peters, *Crime and Punishment in Islamic Law: Theory and Practice from the Sixteenth to the Twenty-First Century* (CUP, Cambridge, 2005) 160; Dr Nasim Hasan Shah, (Retd.) Chief Justice of Pakistan & President SAARC LAW, 'Islamisation of Law in Pakistan' (Lecture delivered at the National Law School of India University, Bangalore, December 1994).
[44] M Lau, *Islam and Constitutional development in Pakistan'* in I Edge (ed), *Comparative Law in Global Perspective* (New York, 2000).
[45] T Wasti, *The Application of Islamic Criminal Law in Pakistan—Sharia in Practice* (BRILL, Leiden 2009) 94.
[46] ibid 96.

Thus, various issues arose from the promulgation and implementation of the Qisas and Diyah Ordinance in Pakistan, which are best understood from a study of the cases that have been decided in the light of this Ordinance.

F. Problems Emerging from the Qisas and Diyah Ordinance 1990: An Analysis of the Case Law

Pakistan is a country with a high incidence of intra-family violence. Often, it is found that members of the same family gang up on a particular family member and devise ways to dispose of them. Dowry murders and stove-burning cases are a common feature in this respect.[47] Pakistan being a highly patriarchal society, cases of domestic violence too often lead to homicide or serious wounding. Another common cultural feature are crimes of 'honour'.[48] In the traditional and highly conservative quarters of Pakistani society, it is common to find cases of homicide in which men have murdered their wives, sisters or other female relatives on suspicion of adultery or other acts that are deemed to have dishonoured the family. Women are largely discriminated against and are the primary victims of these crimes.

The Qisas and Diyah Ordinance was pre-empted by two draft Ordinances in 1980 and 1981 respectively, both of which fell short on various accounts. In December 1980, the Ministry of Law asked the Women's Division, Research Wing; Secretariat of the Government to gather views from various women's organizations on the draft law. However, once these comments were issued, they were never taken into account.[49] Hence, while practicing their prevalent culture under the guise of Islamic law, the Qisas and Diyah Ordinance has resulted in aggravated intra-family violence and further abuse of women in particular.

According to some, this 'privatization' of crimes of homicide and assault by virtue of the Qisas and Diyah Ordinance has had extremely damaging consequences in cases of intra-family violence. The enactment of *diyah* laws has allowed families to evade punishment altogether by offering and accepting monetary compensation for cases of homicide.[50] However, the fact is that the enactment of *diyah* laws did not allow the families to evade punishment altogether but permitted them to replace the death penalty under *qisas*, with the blood money as compensation for the cases of homicide

---

[47] http://www.dailytimes.com.pk/default.asp?page=2006%5C03%5C06%5Cstory_6-3-2006_pg7_33 , http://www.womensenews.org/article.cfm/dyn/aid/1085/context/archive.

[48] http://www.amnesty.org/en/library/asset/ASA33/018/1999/en/dom-ASA330181999en.pdf.

[49] Wasti (n 45) 126.

[50] Human Rights Watch Report, '*Crime or Custom? Violence Against Women in Pakistan*' (August 1999).

(which is also a punishment). Further, according to Islamic law the crime of murder is not totally privatized since it is considered a crime against an individual as well as against the society. Therefore, as far as proving the crime of murder is concerned, the State has every right to investigate. Then the parties have been given option either to go for *qisas,* or blood money, or to forgive the murderer. This approach seems to be victim-centered as well as criminal-centred, or equivalent to human-centered. This provision of several options could bring not only an end to the future blood feud and also provide compensation to the family of the victims, but also save the life of the murderer, both of whom could be main breadwinner of their families.

According to the Qisas and Diyah Ordinance Section 299(3) 'Diyah' means the compensation specified in section 323 payable to the heirs of the victim'.[51] Section 323 (1) provides that its value is to be determined 'subject to the injunctions of Islam as laid down in the Holy Quran and Sunnah'. The section also asserts that the 'the financial position of the convict and the heirs of the victim fix the value of *diyah* which shall not be less than the value of thirty thousand six hundred and thirty grams of silver'.[52] The minimum value of *diyah* is to be revised and fixed by the Federal Government each year.[53] However, in practice, in cases of intra-family violence,[54] *diyah* is reduced to a meaningless measure, since the accused and offender are from the same family and the payment flows from one member of the nuclear family to the other.[55] Hence this practice clearly violates section 323(1) of the Ordinance. Moreover, the specification of amount of *diyah* has been provided by the *hadith* of the Prophet Muhammad, and there is no specific mention of reducing the amount in the case of relatives—therefore, it not permitted to be reduced, which clearly contradicts the *hadith.* Judicial discretion plays a highly damaging role here as well, as 'a large degree of judicial discretion embodied in the *qisas* and *diyah* law has been widely criticised in light of the endemic societal and judicial discrimination against women in Pakistan.'[56]

Again, the cultural interpretation of Islamic law in the Ordinance adversely affects the rights of victimized parties. One of many examples is the case, *Fazal Hussain v The State,*[57] in which the accused was the husband of the deceased. A compromise was reached by paying *diyah* and the charge was dropped.

---

[51] S 299 (e); Qisas and Diyah Ordinance, Pakistan Penal Code.
[52] S 323 of the Pakistan Penal Code.
[53] S 323(2) Qisas and Diyah Ordinance.
[54] Human Rights Watch Report (n 50).
[55] ibid.
[56] ibid.
[57] 2002 PCRLJ 1256 Lahore H.C.

Feeble enforcement and investigation mechanisms of laws also lead to injustices. With the passing of the Ordinance, compromise or concession applications poured into the courts and were liberally granted by judges.[58] Often, one finds that without proper investigations or inquiries, these applications were allowed. In *Muhammad Tufail v The State*,[59] the parents of the deceased lied as to their status, as the only legal heirs of the victim, and the court ordered the acquittal of the accused upon their pardon. It was later discovered that two minor legal heirs were also left behind by the deceased. Similarly in *Muhammad Yaqoob v The State*,[60] it was later discovered that the victim's mother was alive and thus it was necessary for her to be included in the decision process of the court, as a legal heir of the victim. However, she was overlooked by the court during the entire proceedings and only discovered after the accused was set free.

In *Ghulam Shabir v Mst Zanib Bibi*,[61] the court acknowledged the common and widespread fraud that existed in various cases of compromise. However, no concrete solution was given. Despite this widespread fraud, there are no guidelines given to judges on how they ought to determine the authenticity of such compromises. As a result, such incidents continue to this day. Additionally, despite understanding the fraud involved in many of these cases, courts have shown no hesitation in awarding compromise applications.[62]

G. *Judicial Neglect of Social Pressures*

A host of societal pressures exist in such cases and often the victim's heirs are urged to reach a compromise even where they are reluctant to do so. Power dynamics in Pakistan are rife, and those with the financial resources exercise unreasonable social power. This being a commonplace occurrence in various walks of life in Pakistan, it is only expected that the courts take this into account when deciding cases. In *Muhammad Suleman v The State*,[63] the High Court acquitted five convicts who had been sentenced to death for murdering three brothers. The three deceased victims' elderly parents were the only surviving heirs, who ultimately waived their right of *qisas*. To this, the Lahore High Court held: 'The compromise entered into

---

[58] For instance, see, *Muhammad Akram v The State* (1992, ALD 383(2)); *Muhammad Ashraf v The State* (1992 ALD 140); *Shabbir Ahmad v The State* (1991, ALD 265); *Sarwar Khan v The State* (1994 SCMR 1262) *Sharafar Ali v The State* (1997 PCrLJ 199).

[59] 1994 SCMR 1211.

[60] 1997 PCrLJ 1979.

[61] 1999 MLD 581.

[62] See eg *Muhammad Nawaz v The State* (1998 MLD 1) where even an absconding offender charged for murder was granted permission to compound the offence with the fugitive and thereby acquitted.

[63] 1992 PCrLJ 1093.

between the parties seems to be genuine. There is nothing on the record to hold that the compromise was the result of any misconception or coercion'. No concrete investigations were held as to the circumstances in which this pardon was issued. The Court did not encompass that the social pressure existing on two elderly parents against five murder convicts and their families was highly coercive given the circumstances.

H. Application of Diyah and the Case of Minors

From a study of the case-law concerning *diyah*, it is evident that there exists a clear and obvious reluctance on part of the authorities, both legislative and judicial, to implement the death penalty. Thus in most cases, the death penalty is sidelined and the offender is sentenced with imprisonment and *diyah*. In cases where the offender is an adult, the courts do not pay much attention to the financial ability of the offender to pay the *diyah* sum, despite the Ordinance's claims that these will be decisive factors.[64] However, in the cases where the juveniles have been involved the attitude of the court has been found quite different, for example, in *Zafar v The State*,[65] some levy was granted to a minor offender when the court held the Government is responsible for payment of *diyah* when neither the accused nor his *wali* had any property for realization of the same. The court also held that in the absence of an able *wali*, the Government must act as the *wali* of a minor offender.[66] Further, the courts began to utilize different methods to relieve offenders with no capacity to pay *diyah*. As mentioned earlier, issuing bail was one such method.

In *Allah Ditta v The State*,[67] the Juvenile Justice System Ordinance 2000 was used by the court. In *Allah Ditta*, the offender was a destitute minor who had served his entire sentence of imprisonment but remained in prison for months due to non-payment of the *diyah*. The offender's *wali*, his father, was also unable to pay the designated *diyah*. The court decided that the accused, even in the event that he found a job, would not be able to raise the money to pay the *diyah* sum for years to come. This created a situation of uncertainty, both for the intended beneficiary of the *diyah* as well as the accused. The judge applied the provisions of the Juvenile Justice System Ordinance to release the offender on probation subject to the furnishing of bonds and surety. The Home Secretary was directed to ensure that the *diyah* amount be deposited in the Trial Court by the State for payment to the legal heirs from a 'Bait ul Maal' fund or any other. The Trial Court was directed

---

[64] S 323 (1) P.P.C.
[65] 2001 YLR 533 Lahore H.C.
[66] S 305, Qisas and Diyah Ordinance, XII, 1993.
[67] 2002 PLD 406 Lahore H.C.

to take necessary steps for the recovery of the amount of *diyah* by attachment or sale or movable or immovable property of the State in accordance with the law. Similarly, in recognition of the injustice being caused, the Lahore High Court in the case of *Abid Hussain v Chairman Pakistan Bait-ul-Maal*[68] said, '[p]utting a human being behind bars for the rest of his life for no other reason than his impoverished financial condition is an idea offensive to the dignity bestowed upon him by God.' The court elaborated by stating that it was the State's responsibility to 'lessen the burden' and 'extend mercy and compassion towards [the offender's] unfortunate predicament wherever and however possible'. However, this highlights the problems and inconsistencies that emerge as a result of incorporating traditional Islamic legal concepts into largely secular systems of law.

Gottesman argues that in any modern government, the enactment of the Islamic concept of *qisas* and *diyah* basically serves to create a shift in the theory of punishment, by empowering the victim or the heirs.[69] In Pakistan, the enactment of the Qisas and Diyah Ordinance has in fact disempowered the citizen even further. At the same time, the Ordinance has further empowered the State authorities, in particular the judiciary. The Ordinance has been drafted haphazardly and hurriedly, resulting in highly impractical consequences that the courts are now attempting to rectify by engaging in some judicial law-making. Due to the legislative lacunae in the Qisas and Diyah Ordinance, the judiciary has had to innovate in the matter of Islamic criminal law. It has struggled to find a balance between a secular system of governance that has existed for many years, and implanted Islamic criminal laws. Thus the shots are being called by the judges, who have become all powerful in deciding cases relating to homicide and wounding. The courts, as the cases above highlight, have more discretion in the matter than ever before.

Another related problem is the case of the wealthy offender, for whom *diyah*, despite its high financial value, does not provide a sufficient deterrent. Further, there are not even any guidelines for judges on how to tackle cases belonging to this category. It is agreed by scholars that as the custodian of the rights of the citizens, the State retains the right to give *tazeer* punishments even in the case of pardon from the victim/heirs, thus in light of legislative reform, the courts could help to rectify this particular situation. *Tazeer* punishments contained in the PPC are vague and left mostly to the discretion of the judge. The PPC contains no concrete expansion of what these *tazeer* punishments might contain (except the prison terms it specifies). The FSC declared that '*tazeer* can be to any extend barring the

---

[68] 2002 PLD 482 Lahore HC.
[69] E Gottesman, 'The Reemergence of Qisas and Diyah in Pakistan' [1992] Columbia Human Rights Law Review 14.

sentence of death as to exact *qisas*'[70] whereas the Peshawar High Court in *Gul Hasan* held that it is perfectly within the rights of the court to extend death penalty as *tazeer* where it deems fit. In the same case on appeal, the Supreme Court held instead that death penalty cannot be included as *tazeer* where victim/heirs have exercised their right to pardon the offender. No doubt that under Islamic law while imposing *tazeer* punishments a judge has discretionary powers and can choose an effective punishment according to the nature and circumstances of a criminal and the crime itself.[71] However, the precondition is that the end of justice has to be served. Accordingly, the limits of the discretion end where the injustice begins.

Another issue that emerges as a result of the implementation of the Qisas and Diyah Ordinance is that of individual responsibility. The Ordinance exempts minors and the insane from *qisas* punishments.[72] Where this exemption occurs, section 308 provides that *diyah* shall be payable either from the offenders property or 'by such person as may be determined by the Court'. In Islamic law, payment of *diyah* by *aqila* is the only exception as to the principle of individual responsibility wherein the *aqila* (nearest parental kin of the accused) has to pay the *diyah*, and the Ordinance does not take into account the *aqila* at all, though it constitutes a prominent feature of Islamic criminal justice relating to homicide and assault. Yet for some reason, the Pakistan Penal Code does not elucidate upon this particular aspect at all, in fact, it is not mentioned in the criminal code to begin with. The PPC speaks of the *wali's* responsibility to pay on behalf of the offender, but this is vague. This effectively means that this area remains unlegislated, and thus court decisions can result in severe injustice and unreasonable burden upon the family of the accused, or they engage in active judicial law-making by trying to reconcile the matter on a case by case basis.

Various cases have emerged highlighting the injustice that is created by virtue of this provision. Effectively, whenever a crime is committed by a minor or insane person, the offender's next of kin are burdened with the payment of *diyah*. In *Muhammad Afzal v The State*,[73] the accused was a 13-year-old who was ordered to pay 175,000 Rupees (approx £1750) as *diyah* to the victim's heirs. The court refused to take his age into account as it stated that no evidence had been produced by the defence to show that the accused was not mature enough to realize the consequences of his act. The decision was appealed and promptly dismissed by the High Court.

---

[70] *Muhammad Riaz v The State* PLD 1980 FSC 54.
[71] S 338, E.
[72] S 306; PPC.
[73] 1999 SCMR 2652.

I. The Child Offenders Act (Bill), 1995

Pakistan ratified the UN Convention on the Rights of the Child (UNCRC) in 1990. However, serious efforts to introduce a uniform juvenile justice law, in force throughout Pakistan, only started in 1994. This was triggered by several factors. The primary reason for this was that when in April 1994, the UN Committee on the Rights of the Child (CRC) evaluated Pakistan's first periodic report on its compliance with the Convention, it observed that it was 'very much concerned about the system of administration of juvenile justice and its non-compatibility with the provisions of the Convention ... and other relevant United Nations standards in this field.' The CRC requested a progress report to be submitted before the end of 1996, while a second periodic report was due on 11 December 1997. This led to the drafting of the Child Offenders Act (Bill), 1995.[74] The bill was an attempt to bring about change in national law in accordance with the UNCRC. On one side the bill made additions to the protections afforded children under domestic law. These included:[75]

1. Requiring provincial governments to establish one or more juvenile courts for each local area, with exclusive jurisdiction over cases involving children.[76]
2. Granting children a right to counsel at government expense, and providing that court-appointed counsel have 'at least three years of standing in the profession.'[77]
3. Requiring the release of children on bail if their trial does not begin within three months of their arrest or does not conclude within a period of one year.[78]
4. Prohibiting the imposition of the death sentence, amputation, or whipping on children, or assignment to hard labor while in a 'borstal or other such institution'.[79]
5. Prohibiting the imposition of handcuffs, fetters, or corporal punishment on children 'at any time while in custody.'[80]
6. Prohibiting the arrest of children below the age of 12 under laws relating to preventive detention or vagrancy. [81]

At the same time, the bill suffered from some glaring deficiencies in some critical areas. For instance, with respect to the definition of a child, the Bill defined a child as somebody who at the time of commission of the crime

---

[74] V Parekh, *Prison Bound: The Denial of Juvenile Justice in Pakistan* (Human Rights Watch, New York, 1999) 91.

[75] V Parekh (n 74) 91.

[76] Child Offenders Act (Bill), 1995, s 4.   [77] Child Offenders Act (Bill), 1995, s 3.

[78] ibid s 9(7).   [79] ibid s 11(1).   [80] ibid s 11(2).

[81] ibid s 9 (6).

had not attained the age of 16 years.[82] Though consistent with the provisions of the Sindh Children Act, it failed to meet the requisite international standards. Further, the bill required joint trial of an adult and child, in ordinary criminal courts, when a child is charged in a case along with an adult who is the principal accused.[83] This provision was not only in conflict with the international norms, but at the same time, it was a weakening of the provincial laws which had eliminated joint trials in case a juvenile court was in existence.[84] However, for several years this bill could not be tabled before the Parliament due to political changes. Ultimately the JJSO was promulgated in 2000.

1. The UNCRC in the national laws

As mentioned above, Pakistan ratified the UNCRC in 1990. As part of its efforts to fulfil obligations under the UNCRC in July 2000 Pakistan promulgated a Juvenile Justice System Ordinance (JJSO).[85]

2. The juvenile justice system in Pakistan: current position and the JJSO

The JJSO was the first ever comprehensive federal juvenile justice law enforced in Pakistan. Some of its significant provisions include:[86]

1. It defines the child in line with international standards as a person below 18 years of age;[87]
2. It provides for the establishment of special juvenile courts exclusively to try juveniles under special procedures suitable for children; [88]
3. It regulates the arrest of children by police as well as bail and probation;
4. It provides that the child has the right to free legal representation;[89]
5. It prohibits the death penalty and the use of fetters and handcuffs for children.[90]
6. It prohibits the joint trial of adults and children. Children can only be tried by a juvenile court which has been especially set up to hear cases involving children. Courts designated as Juvenile courts cannot hear other cases on days when children's cases are fixed for hearings.[91]

---

[82] The Child Offenders Act (Bill), 1995, s 2(b).   [83] S 4 (3).
[84] Parekh (n 74) 97.   [85] Amnesty International (n 14).
[86] ibid.
[87] Juvenile Justice System Ordinance, 2000, No XXII, s 2(b).
[88] ibid s 4.   [89] S 3.   [90] S 12.
[91] S 5.

Though the passing of the JJSO was a very significant landmark in the history of juvenile justice and child rights in Pakistan, it has been explored that in practice it is not been properly enforced.[92] The dismal state of the JJSO is clearly revealed in reports of various international bodies. In 2003, Amnesty International, in its report on juveniles, expressed that 'despite the promulgation of the JJSO the rights of young people accused of criminal offences continue to be denied'.[93] The CRC, discussing Pakistan's second periodic report on the UNCRC at its 34th session in October 2003, expressed its concern at the poor implementation of the JJSO and gave several suggestions for measures to improve Pakistan's child rights record. These include the setting up of an independent and effective mechanism to monitor the implementation of the UNCRC and receive and address complaints from children in a child-friendly and expeditious manner; scrutiny of existing laws including the Hudood Ordinance with a view to bringing them in conformity with the UNCRC; and the implementation of child rights protection in the Northern and tribal areas.[94] Even more recently, in its 2007 annual report, the Human Rights Commission of Pakistan reported that the ordinance 'remained un-implemented in most of the country,' noting that Sindh still lacked a juvenile court and the government had given no directives for implementing the ordinance in the Federally Administered Tribal Areas.[95] In this regard the CRC observed that: 'Laws implementing the Convention on the Rights of the Child are not de facto applied in the Northern Tribal Territories, and therefore children living in these territories do not fully enjoy their rights under the Convention'. [96]

The CRC expressed its concern that: 'Legislative changes might not be fully implemented and recognized within the State party and that some existing laws may still need to be reviewed.' Accordingly the Zina and Hudood Ordinances are in conflict with the principles and provisions of the UNCRC.[97] The CRC also expressed its apprehension about torture and other cruel, inhuman or degrading treatment or punishment.[98] It expressed that despite the fact that for promoting respect for children's rights, the State party is undertaking

---

[92] Amnesty International, 'Pakistan: Protection of Juveniles in the Criminal Justice System Remains Inadequate' http://www.amnesty.org/en/library/info/ASA33/021/2005/en, accessed 15 October 2009.

[93] Amnesty International (n 14).

[94] Amnesty International (n 93); Amnesty International (n 14).

[95] Human Rights Commission of Pakistan, 'State of Human Rights in 2007' 167–168, http://hrcp-web.org/5-2%20children.pdf, accessed 25 May 2008.

[96] Committee on the Rights of the Child (34th Session) 'Consideration of Reports Submitted by States Parties under art 44 of the Convention' (27 October 2003). CRC/C/15/Add.217.

[97] ibid 2 paras 11–12.

[98] ibid 8 para 38, 39.

some training of police officers and other professionals who work with children, the CRC is deeply concerned about the numerous reports of torture, serious ill-treatment and sexual abuse of children.[99] The CRC recommended that the State adopt measures to certify that adequate financial and human resources have been allocated to the Pakistan Commission for the Welfare and Protection of the Rights of the Child. Furthermore, the State should strengthen coordination mechanisms between all the authorities involved in human rights and children's rights at both national and local levels. Furthermore, the CRC observed the cooperation between the State and NGOs, but expressed its concern that to a great extent, this cooperation is project based and may lack long-term planning and goals.[100]

In practice it lacks of proper implementation of the JJSO has been found in the following areas:

i) Lack of special care and assistance in sentencing practice

Even though the JJSO and UNCRC call for special care to be exercised by Courts while trying and sentencing juvenile offenders, this seems difficult to implement in Pakistan. The Courts have been seen to impose imprisonment of extraordinary length and fines of extraordinary amounts on young offenders, without giving any due consideration to their age or maturity at the time of commission of the crime.[101]

ii) There are several ambiguities with respect to the jurisdiction of the juvenile courts

Though all juvenile offenders are to be tried by juvenile Courts under the JJSO, several jurisdictional problems arise in cases which attract exclusive jurisdiction of more than one Court. For instance, the case of Muhammed Jahangir was being tried by an Anti-Terrorism Court in Lahore despite the fact that he was a minor. Such jurisdictional conflicts still remain unresolved and children continue to be denied their right to juvenile justice. [102]

iii) Joint trials of adult and child offenders continue to take place

Even though article 5 of the JJSO provides for mandatory separation of trials of adults and children, the Courts in Pakistan seem to pay no heed to this provision of law.

However, two of the most controversial issues plaguing the juvenile justice system in Pakistan are the laws related to age of criminal responsibility and death penalty for juvenile offenders. These are elaborated upon below. [103]

---

[99] ibid 8 para 40.
[100] ibid 3 para 13.
[101] Amnesty International (n 93).
[102] Amnesty International (n 93).
[103] ibid.

III. AGE OF CRIMINAL RESPONSIBILITY

The Pakistan Penal Code, section 82 establishes the minimum age of criminal responsibility at seven years. It has been argued that determining the age of criminal responsibility at seven years is too low. Furthermore, section 83 declares that between seven and 12 years a child can only commit an offence when he has 'attained sufficient maturity of understanding to judge of the nature and the consequences of his conduct'. However, the law does not provide any guidelines as to what is maturity and when it is attained. Consequently, concerns have been raised with regard to the vagueness of the phrase 'sufficient maturity of understanding' and the arbitrariness of the authority that is vested in the court to hold a child between seven and 12 years criminally liable.[104]

Under the 1979 Hudood Ordinances, there are provisions that give special consideration to children while determining the type of punishment.[105] However, no specific age has been mentioned and children are defined as those who have not attained puberty.[106] The most pressing problem with puberty being used as a determinative criterion for criminal responsibility, is that it is too subjective and also promotes discrimination against girls who most often attain puberty at an earlier age than boys. Further it fails to take into account the degree of mental and emotional maturity of children.[107] Usually, the federal laws override the provincial laws. However, both the Pakistan Penal Code and the JJSO are federal laws with conflicting definitions of a child with respect to age. Further, the JJSO is in addition to and not in derogation of any other law in Pakistan.[108] The Offence of Zina (Enforcement of Hudood) Ordinances, 1979 overrides all other laws in Pakistan.[109]

A positive step towards a standard definition of a child was taken through the Juvenile Justice System Ordinance 2000, which set the definition of a child at 18 years of age, raising it from 15 and 16 years in the provincial laws. However, the age of criminal responsibility continued to

---

[104] S Berti, Rights of the Child in Pakistan, Report on the Implementation of the *Convention on the Rights of the Child by Pakistan*, OMCT, Geneva, May 2003, available at www.omct.org/pdf/cc/PakistanCRCreport.en.doc, 23.

[105] UNICEF, South Asia and the Minimum Age of Criminal Responsibility, Kathmandu, Nepal, July, 2005, http://www.unicef.org/rosa/Criminal_Responsibility_08July_05 (final_copy).pdf

[106] S 2 (a), Offences Against Property, Hudood Ordinance VI, 1979; Offence Of Zina, Hudood Ordinance VII, 1979, s 2(a).

[107] Committee on the Rights of the Child (6th Session) 'Summary Record of the 134th Meeting: Pakistan' (6 April 1994) 134, para 5 CRC/C/SR., available at http://www.unhchr.ch/tbs/doc.nsf/0/6d28f3c73f6e9beb802565e1004e280f?Opendocument, accessed on 9 October 2009.

[108] Burfat and Ahmed (n 2) 167.

[109] S 3.

remain at seven years. In 2003, the CRC once again expressed its concern with regard to the low age of criminal responsibility that is prevalent in Pakistan.[110] Therefore, increasing the minimum age of criminal responsibility from seven years and bringing it in conformity with the international standards will be a significant step towards reforming the juvenile justice system in Pakistan.[111] Besides this, measures need to be taken to ensure the effective enforcement of such laws as the problem of the lack of birth registration in Pakistan makes any change in the minimum age of criminal responsibility almost meaningless, because if children are unable to provide a concrete proof of their age, it will expose them to charges of criminal liability under ordinary laws meant for adults.[112] Another concern of the CRC was lack of proper birth registration. The considered that although efforts have been made by the State party to promote timely birth registration. However, the CRC observed the fact that even then considerable number of children are not registered at birth, which could adversely affect the full enjoyment of fundamental rights and freedoms by the children.[113] One of the reasons for this problem could be that even though in every city and town compulsory birth registration is required, old traditions remain dominant and a number of births still take place at home. For this reason, determination of the exact date of birth seems extremely difficult to obtain. As a result, for determining the approximate age, resort has to be made to medical examination or school register. However, in *Muhammad Anwar and others v State*, 1976 P Cr.LJ 1325, the court held that in order to determine the age, medical opinion cannot override the evidence provided by the birth certificate.[114]

It is a fact that, even when based on ossification tests, could not be considered conclusive, because different charts have been prepared for such tests. Further, its process depends on various factors, which include environment, climate, eating habits, and heredity.[115]

Nevertheless, in another case the court held that the evidence given by a radiologist to be preferred to a school certificate:[116] '[B]irth certificate and school certificates are not conclusive proof of the age of the petitioner'.[117]

[110] UN Doc CRC/C/15/Add.217, 27 October 2003.

[111] S Berti, 'Rights of the Child in Pakistan: Report on the implementation of the Convention on the Rights of the Child by Pakistan' (OMCT, Geneva, May 2003) available at www.omct.org/pdf/cc/PakistanCRCreport.en.doc, 23.

[112] UNICEF, 'South Asia and the Minimum Age of Criminal Responsibility' (Kathmandu, Nepal, July, 2005) http://www.unicef.org/rosa/Criminal_Responsibility_08July_05 (final_copy).pdf accessed 15 October 2009.

[113] Committee on the Rights of the Child (34th Session) 'Consideration of Reports Submitted by States Parties under Article 44 of the Convention' (27 October 2003) 8, para 38, 39. CRC/C/15/Add.217.

[114] Khan (n 17)16.   [115] ibid.

[116] PLD. 1972, Pesh.27; Khan (n 17)17.

[117] PLD. 1960 Lah. 11 23; Khan (n 17) 17.

With regard to the determination of age, the JJSO 2000 states that: 'If a question arises as to a person before it is a child for the purposes of this Ordinance, the Juvenile Court shall record a finding after such inquiry which shall include a medical report for determination of the age of the child'.[118]

The CRC recommended strengthening and increasing the measures to guarantee the timely registration of all births, in accordance with article 7 of the UNCRC.[119]

IV. THE DEATH PENALTY IN PAKISTAN

A person can be sentenced to death in Pakistan for a wide range of offences. These include murder, *dacoity* (robbery), *zina* (sexual intercourse between partners not married to each other), rape, etc.[120] There are also various channels available for appeal against capital punishment based on the type of offence committed. For instance, in case of an offence that is not tried under the *hudood* laws,[121] there is an automatic mandatory appeal to the appropriate provincial High Court. If the sentence is confirmed by the High court, the prisoner can appeal to the Supreme Court. This possibility of such a further appeal however is discretionary, as the Supreme Court may not accept a case for appeal. On the other hand, when the death penalty is imposed under *hudood* laws, appeal lies to the Federal Shariat Court, and not to the provincial High court. The ultimate appeal in such cases lies to the Shariat Appellate Bench of the Supreme Court. However, there is a huge backlog of cases and the time prisoners spend in death cells, awaiting appeal and execution, may be very long.

Besides appeals, the President of Pakistan can use his power to grant clemency in the case of a death sentence under article 45 of the Constitution which states, 'The President shall have power to grant pardon, reprieve and respite, and to remit, suspend or commute any sentence passed by any

---

[118] S 7.

[119] Burfat and Ahmed (n 2) 167.

[120] In Pakistan, death penalty is most frequently imposed for murder and the real number of death sentences and executions may be much higher than that reported in the media. See Pakistan—the Death Penalty, http://asiapacific.amnesty.org/library/Index/ENGASA33010 1996?open&of=ENG-333 accessed 15 October 2009.

[121] These laws have come under increasing scrutiny and debate both within Pakistan and internationally especially with regard to their impact on civil liberties, human rights and equal treatment of citizens. On December 1, 2006: The 'Protection of Women (Criminal Laws Amendment) Bill, 2006', also informally called the Women's Protection Bill, was passed by the National Assembly on November 15, 2006, and by the Senate on November 23, 2006. The President granted assent to the Bill on December 1, 2006. This Bill makes significant amendments to the Hudood laws and other criminal statutes, http://www.pakistani.org/pakistan/legislation/hudood.html

court, tribunal or other authority.' However, these powers are restricted only to specific kinds of sentences as per the interpretation given by the higher judiciary. To illustrate, death sentences imposed as *hudood* punishments[122] cannot be commuted by the federal or provincial government or the President as provided for in the Code of Criminal Procedure in relation to other judgements.[123]

A. Death Penalty for Juvenile Offenders in Pakistan

Pakistan is a State party to the UNCRC. In line with its obligations under the UNCRC, in July 2000 the government issued a Juvenile Justice System Ordinance banning the death penalty for crimes committed by persons under 18. Article 12(a) of the Juvenile Justice System Ordinance 2000, states that 'no child shall be awarded punishment of death [...]'. Since the promulgation of the Juvenile Justice System, many cases of children in death row have been reviewed. In December 2001, it was announced that the death sentences of around 100 young offenders would have been commuted to imprisonment.[124] In July 2002, Punjab's Law Minister Rana Ijaz Ahmad Khan affirmed that the death sentences of 74 juvenile delinquents had been converted into life imprisonment. On July 27, 2007, the Peshawar Federal Shariat Court commuted to life imprisonment the death sentences against Sohail Fida and Mohammad Rafique. On July 23, 2002, a trial court had sentenced them to death for a murder that took place in May 2000, when they were both under 18. In April 2003 the Peshawar High Court declined to rule on their appeal, saying the Shariat Court had jurisdiction because they had been charged under the Offence against Property (Enforcement of Hudood) Ordinance of 1979.[125]

Despite such measures, the death penalty remains a bane for juvenile offenders. Though Pakistan has abolished the juvenile death penalty, there have been problems in nationwide compliance with the law.[126] Implementation remains very inadequate because many areas lack the underlying courts and structures called for in the new laws. This was reflected in the statement of the CRC on October 3, 2003 where it

---

[122] There is no plea-bargaining or reducing the punishment for a *hudood* crime. *Hudood* crimes have no minimum or maximum punishments attached to them. http://muslim-canada.org/Islam_myths.htm

[123] Amnesty International (n 14).

[124] Presidential Commutation Decree, Official Gazette of Pakistan, December 13, 2001; RG Hood, *The Death Penalty: A Worldwide Perspective* (3rd edn, OUP, Oxford, 2003) 115. Under Pakistani law, life imprisonment is for a maximum period of 25 years and a minimum period of 15 years.

[125] Human Rights Watch 'Enforcing the International Prohibition on the Juvenile Death Penalty', www.juvenilejusticepanel.org/.../HRWEnfIntProhibJuvDPenalty08EN.pdf accessed online on 15 October 2009.

[126] Amnesty International (n 93).

expressed deep concerns about reports of juvenile offenders sentenced to death and executed, even after the promulgation of the Juvenile Justice Ordinance. Despite Pakistan's obligations under the UNCRC, in March 1999, the Peshawar High Court confirmed the death sentence handed down to 17-or-18 year old Sher Ali, convicted of the abduction and murder of a girl in 1993. At the time of the alleged offence Sher Ali would have been 12 or 13 years old. The High Court held that Sher Ali had the ability to differentiate between the right from wrong. It also refused to exercise leniency because of the brutality with which the girl was killed. He was hanged in November 2001.[127]

Another associated issue is that with only 30 per cent of births registered, juvenile offenders find it impossible to convince a judge they were children at the time of the crime, thereby being unable to benefit from reforms.[128] On June 13, 2006, Mutabar Khan was hanged. He was sentenced to death for murder in 1998 and all his appeals to overturn the sentence were consequently dismissed by superior courts. As Mutabar Khan was reportedly aged 16 when he was arrested in 1996, he should have benefited from the Presidential Commutation Order of 2001, which overturned the death sentences of all juveniles then on death row. However, this commutation did not apply to him because of the dispute over his age.[129]

B. Revocation of JJSO by the Lahore High Court

On 6 December, 2004, the Juvenile Justice System Ordinance (JJSO) was revoked by a full bench of the Lahore High Court on the grounds of it being 'unreasonable, unconstitutional and impracticable.'[130]

1. Background of the case

This case resulted out of an application filed by a man called Farooq Ahmed, whose 8-year-old son had been sodomized and murdered. Two of the accused men claimed to be juveniles and demanded that they should be treated in accordance with the provisions of the JJSO. The challenge of their claim by Farooq Ahmed led to a medical examination which established that the accused were not juveniles. Farooq Ahmed then filed a revision

---

[127] Amnesty International (n 14).

[128] Human Rights Watch, *The Last Holdouts: Ending the Juvenile Death Penalty in Iran, Saudi Arabia, Sudan, Pakistan, and Yemen* (2008) available at http://www.hrw.org/en/reports/2008/09/10/last-holdouts-0, accessed 13 October 2010.

[129] M Khan, 'Pakistan: Further information on death penalty:' http://www.amnesty.org/en/library/asset/ASA33/023/2006/en/072fdc2a-d41d-11dd-8743-d305bea2b2c7/asa33023 2006en.html, accessed 3 March 2010.

[130] *Farooq Ahmed v Federation of Pakistan*, PLD 2005, Lahore 15.

petition against declaring the accused to be juveniles. On 8 November 2002, he also moved a writ petition for declaring that the JJSO was unconstitutional. He argued that the JJSO was unduly protecting offenders and being greatly misused. He also argued that the JJSO usurped the right of the family of a murder victim to 'compound' an offence, ie pardon the offender and cease criminal proceedings, and that it provided a lesser punishment without the consent of the heirs of the victim.[131]

2. Arguments of the Courts

According to the Court, the law prior to the promulgation of the JJSO was adequate to protect juveniles and that courts were sufficiently sensitive to the needs of juvenile offenders.[132] Highlighting the flaws in the JJSO, the Court held that the ban on the death penalty had resulted in children being provoked by adults to carry out capital offences, as they would be treated leniently under the JJSO, thus increasing the crime rate. Moreover, the JJSO had encouraged corruption on a large scale as families of accused had procured fake birth, school and medical certificates to establish that the accused were juveniles. The judgment moreover held that the preferential treatment of juveniles violates the constitutional guarantee of equality before the law and equal protection of the law.[133] The judgment also said that in practical terms trying a juvenile separately from adults presented difficulties as juvenile courts and courts trying adults had on occasion reached different conclusions.[134] Lastly, the Lahore High Court argued that the death penalty for juveniles needed to be retained in order to deter crime.[135]

3. Implications and the way ahead

The direct implication of this decision would be the abolishment of juvenile courts. Therefore children would once again be tried in the same system as adults and could be subjected to capital punishment as well. Amnesty

---

[131] Amnesty International, 'Amnesty International's comments on the Lahore High Court judgment of December 2004 revoking the Juvenile Justice System Ordinance' http://asiapacific. amnesty.org/library/Index/ENGASA330262005?open&of=ENG-403, accessed on 15 October 2009.

[132] Critics argue that an analysis of existing law and a review of specific cases shows both claims to be untenable.

[133] Critics argue that the Constitution of Pakistan explicitly allows special provisions for the protection of women and children without diminishing the rights of others.

[134] Amnesty International, 'Pakistan: Death Penalty for Juveniles Reintroduced' (9 December 2004). http://www.amnesty.ca/resource_centre/news/view.php?load=arcview&article=2051 &c=Resource+Centre+News, accessed 3 March 2010.

[135] Amnesty International believes that none of the arguments adduced by the Lahore High Court provide a sufficient basis for revoking the JJSO.

International demanded that '[t]he government of Pakistan must abide by its commitments under the Convention on the Rights of the Child and take immediate action to appeal to the Supreme Court to review the judgment and stay its implementation.'

Upon appeal by the Federal Government and a child-friendly NGO called SPARC, the Supreme Court of Pakistan on 11 January 2005 stayed the High Court. The Attorney General argued that the High Court's findings were not consistent in law as they were based on extra-legal grounds.[136] While the appeals are pending in the Supreme Court the JJSO has been temporarily restored pending a decision. However if Pakistan is to fulfill its commitment to the UNCRC, the JJSO needs to be in enforced with immediate effect.[137]

V. CONCLUSION

Assessing the legal system of Pakistan, what emerges is an ever-burgeoning gulf between those the haves and the have-nots. In this climate it is clear that the enactment of *diyah* in present day Pakistan brings about more discrimination and inequality than the justice and fairness it aims to establish. 'It has been argued by many that the Pakistani law of *qisas* and *diyah* can be blamed for allowing the rich and influential to get way with committing certain crimes, the necessary corollary of which is that the poor tend to get punished.'[138] The case of *Muhammad Arif v The State*,[139] illustrates this point entirely. The Plaintiff, employed as a tube well operator with an annual salary equivalent of £150, was asked by the Court to pay the equivalent of £1706 in *diyah*. The Pakistani legal system fails to recognize and operate with proportionality when adjudicating on cases of this nature. The setting of *diyah* seems to bear no relation to the actual ability of defendants to pay such vast sums.

The introduction of the Qisas and Diyah Ordinance was an attempt by the legislators to address the deficits in the current system of application, and make the legal system more compliant with Islamic principles of justice and fairness. However, its enforcement has led to further levels discrimination against the impoverished classes.[140] Instead of empowering more of the Pakistani population, as was its stated aim noted by Gottesman,[141] it has

---

[136] Burfat and Ahmed (n 2) 175.
[137] http://www.southasianrights.org/pdf/SAHR.Death%20Penalty%20Report-Final.pdf accessed online on 15 October 2009.
[138] Wasti (n 45) 232.
[139] 1999 MLD 2271.
[140] Wasti (n 45) 9.
[141] Gottesman (n 35).

concentrated the authority of judges in criminal cases by awarding them higher levels of discretionary powers in adjudication. The consequential ambiguity created in judicial decisions has left Pakistani citizens in no better a position than before the introduction of these Ordinances. Gottesman illustrates this predicament as follows: 'The final and least attractive scenario is continued uncertainty. Unless the Pakistan government or its judiciary develop a fair and consistent pattern of overseeing the *qisas* and *diyah* process, the Ordinance might lead to confusion and inequity and result in society's disillusionment with judicial arbitration.'[142]

The juvenile justice system in Pakistan is still underdeveloped, and needs to address several key areas if it is to be in compliance with international standards. By which specifically referring to articles 37, 40 and 39 of the UNCRC to which Pakistan is a signatory, the United Nations Standard Minimum Rules[143] for the Administration of Juvenile Justice (the Beijing Rules), the United Nations Guidelines for the Prevention of Juvenile Delinquency (the Riyadh Guidelines), the United Nations Rules for the Protection of Juveniles Deprived of Their Liberty and the Vienna Guidelines for Action on Children in the Criminal Justice System, and the CRC's 1995 discussion day on the administration of juvenile justice (CRC/C/46). The CRC noted many serious violations to international standards, including the sentencing of the death penalty against juveniles, holding the age of criminal responsibility at seven years, the detention of juveniles amongst adult prisoners, and poor and unsanitary prison conditions.[144]

The Juvenile Justice System Ordinance (2000) has been welcomed by the UN and human rights activists for reflecting the specific needs of juvenile defendants. However its implementation is still not uniform across the country, there are still many provinces in the tribal areas of Pakistan that have yet to implement the ordinance.[145] The CRC made many recommendations to the State of Pakistan in improving its juvenile justice system. As a top priority they note the increasing the age of criminal responsibility to and 'internationally acceptable level that ensures that children below the age of 18 years are accorded the protection of juvenile justice provisions and are not treated as adults'.[146] Ensuring that juveniles were imprisoned for the shortest period of time and only as a last resort, and to provide children in conflict with the law appropriate legal assistance and defence was

---

[142] ibid.
[143] Committee on the Rights of the Child (34th Session) 'Consideration of reports submitted by State Parties under article 44 of the Convention' 18, para 80 (27 October 2003). CRC/C/15/Add.217 27.
[144] ibid para 81.
[145] ibid 18 para 81.
[146] ibid 19.

also noted.[147] The Juvenile Justice Ordinance 2000 abolished the death penalty against those under 18, however the CRC states that there should also be revocation of all death penalty cases involving minors, including those decided before the 2000 Act, noting that to act otherwise would be in violation of article 37(a) and 6 of the UNCRC.[148]

[147] ibid.   [148] ibid.

CHAPTER 11

Criminal Law and the Rights of the Child in Spain*

I. INTRODUCTION

Despite the fact that the murder rate committed by minors in Spain may be considered low,[1] there has been an increase in the number of murders committed in street fights. This is associated with the proliferation of juvenile gangs, mainly with Latin-American backgrounds.[2] Indeed, those responsible for half of the murders committed in 2007 come from the American continent.[3]

Despite murder by stabbing following street fights being the most common method used among minors, there has been a series of cases of an extreme cruelty that should be mentioned. Probably, one of the most deplorable crimes was the murder of Sandra Palo. According to the judgment 169/2003 of 13 October of the Juvenile Court no 5 of Madrid, three

---

* Mónica Sánchez-Obrero, Licensed Member of the Bar Association in Madrid (Spain), no 67828, July 2009.

[1] Twenty-five murders committed in 2007 in all the territory of the State, according to the information provided by the *INE* (National Institute for Statistics), available at http://www.ine.es/jaxi/tabla.do [7 May 2009].

[2] According to C Defez Cerezo, 'Delincuencia juvenil', 2006, available online at http://www.iugm.es/investcriminal/TRABAJO%20CURSO%20IUGM.pdf [10 June 2009], 27, up to five Latin-American different gangs have been identified in Spain. These gangs call themselves: *Latin Kings, Ñetas, Dominican Don't Play, Latinos de Fuego* and *Dark Latin Globbers,* the first two being the most violent. The *Latin Kings* is one of the most organized gangs in the world with more than 25,000 members in the United States. Yet, its implementation in Spain has followed a more flexible approach and they are more involved in street fights and less in drug trafficking. In addition, in Spain they are mainly made up of youths coming from Ecuador, Colombia and the Dominican Republic and are also open to national members. According to experts, they are hierarchically organized around a 'king', who is the highest authority and the roles of its members are perfectly defined. It is worth noting that the *Latin Kings* were granted registration as a cultural association in the Autonomous Community of Catalonia in August 2006, after they expressly renounced the exercise of any kind of violence. Conversely, the Provincial Court in Madrid in its judgement of 21 June ordered the dissolution of the *Latin Kings* in the Autonomous Community of Madrid, for being considered an illicit association. The other main gang is the *Ñetas*, mainly coming from Puerto Rico, whose members also follow a dress code and ritual gestures and try to impose their power on certain neighbourhoods.

[3] According to the information provided by the *INE* (National Institute for Statistics), available at http://www.ine.es/jaxi/tabla.do, 11 murders were committed by Spanish citizens, 12 by Latin Americans and two by Africans.

minors and an adult abducted the 22-year-old Sandra Palo and at least two minors and the adult repeatedly raped her. Then, they ran her over with their car eight or 10 times and eventually poured petrol over the body of the victim and burnt it.

Particularly shocking was also the case of Clara García who was brutally murdered by two fellow colleagues and supposedly, friends, on 26 May 2000. Both offenders were minors at the time of the crime. In accordance with the Provincial Court of Cadiz (section 1) judgement of 5 June 2001, the offenders met their friend Clara to have a drink and afterwards they stabbed her to death following a premeditated plan. A further example of cruelty was the case of María Rosario Endrinal, a homeless woman burnt to death while asleep by a 17-year-old minor accompanied by an 18-year-old adult in Barcelona on 15 December 2005.

According to experts, a young offender is normally a man of an average of 16 years old who is impulsive, attention-seeking, and aggressive. He also has low self-esteem, is socially maladjusted, has no emotional control and tends to feel frustrated. He is in most cases the subject of school failure, lacks social abilities and regularly takes drugs. In relation to their social environment, young offenders usually come from dysfunctional families of the lower social stratum and feel a lack of care and affection.[4] They are mostly nationals from Spain although there is a high percentage of them who are immigrants coming mainly from Romania, Morocco or Latin American countries, entering Spain alone and having no family in the country. This is the classical profile of a young offender and they primarily engage in low-scale drug trafficking, shoplifting and petty theft.

However, experts have identified new profiles of juvenile offenders in recent times.[5] Particularly shocking is the case of minors abusing their parents. Abuse may be verbal, through insults and threats, and even physical (kicks, push and shove, etc). This new type of offense is growing dramatically and is causing great concern among experts. It is more common in dysfunctional families, not necessarily economically deprived, where sometimes children feel trapped in the middle of conflicts between their separated or divorced parents. This conflict-rich family situation very often results in an inconsistent upbringing and a lack of parental control. School failure is very frequent in these minors. In addition, drug abuse is a

---

[4] J Morant Vidal, 'La delincuencia juvenil' (2003) Noticias Jurídicas, online publication available at http://noticias.juridicas.com/articulos/55-Derecho%20Penal/200307-585515236 10332031.html accessed 8 May 2009, 3 and M Capdevila Capdevila paper 'Justicia juvenil y reincidencia: apuntes de los estudios de investigación en Cataluña' submitted to the *I Congreso Internacional de Responsabilidad Penal de Menores* conference, 212.

[5] This is for example the case of gangs formed mainly by Latin American members, whose profile coincides with the one previously described in this report. They mostly commit assault and robbery using a great deal of violence. It should not be ignored that nationals are also sometimes integrated in these gangs.

very important risk factor. In other cases, psychological disorders leading to impulsive behaviour and lack of control are also contributing factors.[6]

The profile of young offenders previously described is not exhaustive. It simply reflects a general pattern that may differ from one case to another. There is no consensus among experts on the possible risk factors which may bring a child into conflict with law, thus it would be more sensible to conclude that it is a combination of the following:[7]

- Dysfunctional families, which lead to the lack of limits to be imposed on children and the waiver of parental control;[8]
- Social deprivation;
- Immigration. The existence of immigrant minors that enter illegally in the country alone has become an important risk factor following the immigration wave suffered by Spain during the last 15–20 years. The fact that these minors find themselves alone outside their home countries, homeless, unemployed and unable to communicate in a different language contributes highly to bring them into conflict with law;[9]
- Gang membership: Some immigrants see it as a way to reaffirm national identity and a sense of belonging;
- School failure;
- Unemployment;

[6] C Rechea Alberola and AL Cuervo García, *Menores Agresores en el Ámbito Familiar (Estudio de Casos)* Report, (2009) available online at: http://www.uclm.es/criminologia/pdf/17-2009.pdf, accessed 8 July 2009.

[7] Information extracted from: C Rechea Alberola report elaborated under commission of the CGPJ (Judicial Power governmental organ) 'Conductas Antisociales y Delictivas de los Jóvenes en España' (2008) Available online at http://www.uclm.es/criminologia/pdf/17-2009.pdf, accessed 8 June 2009; *Memoria Fiscalía* 2008 (Prosecution Service Annual Report 2008); A Andrés Pueyo, 'Violencia juvenil: realidad actual y factores psicológicos implicados' (2006) 29 Revista ROL de Enfermería 1; JM de la Rosa Cortina, 'El Fenómeno de la delincuencia juvenil: Causas y tratamientos' (2003) Encuentros Multidisciplinares 13. 9–10, available online at http://www.encuentros-multidisciplinares.org/Revistan°13/José%20Miguel%20de%20la%20Rosa%20Cortina.pdf, accessed 5 June 2009; Papers submitted to the *I Congreso Internacional de Responsabilidad Penal de Menores* (I International Conference on Criminal Responsibility of Minors) celebrated in Madrid in February 2008; Defez (n 2); and Morant (n 4).

[8] However, the waiver of parental control has also been observed in 'normalized' families that, due to a desire to give their children a less strict upbringing than they received, have found themselves trapped in a situation where they are unable to exercise any control over their children. This is also the case of families that influenced by the excessive consumerism of modern society who raise spoilt children who don't take 'no' for an answer. On the other hand, it has also been detected that an excessive control over children has led them to come into conflict with the law as a 'way of escape' as well.

[9] Despite these particular situations and contrary to the public opinion, it cannot be said that being an immigrant or the children of immigrants in Spain is per se a risk factor. It is however, the combination of other factors which may bring immigrant minors into conflict with the law.

- Drug or alcohol abuse is a significant risk factor;[10]
- Psychological factors such as lack of concentration, impulsive behaviour or hyperactivity leading to a lack of self-control;
- Negative influence of the media. The media is accused of creating the feeling among juveniles that violence is socially accepted;[11]
- 'Feeling of impunity'. There is an extended feeling among society that minors are overprotected by the law. The media has actively contributed to this feeling by distorting reality.

II. HISTORICAL OVERVIEW OF THE SPANISH CRIMINAL LAW IN RELATION TO CHILDREN

The Spanish criminal system in relation to children evolved historically from a 'classic model' to a 'tutelary system' to eventually a more modern and coherent 'responsibility system', which is the one currently in force.[12]

The first system or 'classic model' was adopted in the Spanish Criminal Codes of 1822, 1848–50 and 1870, with slight alterations. The basis of this system was the absence of *culpa* in the actions of those aged between seven and nine years and the consideration of the awareness capacity of those aged between seven to nine and 15 to 16 years. Therefore, only where the discernment test evidenced that minors, in the period aforementioned, were acting fully aware of the repercussion of their actions, they could be held accountable under criminal law. Penalties imposed were similar to those imposed upon adults, although reduced.

The Spanish Penal Code of 1928 introduced what could be called the 'tutelary model'. This model was characterized by excluding minors from the criminal responsibility system applicable to adults through a mechanism purely based on a chronological or biological criterion. Offenders over 16 years were criminally accountable although being aged between 16 and 18 years was considered an extenuating circumstance.[13]

---

[10] It is very significant that according to a survey made in the Juvenile Internment Centre 'El Laurel' in Madrid in 2007, 80 per cent of the juvenile interned had taken illegal drugs. LG Cieza paper 'Programa de intervención por maltrato familiar ascendente de la Agencia de la Comunidad de Madrid para la reeducación y reinserción del menor infractor: resultados y proyectos' submitted to the *I Congreso Internacional de Responsabilidad Penal de Menores* conference, 149.

[11] Defez (n 2) 40, states that according to the International Congress 'The TV We Want' celebrated in Huelva University in November 2005, Spanish TV broadcasts 670 homicides, 12,000 violent acts, 14,000 sex references and 2,000 commercials promoting the consumption of alcohol, every week.

[12] J Sáinz-Cantero Caparrós, 'Fundamentos Teóricos y Antecedentes del Sistema de Responsabilidad Penal de los Menores' available online at: http://www.cej.justicia.es/pdf/publicaciones/secretarios_judiciales/SECJUD24.pdf, accessed 5 June 2009, 5138–5152.

[13] ibid and 'Imputabilidad y edad penal' available online http://www.porticolegal.com/pa_articulo.php?ref=271, accessed 11 May 2009.

The reform of the Penal Code operated in 1963, during the dictatorship of Franco, provided for the adoption of governmental measures against those minor offenders who, having committed a crime before the age of 16, were not suitable cases for re-education. Unfortunately, this period saw the proliferation of Reformatories that regrettably were reproductions of prisons and which instead of having a rehabilitative effect led to the stigmatization of youngsters.

The system remained in force after the end of the Dictatorship in 1975 and during the beginning of the Democratic period.[14] The milestone was the Constitutional Court judgment 36/1991 of 14 February, which declared article 15 of the 1948 *Ley de Tribunales Tutelares de Menores* (1948 Tutelary Tribunals for Minors Act) contrary to the 1978 Spanish Constitution for violating fundamental rights such as the right to an impartial judge, the right to be informed of the charges brought against him, and the right to the presumption of innocence. [15]

The long-awaited change came with the proclamation of the Spanish Penal Code of 1995.[16] The new system was called the 'responsibility model' and its foundation is the consideration of minors as individuals fully responsible for their actions. However, considering their special characteristics, as human beings still in development and the socialization process, they require special protection and may not be submitted to the same legal framework as adults.[17]

Unfortunately, the system established by the Penal Code of 1995 was not complete, as it set the minimum liability age at 18 years, leaving the regulation of the liability of those under 18 years of age to a future law on the criminal responsibility of minors. Regrettably, five years passed until the Organic Law 5/2000 of 12 January on the Criminal Responsibility of Minors (hereinafter CRMA) was passed and the legal framework clearly defined.[18]

---

[14] After the death of the Dictator Francisco Franco on the 20 November, 1975, Spain entered a transitional process towards democracy. It was the Spanish Constitution (hereinafter SC) passed by the Cortes Generales in Plenary meetings of the Congress of Deputies and the Senate held on October 31, 1978 and ratified by the Spanish People in the Referendum of December 7, 1978, that proclaimed Spain as a social and democratic State, subject to the rule of law, advocating as higher values of its legal order, liberty, justice, equality and political pluralism. The SC is the supreme norm of the Spanish legal order and citizens and public authorities are bound by the Constitution and all other legal provisions.

[15] The Constitutional Court was established by the Spanish Constitution of 1978 and developed by Organic Act 2/1979 of 3 of October. It is the supreme interpreter of the Constitution, and an independent judicial organ from the rest of the Spanish Judiciary, bound only by the Constitution and its law. The declaration of unconstitutionality implies the nullity of the provision(s) scrutinized, as well as of all those included in the same law connected to it/them. The judgments of the Constitutional Court have the validity of *res judicata* from the day following their publication, and no appeal may be brought against them.

[16] The 1995 Penal Code was passed by Organic Act 10/1995 of 23 November.

[17] Sáinz-Cantero (n 12) 5146–5148.

[18] In the meantime, the loophole was filled by maintaining the preceding system whereby

A. The Spanish Legal System and International Treaties

Contrary to other legal systems, which require the passing of a law implementing international treaties, Spain follows an automatic implementation system from official publication of international treaties validly concluded.[19]

The Spanish Constitution (SC) does not expressly include any provision for the status of international treaties within the Spanish legal order. However, the doctrine has interpreted the impossibility of amending, repealing or suspending the provisions of international treaties by national law included in the SC[20] as evidence of the 'supra-legality' of treaties.[21] Nevertheless, there is no doubt about the 'infra-constitutionality' of international treaties, which means that no international treaty may oppose the provisions contained in the SC, the supreme norm of the Spanish legal order.[22]

With regard to the conclusion of international treaties, only by means of an organic law[23] authorization may be granted for concluding treaties.[24] Additionally, the State shall require the prior authorization of the *Cortes Generales* before contracting obligations by means of treaties or agreements of special relevance, such as treaties affecting the fundamental rights and duties recognized in the Constitution, like the United Nations Convention on the Rights of the Child (UNCRC).[25]

In addition to this mechanism of scrutiny of the constitutionality before the conclusion of international treaties or agreements, there is also a judicial procedure named *'recurso de inconstitucionalidad'* (appeal against

---

an offender between the ages of 16 and 18 was subject to the adult judicial system, although with a lesser degree of criminal responsibility.

[19] In fact, the Spanish Supreme Court *(Tribunal Supremo)* has expressly rejected the obligation to transform international law into national law as a condition for their application in Spain. Therefore, according to art 96.1 of the SC: 'Validly concluded treaties, once officially published in Spain, shall form part of the internal legal order.'

[20] ibid. It further states: 'Their provisions may only be repealed, amended or suspended in the manner provided in the treaties themselves or in accordance with the general rules of international law.'

[21] JD González Campos et al, *Curso de Derecho Internacional Público* (5th edn, Servicio Publicaciones Facultad Derecho Universidad Complutense Madrid, 1992) 239.

[22] SC arts 95.1 and 161.1.a). Cosculluela states that the SC prevails over all powers, including the legislative power. L Cosculluela Montaner, *Manual de Derecho Administrativo Tomo I* (19th edn, Thomson Civitas, Madrid, 2008) 71.

[23] Organic laws are those reserved to regulate highly sensitive matters, such as the development of fundamental rights and liberties

[24] SC art 93.

[25] According to SC art 94.1, authorization of the 'Cortes Generales' is required in the following cases: a) treaties of a political nature; b) treaties or agreements of a military nature; c) treaties or agreements affecting the territorial integrity of the State or the fundamental rights and duties established under Title I; d) treaties or agreements which imply financial liabilities for the Public Treasury; e) treaties or agreements which involve amendment or repeal of some law or require legislative measures for their execution.

unconstitutionality) for the control of those officially published.[26] The declaration of unconstitutionality implies the nullity of the provision(s) scrutinized, as well as of all those included in the same treaty connected to it/them.[27]

Once international treaties have been integrated into the Spanish legal order, citizens and public authorities are bound by them in the same way they are bound by the Constitution and all other legal provisions.[28]

B. Age of Criminal Liability

The legal minimum age of criminal liability under the Spanish Penal Code is 18 years.[29] If a person younger than 18 years of age commits a criminal act he may be held responsible in accordance with the law which governs the criminal responsibility of minors, which is the CRMA. Accordingly, article 1.1 of the CRMA states that 'it will be applied demanding that those persons older than 14 and younger than 18 years of age take responsibility for their own actions if committing a criminal offence according to the Penal Code'. In order to determine the applicable law, the age to consider is that of the person when the action was committed.[30]

In relation to the minimum age to be held accountable under the CRMA, article 3 establishes that 'when the perpetrator of a criminal act is younger than 14 years old criminal responsibility will not apply in accordance with current legislation. In this case, the minor will be subject to the system for the protection of children as prescribed by the Civil Code'.

C. The Rights of the Child in Criminal Matters in the Spanish Legal System

The Spanish system of criminal liability of minors follows a special procedure, regulated by the CRMA, separate from that applicable to adults. The CRMA outlines a legal proceedings characterized by the absolute respect for the legal guarantees recognized in the Constitution and the pre-eminence of the minor's interests. It is also a flexible procedure, which allows the search for the best possible available option, aimed at the re-education of minor

---

[26] Organic Act 2/1979 of 3 October on the Constitutional Court, art 27.Second.c).

[27] ibid art 39. One.

[28] SC art 9.1

[29] According to Penal Code art 19: 'Those offenders younger than 18 years of age will not be held criminally responsible'.

[30] CRMA art 5.3. The system is based on biological age, which leaves no room for interpretation by courts and tribunals. In the absence of official identity documents, it is necessary to resort to documents such as birth or christening certificates or ultimately to a forensic report if age determination is not possible by the previous means. The alternative use of modern medical techniques such as DNA test has also been suggested.

offenders, in every phase of the proceedings. In addition, the system requires that everyone involved in the cases including the court, the prosecutor, the lawyers, police and social services are minor specialists.[31]

The principles informing regulation that may be extracted from the Preamble of the CRMA, are the following:

- The supremacy of the interests of the minor. The aim is not 'punishing' but 'rehabilitating' the minor, providing them with psychological and socio-educational skills for redressing the imbalance that led them to anti-social behaviour;[32]
- Absolute respect for the legal guarantees recognized in the SC. The CRMA guarantees respect for the following principles;
- The accusatory principle. It may be defined as a rule according to which proceedings may only be initiated on the basis of the appropriate request, the indictment, by an authorized prosecutor;
- The right to defence. Minors under detention have the right to those exercising legal guardianship being immediately informed of the detention and the place of custody;[33]
- The right to the presumption of innocence;
- The right of access to a judge;
- Establishment of different age groups for procedural and punishable purposes. The special system introduced by the CRMA, which keeps minor offenders out of the adult system, applies to minors between 14 and 18 years old. However, measures will be imposed more severely on those aged between 17 and 18 years than on those aged between 14 and 16, due to the higher level of maturity attributed to the former group;
- Principle of flexibility. The flexibility is manifest in the possibility of the judge to modify or substitute the measures imposed, which is not possible in adult jurisdiction;[34]

---

[31] CRMA, Final Disposition Fourth.

[32] The Spanish Supreme Court has declared that the principle of the superior interests of the minor means that the law must be interpreted in the most favourable way to the minor. Therefore the Supreme Court judgement of 20 April 1987 states: '(...) debe procurarse, ante todo, el beneficio o interés de los menores, en orden a su desarrollo personal y a la satisfacción de sus derechos legalmente sancionados, por encima de los legítimos intereses de los progenitores, constituyendo, este principio de protección integral y preferente de los hijos menores, un criterio teleológico de interpretación normativa que debe presidir la aplicación de la ley' citing the *Audiencia Provincial* of Asturias judgement of 26 September 2002.

[33] CRMA, art 17.1.

[34] It is worth mentioning CRMA, art 7.3 when saying that in the election of the measure/s to be imposed, both the Prosecutor and the offender's legal counsel in their pleadings, and the judge in his judgment must consider in a flexible way not only the evidence submitted and the legal interpretation of the facts, but specially the age, social and family circumstances, the personality and the best interests of the minor.

- Principle of opportunity. Closely related to the principles of flexibility and the best interests of the minor, the principle of opportunity brings the possibility of the Juvenile Prosecutor not to prosecute a case under certain circumstances;[35]
- Principle of proportionality. The CRMA system seeks to achieve proportionality between the measure imposed and the age and other psychological, personal and domestic situation of the offender;[36]
- Principle of minimum intervention. The CRMA provides for an extra-ordinary mechanism of extra-judicial dispute resolution through mediation, not available so far in adult jurisdiction;
- Respect for the victim's interests. The victims may exercise the private prosecution of the case. The CRMA also regulates a simultaneous civil procedure for damages declaring the joint liability of parents, tutors, foster parents or guardians of the minors.[37]

D. Rights of the Juvenile Held in Juvenile Centres

In case of detention, fundamental rights shall always be respected both at the time of arrest and during the period the minor remains under detention. The detainee has always the right to be assisted by a lawyer and to be accompanied by their legal guardian or by other Juvenile Prosecutor, in their absence, while providing any statement.[38] During the time under detention, the minor shall also be provided with food, clothes, and the appropriate security, health and privacy conditions.[39] Furthermore, they shall be retained in custody in appropriate and separate facilities to those used for adults and they shall be protected and provided with any social, psychological, medical and physical assistance they may require taking into account their age, gender and other individual circumstances.[40] The Police have 24 hours to place the detainee under the authority of the Prosecutor.[41]

In particular, the CRMA recognizes the following rights for juvenile offenders:[42]

---

[35] According to CRMA, art 18, the Juvenile Prosecutor may decide not to prosecute a case taking into account the sporadic nature of the actions, the less gravity of the offense, the lack of criminal records, the mental age of the minor and any other circumstances.

[36] JA Blanco Barea, 'Responsabilidad Penal del Menor: Principios y Medidas Judiciales Aplicables en el Derecho Penal Español' [2008] Revista de Estudios Jurídicos nº 8/2008 (Segunda Época) 15.

[37] CRMA, Title VIII, arts 61 to 64.

[38] Royal Decree 1774/2004 of 30 July on the Criminal Responsibility of Minors, art 3.

[39] ibid art 4.

[40] CRMA, art 17.

[41] ibid art 17.4.

[42] ibid art 56.

- Right to respect of personality;
- Right to freedom of religion and thought;
- Right to life, to health and to physical integrity. Under no circumstances may they be subjected to torture or to inhuman or degrading punishment or treatment. Neither may they be subjected to arbitrary or excessive severity in the application of the norms;
- Right to receive appropriate educational or vocational training;
- Right to dignity and privacy;
- Right to exercise their political, civil, social, religious, economical and cultural rights provided they are compatible with the measure imposed;
- Right to be interned in the institution closest to their permanent address;
- Right to health assistance and to compulsory education;
- Right to participate in the programmes of the institution;
- Right to freedom of communication;
- Right to employment, if compatible;
- Right to information;
- Right to be accompanied by their under three-year old children, according to the terms and conditions laid down by the applicable regulation.

E. Special Procedures for Juveniles

The competent judicial organ to hear a criminal offense allegedly committed by a minor is the *'Juzgado de Menores'* (Juvenile Court), a specialized judicial authority which has a separate jurisdiction to that of adults.[43] The CRMA provides for the specialization of judges, prosecutors and legal counsel participating in legal proceedings involving minors.[44] Specialization within the police is offered by the *GRUMES* (Special Agents of the National Police for Minors) and the *EUMES* (Special Agents of the *Guardia Civil*[45] for Minors).

Whereas in adult jurisdiction, the *'Juzgado de Instrucción'* (Examining Court) is the competent organ to prosecute a case, it is the Prosecutor who carries out this task in the juvenile jurisdiction. Should the Juvenile Prosecutor consider there is no evidence of criminal offence, the minor should be freed immediately or no later than after the first 48 hours following detention.[46] The Juvenile Prosecutor may also decide to discontinue the prosecution under certain circumstances.[47]

---

[43] ibid art 2.
[44] ibid Preamble, para II.17 and art 54.1.
[45] Spanish Gendarmerie.
[46] CRMA, art 17.5.
[47] ibid art 19. Where the accused has committed a lesser non-violent crime and has not caused serious physical injury, provided that one of the following circumstances has also

In the case of the Juvenile Prosecutor finding evidence of a criminal offence, he can try to reach a friendly settlement assisted by a Technical Support Team formed of psychologists, social workers and educators, appointed to the Prosecution Service. Should this extrajudicial settlement succeed, the Prosecutor will declare the termination of the proceedings.[48]

Where an extrajudicial settlement is unsuitable, the Prosecutor shall conduct the investigation of all the circumstances surrounding the case assisted by the Police and other experts.[49] In the meantime and only where considered appropriate, the Juvenile Prosecutor may request from the Juvenile Court the adoption of precautionary measures against the accused such as custody,[50] probation, sharing a residence with an educational group or restraining order.[51]

After the assessment of the situation by a psychologist, a social worker and an educator, the Technical Support Team would elaborate a report comprising a description of the psychological, educational and domestic situation of the minor, together with an assessment of the social context as well as any other circumstances considered relevant and that may have influenced the action attributed to the underage person.[52] The Technical Support Team may also recommend the imposition of socio-educational tasks, a restoration activity, the attempt of reconciliation with the victim and even the discontinuance of the proceedings, where this would result in the best interests of the minor.[53]

Once the investigation process is complete, the Juvenile Prosecutor may request from the Juvenile Court the dismissal of the proceedings or, on the contrary, may decide the committal for trial to the Juvenile Court.[54] Should the case be referred to the Juvenile Court for trial, the Juvenile Judge may immediately issue a judgment imposing a measure provided this has been previously agreed by all the parties.[55] Where there is no such agreement, the Court will call for a public hearing.[56] Under no circumstances is the media

---

occurred: 1. The minor has been reconciled with the victim. 2.The minor has committed to make good the harm caused to the victim. 3. The minor has agreed to follow an educational programme.

[48] ibid.   [49] ibid art 23.

[50] According to CRMA, art 28.2 and 3, for the adoption of this precautionary measure there must be considered the gravity of the offense allegedly committed, the personal and social circumstances of the minor, the possibility of an attempted escape and especially if the minor has committed the same type of offence in the past. In any case, the precautionary measure of internment can initially exceed six months, extended for a maximum of another three months.

[51] ibid art 28. These precautionary measures may only be requested where there is circumstantial evidence of committing a crime and of the intention of the minor to elude or obstruct the course of the justice, or to make an attempt against the legal rights of the victim.

[52] ibid art 27.   [53] ibid.
[54] ibid art 30.   [55] ibid art 32.
[56] ibid art 34.

authorized to obtain or disseminate any images or any data that would allow for the identification of the minors.[57]

During the public hearing the parties will submit evidence and the judge will hear them all (including the Technical Support Team, the victim and the minor accused).[58] Then he will issue a sentence always bearing in mind the best interests of the minor, considering the reports provided by the experts.[59]

Regarding the length of the measures, some rules must be observed.[60] Under no circumstances may the length of the measures exceed that applied to a crime committed by an adult according to the Penal Code.[61]

1. Re-examination of the means of punishment is one of the main features of the CRMA[62]

Should the minor reach the legal age (18) under one of the measures of protection mentioned above, they will remain applicable until the achievement of the objectives set up in the sentence. However, if the minor reaches

---

[57] ibid art 35.2.

[58] Following the 2006 reform of the CRMA, the victims may participate in all phases of the proceedings. Therefore, they may submit written and oral pleadings as well as evidence and must be informed at all time of the course of the proceedings.

[59] According to CRMA, art 7.1, The measures to be imposed are the following: a) Closed internment in a young offenders' institution. b) Semi-open internment in a young offenders' institution. c) Open internment in a young offenders' institution. d) Therapeutic internment (in closed, semi-open or open institution). e) Treatment as an outpatient. f) Attendance of a day centre. g) Weekend restriction. h) Probation. i) Restraining order. j) Sharing a residence with another person, family or group. k) Community service. l) Completion of socio-educational tasks. m) Admonishment or warning. n) Driving ban. o) Disallowance for public service.

[60] Following CRMA, art 10, internment in a closed prison may only be imposed: a. Where the facts constitute a serious criminal offence according to the Penal Code. b. Where despite being considered a less serious criminal offence, violence and intimidation was inflicted upon people or they were at high risk of physical harm. c. Where the facts were committed by a group or the minor belonged to a criminal organization. In the case of serious criminal offences, the following rules apply: Should the minor be 14 or 15 when the offence was committed, the measure imposed may last for three years and between one and six years if the person was 16 or 17 years old. Where the offence constitutes homicide, murder, rape, terrorism or any other criminal offence for which imprisonment for fifteen or more years may be imposed according to the Penal Code, the judge shall impose the following measures: 1. Internment in closed prison between one and five years if at the time of the crime the minor was 14 or 15 years old; between one and eight years if at the time of the crime minor was 16 or 17 years old; in the case of multiple offences of this kind, closed internment may be imposed for up to 10 years on those aged over 16 and up to six years on those between 14 and 16 years, followed by probation.

[61] ibid art 8.

[62] ibid art 13 establishes that 'the judge may at the request of the Juvenile Prosecutor, the offender's legal counsel or the public body responsible for the protection of minors, at any time reduce or amend a sentence, provided such amendment is in the interests of the minor and the minor expresses regret for his behaviour.'

the legal age while under closed internment, the Juvenile Judge may decide to transfer the offender to a prison for the remaining time.[63]

Appeals may be lodged before the specialized organs of the higher tribunals.[64] The implementation of the imposed measures is also of the competence of specialized organs within the Autonomous Community where the Juvenile Court issuing a judgment is based.[65] The Autonomous Community must undertake all necessary endeavours to establish, organize and manage the institutions, services and adequate programmes to guarantee the correct execution of the measures incorporated in the CRMA.[66] It has been common practice the Autonomous Communities entering into agreements with non-profit organizations for the execution of such judicial measures.

F. Social Counsellors

The role of the Technical Support Team is also very relevant during the process, as they may advise both the Juvenile Court and the Juvenile Prosecutor on the most adequate type of judicial measure from an educational point of view as well as about the changes, replacements, reduction or cancellation of the measures previously undertaken.[67]

The work of the Technical Support Teams is also key to achieving the objectives of social rehabilitation and re-education established in the law. They play that important role, inter alia, by giving some orientation to the offenders' families, especially on the Social Services' resources available to them.

In relation to the victims' families, wide support is given by the State through crime victim support bureaux located at the seats of courts.[68] Support given includes economic aid to victims of violent crimes or sexual offences, as well as all kind of assistance such as legal or psychological aid

---

[63] The same will apply in cases where closed internment was imposed when the offender was 21 years old or reaches that age during internment, unless the judge decides otherwise. The judge will make this decision after considering the opinion of the Juvenile Prosecutor, the offender's legal counsel, the Technical Support Team and the public body responsible for the protection of minors.

[64] The sentence handed down by the Juvenile Court is subject to remedy of appeal before the juvenile division or section of the corresponding *Audiencia Provincial (*Provincial Tribunal) or *Tribunal Superior de Justicia* (High Court of Justice) and the issue shall be settled after the holding of a public hearing that must be attended by the parties. Sentences handed down on appeal by the juvenile divisions of the High Courts of Justice are subject, according to certain conditions, to remedy of appeal to vacate the judgement for unification of doctrine before the second division of the *Tribunal Supremo (*Supreme Court).

[65] CRMA, art 45.   [66] ibid.   [67] ibid art 27.
[68] The provision of support and assistance to victims of crime is regulated by Act 35/1995 of 11 December, on support and assistance to victims of violent crimes and sexual offences.

provided by a full range of experts, including lawyers, psychologists, social workers, etc.[69]

G. Spanish Laws Concerning Juvenile Offenders and the UNCRC

The State fulfilled its positive obligation to protect UNCRC rights in different ways. The first one is by the insertion in the SC of the right of children to the protection provided for in the international agreements which safeguard their rights.[70] Also by the express recognition in article 1.2 of the CRMA of the rights enunciated in the UNCRC of 20 November 1989 and any other rules on the protection of minors included in international treaties ratified by Spain.

Secondly, the State also fulfils this obligation to implement UNCRC rights through the application of the UNCRC by national courts, playing a double function: On the one hand, the UNCRC may be directly invoked before national courts as it forms part of our legal order.[71] On the other hand, it may serve as interpretation guide of fundamental rights provisions contained in the CRMA.[72]

Thirdly, the State also protects international law rights by the incorporation in the CRMA itself of the full catalogue of fundamental rights and liberties recognized in the UNCRC and other relevant instruments such as the Beijing Rules on the Administration of Juvenile Justice,[73] the United Nations Regulations for the Protection of Minors in Detention,[74] and the

---

[69] The Police offer this service to victims immediately after they report a crime. Currently, there are more than 80 crime victim support bureaux in the territory of Spain.

[70] SC, art 39.4.

[71] ibid art 96.1. As an example invocation of the UNCRC: Judgment of the *Audiencia Provincial* of Ourense of 18 February 1998; resolution of the *Audiencia Provincial* of La Rioja no.131/2003 of 7 July; Constitutional Court judgement no. 36/1991 of 14 February; and judgement of the *Audiencia Provincial* of Jaén no. 3/2003 of 30 January.

[72] This interpretative value is recognized in the SC, art 10.2 which declares that 'the principles relating to the fundamental rights and liberties recognized by the Constitution shall be interpreted in conformity with the Universal Declaration of Human Rights and the international treaties and agreements thereon ratified by Spain' including the UNCRC. The Constitutional Court judgment 38/1981 of 23 November declared that once the interpretative criteria contained in the SC itself have been exhausted without sufficient clarification of the scope of certain fundamental rights, international treaties must serve as a source of interpretation of the constitutional provisions. Therefore, although human rights enunciated in international instruments, such as the UNCRC, do not have constitutional status in Spain unless they are also articulated in the SC, art 10.2 imposes a duty to interpret fundamental rights according to those international treaties and agreements that, in practice, equates to define the constitutional content of the rights. Indeed, the Constitutional Court in its judgments 36/1991 of 14 February and 254/1993 of 20 July recognized that in some cases international treaties define the exact content of constitutional rights

[73] Adopted by UN General Assembly resolution 40/33 of 29 November 1985.

[74] Adopted by the UN General Assembly in resolution 45/113 passed on 14 December 1990.

United Nations Guidelines for the Prevention of Juvenile Delinquency (the Riyadh Guidelines).[75]

To summarize, the implementation of the UNCRC and other relevant international instruments in the Spanish legal order is threefold: Firstly, international conventions form part of the Spanish legal order since their ratification. Therefore, their provisions are binding on all citizens and public authorities. Secondly, they widen the essential content of the fundamental rights and liberties constitutionally recognized through the direct invocation of international law by the Spanish national courts. Thirdly, implementation operates through the full incorporation into the Spanish criminal responsibility of minors' regulation (CRMA) of the mandates introduced by international law regarding children.

H. Death Penalty

Capital punishment under any circumstances was abolished in Spain in 1995. The SC stated that the death penalty shall be abolished, except as provided for by military criminal law in times of war.[76] However, the Organic Law 11/95 of 27 November modified the Military Penal Code replacing capital punishment by 30 years imprisonment and abolishing definitively the death penalty in Spain.

I. Recommendations

Focusing on the UN Committee on the Rights of the Child (CRC), Spain submitted its second periodic report on 12 October 1998 under article 44 of the UNCRC.[77] In this report, Spain provided information on what, at that moment, was a Draft Organizational Act on the penal responsibility of minors. The Spanish report stated that the draft was based on the following general principles:

(a) The non-penal but corrective and educative nature of the procedure and measures applicable to juvenile offenders, which should be oriented towards effective reintegration, with the overriding interests of the juvenile in mind;
(b) Express recognition of all the guarantees founded upon respect for constitutional rights and the special requirements imposed by the juvenile's interests;

---

[75] According to Blanco (n 36) 3.   [76] SC, art 15.
[77] 'Committee on the Rights of the Child, 'Consideration of Reports Submitted by States Parties Under Article 44 of the Convention' Periodic Reports of States Parties due in 1999: Spain' CRC/C/70/Add.9, available online at http://www.unhchr.ch/tbs/doc.nsf/(Symbol)/CRC.C.70.Add.9. En?OpenDocument, accessed 8 July 2009.

(c) Differentiation for procedural and corrective purposes between various types within the category of juvenile offenders;

(d) Flexibility in the adoption and execution of the measures suggested by the circumstances of each specific case;

(e) Competence of the autonomous bodies for the protection of juveniles to implement the measures prescribed in the sentence;

(f) Judicial supervision of their implementation.

After consideration of the Pre-Sessional Working Group of the Committee on the Rights of the Child, 30th Session, the State was requested to submit in written form additional and updated statistical data (including, where relevant, by gender, age, type of crime) covering the period between 1999 to 2001, on:[78]

a) the number of juvenile courts and their location within the country;

b) number of minors who allegedly committed a crime reported to the police;

c) number of minors who were sentenced by Courts to sanctions, and the nature of sanctions (community service; detention; other types of sanctions);

d) the number of juveniles detained and imprisoned, the location of their detention or imprisonment (eg police station, jail or other place) and the lengths of their detention or imprisonment, including pre-trial detention;

e) percentage of recidivism cases.

The CRC also asked Spain to provide further information on measures taken to implement effectively the laws recently adopted in order to ensure compliance with the UNCRC, in particular Act 1/1996 on the Legal Protection of the Minor and Act 5/2000 on the Penal Responsibility of the Child.[79]

Spain submitted its written replies supplying the updated statistical data required.[80] In relation to general measures of implementation, Spain stated that most of the Autonomous Communities had already put into practice specific programmes for minors in accordance with Organic Act 1/1996 on

---

[78] CRC/C/Q/SPA/2, Implementation of the Convention on the Rights of the Child, 'List of issues to be taken up in connection with the consideration of the second periodic report of Spain (CRC/C/70/Add.9)' available online at: http://www.unhchr.ch/tbs/doc.nsf/(Symbol)/ CRC.C.Q.SPA.2. En?OpenDocument, accessed 8 July 2009.

[79] Bear in mind that at the time the report was considered by the Committee the CRMA (Act 5/2000) had already been passed.

[80] The written response of Spain is available online at: http://www.unhchr.ch/html/menu2/6/ crc/doc/replies/wr-spain-2-sp.pdf, accessed 8 July 2009.

the Judicial Protection of Minors. Regarding the CRMA, it was reported that the Royal Decree regulating its implementation was still in progress.

The CRC, at its 804th meeting, held on 7 June 2002, adopted, among others, the following concluding observations included in the report of the 30th Session:[81]

> The Committee welcomes the great progress and achievements made by the State party since the examination of the initial report to the Committee in 1994. It notes with appreciation that it has made the protection and promotion of the rights of the child a general rule in the society.
>
> The Committee welcomes the new laws adopted at the national and the Autonomous Community levels to ensure better compliance of the domestic legislation with the provisions of the Convention, in line with its previous recommendation.[82] In particular, it notes the Organizational Act 1/1996 of 15 January on the legal protection of minors, the partial amendment of the Civil Code and the Civil Proceedings Act (the Protection of Minors Act), the Organizational Act 5/2000 of 12 January on penal responsibility for minors, and the amendments to the Criminal Code with reference to offences against sexual integrity (Act 11/1999) and protection of victims of ill-treatment (Act 14/1999).
>
> The Committee notes with satisfaction that, in line with its previous recommendation on coordination mechanisms (ibid para 12), the State party established the Observatory for Children in 1999. It further notes that some Autonomous Communities created institutions or services specifically responsible for children, among others the Council of Children's Affairs of Andalusia, the Office for the Defence of the Rights of the Child of the Balearic Islands, the provincial coordination committees for the care of children in Castilla-La Mancha, and the Institute for Children and the Family of Madrid, and that a network of Municipalities for children's rights was established in 1996.

However, regarding the administration of juvenile justice more specifically, the Committee expressed the following concerns:[83]

---

[81] Committee on the Rights of the Child, (30th Session) 'Consideration of reports submitted by States parties under art 44 of the Convention' Concluding observations of the Committee on the Rights of the Child: Spain' CRC/C/15/Add.185, available online at http://www.unhchr.ch/tbs/doc.nsf/(Symbol)/ CRC.C.15.Add.185.En?OpenDocument, para 470–47, accessed 8 July 2009.

[82] CRC/C/15/Add.28 of 24 October 1994, para 18.

[83] ibid para 520.

The Committee welcomes the adoption of the Organizational Act 5/2000 of 12 January on penal responsibility for minors and its educational character, but notes that it would need additional human and financial resource to be implemented effectively. It further notes with concern that the Organizational Act 7/2000 on terrorism increases the period of police custody and the length of prison terms for children accused of terrorism (to up to 10 years). It expresses its concern also at the fact that deprivation of liberty is not used as last resort and that in some cases detention centres are overcrowded.

Accordingly, it made the following recommendations:[84]

In light of articles 37 to 40 and other relevant international standards, the Committee recommends that the State party:
(a) Allocate adequate human and financial resources in order to ensure the full implementation of the Organizational Act 5/2000;
(b) Align the period of police custody for children accused of terrorism with the provisions of the Act and review the length of prison terms for children accused of terrorism;
(c) Provide training on the new juvenile system to those responsible for administering juvenile justice;
(d) Encourage the use of alternative measures to the deprivation of liberty.

III. CONCLUSION

Judges as well as other experts interviewed[85] are very optimistic in relation

---

[84]   ibid para 521.

[85]   List of experts interviewed: *Excmo. Sr. D. Arturo Canalda González. Defensor del Menor de la Comunidad de Madrid* (Madrid Autonomous Community Ombudsman for Children). Date: 19 June 2009. *Ilma. Sra. Dña. Concepción Rodríguez González del Real,* Magistrate-Judge of Juvenile Court no 1 of Madrid. Date: 19 June 2009. *Ilmo. Sr. D. Víctor Embid Marco,* Magistrate-Judge of Juvenile Court no 7 of Madrid (Executing Court). Date: 22 June 2009. *D. José Luis Segovia Bernabé,* Professor of Law at *Universidad Pontificia de Salamanca* (Madrid) and Criminologist. Date: 25 June 2009. *Dna. Petra Tabanera Herranz,* Judicial Psychologist, member of the Juvenile Courts of Madrid Technical Support Team no. 8. Date: 26 June 2009. *D José Ángel Blanco Barea, Jefe del Servicio de Justicia de la Delegación de Justicia y Administración Pública de Jaén* (Head of Justice Division, Delegation of Justice and Public Administration, province of Jaén). Date: 29 June 2009. The researcher also attended public hearings in the Juvenile Court no 4 of Madrid on the 24 of June 2009 and had the opportunity to benefit from the explanations and comments from: *Ilma. Sra. Dña. Victoria Rojo Llorca,* Magistrate-Judge of Juvenile Court no 4 of Madrid. *Ilma. Sra. Dña. Nuria Martín García,* Clerk of Juvenile Court no 4 of Madrid. *Ilma. Sra. Dña. Sonsoles Cabal Cuesta,* Juvenile Prosecutor Provincial Court of Madrid. *D. Tomás Sánchez Romero,* on behalf of the *Agencia de la Comunidad de Madrid para la Reeducación y Reinserción del Menor*

to the effectiveness of the system of criminal responsibility introduced by the CRMA. They all believe the CRMA is a very flexible piece of law that provides a wide range of options to attain at all times the best interests of minors in conflict with the law. The wide discretionary power of the Judge is highly appreciated. One of the judges interviewed defined it as 'a penal law personalised'. It has also been described as a versatile law. Experts judge very positively its educational aim and the legal tools provided to achieve it. Moreover, they all believe that, despite inevitable exceptions, the system is obtaining very positive results in the re-socialization of minor offenders.[86]

Accordingly, judges interviewed do not seem to blame the legal system for the existence of juvenile delinquency but consider the solution to this problem relies on two concepts: education and integration. According to one of the judges, education is the key to avoiding juvenile delinquency. Parents' behaviour must be an example to their children. They must show affection and offer protection to them but they must also follow consistent educational patterns establishing clear limits. The combination of both affection and limits would provide children with the confidence they need at an early age. Integration is also a very important notion due to the current evolution towards more inter-cultural societies. It is, therefore, of the utmost relevance that we promote better understanding among different cultures, avoiding at all costs intolerance to other cultural, religious, ethnic, etc, backgrounds that in many cases inevitably lead to social exclusion and ultimately to delinquency.

Following the opinion of the experts interviewed, there are no significant gaps in legislation or difficulties in its enforcement. Hence, some others think that, despite the positive evaluation, more resources or a better resource optimization are needed to achieve a better correlation between law and practice. According to them, the lack of appropriate resources may somehow undermine the enforcement of the law, by for example delaying proceedings. Nevertheless, it is inevitable that some disparity may occur between the territories of the State, as a consequence of the attribution of competence to the Governments of the Autonomous Communities regarding the enforcement of the measures imposed. Obviously, a better correlation between law and practice will take place in those territories providing more resources to this end.

Infractor (Autonomous Community of Madrid Agency for the Re-education and Rehabilitation of Minor Offenders) (ARRMI). *Dña. Petra Tabanera Herranz,* Judicial Psychologist (ARRMI), member of the Juvenile Courts of Madrid Technical Support Team no. 8.

[86] Indeed, according to the Annual Report 2006 Autonomous Community of Madrid Agency for the Re-education and Rehabilitation of Minor Offenders the percentage of re-socialization in Madrid was 83 per cent in 2006.

The evaluation of the State's (including Central and Autonomous Communities governments) social policies was also found to be positive by all the interviewees. However, it is undeniable that more effort should be made in order to promote integration among citizens from different cultural backgrounds. It is also worth noting the benefit of promoting social policies aimed at developing a more extensive voluntary sector capable of providing support to a wide range of people in need. A wider presence of social educators in problem areas providing youngsters with alternatives to delinquency is also desirable.

In relation to the better strategies for improving the rights of juvenile offenders, the suggestions of the interviewees may be summarized as follows:

1. Prevention. Some of the interviewees have shown concern about the existence of individuals under the age of 14 already in conflict with the law. According to the Spanish legal order, minors below the age of 14 are not subject to the CRMA, which means that they are exempt from any criminal responsibility. Therefore, where an under 14-year-old commits a crime, the Juvenile Prosecutor has no option but to refer the case to the Social Services, as the minor is not liable. However, socio-educational measures imposed by the Social Services are not compulsory, which render them inefficient if the minor is not willing to undertake them.

   Despite the fact that, fortunately, these cases are not very numerous, experts feel particularly concerned as they may constitute early evidence of a future 'criminal career'. Nevertheless, all the experts interviewed agree that the minimum age limit at 14 is appropriate and do not suggest lowering it.

2. Special protection to juvenile offenders between 18 and 21 years. Some of the experts interviewed clearly stand for a differentiated treatment of juvenile offenders between 18 and 21 years old, according to the mandate imposed by international law. Most of the interviewees think that youngsters at this age are still capable of re-education and consequently deserve special protection. However, one of them admits that, relying on the 'discernment test' to conclude if offenders were fully aware of their actions in order to determine the applicable law (CRMA or Penal Law), would create a system based on exceptions that may lead to legal uncertainty. Another expert maintains that juvenile offenders between 18 and 21 years old at least should receive differentiated treatment in prison.

   Almost the same reasoning is behind the opinion of the experts in relation to the possibility of minor offenders being transferred to an adult prison after reaching the age of legal majority at

18.[87] Whereas most of the interviewees strongly oppose this option,[88] there is only one expert who considers it appropriate in the case of very serious crimes committed by minors almost 18 years old, subject always to the principle of proportionality.

3. Better interaction between public authorities. One of the experts considers that better interaction through agreements between public authorities would be more beneficial for minor offenders. It would be desirable to provide support from a comprehensive scope, involving not only the justice system but also other public authorities such as those in charge of health, education, employment, etc, that may play a very important role in the process of re-education or re-socialization of minor offenders.

4. Better social policies aimed at providing juveniles in conflict with the law alternatives to delinquency. Supporting juvenile offenders after compliance with judicial measures is very important to avoid reoffending.[89] This support must be orientated to the social and family environment of these juveniles as in most cases this plays a decisive role in their conflictive behaviour.

Most of the experts interviewed believe that imposing severe punishments on young children is not an appropriate strategy. Indeed, there are experts who agree that the CRMA went slightly backwards by tightening up measures to be imposed after every reform and deem excessive the length of closed interment (up to 10 years in multiple extremely serious crimes).[90] To these experts, lengthy measures would very much resemble punishment under adult jurisdiction and the aim of the CRMA is to provide a differentiated

---

[87] See section II.E.1. of this chapter.

[88] Indeed, one of the interviewees defined prison as a place for 'delinquency training'.

[89] Currently, there is no further control or supervision of the juvenile offenders once they have complied with the judicial measures imposed.

[90] Whereas the CRMA was a long awaited legal instrument demanded by doctrine and politicians, it could be said that its subsequent reforms were directly imposed by society. Particularly, it was the case of Sandra Palo (page 1 of this report) that created great 'public alarm' and generated a unanimous feeling of impunity among society. Two of the minors were sentenced to eight years internment in closed institutions followed by five years probation. The third minor was sentenced to four years interment in a closed institution (that finished in June 2007) followed by three years probation. Public reaction that followed this case opened the debate and forced central government to address an important reform of the CRMA that reverses the feeling of impunity extended among society after such an atrocious crime. Indeed, the Preamble of the Organic Law 8/2006 of 4 December, reforming the CRMA, clearly referred to the effect produced on society by very recent violent crimes and stated that the supreme interests of the minor is perfectly compatible with the adequate proportionality between the gravity of the crimes and the measures to be imposed. Otherwise the supreme interests of the minor would exclude the protection of other rights, implicitly referring to the rights of the victims and the society as a whole. The outcome of this reform was the tightening up of measure to be imposed in the case of serious crimes.

treatment. However, other expert considers that the reforms constituted an adequate response to a legitimate social call for protection after the proliferation of crimes committed by gangs as well as the public outcry created by extremely serious crimes.

There is only one interviewee that considers the measures to be imposed in extremely serious cases under the CRMA a bit short. In words of this expert: 'extraordinary measures shall be imposed in extraordinary serious crimes'. However, the remaining interviewees believe the aim of the law should not be to punish, but to educate, and that the tightening up of measures would contradict the spirit of the law. They all agree that the perception of time is different between youngsters and adults and extending the length of judicial measures would not achieve any successful result in the re-socialization process of minor offenders. On the contrary, it may negatively affect their process of personal development. Nevertheless, one of the experts believes that a long period of closed internment acts as a deterrent or 'Sword of Damocles' and therefore it is appropriate, although it does not necessarily mean it has to be imposed very frequently but only in extremely serious cases.

To conclude, it could be said that the system introduced by the CRMA offers adequate protection to children who come into conflict with the law. Essentially, because it excludes children from adult jurisdiction and creates a comprehensive system that clearly gravitates towards the best interests of minors. Considering that the best interests of minors is their re-education and re-socialization and not their punishment, the law provides for a full catalogue of educational measures to this aim. Only in the case of serious crimes internment is imposed, but always for the shortest period of time and without forgetting the educational aspect. Respect for their fundamental rights, protection, care and support is also guaranteed by the CRMA.

Notwithstanding the positive feedback of the system obtained and adopting a more cautious approach exempt from triumphalism, measures to improve juvenile delinquency problem would include: 1. Formulating better social policies aimed at preventing juvenile delinquency by promoting open dialogue among society. 2. Providing adequate resources for the successful implementation of the educational aim of the law. 3. Achieving better interaction between public authorities supplying support to juvenile offenders in the process of re-socialization from a wider perspective, including health, employment, education, and housing.

CHAPTER 12

Criminal Law and the Rights of the Child in Turkey[*]

I. INTRODUCTION

The Turkish Republic was founded in 1923 by Mustafa Kemal Atatürk, who instituted an ambitious programme of reforms designed to orient the political, social and economic structure of the country towards Western countries and neighbouring Europe in particular. It is one of the 20 most populous countries in the world. The first census of 1927 recorded a total population of 13.8 million, whereas a total of 71.5 million was returned by the last census in 2008. Children are the country's largest demographic group. The current estimated total of 27 million people under 19 years of age represents 36 per cent of the total population with under 15s and under-five-year-olds constituting 28 per cent and nine per cent of the total respectively.[1]

In its attempts to accede to the European Union, the Turkish Government is following the National Program for the Adoption of the Acquis Communautaire. As a result, Turkey is currently going through a process of major political, legal and institutional reforms. This has been reflected by the enactment of a new Penal Code[2] that entered into force on 1 June 2005, a Criminal Procedure Code, a Misdemeanours Law and an Enforcement Law. The Juvenile Courts Law has been replaced by the Child Protection Law (Act No 5395), hereinafter referred to as the CPL, which entered into force on 3 July 2005. It implemented the UN Convention on the Rights of the Child (hereinafter referred to as the UNCRC) and the 10 fundamental principles of the Beijing Rules.[3] The legislation was aimed at minimizing custody and imprisonment, accelerating trials, ensuring privacy, preventing interruption to children's education, encouraging rehabilitation and ensuring that child suspects and offenders are handled only by police

---

[*] Dr M Hakan Hakeri, Professor of Criminal Law, Dean of the Law School, University of Ondokuz Mayis, Samsun , Turkey.

[1] http://www.unicef.org/turkey/ut/ut2_2010.html#nt26.

[2] Available in English at: http://www.legislationline.org/documents/action/popup/id/6872/preview, accessed 25 February 2010.

[3] J Zermatten, 'Introduction' in J Zermatten (ed), *Training Course On Juvenile Justice for Officials from Turkey*, Working Report 2-2003, 5–6 available at: http://www.childsrights.org/html/documents/Publications/WRTurquie2003.pdf, accessed 25 February 2010.

child branches, child courts, child penitentiaries and professionals and personnel trained in dealing with children.[4] This law was particularly necessary as the last decade has shown considerable increases in reported offences by juveniles in many countries.[5] Indeed, young people commit more offences than adults although these are rather minor offences such as shoplifting and vandalism. According to criminologists, this is a universal phenomenon.

The new Child Protection Law provides protection and rehabilitation measures for children who have been exploited or forced into criminal activity and guarantees their rights to counselling, education, childcare, healthcare and housing. The Ministry of Justice was the coordinating institution for its implementation. The Ministries of Health, Labour and National Education, the General Directorate of Social Services and Child Protection[6] and various municipalities were also involved in implementing measures to protect and support children.[7]

II. NATIONAL LEGAL FRAMEWORK

At the outset, it should be noted that Turkish law follows the Civil Law tradition of continental Europe, which had its origin in Roman law, and is based on statutory or legislative enactments.[8] For example, the first Turkish penal code, enacted in 1923, was based on the Italian Penal Code of 1889.

In 1979, Turkey enacted Law No 2253 on the Establishment, Duties and Trial Procedures of Juvenile Courts, which essentially dealt with procedural matters. Thus, one of the problems encountered by the criminal justice

---

[4] 'Plus 5' Review of the 2002 Special Session on Children and World Fit for Children Plan of Action, National Progress Report, Turkey, January 2007, 17 available at: http://www.unicef.org/worldfitforchildren/files/Turkey_WFFC5_Report.pdf, accessed 25 February 2010.

[5] Dr R Miklau, 'New Tendencies and Politics in Juvenile Justice, A Challenge for The Legislator' in J Zermatten (ed) *Training Course On Juvenile Justice for Officials from Turkey* Working Report 2-2003, 9, accessed 25 February 2010.

[6] Established by Act No 2828 on Social Services and the Child Protection Agency, dated 24 May 1983.

[7] Hancı, United Nations Committee on the Rights of the Child, (42nd Session) 'Summary Record of The 1129th Meeting' (Chamber B) 2, available at http://www.unhchr.ch/tbs/doc.nsf/898586b1dc7b4043c1256a450044f331/c0418bef762dfbefc1257185002e697c/$FILE/G0642 246.pdf, accessed 25 Febuary 2010.

[8] Ü Şeref, 'Turkish Legal System and the Protection of Human Rights' SAM (Stratejik Araştırmalar Merkezi) Papers, No 3/99, 3. A new Civil Code was adopted by Parliament in November 2001 and entered into force in January 2002. The new Civil Code incorporates some amendments regarding the protection and rights of the child. See Commission of the European Communities, 2002 Regular Report on Turkey's Progress Towards Accession, 20, 40 and 45 available at: http://ec.europa.eu/enlargement/archives/pdf/key_documents/2002/tu_en.pdf, accessed 25 February 2010.

system was the lack of specific legislation relating to the protection of juveniles. As a result, the Ministry of Justice worked towards enacting a separate piece of legislation relating to children within the framework of the UNCRC and other international instruments, such as the United Nations (Havana) Rules for the Protection of Children Deprived of their Liberty and the United Nations Standard Minimum Rules for the Administration of Juvenile Justice (Beijing Rules). In addition, a number of laws were been enacted to monitor the judiciary. For example, Law No 4675 on Supervisory Judges, which entered into force on 16 May 2001, ensures that objections and complaints relating to services and practices in institutions are overseen by an independent judicial organ. Law No 4681 on Monitoring Boards for Penal Institutions and Detention Houses, which entered into force on 21 June 2001, requires that institutions be inspected at regular intervals by civil society organizations and reports drawn up further to these inspections be delivered to the Turkish Grand National Assembly and to various executive organs, such as Ministries and General Directorates, in order to take the necessary steps.

These new laws reconstructed the juvenile justice system with the aim of rendering it more child-friendly. The definition of child protection and principles governing children's rights are now more complete and in line with international instruments. A clear distinction between child delinquency and child protection has been made.[9] Article 3(1)(a) of the CPL provides the major definitions:

1. Juvenile in need of protection: any juvenile whose physical, mental, moral, social or emotional development and personal safety is in danger, who is neglected or abused, or who is a victim of crime.
2. Juvenile pushed to crime: any juvenile about whom an investigation or prosecution is carried out on the allegation that he/she has committed an act which is defined as a crime in the Laws, or any juvenile about whom a security measure has been decided due to an act he/she has committed.

    The purpose of the CPL is to regulate the procedures and principles protecting juveniles who are in need of protection or who are pushed to crime, and ensuring their rights and well-being.[10] It entails:

    •   the types of protection measures regarding children in need of protection;

---

[9] Seminar on Juvenile Justice Procedures, TAIEX Workshop, 3.

[10] Art 1 CPL 2005, available at: http://www.law.yale.edu/rcw/rcw/jurisdictions/asw/turkey/Turkey_juv_prot_law_Eng.pdf, accessed 25 February 2010.

- the institutions and organizations that are to apply these measures;
- the courts that have jurisdiction;
- the qualifications required for the appointment of judges, prosecutors and social workers who are to function in these courts;
- enforcement procedures;
- a supervision mechanism of protection orders given by the Courts.

This law also provides for a broader application of 'conciliation'[11] and introduces two important procedures, namely the possibility of suspending the pleading of the criminal case and the announcement of the verdict.[12] A child can apply to Social Services when he/she wishes to be taken by the agency. It recognizes the right of the juvenile of adequate capacity to participate in the proceedings, by taking his opinion into consideration, and to be informed about them. The question of capacity is not defined by age but is rather a factual question to be decided by the judge.[13]

One of the main goals behind the legislation was the reorganization of the services provided to children in light of international instruments, namely the UNCRC, and scientific developments.[14] In order to attain this goal, all Turkish facilities and services directed at children should ensure that:

a. they are equipped with the knowledge and resources to meet their own basic humanitarian needs and develop the potential they have;
b. the damage done to a child's psychological, social and physical integrity by the event that resulted in the restriction of their liberty is identified and undone;
c. children undergo a social, cultural, vocational, psychological, medical and physical treatment as required by their age, gender and personality, which will be aimed at their reintegration into society, will develop their esteem and trust and will reinforce their respect of the rights and freedoms of others;
d. children are brought up to be physically, intellectually, morally and emotionally healthy individuals who are aware of the importance of working and assuming a constructive role in society and who have learned to live without causing any damage to others;

---

[11] Report presented by the Minister of Justice of Turkey, in: 28th Conference of European Ministers of Justice, Lanzarote (25–26 October 2007), 5, available at: http://www.coe.int/t/dghl/standardsetting/minjust/mju28/MJU-28%282007%2914E-Turkey.pdf, accessed 25 February 2010.

[12] Arts 19 and 23 CPL 2005.

[13] http://www.law.yale.edu/rcw/rcw/jurisdictions/asw/turkey/frontpage.htm, accessed 25 Feb 2010.

[14] United Nations Children's Fund Executive Board First regular session 2006, 16-20 and 23 January 2006, Revised country programme document, Turkey, 3 available at: http://www.unicef.org/about/execboard/files/Turkey-CPD_Rev1.pdf, accessed 25/02/2010.

e.   children strengthen their relationships with their family and society;
f.   children are integrated into society by approximating life in institutions to social life and seizing every opportunity to maintain their relationship with society.[15]

In addition to the aforementioned laws, provisions on the special status of children with regards to law enforcement and procedural rights are now provided for in the Penal Code,[16] Misdemeanours Law, the Criminal Procedure Code and the Law on the Execution of Criminal and Security Measurements. Following Turkey's ratification of the UNCRC in 1995 and in line with the amendments made to its legislation thereafter, article 19 of the Regulations on Apprehension, Custody and Taking of Statements now contains special provisions concerning minors: apprehension and statement-taking powers are restricted and provision is made for juveniles to benefit from the assistance of a lawyer, for their parents or guardians to be able to choose a lawyer and for statements to be taken from under-age suspects on condition that their lawyer is present.

The draft law on 'the Organization and Duties of the General Directorate of Penal Institutions and Detention Houses', which relevant authorities are currently working on, would allow:

- a Child and Youth Services Department to be established to provide services to children in the 12–18 age group and youth in the 19–21 age group, with a single management;
- Observations and Measures Centres to be established to make up for the deficiencies in infrastructure at the trial stage;
- Education services to be inspected by the Ministry of National Education and health services by the Ministry of Health in order to make institutional services more effective.

Furthermore, works have commenced on a comprehensive regulation aiming to standardize the services provided to children who are under the supervision of General Directorate of Prisons and Detention Houses and to bring these services in line with provisions contained in international instruments. The draft regulation has been submitted to institutions, organizations and professionals. The studies were to be completed by 23 April 2002.[17]

---

[15] N Nursal, 'Juvenile Justice and treatment in Turkey' in J Zermatten (ed) *Training Course On Juvenile Justice for Officials from Turkey* Working Report 2-2003, 69, available at http://www.childsrights.org/html/documents/Publications/WRTurquie2003.pdf, accessed 25 February 2010.
[16] For example: abandonment (art 97), failure in the duty of assistance or notification (art 98), maltreatment (art 232), breach of family law obligations (art 233), kidnapping and detention of a child (art 234).
[17] See (n 15) 73.

There are three models that inspire the juvenile courts' system:[18] the welfare model, the justice model and the restorative model.[19] The welfare model places the emphasis on the person of the young offender. The latter is seen as a victim rather than an offender so that the criminal justice system should not punish him, but rather look for the causes that might explain his behaviour. The justice model is based on the idea that a young offender is responsible for his acts so that when he commits an offence he has chosen to misbehave. He therefore has to pay for it in the form of retributive punishment. The last model, the restorative justice model, focuses on re-integrating the victim into society. The young offender has to face his victim(s) and do something in order to repair the damage he has caused. Thus, mediation and service community orders are frequently used. The Turkish model is a mixture between the welfare and the justice model. Young offenders are not only sanctioned by the criminal law but also by family and welfare law laws.[20] Since 2005 however, a restorative justice model has also appeared through the use of mediation.

III. INTERNATIONAL LEGAL FRAMEWORK

Turkey ratified the European Convention on Human Rights (ECHR) on 18 May 1954[21] and has accepted the competence of the European Court of Human Rights to receive individual complaints. It signed the UNCRC on 14 September 1990 and ratified it on 9 December 1994.[22] The Social Services and Child Protection Agency (SHCEK) is the coordinating directorate for the implementation of the UNCRC. The CPL is in conformity with the UNCRC and efforts to ensure that it is fully implemented continue. Research is being conducted on the need for further legislative changes to ensure that all legislation affecting children is UNCRC-compliant.[23] Turkey

---

[18] J Zermatten, 'Face à l'évolution des droits de l'enfant, quel système judiciaire: système de protection ou système de justice?' (1994) Revue internationale de criminologie et de police technique 2.

[19] H İbrahim Bahar, Mehmet Arıcan, 'Dünya'da ve Türkiye'de Çocuk Adaletinin Gelişimi: Temel Sorunlar, Modeller ve Arayışlar' in Kriminoloji Dergisi (Turkish Journal of Criminology and Criminal Justice) (2009) CI, SI, 64–66. Also see Zermatten (n 4).

[20] See (n 5) 11.

[21] http://conventions.coe.int/Treaty/Commun/ChercheSig.asp?NT=005&CM=&DF=&CL= ENG, accessed 25/02/2010.

[22] The convention became a national legal instrument after having been ratified by Law No 4058 published in the Official Journal No 22184 of 27 January 1995. It should be noted that Turkey made a number of reservations to the Convention, which remain today. For details see: http://treaties.un.org/Pages/ViewDetails.aspx?src=TREATY&mtdsg_no=IV-11&chapter= 4&lang=en#EndDec, accessed 25/02/2010. Y Solmaz Balo, 'Teori ve Uygulamada Çocuk Ceza Hukuku' 2.B., (Ankara, 2005) 89.

[23] ibid (n 4) 4. See also art 45(1) of the CPL.

has also ratified the European Convention on the Exercise of Children's Rights on 10 June 2002[24] and the Optional Protocol to the Convention on the Rights of the Child on the involvement of children in the armed conflict on 4 May 2004[25] following a decision of the Council of Ministers on 16 October 2003 (Decision No: 4991). According to the Turkish Constitution, international human rights instruments duly ratified by Parliament have priority over national laws in case of conflict.[26] Since international conventions take precedence, they directly protect human rights in Turkey. Furthermore, the best interests of the child are guaranteed by several provisions of the Turkish Constitution:[27]

- Article 42(2) of the Constitution stipulates that 'the State will adopt appropriate measures for protecting children and establish the institutions needed therefore.'
- Article 50(2) states that 'Minors, women and persons with physical and mental handicaps will be protected by special provisions as to their working conditions.'

Thus, it can be said that Turkish law ascribes a great deal of importance to child protection. The UN Committee on the Rights of the Child (CRC) noted with appreciation the CPL, the designation of the General Directorate of Social Services and Child Protection Agency as the coordinating organization responsible for monitoring and implementation of the UNCRC and its Optional Protocol, and the amendments to the Constitution allowing for direct application of the Optional Protocol to domestic legislation and the training activities undertaken by the State party in order to enhance the awareness of the issues covered by the Optional Protocol.

---

[24] http://conventions.coe.int/Treaty/Commun/ChercheSig.asp?NT=160&CM=&DF=&CL=ENG, accessed 25/02/2010.

[25] http://treaties.un.org/Pages/ViewDetails.aspx?src=TREATY&mtdsg_no=IV-11-b&chapter=4&lang=en, accessed 25/02/2010.

[26] Art 90(5) of the Turkish Constitution: 'International agreements duly put into effect bear the force of law. No appeal to the Constitutional Court shall be made with regard to these agreements, on the grounds that they are unconstitutional. In the case of a conflict between international agreements in the area of fundamental rights and freedoms duly put into effect and the domestic laws due to differences in provisions on the same matter, the provisions of international agreements shall prevail'.

[27] The Constitution is available in English at: http://www.anayasa.gov.tr/images/loaded/pdf_dosyalari/THE_CONSTITUTION_OF_THE_REPUBLIC_OF_TURKEY.pdf, accessed 25 February 2010.

IV. DOMESTIC LEGISLATION ON THE PROTECTION OF THE RIGHTS OF
THE CHILD IN CRIMINAL LAW

A. The Age of Criminal Liability

According to article 1 of the UNCRC, 'a child means every human being below the age of eighteen years unless under the law applicable to the child, majority is attained earlier'. The new Penal Code defines a child as any person under the age of 18,[28] a definition in line with that of the UNCRC.[29] Article 3(1)(a) of the CPL defines a juvenile as 'any individual that has not yet completed the age eighteen, regardless of whether they have reached full legal age earlier'. Thus, the upper limit for the application of the special provisions of the CPL has been fixed at 18.

In the old Turkish Penal Code the minimum age of criminal liability was 12 years of age. Under article 31(1) of the new Code however, 'minors under the age of thirteen are exempt from criminal liability'. This is in line with most legal systems nowadays which provide for a criminal threshold between 13 and 15 years of age.[30] Thus, between the ages of 13 and 18, the juvenile's responsibility varies depending on his/her mental development. In some European countries, there is an interesting discussion about applying some provisions of juvenile laws to young adults, referring to the age groups of 18 to 21 and 21 to 24, but this has not been the case in Turkey.

1. Consideration given to the age of the child

As mentioned, criminal sanctions cannot be applied to a juvenile who at the time of committing an offence was under the age of 13. While such minors cannot be prosecuted, security measures may be imposed to them.

Different sanctions apply according to the age group of the juvenile offender. Where a minor is older than 12 but younger than 15 at the time the offence was committed, and he is either incapable of appreciating the legal meaning and consequences of his act or his capability to control his behaviour is underdeveloped, then he shall be exempt from criminal liability. However, such minors shall be subjected to security measures specific to children. Where the minor has the capacity to comprehend the legal meaning and result of the act and to control his behaviour in respect thereof, a term of 12 to 15 years of imprisonment shall be imposed for offences requiring a penalty of aggravated life imprisonment and for offences that

---

[28] Art 6(1)(b).

[29] In the old law on the 'Establishment, Duties and Trial Procedures of Juvenile Courts' the competence of the courts was limited to juveniles aged 12 to 15. Consequently, juveniles between 16 and 18 were tried by ordinary courts.

[30] ibid (5) 11.

require a penalty of life imprisonment, a term of nine to 11 years imprisonment shall be imposed. Otherwise, the penalty to be imposed shall be reduced by half, save for the fact that for each act such penalty shall not exceed seven years.[31] Where a minor is older than 15 but younger than 18 years at the time the offence was committed, then for crimes that require a penalty of aggravated life imprisonment a term of 18 to 24 years of imprisonment shall be imposed and for offences that require a penalty of life imprisonment 12 to 15 years of imprisonment shall be imposed. Otherwise, the penalty to be imposed shall be reduced by one-third, save for the fact that the penalty for each act shall not exceed 12 years.[32] According to article 107(5) of the Code of Execution of Punishments and Security Measures, when the offender is a juvenile a day in prison counts as two days served. Thus, article 31 of the Turkish Penal Code illustrates that the Turkish juvenile justice system is a mixed one. For the juvenile offender under 13, a welfare model is in place. For the juvenile offender aged between 13 and 16, a welfare and justice model prevails and aged between 16 and 18 the justice model governs. Some elements of the restorative justice model also exist through mediation.[33]

The security measures mentioned above are protective and supportive measures regulated by the CPL. They are juvenile-specific safety measures aimed at juveniles who are pushed to crime and who do not have criminal liability.[34] They are enumerated in article 5 of the CPL and include education, care, health and shelter. They are flexible measures and their duration is not determined by law. The court must monitor their implementation[35] and may vary them if they are deemed inappropriate.[36]

B. Deprivation of Liberty and Conditions of Detention

1. Pre-trial arrest and detention

As regards juvenile suspects, the following rules apply.[37] Children who are under the age of 13 at the time of the offence and deaf or mute minors who are under the age of 16 at the time of the offence may not be apprehended for any offence. As soon as their identity has been established, such minors shall be released. The public prosecutor's office shall immediately be informed of the minor's identity and offence. Minors shall not on any account be used in establishing the nature of an offence. Children between the ages of 13 and 18 may be apprehended for an offence. Their relatives and lawyers shall be informed of their apprehension and they shall immediately

---

[31] Art 31(2) Penal Code.
[33] Art 24 CPL 2005.
[35] Art 8(2) CPL 2005.
[37] ibid (n 11) 6.

[32] Art 31(3) Penal Code.
[34] Art 11 CPL 2005.
[36] Art 7(5) CPL 2005.

be brought before the public prosecutor. The preliminary investigation shall be conducted by the chief public prosecutor in person or a public prosecutor appointed by him.[38] Detained juveniles shall be kept at the juvenile unit of the law enforcement facility.[39] In situations where the facility does not have a juvenile unit, juveniles shall be kept separate from detained adults.[40] Chains, handcuffs and similar tools cannot be put on juveniles. However, when necessary, the police may take necessary measures to prevent the juvenile from escaping or endangering his life or physical integrity or that of others. If the offender is under the age of 18 at the time he begins serving his sentence, his liberty depriving sentence will be served in a reformatory or in a special section of the adult penitentiaries.[41] If, at the time of the trial, the juvenile offender is an adult, there are no specific rules, except reducing the punishment.

2. Measures that can be taken against a juvenile offender

At the investigation or prosecution stages related to juveniles pushed to crime, the court may decide for one or several of the measures listed below to be taken:

a)   No moving outside specified peripheral boundaries;
b)   No access to certain places or access to certain places only;
c)   No contact with specified persons and organizations.[42]

However, if these measures do not bring about favourable outcomes or are violated by the juvenile, the court may decide to issue an arrest warrant.[43] According to article 107(5) of the Code of Execution of Punishments and Security Measures, a day in prison for a juvenile counts as two days served. It should be borne in mind that an arrest warrant cannot be issued for juveniles who have not yet completed the age of 15 for acts that require an imprisonment penalty with an upper limit of five years.[44] Criminal sanctions available against the juvenile are juvenile custody and security measures.

---

[38] Response of the Turkish Government to the report of the European Committee for the Prevention of Torture and Inhuman or Degrading Treatment or Punishment (CPT) on it visit to Turkey from 7 to 15 September 2003, p. 7 and 22, available at http://www.unhcr.org/refworld/country,,COECPT,,TUR,4562d8cf2,4718b94e2,0.html, accessed 26 February 2010.

[39] Art 16(1) CPL 2005.

[40] Art 16(2) CPL 2005.

[41] F Gölcüklü, S Feyyaz, and S Cin Şensoy, 'Criminal Law' in T Ansay and D Wallace (eds) *Introduction to Turkish Law* (5th edn, Wolters Kluwer, The Hague 2005) 173.

[42] Art 20(1) CPL 2005.

[43] Art 20(2) CPL 2005.

[44] Art 21 CPL 2005.

3. Education and training while in detention

Children in reformatories benefit from all types of education and training activities. Juveniles placed in reformatories whose age and other particulars are appropriate may attend institutions of primary, secondary and higher education; participate in social and sports activities that take place in their respective schools; take, in connection with their education, foreign language, computer and vocational courses and courses given to prepare students for university examinations; take an examination conducted outside the institution to enter distance education institutions and universities; and attend social activities such as plays, concerts and sports events under the supervision of the institution's educators.[45]

The workshops in the Juvenile Reformatory in Ankara were closed down in 1995. According to new regulations, children older than 15 years of age for whom it is impossible to attend formal education are guided towards an appropriate occupation taking into consideration their wishes, abilities as well as the availability of vocational training centres and employment opportunities in their future place of residence. These juveniles may then attend vocational training centres attached to the Ministry of National Education under the Apprenticeship and Vocational Training Law (Act No 3308). Students who are employed within the framework of the vocational training program receive a certain portion of their monthly wages to be used for their personal expenses and the remaining amount is deposited in a bank and kept in a safe custody account to be delivered to children on their release.[46]

4. Post-release measures

New laws in place since 2005 have helped to address some of the concluding observations of the CRC, (example: the provision of a probation mechanism for children).[47] Prior to 2005, there was no specific legislation in Turkey dealing with the situation of children released from care. Therefore, Law No 5402 on Probation and Help Centre and Protection Boards was enacted to this effect and came into force on 20 July 2005.

The enactment of the new law represents an important part of the reform of the Turkish criminal justice system. With this new system, juvenile offenders are placed under supervision and measures to enable the resettlement of the children under the supervision of an expert are introduced. This

---

[45] This is in line with art 19, CRC.
[46] ibid (n15) 71.
[47] United Nations Children's Fund Executive Board, First regular session 2006, 16–20 and 23 January 2006, Revised country programme document, Turkey, 3, available at http://www.unicef.org/about/execboard/files/Turkey-CPD_Rev1.pdf, accessed 26 February 2010.

change also allows children released from prison to be supervised. Since 2005, probationary measures that apply to both adults and juveniles are in place. However, there is still no exclusive regulation for juveniles, except article 36 of the CPL: 'the court may decide to take under supervision the juvenile about whom a protective and supportive measure have been decided, about whom the decision to defer the commencement of a public prosecution action has been approved, and about whom it has been decided to put off the announcement of verdict'.[48]

One of the most important problems faced by children released from care was the failure to maintain the confidentiality of 'records of convictions' especially for juveniles aged 16–18. This places a number of barriers for juveniles seeking employment, benefiting from credit and hostel facilities in higher education, attending certain education institutions and those being called up for military service.[49] There is now a better regulation in place, which provides that the criminal records of juveniles can only be given to the Public Prosecutor Services and the courts.

C. Procedural Rights

1. Specialized institutions and procedures

Juveniles are treated as criminal offenders but subject to different, sometimes reduced, sanctions to adults. The CPL governs procedures regarding juvenile delinquents so that the general criminal law is only subsidiary.

a) The courts

In Turkey, there are lay judges in neither the adult courts nor in the juvenile courts.[50] Juvenile courts are composed of a single judge and are found in each provincial centre. Where required due to heavy workload, more than one chamber may be established. They administer actions filed with regard to juveniles pushed to delinquency, for crimes falling under the jurisdiction of basic penal courts and penal courts of peace.[51] The Public Prosecutor shall not be present at the hearings administered at juvenile courts but may appeal their decisions.[52]

Juvenile heavy penal courts[53] also exist. They are composed of one presiding judge and two members.[54] They administer suits related to crimes

---

[48] Also refer to arts 37, 39, 40 and 41 CPL 2005.   [49] ibid (n 15) 72.
[50] On the appointment of judges see art 28 CPL 2005.
[51] Art.26(1) CPL 2005.
[52] Art 25(1) CPL 2005.
[53] During Parliamentary debates, it was argued that the maintenance of these courts was counter to the CRC. However, they remained in place. See Ms Seda Akco in Balo, (n 23) 602.
[54] Art 25(2) CPL 2005.

committed by juveniles, involving a penalty of over five years imprisonment, and falling under the jurisdiction of the heavy penal court.[55]

b) Public prosecutor's juvenile bureau

A juvenile bureau at the Chief Public Prosecutor's Offices has been put in place.[56] Its main duties are (i) carrying out the investigation procedures related to juveniles pushed to crime, (ii) ensuring that necessary measures are taken without any delay, in cases which require measures to be taken with regard to juveniles and (iii) working in cooperation with the relevant public institutions and organizations and non-governmental organizations for the purpose of providing the necessary support services to juveniles in need of assistance, education, employment or shelter and to notify such and similar cases to the authorized institutions and organizations.[57] In cases where delay is considered risky, these duties may also be carried out by Public Prosecutors who are not assigned to juvenile bureaus.[58]

c) Juvenile unit of the police

Law enforcement duties related to juveniles are carried out by the juvenile units of the police.[59] When starting a procedure related to juveniles in need of protection or pushed to crime, the juvenile unit must notify the situation to the juvenile's parent(s) or guardian, or to the person who has undertaken the care of the juvenile, to the Bar and the Social Services and Child Protection Agency. If the juvenile is residing in a public institution, the representative of that institution should be notified. However, any relatives of the juvenile who are suspected of soliciting the juvenile to commit the crime or of abusing the juvenile should not be given any information.[60] If the juvenile is detained by the police, he/she may be accompanied by a next of kin.[61]

The personnel at the juvenile unit of the police should be provided with training on topics such as juvenile law, prevention of juvenile delinquency, child development and psychology, social services and so on, by their own agencies.[62] They must attend 60 hours of elementary training and 90 hours of expert training.[63]

---

[55] Art 26(2) CPL 2005.   [56] Art 29 CPL 2005.
[57] Art 30(1) CPL 2005.   [58] Art 30(2) CPL 2005.
[59] Art 31(1) CPL 2005. As of January 2002, all 81 provinces had police child branches and 43 had fully equipped childcare units. Separately, crime prevention centres for children have been established in major cities, 'Plus 5' Review of the 2002 Special Session on Children and World Fit for Children Plan of Action National Progress Report TURKEY January 2007, 17, available at http://www.unicef.org/worldfitforchildren/files/Turkey_WFFC5_Report.pdf, accessed 26 February 2010.
[60] Art 31(2) CPL 2005.   [61] Art 31(3) CPL 2005.
[62] Art 31(4) CPL 2005. See also art 32 CPL 2005.
[63] 30 hours on Child trafficking and child abuse, 30 hours on Juvenile Justice System and 30 hours on Child Protection.

If the juvenile is in need of protection or if reasons exist indicating that waiting for a court decision would be against the interests of the juvenile, the juvenile unit of the police should secure the safety of the juvenile by taking the necessary measures in those circumstances and delivering the juvenile to the Social Services and Child Protection Agency as soon as possible.[64]

Following ratification of the UNCRC in 1994, Turkey established a 3500 member juvenile police force. The duties and responsibilities of the gendarmerie were similar to those of the police. The gendarmerie operates mainly in rural areas and cooperates with the General Directorate of Social Services and Child Protection, particularly in the implementation of action plans relating to children's rights. The General Directorate assesses the situation of children taken into gendarmerie custody on a case by case basis and, if necessary, refers them to the relevant support units within the Directorate.[65] A new, separate and specifically trained police organization has been established to deal with juvenile crime in 84 cities. It is not only dealing with juvenile delinquency but also helping street children and other children who live in difficult circumstances. In Istanbul alone, eight juvenile protection centres have been established. The police is also implementing a 'foster family' project via the project 'Volunteer families provide for street children'.[66]

d) Investigation

Crimes committed by juveniles first come to the police. The police must, however, pass the case on to the Public Prosecutor immediately. The police may do nothing, besides collect and secure the evidence. As noted above, there is a special police unit for juveniles that they may arrest juvenile offender if necessary.[67] Following the enactment of the CPL, investigations related to juveniles pushed to crime are carried out by the Public Prosecutor assigned at the juvenile bureau[68] or by assistants appointed by him.[69] He must be present during all activities and procedures conducted as part of a preliminary investigation concerning minors. In theory, he must take over responsibility at the outset. In practice however, he only does so in serious cases. During interrogation and other procedures related to the juvenile, the

---

[64] Art 31(5) CPL 2005.

[65] Unveren, United Nations Committee on the Rights of the Child, (42nd Session) 'Summary Record of The 1129th Meeting' (Chamber B) 8, available at: http://www.unhchr.ch/tbs/doc.nsf/898586b1dc7b4043c1256a450044f331/c0418bef762dfbefc1257185002e697c/$FILE/G0642246.pdf, accessed 26 February 2010.

[66] ibid (n 15) 81.

[67] Dr H Hakeri, 'The Prosecution Service Function within the Turkish Criminal Justice System' [2008] Eur J Crim Policy Res 353.

[68] Art 15(1) CPL 2005.

[69] Art 19 of the Regulations on Apprehension, Custody and Taking of Statements.

juvenile may be accompanied by a social worker.[70] If necessary, the Public (rosecutor may file a request to the juvenile judge for a protective and supportive measure to be taken regarding the juvenile.[71] This would enable his/her positive social integration.

In order to ensure a sensitive approach to matters regarding juveniles, four separate circulars have been issued on the responsibilities of the juvenile police entitled, The Use of Handcuffs, Protection of Minors, Protection of the Family, and The Juvenile Police.

e) Prosecution

The Juvenile Prosecution Offices are not separately organized from the general prosecution offices but they are settled within the structure of general prosecution offices.[72]

According to article 170(2) Criminal Procedure Code, 'the public prosecutor must undertake criminal prosecution if there is evidence that the crime which is prosecuted ex officio, has been committed'. However, an exception exists in juvenile cases whereby the commencement of a public prosecution for an act, which carries a penalty of imprisonment of three months to two years, may be deferred for five years.[73]

In situations where juveniles have committed a crime together with adults, the investigation and prosecution shall be carried out separately.[74] If considered necessary, the court may delay the juvenile's trial until a verdict has been reached on the adult's case.[75] Where it is thought that the trials must be carried out together, the general courts may decide, at any stage, to consolidation the trials, on the condition that such consolidation is found appropriate by the courts. In such an event, the joint cases shall be administered at general courts.[76]

f) Hearing

The juvenile, his/her parent, guardian, court-assigned social worker, the family that has assumed the care of the juvenile, or if the juvenile is cared for by the Agency, the representative of the Agency may be present at the hearing.[77] The juvenile present at the hearing may be taken outside the courtroom if his/her interests so require so. Additionally, a juvenile whose interrogation procedures have been completed may be dispensed from attending the hearing.[78]

---

[70] Art 15(2) CPL 2005.
[71] Art 15(3) CPL 2005.
[72] ibid (n 7) (TIII).
[73] Art 19 CPL 2005.
[74] Art 17(1) CPL 2005.
[75] Art 17(2) CPL 2005.
[76] Art 17(3) CPL 2005.
[77] Art 22(1) CPL 2005.
[78] Art 22(3) CPL 2005.

g) Putting off announcement of the verdict

If the penalty determined after the trial procedures carried out with respect to the crime with which the juvenile is found guilty is imprisonment for maximum three years or judicial monetary fine, the court may decide to put off the announcement of the sentence.[79] In case of a decision to put off the announcement of the sentence, the juvenile will be subjected to a measure of supervised freedom (probation) for a period of three years.[80]

h) The right to a lawyer

The right to a lawyer is unrestrictedly stated and mandatory in any procedure against a juvenile. According to article 150(2) of the Criminal Procedure Code, a juvenile must have a defence counsel from the outset of the preparatory proceedings, regardless of whether he demands one. He must be present from the very first examination. If the juvenile or his legal representative does not engage an attorney, the police/public prosecutor/judge will appoint one for him. Declarations made to the police in the absence of the lawyer have no evidential value.

In addition, there are child rights committees and child centres established by bar associations. They are accessible to all of children wishing to file a complaint or looking for attorneys. Their assistance is free of charge.[81]

i) The right to be heard

According to article 12 of the UNCRC, a child who has the ability to express him/herself freely has the right to express himself freely on every matter related to their own selves. In order for this right to be effective, listening to the child, either directly or through a representative or an appropriate authority, is to be especially provided for in judicial or administrative investigations that affect the child. In conformity with this principle, article 13(2) of the CPL states that 'before rendering a decision, the opinion of the juvenile having adequate capacity shall be taken.'

j) Privacy

Juveniles are also protected from media exposure and attacks on privacy. The media is not allowed access to judicial proceedings. As per article 185 of the Criminal Procedure Code, the trial of a juvenile is not open to the

---

[79] Art 23(1) CPL 2005.   [80] Art 23(3) CPL 2005.

[81] The offices of the various bar associations are being criticized for not being very efficient. Sixty Bar offices across the country had offices known as 'Child Rights Commissions' but only 40 of these are actually active: UNHCR, Report of Fact-Finding Mission, 11–20 February 2008, Turkey, 57 available at: http://www.unhcr.org/refworld/topic,45a5fb512,4652f4a02,489c167e2,0.html, accessed 26 February 2010.

public and the verdict is announced in a closed session. Only the judge(s), victim, lawyers, parents and social workers[82] are present during proceedings. This protects juveniles, forestalls their stigmatization and stimulates their future social integration. This is one of the most important principles of criminal procedure.

k) Discrimination between boys and girls

There are no gender specific issues when it comes to child protection. Also, there is no discrimination between boys and girls in the Turkish Penal Code, the CPL and the Turkish criminal justice system as a whole. Boys and girls have equal access to justice.[83]

Turkish legislation is governed by the egalitarian philosophy of the Constitution. The principle of equality is enshrined in article 10 of the Constitution as an inalienable human right. According to this article, 'Everybody is equal before the law irrespective of his or her language, race, sex, political and philosophical belief, religion, sect and other differences.' Privileges cannot be granted to any person, family, group or class. All State organs and administrative authorities are under the obligation to comply with the principle of equality before the law in all their actions. Law No 2828 on Social Services and Child Protection Agency reiterates the principle of equality by stating in its article 4(d) that 'Differences in class, race, religion, sect or region may not be considered in the provision of social services.'

l) Limits to protection

It was possible in Turkey, that children over 15 to be tried in special heavy penal courts for acts of terrorism. This regulation was a clear violation of UNCRC. The law has been amendment in July 2010. According to new article 250/4 Code of Criminal Procedure children can be no more tried in special heavy penal courts. All of the children must be tried in children courts.

2. Possible risk factors

Alongside industrialization, urbanization, economic development and modernization, Turkey is also experiencing rapid social change. This change, no doubt influenced by the ideal of joining the European Union, can be seen at all levels of society.

---

[82] Social workers have to be present during proceedings as per arts 33–34 CPL 2005.

[83] In fact, only 2.3 per cent of convicted juveniles are girls; H Hancı, Hamit, B Eşiyok, Filiz Ans B Ulukol, 'Cezaevinde Bulunan Çocukların Temel Özellikleri ve Suç Tipleri' in III *Ulusal Çocuk ve Suç Sempozyumu, Bakım, Gözetme ve Egitim*, 22–25 Ekim 2003, Bildiriler (Akyüz, Uluştekin, Acar, Öntaş (eds), (Ankara 2005) 404.

The possible risk factors which bring a child in conflict with the law are difficulties created by rapid urbanization[84] and industrialization, migration and economic crises, confusion created by changing values and moral rules, inadequate training, lack of love[85] and family breakdown.[86] In the Turkish context, domestic migration from rural areas to metropolitan cities is one of the leading factors that increase the number of children living and working on the streets.[87] Figures from the Ministry of Justice also show that following the recent economic crisis, the number of children who commit crimes has increased.[88]

Police officers are of the opinion that the main risk factor is familial problems. When a family breaks down, children are the first to suffer. Those that live in an unhealthy family environment, for example those who have an alcoholic parent or suffer from domestic violence,[89] often end up in the street[90] and begin to commit crimes, in a bid to anger the family. This normally stems from lack of love, care and attention given by the family.[91] Judges are of the same opinion. Children of divorced or single parents, those who live away from their parents or those who live in care institutions commit more offences than children who live with both parents.[92] They normally live in poor conditions and drop out of school at a very early age. Indeed, burglary and rape are mostly being committed by children who are poor, uneducated and have always had problems. Finally, children who come from large families commit more crimes than children with fewer siblings.[93]

---

[84] According to research results of children in juvenile reformatories, 79 per cent of young offenders are from cities, H Yokuş-Sevük, *Uluslar arası Sözleşmelerdeki Ilkeler Açısından Çocuk Suçluluğu ile Mücadelede Kurumsal Yaklaşım* (Istanbul, 1998) 60.

[85] ibid 14 (TI), 68.

[86] H Dayıoglu and M Dayıoglu, in Kriminoloji Dergisi (Turkish Journal of Criminology and Criminal Justice) (2009) CI, S.I, Ocak 41.   [87] ibid 42.

[88] http://bianet.org/english/english/children-of-turkey-in-2004, accessed 26 February 2010.

[89] Y Çor, Aile Içi Şiddet, in H İbrahim Bahar (eds), *Suç Magdurları* (Ankara 2006) 87–103.

[90] The findings show that children working on the streets do not get sufficient support from their families. They also experience significant hardship at school. Children from rural families newly urbanised make up the majority of the children working on the streets. Dayıoğlu, and Dayıoğlu (n 88) 36.

[91] H Yılmaz Çocuk, 'Suç ve Mağduriyet: Suçlu Olan Çocuk Yoktur, Suça Itilen Çocuk Vardır' in H Ibrahim Bahar (ed), Suç Mağdurları (Ankara, 2006) 135–149. Based on interviews, a typical child working on the streets of Ankara, Turkey is a 12 year-old boy, who attends a low profile public school, showing poor academic performance and most likely to have fallen behind his peers; lives with his parents in the same household, but unfortunately is not getting enough attention and support from his family; works as a street vendor (selling napkins, flowers, pretzels, etc); might smoke but has not yet taken drugs; was registered in an eastern or South eastern province of Turkey at birth, meaning that his family moved from these regions probably due to ethnically oriented incidents and economic problems. Dayıoglu and Dayıoglu (n 88) 51.

[92] According to research results, 42.1 per cent of the 974 young offenders come from a fragmented family. Yokuş-Sevük, Uluslar arası Sözleşmelerdeki Ilkeler Açısından Çocuk Suçluluğu ile Mücadelede Kurumsal Yaklaşım (Istanbul, 1998) (n 86) 46.

[93] Yokus Sevük (n 86) 50.

Thus, working with child offenders in breaking the cycle of offending is important in the prevention of recidivism. Children more often become recidivist if effective intervention programmes have not been implemented. Early intervention will help prevent re-offending, reduce unnecessary over-crowding in prisons, and play an important part in the rehabilitation of juvenile and young offenders into the community.[94]

3. Awareness-raising efforts

Turkey's ratification of the UNCRC led to an awareness raising campaign on children's rights. This was followed by a National Children's Congress in 2002. The Congress in turn decided to set up a National Children's Forum, which was to consist of one boy and one girl from each province. The Forum was initiated by SHCEK, the national agency responsible for monitoring the implementation of the UNCRC, and meets every year. Children attending the seventh annual gathering of the Child Forum in 2006 launched a new campaign to promote and raise awareness about children's rights and to boost children's participation in decision-taking at all levels. The 'Rights of the Child Promotion Campaign' went ahead in 25 provinces spanning the entire country. The first phase of the campaign lasted until 20 November 2007 and was managed entirely by children. The provinces in question were chosen because they had active children's rights committees and/or were candidates for the Child Friendly City initiative being conducted by the Ministry of the Interior.

Information on the rights of the child, particularly rights that had been affected by recent changes in legislation, are being widely disseminated to the public.[95] Children are being taught about their rights as part of the national school curriculum. Many national and international conferences, symposia, panels and other events have been organized to raise awareness of children's rights.

Finally, the Ministry of Justice of Turkey has developed and executed a National Judicial Network Project (NJNP) (UYAP) by using every modern technology necessary to accomplish inner automation of the entirety of the judiciary and judicial support units and to accomplish external unit integration with public bodies and organizations. As a result of the contributions of NJNP to the judicial system, juveniles may be tried in a reasonable time period, accurate policies may be developed by receiving crime reports

---

[94] http://ec.europa.eu/enlargement/pdf/turkey/ipa/tr_07_01_01_work_with_juveniles_victims_ by_the_tk_probation_service_en.pdf, p.4-5, accessed 26 February 2010.

[95] An agreement had been concluded with the Turkish radio and television authorities to produce 12 human rights-related programmes, one of which would focus exclusively on child rights and abuse. (The author has also participated in one of these programmes on 'the right to life and the right to liberty and security'.)

of juveniles, it is easier to prevent impunity for those who commit crimes against children, and to stop crimes against children by an effective, transparent, fair and speedy performance of the judiciary. Legislations relating to children are accessible any time with their up to date status. Studies are being conducted swiftly by the judicial authorities for the establishment of precautions that aim to improve, protect and support the rights and well-being of children and vulnerable groups.[96] Systematic data collection and analysis are needed to provide the basis for improved policies and programs for children. Awareness of child rights among policy and decision-makers, service providers, caregivers and children will enhance the effectiveness of their participation in policy discussions.[97]

D. The Death Penalty

There is no death penalty in Turkey for adults or juveniles. The last execution in Turkey occurred in 1983 (after the 1980 military coup). Even if the death penalty was still in place, it would be inapplicable to children.

V. CONCLUSION

In its efforts to accede to the European Union, Turkey has made remarkable improvements to its juvenile justice system, mainly through the enactment of the CPL and the amendment of several of its laws, rendering them UNCRC-compliant. Indeed, a separate piece of legislation, wholly dedicated to child protection, is now in place. Specialized institutions, such as courts and juvenile police branches, have been set up. Activities are provided to those in detention and post release measures, such as probation, have been put in place. These changes have been welcomed by the CRC.

However, a number of problems remain in practice, an important one being the insufficiency of resources allocated to SHCEK and children's services as a whole. In terms of legislation, some provisions of the anti-terrorism law remain in violation of the UNCRC. They should be amended or abrogated as soon as possible. An independent Ombudsman, who would ensure that children's rights are being respected and that their individual complaints are being dealt with is still not in place. Finally, it should be noted that although the CPL provided for juvenile courts to deal with cases

---

[96] See (n 11) 8.

[97] United Nations Children's Fund, Revised country programme document Turkey, 31 October 2005, 9 available at: http://www.unicef.org/spanish/about/execboard/files/Turkey-CPD_Rev1.pdf, accessed 26 February 2010.

involving children, these are insufficient in number so that some cases are still being dealt with in ordinary courts. This raises concerns as the personnel in those courts is not specially trained to deal with child-specific issues. Although the number of children receiving custodial sentences fell from 6,254 in 2000 to 4,523 in 2004, juvenile courts had still not been expanded throughout the country so that only 34 per cent of children were tried by juvenile courts.[98] The others were tried by ordinary courts that apply the CPL. Moreover, trials take a long time and this is in direct violation of article 40 of the UNCRC. The Ministry of Justice reports the average duration of proceedings to be longer in juvenile courts than in other courts (755 days in 2000).[99] And finally, the judicial system is faced with a large backlog. In 2002 there were 1,153,000 criminal cases and 548,000 civil cases pending.[100] In Diyarbakır, some 4,000 cases are awaiting action in the new juvenile court, hearings are being put off for a year and some changes for the benefit of juvenile offenders have yet to take effect.

[98] There are 73 juvenile courts and 20 juvenile felony courts established within the country for 75 million inhabitants but not all of them are working which effectively means that there are currently only 68 juvenile courts and 13 juvenile felony courts that are active.

[99] Commission of the European Communities, 2002 Regular Report on Turkey's Progress Towards Accession, 21 available at: http://ec.europa.eu/enlargement/archives/pdf/key_documents/2002/tu_en.pdf, accessed 26 February 2010.

[100] ibid 77.

CHAPTER 13

Criminal Law and the Rights of the Child in the United Arab Emirates (UAE)[1]

I. INTRODUCTION

The population of the United Arab Emirates (UAE) reached 4.8 million in mid-2008,[2] compared with 4 million at the end of 2003, which was itself an increase of 7.6 per cent from the previous year.[3] The increasing population and changing society, in which the majority is composed of male expatriates from various backgrounds, has posed a great challenge to the country's criminal justice system and the criminal justice infrastructure must readily adapt to these changes.[4] The following report will provide an introduction the UAE legal framework, where it is significant to note that the UAE is a fairly new State and the promulgation of many of its laws are approximately 30 years old.

The phenomenon of juvenile delinquency is on the increase in the UAE. Reports found that in 2008, 315 crimes were committed by juveniles whereas in 2003, only 240 crimes were committed.[5] However, despite the increase in juvenile crime, a significant amount of research has been conducted in order to understand and address the causes of increasing juvenile delinquency.[6] Juvenile crime in the UAE is generally treated as a

---

[1] Ayla Karmali, Legal Consultant.

[2] UAE population to grow six per cent in 2009, posted on 19 May 2009, UAE Interact. Available at: http://www.uaeinteract.com/docs/UAE_population_to_grow_6_in_2009_/ 35846.htm

[3] 'UAE Population Topped Four Million In 2003' (13 April 2004), *Middle East Online*, available at: http://www.middle-east-online.com/english/?id=9623

[4] ibid.

[5] "الاجتماعية" تكشف عن دراسة قانون جديد خاص بالأحداث الجانحين الاحد 13 صفر 1430 هـ الموافق 8 شباط" 2009, (فبراير), http:// www.emasc.com/content.asp?ContentId=17839; Arab delinquents in detention separated from non-Arabs,' Amira Agarib and Afkar Ali, 13 July 2009 available at: http://www.khaleejtimes.com/DisplayArticle08.asp?xfile=data/theuae/2009/July/theuae_ July287.xml&section=theuae and www.uaepulse.net/vb/showthread.php?t= 65892; 'Call for innovative solutions to check juvenile delinquency' November 23 2004, WAM, Inter Press Service News Agency (http://ipsnotizie.it/wam_en/news.php?idnews=1587)

[6] محمد رياض الخاني . جنوح الأحداث في دولة الإمارات العربية المتحدة : أسبابه وطرق علاجه : دراسة مقارنة .- عجمان : جمعية أم المؤمنين النسائية ، 1989 .- 216 ص؛ محمد مراد عبد الله . جناح الأحداث في دولة الإمارات العربية المتحدة من منظور شرطي .- ص ص 17 - 75 .محمد هويدي . ظاهرة جناح الأحداث في مجتمع الإمارات .- الشارقة : جمعية الاجتماعيين

community problem, and commenting in 2005, the Deputy Director of Al Mamourah Police Station in the Emirate of Rass Al Khaimah, stated that the increase in juvenile crime 'isn't a security problem in the first degree. It is a social problem that needs to be addressed by all the public and private institutions.'[7]

To this effect, the authorities appear to place considerable emphasis on the social causes of juvenile crime. In July 2008, Lt Col Arif Baqer, Director of Dubai Police's Family Security Department of Human Rights commented that broken families and peer pressure were the two main reasons behind juvenile delinquency.[8] Other causes and risk factors noted by Bushra Qaed, Director of the Juvenile Department at the General Directorate for Punitive and Corrective Establishments of Dubai Police include poverty and pursuit of luxury (for theft cases) and in 2005, drug abuse was becoming an increasingly common factor.[9] Interestingly, of the crimes committed in 2008, 64 were related to violence, 64 to assault, and 36 were theft-related.[10] With regard to female juveniles, it has been found that an unstable domestic environment was one of the key factors that led girls to crime.[11] Statistics released by the Sharjah Police found that 45 girls were arrested during the 18 months prior to July 2009 and most were charged with 'immoral acts and thefts, and a majority of them are under 16 years of age.'[12] The Director of the Juvenile Centre in Sharjah, Khalil Al Buraimi and Mohammed Hassan Fayeq, a psychiatrist consulted for the report, both found that delinquent juvenile girls came from broken families and that 25 per cent of female juveniles had divorced parents while nine per cent had parents who were separated.[13] Another media report of 2005, reported that in Dubai, 26 per cent of juvenile offenders lived with divorced parents and nine per cent live with separated parents.[14]

، 1988 -. 450 ص (سلسلة الدراسات الاجتماعية - 1).؛ منى جمعة عيسى البحر . الأسرة وجنوح الأحداث في مجتمع
see generally): الإمارات العربية المتحدة .- الشارقة : جمعية الاجتماعيين ، 1991 -. 176 ص (سلسلة الرسائل العلمية
http://www.libs.uaeu.ac.ae/ UAE%20Bibliography/Biobl14.html

[7] Khaleej Times, 'Strict Measures Needed To Curb Juvenile Delinquency' Sadiq A Salam (22 June 2005), http://www.khaleejtimes.com/DisplayArticleNew.asp?section=theuae&xfile=data/theuae/2005/june/theuae_june629.xml

[8] A Agarib and A Ali, 'Arab Delinquents in Detention Separated from non-Arabs' (13 July 2009), available at http://www.khaleejtimes.com/DisplayArticle08.asp?xfile=data/theuae/2009/July/theuae_July287.xml&section=theuae.

[9] L Abdul Rahman 'Juvenile Crimes on the Rise' *Khaleeji Times* (23 September 2005), available at http://www.khaleejtimes.com/Displayarticle.asp?section=theuae&xfile=data/theuae/2005/september/theuae_september707.xml.

[10] See (n 8).

[11] 'Domestic Instability May Push Girls Towards Crime' *Khaleeji Times* (13 July 2009) Available at: http://www.khaleejtimes.com/DisplayArticleNew.asp?col=&section=theuae&xfile=data/theuae/2009/July/theuae_July288.xml

[12] ibid.   [13] ibid.

[14] Abdul Rahman (n 9).

It has been suggested by the Minister of Social Affairs, Head of Protection, that the reason for the increase in juvenile offences is due to rapid social changes in the society.[15] Indeed, the UAE is a rapidly growing State.

II. NATIONAL LEGAL FRAMEWORK

A. *The UAE Legal System and International Treaties*

The UAE is a federation of seven Emirates and governed by a Constitution which came into effect in 1971. The federal State is composed of seven separate Emirates and the UAE Constitution allows for each Emirate to retain power over specific areas of governance and administration, including the judicial system. Therefore, each Emirate has both federal Courts and local/federal Courts.[16] The Federal Courts and the local courts apply UAE federal law legislated by the UAE Supreme Council, but there are also local laws and regulations enacted by the rulers of each Emirate.[17] Each Emirate has three types of courts: Civil, Criminal and Sharia. Civil Courts in the UAE deal with civil/commercial matters, Criminal Courts with criminal matters, and the Sharia Court with certain family matters between and among Muslims.[18] It is important to note that Sharia law does not apply in criminal matters.

Within the UAE, Law No 9 of 1976 is a federal law and applies in all criminal courts across the UAE. Each emirate in the UAE has its own criminal court and there are three stages for litigation which include the Courts of First Instance, the Courts of Appeal and then the Federal Supreme Court.[19]

Along with a new law related to juvenile offenders and criminal law,[20]

---

[15] http://www.msa.gov.ae/MSA/AR/News/Pages/NewsDetails.aspx?NewsID=194 8 February 2009.

[16] R Price and E Al Tamimi, *United Arab Emirates Court of Cassation Judgments 1998–2003*, (Brill, Leiden, 2005) vii; For further information on the political background of the UAE, please also see 'Arab Political Systems: Baseline Information and Reforms—UAE,' Carnegie Endowment for International Peace available at: www.carnegieendowment.org/arabpoliticalsystems

[17] ibid viii; Should the local law conflict with the Federal Law, the Federal Law will prevail. Within the UAE, each Emirate has three types of courts: Civil, Criminal and Sharia. Civil Courts in the UAE deal with civil/commercial matters, Criminal Courts with criminal matters, and the Sharia Court with certain family matters between and among Muslims. ibid ix.

[18] ibid ix.

[19] For more information on the Dubai Courts and the history of the Dubai Courts, please see the Dubai Courts website: http://www.dubaicourts.gov.ae/portal/page?_pageid=53,72555, 53_72567: 53_78353&_dad=portal&_schema=PORTAL

[20] الاجتماعية" تكشف عن دراسة قانون جديد خاص بالأحداث الجانحينالاحد 13 صفر 1430 هـ الموافق 8 شباط
2009 (فبراير) http://www.emasc.com/content.asp?ContentId=17839

the UAE is also issuing a new law aimed at the protection of children with specific intention to bring the UAE laws in accordance with the UN Convention on the Rights of the Child (UNCRC).[21]

III. THE INTERNATIONAL FRAMEWORK AND THE UNCRC

The UAE appears, in practice, to adopt a monist doctrine.[22] According to the Constitution of the UAE, international instruments ratified by the State are binding on all federal authorities of the State. Furthermore, 'all State institutions, including the courts, are bound in many cases to apply the provisions of the international instruments even if domestic legislation has not been adopted to that effect.'[23] The UAE signed and ratified the UNCRC on January 3, 1997, entering reservations against articles 7, 14, 17 and 21.[24] The reservations against article 14, 17 and 21 are related to the preservation and respect of the UAE's culture and religion[25] however, none of these relates directly to the rights and protection of juvenile offenders.

IV. PROTECTION OF JUVENILES UNDER THE CRIMINAL JUSTICE SYSTEM AND COMPATABILITY WITH THE CONVENTION ON THE RIGHTS OF THE CHILD (UNCRC)

A. Age of Criminal Liability

The UAE is a relatively new State and Federal Law No 9 of 1976 on Homeless and Delinquent Juveniles, which applies to juvenile offenders, was issued following the independence of the union. As a comparison, the Provisional Constitution was adopted on 2 December 1971, the Criminal Code was issued in 1987 under Federal Law No 3 of 1987 and the Law of Criminal Procedure was issued in 1992 under Federal Law No 35 of 1992.

The Federal Law No 9 of 1976 ('the Law') on the Homeless and Delinquent Juveniles applies to all persons under the age of 18 at the time

---

[21] 'UAE preparing comprehensive law on protection of children's rights: FNC member' posted on 23 June 2009 and available at: http://uaeinteract.com/docs/UAE_preparing_comprehensive_law_on_protection_of_childrens_rights_FNC_member/36430.htm. More reports on the new law include: http://www.zawya.com/Story.cfm/sidZAWYA20090427064331/UAE%20drafts%20new%20law%20to%20protect%20children's%20rights/; http://www.crin.org/resources/infoDetail.asp?ID=18733.

[22] UN Security Council, Commission on Counter Terrorism, S/2003/280, 8.

[23] ibid 3–4.

[24] United Nations Treaty Collection, Declarations and Reservations available at: http://www.unhchr.ch/html/menu3/b/treaty15_asp.htm

[25] Art 14.

the 'event'/ 'action' took place.[26] This provision is in accordance with article 1 of the UNCRC states that 'a child means every human being below the age of eighteen years unless under the law applicable to the child, majority is attained earlier.'[27]

Article 2 of the Law requires that the age of the offender must be verified by official documentation or scientifically determined and article 3 further clarifies that the Gregorian calendar will apply when determining the age of the alleged offender.

The minimum age for criminal liability is seven, and article 6 provides that a criminal case cannot be opened if the offender is under the age of seven. However, where a child under the age of seven is found to have committed a crime, the authorities mentioned in the law have the right to look into applying necessary disciplinary, educations or medical measures.[28] The Committee on the Rights of the Child (CRC) however, were of the view that the minimum age of criminal responsibility was actually too low.[29]

Where the alleged juvenile offender is between the ages of seven and 16, article 7 of the Law provides that if the juvenile offender has committed a crime punishable by law, the judge has the discretion to take any measures it deems fit. With regard to older juvenile offenders between the ages of 16 to 18, the judge only has discretion to apply Law No 9 of 1976 as per article 8 of the law. This is in accordance with article 40(3)(b) of the Convention, as the law allows the authorities to take measures educational, disciplinary or medical measures deemed necessary for the juvenile's development.[30]

B. Measures Which Can Be Taken Against a Juvenile Offender

The language of Law No 9 of 1976 is very precise in that the law does not refer to the actions committed by juvenile offenders as crimes and does not provide for punishments but rather, 'corrective measures.' Therefore, the Law may be seen to take specific consideration of the fact that the juvenile offender is a child. Significantly, article 9 of the Law expressly provides that a juvenile offender cannot be punished with execution, imprisonment or a fine.

---

[26] Law No 9 of 1976, art 1.
[27] Convention on the Rights of the Child, Article One available at: http://www.unhchr.ch/html/menu3/b/k2crc.htm.
[28] See also para 89.
[29] Concluding observations of the Committee on the Rights of the Child: United Arab Emirates, CRC/C/15/Add.183 13/06/2002, para 42.
[30] ibid.

Article 15 of the law summarizes the measures which may be taken against a juvenile offender. These include: reprimand, surrendering to the parent/guardian/suitable carer, judicial probation, prohibiting the offender from certain places, prohibiting offender from engaging in certain actions, compulsory education/training, depositing the offender in a medical care home, rehabilitations centre or educational facility depending on the act, and deportation.

C. Deprivation of Liberty and Conditions of Detention

Measures requiring the deposition of the juvenile offender in a juvenile rehabilitation centre require special regulation and provision. Article 40 of the Convention stipulates that:

> States Parties recognize the right of every child alleged as, accused of, or recognized as having infringed the penal law to be treated in a manner consistent with the promotion of the child's sense of dignity and worth, which reinforces the child's respect for the human rights and fundamental freedoms of others and which takes into account the child's age and the desirability of promoting the child's reintegration and the child's assuming a constructive role in society.

Therefore, State Parties must ensure that:

> 4. A variety of dispositions, such as care, guidance and supervision orders; counselling; probation; foster care; education and vocational training programmes and other alternatives to institutional care shall be available to ensure that children are dealt with in a manner appropriate to their well-being and proportionate both to their circumstances and the offence.

When it comes to juvenile detention, UAE laws and regulations provide a number of provisions to ensure the protection of juveniles and the administration of juvenile rehabilitation centres.

1. Limits to criminal sentencing

Article 10 of the Law No 9 of 1976 ('the Law') specifically limits the types of criminal sentences that can be taken against a juvenile offender. Article 10 states:

> 1. In cases where a criminal sentence can be imposed upon a minor, the applicable penalties of death or imprisonment shall be replaced by a custodial sentence.

2. The term of the custodial sentence shall not exceed one half of the statutory maximum sentence.

3. Any custodial sentence handed down against a minor in accordance with the terms of the present article must be served in a special institution that offers social welfare and educational facilities.

Article 69 of the Criminal Code No 3 of 1987 specifies that:

Detention means the placement of a convicted person in a penal institution legally established for that purpose for the period stated in the sentence. Unless otherwise specified herein, a term of detention must not be less than a minimum of one month or more than a maximum of three years.

It is evident from the above that even where the juvenile offender has committed a serious crime and a criminal penalty would normally apply, the juvenile is given a more lenient penalty and the emphasis of the detention is still on the rehabilitation of the juvenile offender, though also to deter or intimidate the juvenile from repeating crimes in the future.[31]

2. *Judicial probation—suspended sentencing*

The Law provides further clarification as to the circumstances and nature of juvenile detention. Article 18 of the Law provides that where it is permissible to announce judgment that allows the offender to be deposited in a detention centre, the judge can suspend to measure for no less than one year and for no more than three years. This is known as judicial probation, and it also involves putting the minor under supervision and other restrictions required to examine him judicially. If the minor passes this period of examination successfully, the allegations will be considered as if they never happened, otherwise the case would be reheard.[32]

3. *Suitability of juvenile rehabilitation centres*

Article 23 of the Law states that a juvenile offender can only be deposited in a government detention centre, a suitable rehabilitation centre, or an education facility specifically designated by or recognized by the State. The UAE report to the CRC clarifies that the juvenile offender can spend 'no

---

[31] The Initial reports of States parties due in 1999: United Arab Emirates, CRC/C/78/Add.2, 24 October 2001, para 103.

[32] Written replies by the government of the United Arab Emirates concerning the list of issues (CRC/C/Q/UAE/1) received by the Committee on the rights of the child relating to the consideration of the initial reports (CRC/C/78/Add.2), 26 April 2002, 14.

more than one and a half years, the equivalent of half of the maximum sentence prescribed by the Penal Code' in a rehabilitation or detention centre.[33] During the course of the judicial order for rehabilitation, the juvenile may be released on the basis of reports submitted to the judge from the institutions.[34] However, if the offender turns 18 during this period of detention, he cannot remain in these detention centres and he is then transferred to a detention centre for adults. Within the UAE prison system, there are specially allocated units for young adults.

4. Limits on pre-trial detention

With regard to pre-trial detention, article 28 states that precautionary detention is prohibited (pre trial). If circumstances dictate that detention is needed, the public prosecution can decide to detain the juvenile for a maximum of one week in a rehabilitation facility unless the court approves another the period. Instead of depositing the subject at a place of detention, the minor can be left under the care of his or her parent/guardian or family if they agree to be responsible to present him or her to the authorities when required.

5. Special circumstances

The Law also makes provision for juvenile offenders who may be deemed to suffer a mental illness and therefore require special hospitalization. In such cases, article 22 provides that if a juvenile offender is found to be mentally ill, the Court may have him sent to a suitable medical institution for treatment and care. The Court is responsible for monitoring the supervision of the minor for a period not exceeding one year at any one time. The person must be examined yearly and can only be released following a positive medical report recommending release. If the person reaches 21 years of age and she or he is still in need of treatment, she or he must be transferred to a specialist institution for adults.

D. Rights of the Juvenile Held in Juvenile Centers

1. Access to family

Aside from rehabilitation and education programmes, a juvenile offender held in a juvenile correction facility has the right to contact his or her family and even leave the facility when required. Article 18 of the Ministerial

---

[33] ibid (CRC/C/78/Add.2) 14.
[34] ibid 15.

Ordinance No 32/2 of 1983 provides that 'the inmates shall be permitted to visit their families on official holidays if their guardians so request.' The supervisory board created by article 33 also has the power to authorize visits which would allow the detainees to spend holidays with their respective families. Federal Act No 43 of 1992 and its implementing regulations provide in article 51 that juveniles may leave the centres for no more than three days in the event of public holidays, the death of a close family member, or exception circumstances 'at the discretion of the officer in charge of the penal institution, in accordance with the rules laid down by the juvenile rehabilitation board and provided that the juvenile meets the conditions specified in article 91 of the implementing regulations.'[35]

2. Education and training

Under article 34 of Law 43/1992, each detention center must have a religious adviser available to guide and teach the detainees principles and morals. Moreover, a full-time social counselor must be present and along with the prison officers, they are required to study the physical and mental condition of each detainee at regular periods and also offer recommendations. Provisions of the law also provide that teaching and training is required, particularly training in a craft or a skill, and the training must take into consideration the duration of the detention, the age of the detainee, their interests and abilities. After consulting the Ministry of Education, the Ministry of Interior should put in place an education system and programme for the benefit of the detainees. The inmates may also have a library and if an inmate wishes to continue their further education inside the centre, they can register with the Ministry of Education and the centre must obtain the required books for the juvenile to sit the exams.

Article 52 of the Act and articles 98–101 allow juveniles specifically to work in any commercial or industrial establishment outside of the detention centre following approval of the board.

Generally, when it comes to education and rehabilitation, the provisions in the UAE and the regulations in force to ensure their implementation, appear to be in accordance with article 39 of the UNCRC. Article 19, section 5 of the Ministerial Ordinance No 32/2 of 1983 for Juvenile Welfare and Reform Centers refer specifically to the importance of providing 'social, psychological, health, educational, religious, vocational and recreational welfare of all inmates through the activities provided for in the said Statutes.'[36]

---

[35] The Initial reports of States parties due in 1999: United Arab Emirates, CRC/C/78/Add.2, 24 October 2001, para 125.
[36] ibid para 109.

3. Administration and management

When it comes to the administration and management of the juvenile detention/rehabilitation centres, article 34 of Law No 9 of 1976 states that:

> Every institution specialized in the welfare and reform of juveniles, and any other premises intended for their reception, shall be supervised by a board chaired by a representative of the Department of Public Prosecutions and including among its members the director of the institution and a specialist appointed by the Minister for Social Affairs. The persons sentenced to placement in such institutions shall be released only on the recommendation of the said board.[37]

Additionally, article 49 of Federal Act No 43 of 1992 emphasizes the requirement that for juvenile centres, a board of specialists and experts must set up in order to ensure the quality and effectiveness of rehabilitation programmes. Further regulations as provided for in article 33 of Ministerial Ordinance No 32/2 of 1983 ensure that 'every such unit must have a supervisory board, chaired by a representative of the Department of Public Prosecutions within the jurisdiction of which the unit is located and including among its members the director of the unit and a representative delegated by the Deputy Minister, which shall meet once every 15 days and shall exercise the following functions:

(a) Study, and submit to the court, recommendations for the release of convicted persons;
(b) Participate in the formulation of the general policy, and in the organization of the work and activity programmes, of the unit; and
(c) Help to solve any problems that the unit encounters.[38]

The above demonstrates some of the supervisory measures in place required for administering and protecting the rights of juveniles in detention and submissions to the CRC attest to this.[39]

With regard to discplinary measures that may be taken against a juvenile specifically, article 55 of Law 43/1992 provides that only four are permitted. These include: Admonition, verbal warning, suspension of privileges for a period not exceeding two weeks, and suspension of holidays for a maximum of 55 days.

---

[37] The Initial reports of States parties due in 1999: United Arab Emirates, CRC/C/78/Add.2, 24 October 2001, para 104.
[38] ibid para 105.
[39] ibid para 124.

These measures take into consideration the age and interests of juveniles requiring discipline within a detention centre and do not appear to infringe on the rights protected by the UAE laws and regulations.

V. PROCEDURAL RIGHTS OF JUVENILE OFFENDERS

Although there are no special courts, the Law does provide special procedures for juvenile offenders. Moreover, specific judges are assigned to handle criminal cases involving juvenile offenders.[40]

A. *Privacy*

In order to protect the juvenile, article 29 provides that the trial shall remain without media coverage and only attended by the guardians, witnesses, lawyers, ministry of social affairs representatives, institution members, and anyone the court specifically allows to enter. The court can decide to relieve the defendant from appearing, and the witnesses are heard without his/her presence if this is in his/her benefit.[41]

A guilty verdict is not allowed except after explaining to the defendant what happened during their absence, and the utterance of the verdict has to be done in a hearing. Indeed, this is in conformity with article 40(2)(b)(vii) of the CRC.

B. *Social Counsellors*

Once the alleged juvenile offender has been arrested and the file has been forwarded to the prosecution department, a social counsellor is required to undertake an investigation looking into the background of the alleged juvenile offender.[42] If the prosecutor decides to forward the matter to the Courts, the Social Counsellor's report will then play a vital role in the judge's decision making and indeed, the judge cannot issue a judgment without the report. Generally, the report is required to give the judge an idea of the background and character of the juvenile offender, and as the aim of the judicial process here is not to punish the offender but to facilitate rehabilitation and correction, the report will guide the judge in deter-

---

[40] Please see interview with Judge Omar Carmustagy.

[41] Case 93/1997, Criminal, Juvenile, Supreme Court, Sunday 26 October 1997; Case 137/1996, Criminal, Juvenile, Supreme Court, 10 May 1997. In this case the Supreme Court reiterated that a normal criminal trial could have on the psychology of the juvenile to the point that it could even exceed the aim of the measures or penalties that could be used. The Court went on to say that a normal trial could cause irreparable damage to a juvenile.

[42] Please see interview with Judge Omar Carmustagy.

mining the most suitable measures which should be decided in the interests of the juvenile and the wider society.[43]

Article 30[44] of the Law provides that prior to issuing a judgment, the following needs to be investigated by the Social Counsellor and Prosecutor: financial situation, social situation, ability to understand, growing up environment, reasons for committing the crime or the absconding and the possible measures which would be most effective in correcting or rehabilitating the minor. If the court sees that the physical or mental or psychological or social state of the defendant needs further care/attention then this needs to be done in a special and specific centre, or in any other place the court decides on and that is for a period it decides and this continues until the observation/attention ends.

C. Appeals and Temporary Judgments

Article 32 provides that appeals are allowed for sentences except those involving distancing the subject or telling them off or handing them off to their parents or those have custody or responsibility. If an appeal is requesting, it should be made within 30 days from the sentencing if it was made in the presence of the juvenile or offender or from the date of announcement if it was in absentia. The court should then look into the appeal quickly.

Article 31 provides that any procedure set in law should be communicated to the subject via either parent or someone with custody or responsibility over the person depending on circumstances. Those people above have the right to appeal matters to the advantage of the subject.

Where the Court has decided that the juvenile offender must be deposited in a specialist care institution or correctional facility, this decision must be executed even if an appeal has been filed (article 33).

Under article 35, a special provision in the law allows the court to change its judgments after looking into reports submitted by the Department of Public Prosecution, by the juvenile or the juvenile's guardian, the social counsellor or the lawyer. The judge is then permitted to review the measure and stop and cancel the measure, particularly if it is

---

[43] Please see interview with Judge Omar Carmustagy; The Initial reports of States parties due in 1999: United Arab Emirates, CRC/C/78/Add.2, 24 October 2001, para 98–99.

[44] The Initial reports of States parties due in 1999: United Arab Emirates, CRC/C/78/Add.2, 24 October 2001, para 98, translated art 30: 'Before a juvenile is sentenced, the court shall look into his financial and social situation, the extent to which he is capable of acting with discretion, the environment in which he grew up, the reasons that prompted him to commit the offence or to become a vagrant and the measures that would be most conducive to his reform. If the court believes that the juvenile's physical, mental, psychological or social situation necessitates observation and study before a judgement is handed down in his case, it shall order his placement in a surveillance centre, or in any other place designated by the court, for a specified period of time and the proceedings shall be suspended pending completion of the observation and study.'

then found to be inappropriate. Article 35 goes on to state: 'the court shall under no circumstances be subject to appeal and a further petition may not be submitted within three months from the date of the said decision.'[45]

Finally, the rehabilitation centre or institution holding the juvenile offender must provide the Court with a report detailing the person's situation and behavior every six months as an upper limit. This is so that the Court can monitor whether or not the corrective measures are having the desired effect on the minor.[46]

In its report to the CRC, the UAE emphasized the fact that within the Law, a decision could be amended or annulled through more efficient channels. The CRC translated the provisions of article 36 and article 37 as follows:

> If a defendant is sentenced on the assumption that he is over 18 years of age and official documents subsequently prove him to be under 18 years of age, the Department of Public Prosecutions shall bring the matter to the attention of the court that pronounced the sentence so that it can annul the sentence and pass judgement in the case in accordance with the rules and procedures laid down for the prosecution of juveniles.

According to article 37:

> If a defendant is sentenced to any of the measures prescribed for juveniles and official documents subsequently prove him to be over 18 years of age, the Department of Public Prosecutions shall bring the matter to the attention of the court which pronounced the sentence so that it can annul the sentence and pass judgement in the case in accordance with the provisions of the Code of Criminal Procedure.[47]

It should also be noted that while the normal civil and criminal procedure law bars the defendant from raising challenges to procedures which are not challenged at the first hearing, this rule does not apply to juvenile cases.[48]

D. *No Future Criminal Record*

The UAE Criminal Procedure Code, Federal Law No 36 of 1992 provides in article 18.3 that juvenile offenders do not get a criminal record should

---

[45] Initial reports of States parties due in 1999: United Arab Emirates, CRC/C/78/Add.2, 24 October 2001, para 89.
[46] Please see interview with Judge Carmustagy
[47] Initial reports of States parties due in 1999 : United Arab Emirates, CRC/C/78/Add.2, 24 October 2001, para 91.
[48] See Case 93/1997, Supreme Court Judgment referenced below.

they be found guilty of committing a crime as per article 18(3). This allows juveniles to reintegrate with society following the end of the measures they undertake, and does not permanently and irreparably damage future opportunities, thus restoring their honour and reputation.

E. Procedures Depending on Gender

There are no identifiable gender-specific issues or discrimination between male and female juveniles and both have the same access to the judicial system. Both genders undergo the same procedures and have access to rehabilitation centers catering to their specific genders. The Ministry of Labour and Social Affairs runs special centers for males and females, such as the Centre for Girl Minors at Sharjah.[49]

VI. DEATH PENALTY

The death penalty is not applied to juveniles in the UAE as stipulated in article 9 of Law No 9 of 1976. Moreover, murder cases involving juveniles are extremely rare.

VII. CONCLUSION

In general terms it can be noted that the current laws in the UAE offer general protection to the rights of juveniles in conformity with article 40 of the UNCRC. Article 40(a) requires that the juvenile must have 'infringed the penal law' and Law No 9 of 1976 provides in article 7 and article 8 that the law only applies where the juvenile offender has committed an action punishable by the law. Moreover, the requirements set forth in article 40(b) can also generally be found to be fully complied with as illustrated above. Equally important are the variety of dispositions available to juvenile offenders in accordance with article 40(4). In an interview with Judge Carmustagy judge of the Dubai Criminal Court,[50] he emphasized the importance of ensuring that the education and professional training of the juvenile was not disrupted.

Despite the general observance of the UNCRC, one of the main concerns with regard to the protection of juvenile offenders is the lack of special training for police officials, public prosecutors and government officials

---

[49] Committee on the Rights of the Child (30th Session) Summary Record of the 795th meeting (13 May 2002) 9 CRC/C/SR.795.
[50] Please see interview with Judge Carmustagy.

who come into contact with the juvenile. The UAE does not currently have specialized training programmes for police officers, prosecutors and judges that teach them to deal specifically with juveniles and appreciate their psychology. Similarly, the State should ensure that people administering justice, particularly judges, need to understand the various backgrounds of juvenile offenders in order to better appreciate their motives as well as the effect taking certain measures could have on their psychology. Both these recommendations were shared by Judges Ali Shamis Mohamed Shamis Al Madhani,[51] and Omar Carmustagy,[52] as well as Dr Thaera Sha'alan in her comparative study of juvenile justice in the Arab World.[53] The CRC also made a series of recommendations[54] touching upon suitable training, a separate criminal justice system for juveniles including specialized courts and finally, the speedy promulgation of the new law among others.

While it may appear that the current criminal justice in relation to juveniles is largely compatible with the UNCRC, practitioners have themselves noted areas which require further attention and reform in order to properly implement the existing laws and protections. As practitioners within the system, Judges Ali Shamis Mohamed Shamis Al Madhani[55] and Omar Carmustagy[56] both provide specific areas in need of reform including more stringent laws with regard to pre-trial detention, specialized units to deal with juvenile offenders, extra care for privacy during investigation and priority given to training professionals dealing with juveniles. Judge Carmustagy noted that the new law should provide more corrective measures and his secretary offered community service as another option. The judge was also concerned that corrective measures were not properly implemented and that juvenile rehabilitation centres required great regulation. Finally, the judge stated that the role of Social Counsellors ought to be enhanced during the hearing in order to better appreciate the psychology and circumstances of the child offender.

The above recommendations demonstrate that although in general terms the UAE system complies with the UNCRC, the practical implementation requires greater care and accuracy. By paying attention to the comments of practitioners and professionals who also appreciate the culture and norms of the society, the UAE can better enhance juvenile protection.

---

[51] Former judge of the Dubai Courts (civil and criminal) and currently judge of the DIFC Courts.

[52] Interview conducted by the author of the report 13 July 2009.

[53] Dr T Sha'alan, 'Juvenile Justice in the Arab World—Between Theory and Practice' 13 May 2008, available at http://www.crin.org/docs/Juvenile_Justie_Ara.doc (http://www.crin.org/resources/infodetail.asp?id=17309).

[54] Concluding observations of the Committee on the Rights of the Child: United Arab Emirates, CRC/C/15/Add.183 13/06/2002, para 42.

[55] Interview conducted by the author of the report, 22 July 2009.

[56] Interview conducted by the author of the report, 13 July 2009.

CHAPTER 14

*Criminal Law and the Rights of the Child in the United Kingdom**

I. INTRODUCTION

The UK legal system is the result of centuries of legal development, and represents three distinct legal jurisdictions: England and Wales collectively, Northern Ireland, and Scotland. Although politically the UK is run by a centralized parliament located in Westminster, each jurisdiction also operates under a devolved local government structure. This results in differences within the juvenile justice system. The most prominent legal disparity within the United Kingdom is the minimum age of criminal responsibility. Scotland sets it at eight years of age, whereas the rest of the UK sets it at 10 years. In this report, the UK will be analysed as a single legal system. However, where the three jurisdictions diverge in their legal approaches to juveniles, each approach will be discussed in turn.

The UK Home Office recently published statistics on the number of recorded juvenile arrests in England and Wales which revealed an upward trend in the numbers of offending. Between 2003 and 2004, 63,300 arrests of 10- to 17-year-olds were recorded while the following period, 2004–2005, showed an increase in arrests to 76,600.[1] Over the past 12 years of Labour rule, the juvenile justice system has undergone immense reform,[2] most notably through the integration of Social Services, education departments, the Police and the National Health Service in order to tackle issues of youth crime and rehabilitation.[3]

Some of the major risks associated with youth crime were reiterated and identified in the Youth Crime Action Plan 2008.[4] The factors that the UK

---

* Dr Nisrine Abiad, Dr Farkhanda Zia Mansoor.

[1] Table AB 'Persons arrested for recorded crime (Notifiable Offences) by type of offence, sex and age group 2003/04 and 2004/05, 3, Home Office Statistical Bulletin 'Arrests for Record Crime (Notifiable Offences) and the Operation of Certain Police Powers under PACE' England and Wales 21/05, Margaret Ayres and Liz Murray, 16 December 2005. Research Developments and Statistics Directorate. Available at: http://www.homeoffice.gov.uk/rds/pdfs05/hosb2105.pdf, accessed 3 March 2010.

[2] The Crime and Disorder Act 1998, Youth Justice and Criminal Evidence Act 1999, Criminal Justice and Immigration Act 2008.

[3] Crime and Disorder Act 1998 s 39 (5)(a-e), available at: http://195.99.1.70/acts/acts1998/ukpga_19980037_en_5#pt3-pb1-l1g39, accessed 3 March 2010.

[4] http://homeoffice.gov.uk/documents/youth-crime-action-plan/youth-crime-action-plan-082835.pdf?view=Binary, accessed 3 March 2010.

320

A brief summary of the Criminal Justice System of the United Kingdom and Northern Ireland

	England and Wales and Northern Ireland	Scotland
Lower Court	**Magistrates Court:** resolve 90 per cent of cases. They have jurisdiction over (i)summary offences[5] ie offences for which a defendant would not have an automatic right to trial by jury such as speeding and minor assaults and (ii)'either way' offences such as theft. Cases are heard either by three lay magistrates or one District Judge. The lay magistrates, or 'Justices of the Peace', as they are also known, are local people who volunteer their services. They don't have formal legal qualifications, but are given legal and procedural advice by qualified clerks. The maximum punishment a *Justice of the Peace* can issue is a £5000 fine or six months detention.[6] District Judges are legally qualified, paid, full-time professionals.[7] They must have 'at least seven years experience as a Barrister or Solicitor and two years experience as a Deputy District Judge. They sit alone and deal with more complex or sensitive cases e.g. cases arising from Extradition Act, Fugitive Offenders Act and Serious Fraud[8]'.	**The Justice of the Peace Court,** which replaces the Scottish District Court, is presided over by lay people known as 'Justices of the Peace'. They hear 'summary cases' such as motoring offences and minor assaults. They have the power to impose fines of up to £2,500 and custodial sentences of up to two months. In Glasgow, there are also legally qualified Stipendiary Magistrates with the power to pass fines of up to £10,000 and custodial sentences of up to 12 months.[9]

Upper Court	**The Crown Court** have jurisdiction over 'either way' offences. In such cases, the defendant can pursue his right to be heard in Crown Court rather than in the Magistrates' Court or a judge can deem the case serious enough to be heard in Crown Court. It also has jurisdiction over 'indictable offence', such as murder or rape, where there is an automatic right of jury trial. Cases are often heard within the Magistrates' Court and are then referred on a guilty verdict to the Crown Court for harsher sentencing.[10]	**The Sheriff Court:** Crimes in Scotland are divided into 'solemn' where a judge sits with a jury of 15 people or 'summary' where a judge can hear a case alone. They have the authority to pass down sentences of up to 12 months imprisonment and issue fines of up to £10,000 in summary cases. In solemn cases, imprisonment for up to five years[11] can be ordered and there is no upper limit on the amount of the fine that can be issued.
Court of Appeal	The Court of Appeal (Criminal Division).	High Court of the Justiciary

[5] 1 McLeod, *Legal Method* (4th edn, Palgrave Law Masters, Macmillian, 2002) 41.
[6] A Ashworth, *Sentencing and Criminal Justice* (4th edn, CUP, Cambridge, 2005) 2.
[7] http://www.cjsonline.gov.uk/the_cjs/how_it_works/magistrates_court/, accessed 3 March 2010.
[8] Her Majesty's Court Services: http://www.hmcourts-service.gov.uk/infoabout/magistrates/index.htm, accessed 3 March 2010.
[9] Official Scottish Courts Homepage, available at http://www.scotcourts.gov.uk/ district/index.asp, accessed 3 March 2010.
[10] McLeod (n 6) 2.
[11] See (n 9).

government recognized as being risk-inducing in involvement in crime were the following: troubled home life; poor academic achievement, truancy, school exclusion; drug or alcohol misuse; mental illness; deprivation (poor housing or homelessness); and peer group pressure.[12]

The UK Supreme Court was established in October 2009, hearing issues of devolution from the Northern Ireland and Scottish Courts and the Welsh Assembly. It is also the highest court of appeal for Scottish civil law cases and the final court of appeal for England and Wales, replacing the House of Lords. An individual contending that his Convention rights have not been respected by a decision of a United Kingdom court (including the Supreme Court) against which he has no domestic recourse may bring a claim against the United Kingdom before the European Court of Human Rights.[13]

II. NATIONAL LEGAL FRAMEWORK FOR THE PROTECTION OF JUVENILE OFFENDERS

A. The Minimum Age of Criminal Responsibility

1. England and Wales

Under the old law, the minimum age of criminal responsibility was to start on the day a child reached his seventh birthday.[14] Although English Law only recognizes people as legal entities after the age of 18, 'the law posed no such limitation on their ability to commit crimes'.[15] Courtney Stanhope Kenny explains this incongruity thus: 'a child knows right from wrong long before he knows how to make a prudent speculation or a wise will'[16] and this very much exemplifies the position of the legal systems operating throughout the UK. However, the laws of Great Britain were heavily criticized for treating juveniles harshly, as they failed to distinguish between juvenile and adult criminals. Children were tried and sentenced in the same way as adults, regardless of the offence committed, and, more shockingly, were incarcerated in adult criminal facilities.

The British Parliament enacted the Children's Act in 1908, which created the first juvenile court system in Great Britain. The first review of juvenile law came in 1930. It was conducted by the Home Affairs Select Committee

---

[12] See (n 3) 58–59.

[13] http://www.supremecourt.gov.uk/about/the-supreme-court-and-europe.html, accessed 3 March 2010.

[14] D Ormerod, *Smith and Hogan Criminal Law* (10th edn, OUP, Oxford, 2005) 211.

[15] See (n 13).

[16] CS Kenny and JWC Turner, *Kenny's Outlines of Criminal Law* (17th edn, CUP, Cambridge, 1966) 80.

and concluded that a higher age of criminal responsibility should be set. Their findings resulted in the Children and Young Persons Act 1933, which increased the age of criminal liability to eight.[17] In 1960, the findings of another Government Select Committee recommended that the minimum age be increased to 12.[18] A compromise was reached in the 1963 and the age was fixed at 10 years of age by the Children and Young Persons Act 1963. As a result, any child under the age of 10 could not be convicted of a crime as they were *doli incapax* (incapable of committing a crime), even if the requisite *mens rea* and *actus reus* (mental intent and physical act of a crime) could be proven.

With regards to the nature of criminal responsibility, the 1963 Act in conjunction with case law within the UK established different categories of criminal capacity. These categories provided that, depending on the age of the offender, the prosecution could be required to satisfy a heightened burden of proof before certain child offenders were found criminally responsible.[19] The British courts defined three categories of criminal capacity:

1. children under the age of 10 who cannot be held criminally responsible;
2. children between the ages of 10 and 14 for whom the prosecution had to meet a heightened burden of proof before they could be held criminally responsible;
3. children between the ages of 14 and 18 for whom the prosecution bore no additional proof.

2. Scotland and Northern Ireland

The age of criminal responsibility in Northern Ireland is also fixed at 10.

---

[17] Children and Young Person Act 1933, s 50 (amended by 1963 Act), available at: http://www.opsi.gov.uk/RevisedStatutes/Acts/ukpga/1933/cukpga_19330012_en_6#pt3-pb6-l1g52, accessed 4 March 2010.

[18] ibid (n 13) 212. C Lees, 'The Age of Criminal Responsibility, Which Direction?: A Comparative Study of the United Kingdom And Canada' (2000) Thesis, McGill University. The minimum age is 12 in the Netherlands, 13 in France, 14 in Germany, 15 in Sweden and Italy, 16 in Spain and 18 in Belgium. Most US states do not stipulate when children can be prosecuted, but in those that do the age varies between six and 12. Australia followed the English lead and set a minimum of 10, while it is 12 in Canada, 14 in New Zealand and 15 in Japan. Fixing an age of criminal responsibility does not necessarily mean children are jailed. Instead, it leads to young law-breakers being treated as a welfare problem. N Morris, 'The Big Question: At What Age Should Children Be Held Responsible for their Criminal Acts? *The Independent* (London England 5 February 2009).

[19] J Farrington-Douglas and L Durante, *Towards a Popular, Preventative Youth Justice System* (Institute for Public Policy Research, June 2009) 304, available at: http://www.ippr.org.uk/members/download.asp?f=%2Fecomm%2Ffiles%2Fyouthjustice.pdf, accessed 3 March 2010.

Although a comprehensive review of the criminal justice system in Northern Ireland was conducted in 2000 to consider the matter, it did not recommend that the age be increased. It did, however, recommend that children aged 10 to 13 who are found guilty of criminal offences should not be held in juvenile justice centres. Rather, their accommodation needs should be provided by the care system. While legislative provision was made to this effect, it was felt that a non-institutionalized approach would be more appropriate. This view was supported by the judiciary and the Northern Ireland Human Rights Commission. The youth justice system therefore continues to work with a range of partners in the statutory and NGO sectors.[20]

The situation in Scotland differs somewhat. By virtue of the Criminal Procedures Act 1995, the minimum age of culpability is deemed to be eight. In 1964, the Kilbrandon Committee on Children and Young Persons in Scotland, chaired by Lord Kilbrandon, came to this final conclusion:

> The legal presumption by which no child under the age of 8 can be subjected to criminal proceedings is not therefore a reflection of any observable fact, but simply an expression of public policy to the effect that in no circumstances should a child under the age of 8 be made the subject of criminal proceedings and thus liable to the pains of the law. Equally, at various intermediate stages prior to adulthood, the effect of statute law is to exempt juveniles below certain ages from certain forms of judicial action ... It is clear, therefore, that the age of criminal responsibility is largely a meaningless term, and that in so far as the law refers to the age of 8 being the minimum age for prosecution, this is essentially the expression of a practical need for a rule on age of criminal responsibility in the sense of capacity to commit crime. We must stress that our recommendation to abolish a rule that a child below 8 is deemed incapable of being found guilty of an offence is not a proposal to get rid of the entire idea of age of criminal responsibility. Rather the effect of our recommendations is to give greater clarity to the principles on age of criminal responsibility which already exist in Scots law. The existence of two different senses of age of criminal responsibility is a source of considerable misunderstanding and we consider that our proposed reforms will result in the elimination of a confusing anomaly from our law.[21]

---

[20] The Consolidated 3rd and 4th Periodic Report to the UN Committee on the Rights of the Child, para 8.58, available at: http://www.dcsf.gov.uk/everychildmatters/resources-and-practice/ IG00249/, accessed 3 March 2010.

[21] Cited in the Scottish Law Commission Report No 185, 'Report on Age of Criminal Responsibility' January 2002, 6, available at: www.chscotland.gov.uk/pdf/krcy.pdf, accessed 4 March 2010.

The reality of the situation is that more often than not it is the offence that is looked at rather than the offender. When faced with less serious crimes, the courts are often accommodating but when the nature of the offence is aggravated by particular violence, the courts show little leniency in terms of sentencing. The changing political trend in approaching youth crime has meant that the courts are slowly changing their approaches to juvenile offenders. However, progress is slow and the way in which courts approach juveniles is still in contravention to many of the principles of the UNCRC.

B. The Courts

Juveniles who face court proceedings are tried by a Youth Court, which is a section of the Magistrates' court, designed to be less formal. The young defendant, his family and the victim(s) may attend the hearing. However, the trial is closed to members of the general public.[22] If a juvenile is charged with a serious crime or a crime committed alongside an adult, he will be tried in the adult Crown Court under the law pertaining to minors.[23]

The UK Government has stated that custodial sentences should be the last resort for juveniles convicted of crime and a punishment reserved for the most serious crimes. Those cases that are assessed as not meriting court proceedings are now diverted to the Youth Conditional Caution, where a juvenile with no previous convictions who pleads guilty to an offence consents to receiving a caution. The Crown Prosecution Service reserves the right to continue prosecution if the juvenile does not meet the terms of his caution, usually requiring the completion of an activity, the duration of which cannot exceed 20 hours, rehabilitation or providing reparations to a victim.[24] Rehabilitation through behavioural management programmes and drug and alcohol counselling are all ways in which the UK juvenile justice system seeks to protect and promote the rights of juveniles by equipping them with the necessary tools to navigate civil society. However, the stigma of criminal conviction can be very damaging, which is why many youth sentences are recorded as 'spent' so that they will not appear on the juvenile's criminal record nor will he/she need to declare them.[25]

Holding parents formally responsible for providing 'proper care and control'[26] of their delinquent children is another method in which the UK

---

[22] Official Youth Justice Board Website, available at: http://www.yjb.gov.uk/en-gb/yjs/Courts/YouthCourt.htm, accessed 10 February 2010.

[23] See (n 21).

[24] Crime and Disorder Act 1998, Part 1, ss 8–16.

[25] Criminal Justice and Immigration Act 2008, Section 49, available at: http://www.opsi.gov.uk/acts/acts2008/ukpga_20080004_en_7#pt4-pb1-l1g49, accessed 04/03/2010.

[26] White Paper: 'No More Excuses—A New Approach To Tackling Youth Crime In England And Wales' published November 1997, Home Office, available at: http://www.homeoffice.gov.uk/documents/jou-no-more-excusesa8cf.html?view=Html, accessed 4 March 2010.

has tried to address the root problems of juvenile offending. Parenting Orders are given to the parent or carers of children who have received a Referral Order. They do not result in a criminal record for the parent or carer but they ask that they attend counselling guidance sessions for a maximum of three months[27] to support families in reducing re-offending of children.

C. Key Legislation

The Crime and Disorder Act 1998 sets out the aim of the juvenile justice system in England and Wales as the following: to 'prevent offending by children and young persons'.[28] Youth Offending Teams are now a statutory obligation on local authorities[29] and are composed of representatives from the Police, health and education authorities and the probation service.[30] The Youth Justice Board was introduced to monitor the juvenile justice system in England and Wales. It is an executive, non-departmental body composed of members appointed by the Secretary of State for Justice.

The Criminal Justice and Immigration Act 2008 reiterates the role of the youth justice system: 'to prevent offending and re-offending'.[31] It introduces new measures and amalgamates existing diversion measures in order to streamline the system.[32] These include Youth Rehabilitation Orders, which replace 13 previous orders,[33] for juveniles convicted of a serious crime or those who are found to be persistent offenders.[34] Youth Rehabilitation Orders offer the courts different sentencing methods including proscribing activity,[35] unpaid work[36] or attendance to a programme[37] as well as mandatory drug treatment[38] and testing.[39] Orders are subject to proportionality considerations, balancing the severity of the crime committed with the restrictions on liberty imposed.[40] In addition, Referral Orders

---

[27] UK Youth Justice Board: http://www.yjb.gov.uk/en-gb/yjs/SentencesOrdersand Agreements/ParentingOrder/, accessed 04/03/2010.

[28] Crime and Disorder Act (CDA) 1998 Part III, s 37 (1), available at: http://www.opsi.gov. uk/acts/acts1998/ukpga_19980037_en_5#pt3-pb1-l1g37, accessed 04/03/2010.

[29] CDA 1998, s 38 (1)-(4).

[30] CDA 1998, s 39 (5)(a-e).

[31] Criminal Justice and Immigration Act (CJIA) 2008, s 9, available at: http://www.opsi. gov.uk/acts/acts2008/ukpga_20080004_en_3#pt2-pb1-l1g9, accessed 04/03/2010.

[32] See (n 25).

[33] Youth Rehabilitation Orders replace the following: Action Plan Order, Curfew Order. Supervision Order, Supervision Order and conditions, Community Punishment Order, Community Punishment and Rehabilitation Order, Attendance Centre Order, Drug Treatment and Testing Order, Exclusion Order, Community Rehabilitation Order, Community Rehabilitation Order and conditions.

[34] Criminal Justice and Immigration Act 2008, s 1(4)(a)–(c).

[35] ibid s 1(a).
[37] ibid 1(d).
[39] ibid s 1(m).

[36] ibid s 1(c).
[38] ibid s 1(l).
[40] ibid ss 147–148.

are applicable to juveniles aged 10–17 who plead guilty to a crime[41] and allow specialized local youth offender panels to take up sentencing. They consist of an agreed contract with the young offender on a programme of behaviour and his offering reparations to the victim.[42] Under the new law, courts have more say in how Referral Orders operate: they are able to issue them onto parties who previously were not included in the law, such as those who have received a conditional discharge, and they have the power to revoke the order following good behaviour or alternatively extend it.[43]

1. Northern Ireland

During Northern Ireland's years of sectarian violence and civil unrest, the area of juvenile justice was underdeveloped. The Belfast (Good Friday) Agreement in 1998 initiated wide-ranging changes in all areas of civil and political life, including the juvenile justice system. In fact, 'The Review of the Criminal Justice System in Northern Ireland' report resulted from a provision within the Belfast Agreement.[44] It was published in 2000 and made a series of recommendations which later manifested into law. As it stands, the juvenile justice system deals with children aged between 10 and 17. Children younger than 10 who come to the attention of the Police are transferred to Social Services where welfare legislation applies.[45]

Since 1973, specialist police officers from the Northern Ireland Juvenile Liaison Scheme were charged with policing cases involving youth suspects and had some discretion in disposing of certain cases. Four options were available to them, including the possibility of not taking further action. They could also issue 'informal warnings and advice' where juveniles would be warned of the consequences of being involved in criminal activity. Although this action would not be recorded on their criminal record, the police would keep an internal record of warnings issued. Otherwise, a formal caution could be issued, which again would not form part of a child's criminal record although it could be cited in court at a later date. Finally, the Police were able to carry out a full prosecution against a juvenile.[46]

In 2003 and following recommendations made by the Criminal Justice System Review report, the Juvenile Liaison Scheme was replaced by the

---

[41] Powers of Criminal Courts (Sentencing) Act 2000, ss 16–20, available at: http://www.opsi.gov.uk/acts/acts2000/ukpga_20000006_en_4#pt3-pb1, accessed 4 March 2010.

[42] Powers of Criminal Court (Sentencing) Act 2000, ss 23–27.

[43] Criminal Justice and Immigration Act 2008, ss 36–37.

[44] Review of the Criminal Justice System in Northern Ireland (March 2000) 1, available at: http://cain.ulst.ac.uk/issues/law/cjr/report30300.htm, accessed 4 March 2010.

[45] See (n 43) 223.

[46] ibid.

Youth Diversion Scheme, in an effort to consolidate all youth matters that come to the attention of the police such as non-offending behaviour, anti-social behaviour as well as criminal behaviour.[47] The Youth Diversion Scheme or YDS was created under the Justice (Northern Ireland) Act 2002[48] with the concept of restorative justice[49] at its fulcrum.

D. Mental Health and Protection of the Rights of Children

According to a report issued by NACRO, the Crime Reduction Charity, in September 2005, between 46 per cent and 81 per cent of children in custody have a psychiatric diagnosis.[50] The report suggests that the same risk factors that give rise to criminal behaviour also predispose children to psychiatric diagnoses so that there is a general overlap between delinquency and mental health.

The Mental Health Act 2007 regulates the way in which authorities, particularly the police, should act in relation to detained individuals who may have mental health issues. Previously, section 136 of the Mental Health Act 1983 ('MHA 1983') gave the police the power to transfer detainees suffering from mental health issues from a public place to a place of safety for up to 72 hours. Under the newly ratified Mental Health Act 2007, an appropriate person, usually a police officer or social worker, still has the power to do so. Guidance suggests that police stations should rarely be used as places of safety, except in exceptional circumstances. In reality however, annual figures suggest that 11,000 individuals are placed in police stations as places of safety.[51] In a recent report by the Sainsbury Centre for Mental Health, it has been recognized that detention within a police station further instils the stigma of criminalization within the particular individual suffering from mental health issues, even if he has not partaken in criminal activity. The report suggests that in the future, police stations should only be used as a measure of last resort, and that appropriate suites should be built within police stations to accommodate those individuals detained under section 136 MHA 1983. For the vast majority of cases, medical examinations in police stations are performed by medical examiners, forensic

---

[47] 'PSNI Section 75, Equality Impact Assessment, Youth Diversion Scheme' Police Service of Northern Ireland, Published March 2007, 5, available at: www.psni.police.uk/summary_of_youth_diversion_eqia.pdf, accessed 4 March 2010.

[48] The Justice (Northern Ireland) Act 2002, Part 4, available at: http://www.opsi.gov.uk/acts/acts2002/ukpga_20020026_en_7#pt4, accessed 4 March 2010.

[49] ibid 47.

[50] National Association of Care and Resettlement of Offenders,Youth Crime Briefing September 2005, 1, available at: http://www.nacro.org.uk/data/files/nacro-2006071402-104.pdf, accessed 4 March 2010.

[51] P Bather, R Fitzpatrick, and M Rutherford 'Briefing 36: The Police and Mental Health' (Sainsbury Centre for Mental Health, 2008) available at: http://www.scmh.org.uk/publications/police_and_mental_health.aspx?ID=583, accessed 4 March 2010.

medical examiners ('FME') within the police force. The FME will usually assess whether or not an individual should be detained under the Mental Health Act. Children will usually be assessed by a Youth Offending Team Officer ('YOT') who will sometimes, but significantly not always, liaise with the Child and Adolescent Mental Health Services.[52]

The 'Youth Crime Action Plan' published by the UK Government in 2008 identified numerous measures it hoped to implement in relation to youth crime and mental health. Whilst the Plan paid lip service to mental health issues regarding young juvenile offenders, it failed to clearly outline how such goals would be targeted or met.

Schedule 1 § 20(1) of the Criminal Justice and Immigration Act 2008 states that a mental health requirement means 'a requirement that the offender must submit, during a period or periods specified in the order, to treatment by or under the direction of a registered medical practitioner or a chartered psychologist with a view to the improvement of the offender's mental condition.' Such treatments are defined as periods of respite in either an independent hospital or care home, or an appropriate facility. Importantly, under § 20(3) it is stated that the order can only be granted with such an attachment if the mental condition of the individual may be susceptible to treatment but 'is not such as to warrant the making of a hospital order or guardianship order within the meaning of the Act [Mental Health Act 1983]', and moreover that the individual has expressed a willingness to comply with such an order. There are obvious complications with such orders, namely the degree of the gravity of the condition and the willingness on the part of the young offender to undergo treatment.

III. THE INTERNATIONAL HUMAN RIGHTS FRAMEWORK: ITS ADOPTION AND INTEGRATION INTO DOMESTIC LAW

The UK ratified the UN Convention on the Rights of the Child (hereinafter referred to as the UNCRC) with reservations on 16 December 1991.[53] It was incorporated into domestic law by way of statute in 1991. Until recently those reservations remained intact and continued to affect asylum-seeking children residing in the UK. They have since been lifted and the UK may no longer make reservations to the UNCRC. However, the Committee on the UNCRC is

---

[52] Sainsbury Centre for Mental Health, 'The Chance of a Lifetime—Preventing Early Conduct Problems And Reducing Crime' published 23 November 2009, available at: http://www.scmh.org.uk/publications/chance_of_a_lifetime.aspx?ID=604, accessed 10 January 2010.

[53] http://treaties.un.org/Pages/ViewDetails.aspx?src=TREATY&mtdsg_no=IV-11&chapter=4&lang=en, accessed 4 March 2010.

concerned that the principles of the Convention are not duly taken into account in all pieces of legislation throughout the country and that the State party has not incorporated the Convention into domestic law nor has ensured the compliance of all legislation affecting children with it.[54]

One example is the fact the Children's Act 2004, designed to address the issue of children's rights, only applies to England and Wales. It urged the UK Government to provide an 'overarching policy to ensure the full realization of principles, values and goals of the convention'.[55] In an attempt to address the CRC's concerns, the Department for Children, Schools, and Families was established in 2007.

The United Nation's 49th Session on the UNCRC convened on 20 October 2008 in order to analyze the UK government's commitment to implementation of the UNCRC. Whilst it acknowledged that the UK had made efforts to implement certain observations, it regretted that the UK had failed to address the following topics: budgetary allocation; discrimination and awareness of the Convention; non-discrimination; corporal punishment; education; asylum-seekers and refugee children; juvenile justice. In addition, the report highlighted the CRC's mains concerns:

- The low age of criminal responsibility;
- Children between the ages of 16–18 can be tried in an adult court;
- The proportion of children in detention remains high, which suggests that custody is frequently used and is not a measure of last resort;
- The number of children in remand;
- The fact that children in custody do not have a right to education;
- The practice within the Overseas Territories to detain children below 18 in facilities also intended for adults;
- The Youth Crime Action Place (July 2008) which intends to remove reporting restrictions for 16 and 17-year-olds within the criminal justice system;
- The provisions of the Counter-terrorism bill in relation to children and extended pre-charge detention;
- Children within Turks and Caicos held in Jamaica due to a lack of facilities;

---

[54] Committee on the Rights of the Child: 49th Session, *Consideration of reports submitted by State Parties under Article 44 of the Convention, Concluding observations: United Kingdom of Great Britain and Northern Ireland*, 20 October 2008, para 10, available at: http://www2.ohchr.org/english/bodies/crc/docs/AdvanceVersions/CRC.C.GBR.CO.4.pdf. accessed 4 March 2010.

[55] ibid para 14.

- The mental health of children, because of the 10 per cent of children who are diagnosed as having mental health problems, only 25 per cent are receiving medication.[56]

The Committee made the following recommendations:

- Raise the minimum age of criminal responsibility;
- Develop a broad range of alternative measures for children in detention;
- Deal with children within the juvenile justice system and not to treat them as adults;
- Ensuring that all children within detention are separated from adults;
- Provide a statutory right for education within detention facilities;
- Review the Counter-Terrorism procedures in relation to children;
- In respect of Overseas Territories to ensure that those children who are deprived of their liberty are held to have all their article 40 rights.[57]

The UK is also a signatory to the UN Guidelines for the Prevention of Juvenile Delinquency (the Riyadh Guidelines), the UN Guidelines for Action on Children in the Criminal Justice System and the UN Minimum Rules for the Administration of Juvenile Justice (Beijing Rules). The European Convention on Human Rights (ECHR) based on the UN charter, was also ratified into UK domestic law through the Human Rights Act 1998 and is the basis of the UK human rights framework of child protection.

IV. CONTEMPORARY PRACTICE: TWO CASE STUDIES

A. *The James Bulger Murder Trial (1993) and its Implications on the UK Juvenile Justice System*

James Bulger was a 2-year-old toddler murdered by two 10-year-old boys in 1993. His murder trial caused much debate in the UK and had a lasting impact on the juvenile justice system. The two juveniles were found guilty of murder but the case was subject to appeals that ended at the European Court of Human Rights (ECtHR). The Court held[58] that the minimum age of criminal responsibility did not in itself deviate so far from European

---

[56] ibid para 77.
[57] ibid (n 54) para 78.
[58] *V v United Kingdom,* Application No 24888/94, 30 EHRR 121, 16 December 1999, available at: http://cmiskp.echr.coe.int/tkp197/viewhbkm.asp?skin=hudoc-en&action=html &table=F69A27FD8FB86142BF01C1166DEA398649&key=15003&highlight=, accessed 4 March 2010.

practices as to violate human rights standards.[59] However, the Court found that the boys' right to a fair trial had been compromised in various ways because of their inability to adequately understand and participate in legal proceedings. It is questionable the extent to which very young children can meaningfully participate in their own defence in legal proceedings.[60]

Before the historic case of *R v Secretary of State for the Home Department, ex parte V and T,* there was a presumption that youth offenders aged between 10 and 14 were *doli incapax.* When the case was heard, the presumption was rebutted and as a consequence abolished. At the time the case was heard, young offenders convicted of murder were to be automatically detained at Her Majesty's pleasure by virtue of section 53(1) of the Children and Young Persons' Act 1933 which provided:

> [A] person convicted of an offence who appears to the court to have been under the age of eighteen years at the time the offence was committed shall not, if he is convicted of murder, be sentenced to imprisonment for life nor shall sentence of death be pronounced on or recorded against any such person but in lieu thereof the court shall ... sentence him to be detained during Her Majesty's pleasure, and if so sentenced he shall be liable to be detained in such a place and under such conditions as the Secretary of State may direct.

Over the years, the Secretary of State adopted a tariff policy in relation to offenders who were sentenced to life: '[i]n essence, the tariff approach involves breaking down the life sentence into component parts, namely retribution, deterrence and protection of the public. The "tariff" represents the minimum period which the prisoner will have to serve to satisfy the requirements of retribution and deterrence.'[61] The UK does not have the death penalty, nor does it sentence prisoners to corporal punishment.

At trial, Mr Justice Morland sentenced the boys to detention 'during Her Majesty's pleasure in such a place and under such conditions as the Secretary of State may direct'.[62] As was standard procedure, he provided advice to the Home Secretary regarding the length of detention. He wrote:

> If the defendants had been adults I would have said that the actual length of detention necessary to meet the requirements of retribution and general deterrence should have been 18 years. ...

---

[59] For the reasoning of the court, see D Cipriani, *Children's Rights and the Minimum Age of Criminal Responsibility* (Ashgate, London, 2009) 66–67.

[60] http://billofrights.nihrc.org/submissions/submission_323.pdf, 2, accessed 4 March 2010.

[61] *V v United Kingdom*, para 40.

[62] *Ex parte V and T*, HL [1997] 1, available at: http://www.publications.parliament.uk/pa/ld199798/ldjudgmt/jd970612/vandt01.htm, accessed 4 March 2010.

In my judgment the appropriate actual length of detention necessary to meet the requirement[s] of retribution and general deterrence for the murder, taking into account all its appalling circumstances and the age of the defendants when it was committed is 8 years. ... 8 years is 'very very many years' for a ten or 11-year-old.

They are now children. In 8 years' time they will be young men.[63]

Having received advice from both Judge Morland and the Lord Chief Justice, who felt that a tariff of 10 years was more appropriate, the Home Secretary taking into consideration the penal element stated that he:

[T]akes the view that this was an exceptionally cruel and sadistic offence against a very young and defenceless victim committed over a period of several hours. The Secretary of State believes that if the offence had been committed by an adult then the appropriate tariff would have been in the region of twenty-five years and not eighteen years as suggested by the trial judge. For these reasons and bearing in mind your age when the offence was committed the Secretary of State has decided to fix a tariff of fifteen years in your case.[64]

Applications were subsequently made on behalf of both V and T to quash the Home Secretary's Decision. The matter was heard before a Divisional Court headed by Lord Justice Pill and Judge Newman. The sentences were quashed on the basis that the Home Secretary had based much of his decision on the fact that, like adult offenders, a part of their sentence would be composed of a penal element, which they would have to serve before their parole could be considered. Such a decision was however considered unlawful with regard to children. The Home Secretary appealed to the Court of Appeal, and both respondents V and T made, by way of notices, cross appeal for breaches of natural justice and unfairness. On 12 June 1997, the House of Lords, by majority, dismissed the Secretary of State's appeal and allowed the applicants' cross appeal. They further found that it was unlawful for the Secretary of State to have not taken into consideration the 'progress and development of a child detained during Her Majesty's pleasure'[65] when applying the tariff. Lord Hope stated:

A policy which ignores at any stage, the child's development and progress whilst in custody as a factor relevant to his eventual release date, is an unlawful policy. The practice of fixing the penal element as

---

[63] *Ex parte V and T*, HL [1997] 2.
[64] *V v United Kingdom*, para 23.
[65] ibid para 26.

applied to adult mandatory life prisoners, which has no regard to the development and progress of the prisoner during this period cannot be reconciled with the requirement to keep the protection and welfare of the child under review throughout the period which he is in custody.[66]

As a result of the House of Lord's ruling, the Secretary of State informed Parliament on 10 November 1997 that he was applying a new policy in relation to young offenders convicted of murder where the tariff would be kept under review according to their progress and development. He stated:

> I shall continue to seek the advice of the trial judge and that of the Lord Chief Justice in deciding what punishment is required in any case of a person convicted under section 53(1) of the Children and Young Persons Act 1933. I shall then set an initial tariff with that advice, and the offender's personal circumstances in mind; I shall continue to invite representations on the prisoner's behalf and give reasons for decisions.
>
> Officials in my Department will receive annual reports on the progress and development of young people sentenced under section 53(1) whose initial tariff has yet to expire. Where there appears to be a case for considering a reduction in tariff, that will be brought to the attention of the Ministers.
>
> When half of the initial tariff period has expired, I, or a Minister acting on my behalf, will consider a report on the prisoner's progress and development, and invite representations on the question of tariff, with a view to determining whether the tariff period originally set is still appropriate'.[67]

In May 1994, applications on behalf of both boys were made to the European Commission of Human Rights that later became the European Court of Human Rights. Judgment was given on the 16 of December 1999. V, the first applicant, claimed numerous breaches of his rights under the ECHR. Here, discussion will be limited to the alleged breaches of article 3 and 6 and the age of criminal responsibility. The applicant asserted:

> [T]he cumulative effect of the age of criminal responsibility, the accusatorial nature of the trial, the adult proceedings in a public court, the length of the trial, the jury of twelve adult strangers, the physical layout of the courtroom, the overwhelming presence of the media and public; the attacks by the public on the prison van which brought him to court and the disclosure of his identity, together with a number of other factors linked to his sentence gave rise to a breach of Article 3.[68]

---

[66] *V v United Kingdom,* quoting Lord Hope, para 43.
[67] *V v United Kingdom*, para 44.   [68] *V v United Kingdom*, para 63.

Much of the applicant's arguments focused on the minimum age of criminal responsibility and how it was far below that of its European neighbours. He accepted that it was not a breach of the ECHR to prosecute a child of such a young age, but asserted that it was then incumbent on the state to 'ensure that the procedures adopted for the trial and sentencing of such young children were modified to reflect their age and vulnerability'.[69] The applicant further asserted that there was evidence from various psychiatric reports to suggest that at the time of the trial, he was functioning on a level far below that of his biological age.

In response to these allegations, the UK Government stated that there were several Member States whose age of criminal responsibility was much lower than 10 years of age. It added that there were no international instruments that laid down a specific age. It also contended that the applicant was not subjected to inhuman or degrading treatment, as a number of changes were made during the trial process so as to make the process more bearable for the young defendants.

In its decision, the ECtHR stressed the importance of article 3 and emphasised the threshold that must be crossed for a breach to take place:

> Ill-treatment must attain a minimum level of severity if it is to fall within the scope of Article 3. The assessment of this minimum is, in the nature of things, relative; it depends on all the circumstances of the case, such as the nature and context of the treatment or punishment, the manner and methods of its execution, its duration, its physical or mental effects and, in some instances, the sex, age and state of health of the victim.[70]

It then considered whether the age of criminal responsibility in England and Wales could in itself give rise to a breach of article 3. In determining this, it accepted that there is no common minimum age of responsibility amongst the Member States. It then cited examples where the minimum age of criminal responsibility was lower than that of the UK. In addition, it referred to international instruments which only offered guidance but set no formal age at which a child becomes liable. For these reasons, the applicant failed on his article 3 claim.

In relation to article 6, the applicant argued that an individual had to be able to participate effectively in the conduct of his case for the right to be effective. He argued that because of the nature of the trial and the exposure to the public and media, he had had been unable to exercise his right to participate. The Court found that there had indeed been a breach of article 6. It stated that:

---

[69] *V v United Kingdom*, Case No 24888/94, para 63.
[70] ibid para 70.

It follows that, in respect of a young child charged with a grave offence attracting high levels of media and public interest, it would be necessary to conduct the hearing in such a way as to reduce as far as possible his or her feelings of intimidation and inhibition ... It is highly unlikely that the applicant would have felt sufficiently uninhibited, in the tense court-room and under public scrutiny, to have consulted with them during the trial or, indeed, that, given his immaturity and his disturbed emotional state, he would have been capable outside the courtroom of cooperating with his lawyers and giving them information for the purposes of his defence.[71]

It should be noted that both defendants were released in June 2001 follow-ing a decision of the Parole Board approved by the then Home Secretary, David Blunkett. However, they were given compulsory life sentences thus remaining on licence for the rest of their lives. In fact, in early March 2010, Jon Venables was recalled to custody after breaching the terms of his release. The Ministry of Justice did not detail the nature of Venables' breach of his licence.[72]

Thus, the James Bulger case raised the important issue of criminal responsibility in relation to juveniles. Sula Wolff and Alexander A McCall Smith, writing in the Child Psychology & Psychiatric Review, heavily criti-cize the English Courts in their framing of the principle of *doli incapax* to a question of whether the juvenile understood the difference between right and wrong, rather than taking into account their wider psychological condition. They assert that '[t]o limit the concept of culpability to ones intellectual understanding makes no sense'.[73]

B. The Edlington Child Torture Case (2010)

More than 13 years on from the ECtHR's ruling, this case involved two child defendant brothers, known as A and B, who were charged initially with attempted murder but later pleaded guilty to the lesser charges of caus-ing grievous bodily harm, robbery, causing actual bodily harm (two counts) and intentionally causing a child under 13 years old to engage in sexual activity (two counts). A and B's victims were two boys aged nine and 11. Defendants A and B also pleaded guilty to a separate incident against another 11-year-old boy for causing actual bodily harm with a threat to

---

[71] *V v United Kingdom*, para 90.
[72] 'James Bulger murderer Jon Venables returned to Prison' http://news.bbc.co.uk/1/hi/england/merseyside/8546528.stm, accessed 5 February 2010.
[73] S Wolff and R Alexander A McCall Smith, 'Child Homicide and the Law: Implications of the Judgements of Human Rights in the case of the children who killed James Bulger' (2000) 5 Child Psychology & Psychiatric Review 3.

kill.[74] The incident against the nine- and 11-year-olds was described as a 'horrific, violent, sustained physical attack[75] 'that lasted over 90 minutes. Per Mr Justice Keith, 'what it amounted to was torture.'[76]

1. *The judicial process*

The juvenile defendants were arrested and questioned by the police over the incident on 4 April 2009.[77] They were then called to court on 8 April to hear the charges held against them. As A and B were juvenile defendants, their case was heard in the Youth Court, a division of the adult magistrates court which, as already mentioned, tries cases committed by juvenile defendants between 10 and 17 years old. The presiding judge, district judge Jonathan Bennett, refused to grant them bail and A and B were held on remand in the local authority secure accommodation until 14 April. The Court ruled at that stage that the identities of the juveniles in question were not to be released.[78] As the juveniles were charged with an indictable offence, the case could not be heard in the Youth Court and was transferred to the Crown Court, the adult criminal court.

On 22 January 2010, after a closed trial at Sheffield Crown Court, juveniles A and B were sentenced to an indeterminate period in detention, lasting at least five years. The pre-sentencing assessment and psychological evaluations submitted to the court described the juvenile defendants as 'posing a risk of serious harm to members of the public'.[79]

2. *'Indeterminate sentence'*

First introduced under the Criminal Justice Act 2003[80] and amended in 2008 in the Criminal Justice and Immigration Act,[81] indeterminate impris-

[74] P Naughton and A Norfolk, 'Parents of Edlington torture brothers could face charges' *The Times* (22 January 2010) available at: http://www.timesonline.co.uk/tol/news/uk/crime/article6998636.ece, accessed 15 February 2010. —'Young brothers admit boys' attack' *BBC Online* (22 January 2010) available at: http://news.bbc.co.uk/1/hi/england/south_yorkshire/8233822.stm, accessed 15 February 2010.

[75] P Walker, 'Brothers, 12 And 10, Plead Guilty To Attack On Schoolboys' *The Guardian* (3 September 2009) available at http://www.guardian.co.uk/uk/2009/sep/03/brothers-plead-guilty-attack-schoolboys, last accessed 15 February 2010.

[76] Full text of Mr Justice Keith's comments available at http://www.timesonline.co.uk/tol/news/uk/crime/article6998667.ece, last accessed 15 February 2010.

[77] *BBC Online* (n 74).

[78] 'Brothers appear in court over Edlington 'torture' *The Times* (8 April 2009) available at: http://www.timesonline.co.uk/tol/news/uk/crime/article6053832.ece, accessed 15 February 2010.

[79] ibid.

[80] http://www.opsi.gov.uk/acts/acts2003/ukpga_20030044_en_1, accessed 15 February 2010.

[81] See Criminal Justice and Immigration Act 2008, s 19, available at: http://www.opsi.gov.uk/acts/acts2008/ukpga_20080004_en_1, accessed 15 February 2010.

onment for Public Protection is a sentence whereby the convicted individual has 'no automatic right for release'[82] after serving the recommended minimum sentence, also known as the tariff period. Once that period is over, the defendant is assessed by the Parole Board to consider whether he is fit to be released. It should be noted that the release of indeterminate sentence prisoners is entirely a matter for the Parole Board.[83] Under the Powers of Criminal Court (Sentencing) Act 2003, a juvenile convicted of a serious crime may sometimes be sentenced to the same length of detention as an adult.[84]

The fact that children charged with serious crimes may be subjected to the same sanctions as adults is a point of serious contention with child rights advocates. Tim Bateman, spokesman of the National Association for the Care and Resettlement of Offenders, criticized the courts, stating:

Dragging children through a justice system designed for adults is inappropriate and can be harmful. There are lots of less intimidating mechanisms available that are more appropriate for children.

Many have been psychologically damaged and have an undeveloped understanding of the consequences of their actions.

In most other European countries the Edlington boys would have been detained, for their own safety as well as others, but would not have been through the criminal justice system. The age of criminal responsibility in England is among the lowest in Europe.

It is not unusual for children who end up in the criminal justice system to have traumatic and chaotic lives. A quarter of those in custody have suffered violence in the home, sexual abuse or emotional abuse through parental neglect and 85 per cent have signs of personality disorder.

There needs to be a an effective approach for dealing with the welfare needs of young people, which are almost always at the root of serious and persistent youth offending.[85]

3. *The extent of children's criminal responsibility*

At the trial, Mr Justice Keith made some interesting assertions:

---

[82] Her Majesty's Prison Service: http://www.hmprisonservice.gov.uk/adviceandsupport/prison_life/lifesentencedprisoners/, accessed 15 February 2010).

[83] ibid.

[84] Powers of Criminal Court (Sentencing) Act 2000, s 91, available at: http://www.opsi.gov.uk/acts/acts2000/ukpga_20000006_en_8#pt5-ch2-pb2-l1g91, accessed 15 February 2 2010.

[85] Nacro's Youth Crime Policy Officer, Tim Bateman, http://www.nacro.org.uk/news-and-resources/latest-news/nacro-responds-to-edlington-case,302,NAP.html, accessed 5 March 2010.

Against all that has to be put the fact that you are still very young. You can't be expected to have developed the sort of mechanisms which grown-ups have and which make it easier for them to stop behaving badly.

In particular, you never had guidance at home about the way you should behave. You come from a dysfunctional family, where the environment has been described as 'toxic' and the adults were hardly role models.

There was an atmosphere of violence at home. You were never taught what the proper boundaries were, and your bad behaviour was never confronted within the family.

It is not for me to apportion blame, though I do know that criticism has been levelled against social services and various child protection agencies for not intervening earlier.[86]

The Edlington attack has caused much public debate regarding the extent of children's criminal responsibility. The home life of the two juvenile defendants was described as 'toxic' and at the time of the event the brothers were in foster care. Accounts of their life include persistent neglect, domestic violence in the household, drink and drug abuse by both children and parents and exposure to pornography and adult, violent films.[87] These revelations have lead to calls that their parents should also be apportioned responsibility for their part in contributing to the criminal behaviour of their children. Superintendent Ian Bint, of South Yorkshire Police, stated: 'It's something we will be looking at with partners in the light of what has come out in court'.[88]

Controversy also surrounds the fact that key documentation regarding the brothers from social services, who were their custodians, was not available for the judge at trial.[89] It is said that 'in the report a study of the boys' case by a consultant child psychiatrist, Susan Bailey, had found "a causal link" between the failings of the care authorities and the brothers' grotesque violence'.[90] This leads to further questions regarding the culpa-

---

[86] 'Edlington: full text of Mr Justice Keith's comments to torture brothers' *The Times* (Jan 22nd 2010) http://www.timesonline.co.uk/tol/news/uk/crime/article6998667.ece, accessed 15 February 2010.

[87] D Higgens, 'Inquiry Into Case of 'Torture Boys' *Press Association* (26 January 2010) available at: http://www.independent.co.uk/news/uk/home-news/inquiry-into-case-of-torture-boys-1878803.html, accesse 15 February 2010.

[88] C Mackie 'Torture Boys' Parents Could Face Charges of Child Neglect' *The Scotsman* (23 January 2010) available at: http://heritage.scotsman.com/legalissues/Torture-boys39-parents-could-face.6007977.jp, accessed 15 February 2010.

[89] A Norfolk and R Bennett, 'Judge Is Refused Care Authorities' Report In Edlington Torture Case' *The Times* (22 Jan 2010) available at http://www.timesonline.co.uk/tol/news/uk/crime/article6997640.ece, accessed 15 February 2010.

[90] ibid 89.

bility of the convicted juveniles. Nonetheless, the fact that they were found to 'pose a very high risk of serious harm to others'[91] may qualify the detention of the children on public protection grounds.

C. Guidelines Towards Providing an Appropriate Legal And Social Framework for the Better Enforcement of Relevant Laws

As noted above, the UN Committee on the Rights of the Child (CRC) made recommendations regarding the juvenile justice system in the UK. These included increasing the minimum age of criminal responsibility[92] currently set at 10 in England and Wales, eight in Scotland. It also urged improvements to be made with regards to the administration of juvenile justice, such as enhancing the protection of privacy of children in conflict with the law[93] and reviewing specific legal provisions in the Crime and Disorder Act 1998.[94] One of the most radical suggestions came in the form of a recommendation to enact a British Bill of Rights and a Bill of Rights for Northern Ireland, each incorporating the founding principles of the UNCRC.[95] Furthermore, the CRC noted that the State party functions with devolved government arrangements and that this system makes it difficult to have a single body coordinating implementation of the UNCRC. Thus, it advocated for continued national coordination and placed special emphasis on local integration, 'where local authorities have significant powers to determine their priorities and allocate budgets'.[96]

The most recent discourse suggests that there needs to be an emphasis not only on the minimum age of culpability but also on the treatment of offenders in contact with the justice system. What policy analysts have suggested for a long time is a complete overhaul of the criminal justice system in relation to juveniles. In a report published by the Institute for Public Policy Research, there were suggestions regarding developmental interventions whereby young offenders would be exposed to a variety of therapies. These included tailor-made interventions to understand the reasons that pushed the juvenile to delinquency in the first place and the means to prevent further re-offending. The interpersonal skills and relationships of juvenile offenders would be closely scrutinised so that interventions would be tailored to the specific aggravations that may be causing the offending.

---

[91] Mr Justice Keith, http://www.timesonline.co.uk/tol/news/uk/crime/article6998667.ece

[92] UN Committee on the Rights of the Child (31st Session) 'Consideration of Reports submitted by State Parties under Article 44 of the Convention, Concluding Observations: United Kingdom of Great Britain and Northern Ireland' 9 October 2002, para 62, available at: http://www.unhchr.ch/tbs/doc.nsf/898586b1dc7b4043c1256a450044f331/2f2744b7e0d0 15d6c1256c76004b3ab7/$FILE/G0245381.pdf, accessed 5 March 2010.

[93] See (n 91).　　　　　　　　　　　　　　　　　　　　　　　[94] See (n 92).

[95] See (n 53) para 11.　　　　　　　　　　　　　　　　　　　　[96] ibid para 12–13.

Further research suggests that four key barriers must be overcome in order for reform to take place: removing conflicting objectives and incentives; reducing current over-centralization; improving local collaboration; and creating alternative routes which allow young people to be dealt with without recourse to the criminal justice system.[97]

One can see that much of the reforms instigated within the UK juvenile justice system are based on restorative justice models. According to Braithwaite, restorative justice

> is a dominant model of criminal justice throughout most of human history ... remaining today as a resource for cultural diversity that can be drawn upon by European peoples whose justice traditions have been more homogenized and impoverished by central state power.[98]

However, the model implemented in the UK has been heavily criticized for 'experiencing forms of punitiveness that would not be expected from a truly restorative system'.[99] An example given is the manner in which restorative conferencing is conducted, 'becom[ing] dominated by the police officer'.[100] The role played by the victim and the juvenile offender is very limited during the restorative conference.[101] The manner in which reparations are agreed upon can also become punitive, as concluded in a study by Antonopoulos and Winterdyk in 2003: 'the reparations order automatically becomes a punishment. In other words 'the offender may be coerced into reparations'.[102] Indeed, the use of ASBOs and other court orders, which at the outset were techniques to avoid the formal criminal process, have had an inverse effect, bringing many juveniles whose behaviour is not criminal into the criminal justice process.

There is a call for a less punitive type of reform in which a holistic view of the offender and his crime would be addressed by realistic and tailored interventions. Policymakers refer to this method as 'popular preventionism'.[103] 'The new approach would be both progressive, in that it would further social justice and democratic engagement, and preventative, with the aim of reducing crime, while still meeting 'populist' objectives'.[104] Through this approach, the system focuses on a multi-stranded concept of involvement. Importantly, it recognizes that policies born outside of the communities encourage distrust in the criminal justice system. Thus, the

---

[97] See(n 19) 21.
[98] EL Jensen and J Jepsen, 'Conclusions: Themes, Trends and Challenges' in *Juvenile Law Violators and the Development of New Juvenile Justice Systems* (Hart Publishing, Oxford, 2006) 452.
[99] ibid 453.
[100] ibid.
[101] ibid.
[102] ibid.
[103] See (n 18) 23.
[104] ibid 103.

new approach would do away with this traditional method and would instead focus on community involvement.

V. CONCLUSION

The UK's juvenile justice system has undergone a series of developments over the years. Several specific statutes have been enacted and amended to ensure that legislation offers adequate protection to children and is UNCRC-compliant. Specialized courts and institutions have been established to deal with children in conflict with the law. In practice however, children charged with indictable offences are still tried by the adult Crown court. The ECtHR's ruling in the Bulger case called for reforms to be made in this, and other, domains. As a consequence, there is now a concerted policy to make trials more understandable to juvenile defendants. But according to Dr Eileen Vizard, a child psychiatrist with the NSPCC's child offender service, scientific evidence about child development indicates that 10-year-olds are not capable of participating fully or fairly in a criminal trial.[105]

A number of other issues remain of concern, namely the low age of criminal responsibility. Thus, the CRC has urged the UK to increase the age to to ensure better compliance with the UNCRC. Another problem encountered is the focus on the nature of the offence committed rather than on the ways in which offenders are treated. This is a crucial point because juveniles are more likely to avoid re-offending if proper care and advice are available to them. Finally, the two cases discussed are a good illustration of the problems faced by the current system and the reasons why a reform of the law is urgent.

---

[105] M Buckley, 'How Edlington Case Follows Course Paved By Bulger Trial' *BBC Online* (22 January 2010) available at http://news.bbc.co.uk/1/hi/uk/8300034.stm, accessed 15 February 2010.

PART III

CHAPTER 15

Concluding Analysis

I. INTRODUCTION

This chapter will consider the main issues raised in the preceding country reports. It will also provide comparative analysis of the core issues in this research relating to the rights of the child.

II. RISK FACTORS

There are multiple risk factors which lead children into delinquency and criminal activity. After examining a cross-section of Muslim and non-Muslim States, it appears that in all these States, whether secular or religious, there are common causes of juvenile delinquency. These common factors include broken or dislocated families, school truancy and poor education, drug and alcohol addiction, involvement in drug trafficking sometimes combined with gang membership, poor social environment, and a lack of family or parental control, leaving them vulnerable to external influences. A strong theme is the experience of children befriending older ones who have left education, who introduce them to street gangs, and encourage the younger children to commit crime. Further risk factors resulting in childhood delinquency include living in deprived neighbourhoods and densely populated urban areas, lack of a stable place of residence, no source of income within the household, and the proliferation of violence in the media.[1] Political activities, for example in Nigeria where children are drugged and used for political purposes, also represent a major risk factor.

A worrying development has been the abuse of child protection laws by adults in order to circumvent the law. In Lebanon, case law has shown a distressing trend in which children are commissioned to commit crimes on behalf of adults—crimes that would ordinarily carry a death penalty if carried out by adults. An Iranian case also illustrates this pattern. For example, Delara Darabi was persuaded by her boyfriend to confess to his crime and was told that because of her age (17 at the time of the offence) she would be spared execution. She later unsuccessfully retracted her confession and was sentenced to death.

---

[1] See A Andrés Pueyo, 'Violencia juvenil: realidad actual y factores psicológicos implicados' (2006) 29 Revista ROL de Enfermería 1.

III. RESERVATIONS TO THE UNITED NATIONS CONVENTION ON THE
RIGHTS OF THE CHILD

It has been established that with regard to the protection of the rights of the child and their reservations to the UNCRC, the States studied here fall into three categories. The first category includes those States which have ratified the UNCRC without any reservation, such as Lebanon. The second category is comprised of States that have ratified the UNCRC with reservations, but reservations that do not have any direct impact for the purposes of this research. For example, the UAE signed and ratified the UNCRC on 3 January 1997, entering reservations against articles 7, 14, 17 and 21.[2] The reservations relate to the preservation and respect of the UAE's culture and religion. However, none of these reservations have been found to have a direct impact on the rights and protection afforded to juvenile offenders in the criminal justice system, since these reservations are not made against those specific provisions of the UNCRC. Nevertheless, these reservations may have an impact on the overall aim of the UNCRC and in knock-on effect on rights surrounding juvenile justice.

The third category of reservations consists of States that have ratified the UNCRC with specific reservations, but ones that could directly affect the protection the rights of the juvenile offenders. Malaysia has ratified the UNCRC subject to several reservations on various grounds concerning the preservation of its Constitution, national laws and policies, and religious practices. For example, article 37(1)(a)[3] of the UNCRC has a reservation because at present Malaysian law provides for the possibility of the child being subject to 'whipping with a light cane'. Though this is not a widespread practice given its limited invocation in law, nonetheless, article 37 would clearly prohibit its application. Another example of such reservations is that of Iran, which has inserted the reservation that the Iranian State will only observe the rules and regulations of the UNCRC that do not conflict with their internal, jurisprudential, and religious laws. This condition is so broad as to be considered contrary to the objects and purposes of the Convention, and so could be invalid under article 19 of the Vienna Convention on the Law of Treaties.[4]

The present study explored that, albeit to a varying degree, all of these States have taken several positive steps to reform their juvenile justice

---

[2] United Nations Treaty Collection, Declarations and Reservations available at: http://www.unhchr.ch/html/menu3/b/treaty15_asp.htm

[3] Art 37 para (a) provides that 'No child shall be subjected to torture or other cruel, inhuman or degrading treatment or punishment. Neither capital punishment nor life imprisonment without possibility of release shall be imposed for offences committed by persons below eighteen years of age'.

[4] http://tarh.majlis.ir/?ShowRule&Rid=A8228439-C6B7-4150-9E3C-DF7A7D8D78CB.

system, probably in part as a consequence of the UNCRC and other international instruments.

IV. COMPLIANCE WITH INTERNATIONAL LAW

At the national level, all the States considered here have made efforts to make their laws compatible with international legal standards provided for the protection of the rights of juveniles who come into conflict with the law. Each State within the study has made tangible efforts to improve its existing juvenile justice system through statutory reforms. A few key instances will be considered here.

With the aim of supporting its obligations and commitments under the UNCRC in 2005, Afghanistan passed the Juvenile Code. Egypt's latest report to the Committee on the Rights of the Child (CRC) revealed that police officers were being trained in how to address child rights issues. Further, a 2002 Strategy for the Rehabilitation and Reintegration of Street Children was conceptualized, and a new programme was launched to train 200 police officers on how to deal with children in general and street children in particular—evidence of the far-reaching effect of the UNCRC.[5]

UNICEF acknowledged the efforts being made by the Iranian judiciary and the police to initiate and participate in more training courses to highlight the aims of the UNCRC, and to create a better understanding between children and authority figures through educational workshops. For example, in 2009 a close collaboration between the Department of Education of the Iranian Judiciary and UNICEF resulted in a series of workshops and other events, such as training for educators on the subject of the rights of the child and training for judges on the ways of using alternative punishments to custodial sentences.[6] In 2004, with a large parliamentary majority, a bill for the Formation of Juvenile Courts to the Iranian Parliament was passed.[7] Presented by the Iranian judiciary, its success represents a level of commitment to child rights with the Bill providing for restorative justice and diversionary measures as alternative sentencing options within criminal cases, and, most importantly, the opportunity for judges to reassess the mental age of the accused. Another reform-minded act was ratified on first reading by the Government in 2006, though its passage into statute is yet to be finalized, namely the Investigation of Crimes of Juveniles Bill. Various

---

[5] N Ammar, 'The Relationship Between Street Children and the Justice System in Egypt' in the International Journal of Offender Therapy and Comparative Criminology *OnlineFirst* (29 July 2008).

[6] See the Judiciary Newsletter (Maa'va) on 12 July 2009 (in Farsi).

[7] See Amnesty USA 2004 Annual report for Iran at http://www.amnestyusa.org/annual report.php?id=ar&yr=2004&c=IRN, accessed 10 June 2010).

reasons have been attributed to this delay—one of these being the Guardian Council's comments on the Bill, which state that some provisions in the Bill contradict Islamic law. These are article 2(3) of article 33 which proscribes *qisas* sentences for defendants under 18, and article 3 which states that children are exempt from criminal responsibility, referring to a child as a person who has not reached the age of puberty as defined by Islamic law.

The Lebanese government, in response to the recommendations made by the CRC after its second periodic report, took several positive steps, including the establishment of a residential institution for girls in conflict with the law and a specialized police unit for investigating and taking statements of minors.[8] Similarly, with the aim of fulfilling their international commitments, Malaysia drafted the Child Act 2001(Act 611), and the preamble of the Act explicitly refers to several provisions within the UNCRC.[9]

In Nigeria, along with the official training provided in various police institutions, human rights-focused NGOs in collaboration with UNICEF are currently providing training not only to the police but to many actors involved in juvenile justice administration.[10] For example, in 2007, a workshop was held on diversion in juvenile justice at Katsina state where many stakeholders in the juvenile justice system—police, prison officers, Sharia court judges, prosecutors and practising lawyers—were participants in promoting child rights.[11] However, more support and investment is required at the institutional level and extensive legal reform is needed if Nigerian laws are to comply with the international conventions it has ratified, most notably the UNCRC. Pakistan passed in 2000 the Juvenile Justice System Ordinance[12] legislation designed to address criminal law in relation to children.

The Organizational Act 5/2000 is a Spanish statute tackling the issue of penal responsibility for minors. The Act has been widely praised by the CRC who commented that it 'welcomes the great progress and achievements made by the State party since the examination of the initial report to the Committee in 1994. It notes with appreciation that it has made the

---

[8] The CRC has addressed this concern in its recommendations following Lebanon's submission of its periodic report. Such reports have been submitted in 1994, 1998 and 2003. Three sets of Concluding Observations were delivered by the CRC respectively in 1996, 2002 and 2006.

[9] Child Act 2001. Hereafter will be referred to as the '2001 Act.'

[10] For instance, Training Workshop for Key Players in the Juvenile Justice Administration Organized by the League of Democratic Women (LEADS) held at Gusau Hotel, Gusau Zamfara State, December 2006.

[11] See MU Abubakar, (2007) 'Accommodating Diversion in the Nigerian Juvenile Justice Regime' paper presented at a two-day interactive session with Juvenile Justice Administrators organised by LEADS in collaboration with UNICEF Zone 'C'at Katsina Motel, Katsina state, Nigeria, 2–22 November 2007.

[12] Amnesty International, 'Denial of Basic Rights for Child Prisoners' http://www.amnesty.org/en/library/asset/ASA33/011/2003/en/4fb4b9fc-d698-11dd-ab95-a13b602c0642/asa330112003en.html, accessed 15 October 2009.

protection and promotion of the rights of the child a general rule in the society.'[13]

Turkey has made several efforts, including enacting a new Child Protection Law in 2005 and making several amendments to the existing penal code and legislation. Those amendments include minimizing custody and imprisonment, speeding up trials, ensuring privacy, ensuring that child suspects and offenders are handled only by specific police branches for children, child courts, and professionals and personnel trained in dealing with children. In addition, the Towards Good Governance, Protection and Justice for Children in Turkey Project is currently being implemented under the coordination of the Gendarmerie General Headquarters. The general aim of the project is to improve the protective climate for children who are in conflict with the law.[14] The United Arab Emirates issued specific legislations aimed at making theirs laws more compatible with the requirements of the UNCRC and established numerous rehabilitation and care centres for juvenile offenders, particularly in Abu Dhabi and Al Ein. Those facilities have been however found insufficient in practice; the CRC in its 2002 observations urged the UAE to review the promulgation of their legislation on child rights and its effective implementation.

To bring UK laws into conformity with the international standards on child rights, it ratified the UNCRC into its law by way of statute in 1991. The European Convention on Human Rights was also integrated into UK domestic law through the Human Rights Act 1998. Coupled with these legal reforms, a new statute, the Children's Act 2004, was created to address the issue of children's rights. It created the position of the Children's Commissioner for England and Wales, followed by the Children's Act 2006. In response to the concerns of the CRC, the UK Department for Children, Schools, and Families was established in 2007.[15] However, in its 49th session, the CRC revealed its concern that: 'the principles of the Convention are not duly taken into account in all pieces of legislation throughout the country and that the State party has not incorporated the Convention into domestic law nor has ensured the compliance of all legislation affecting children with it.'[16]

---

[13] CRC/C/15/Add.185, Committee on the Rights of the Child (30th Session) Consideration of reports submitted by States parties under Article 44 of the Convention, Concluding observations of the Committee on the Rights of the Child: Spain, available online at http://www.unhchr.ch/tbs/doc.nsf/(Symbol)/_CRC.C.15.Add.185.En?OpenDocument (8 July 2009) para 470–472, 521.

[14] S Report presented by the Minister of Justice of Turkey, in 28th Conference of European Ministers of Justice, Lanzarote (25–26 October 2007) 8.

[15] Committee on The Rights of the Child (31st Session) Consideration of Reports Submitted By States Parties Under Article 44 Of The Convention Concluding observations: United Kingdom of Great Britain and Northern Ireland) CRC/C/15/Add.188, 9 October 2002, 2.

[16] CRC/C/GBR/CO/4, Committee on the Rights of the Child (49th Session) Consideration of Reports Submitted by States Parties under Article 44 of the Convention, 20 October 2008, 3.

One aspect of all these changes in national laws and practices is the increased impact of the child rights movement. This movement is transforming the discourse of child rights, and is providing much of the impetus to legislative and administrative reform within domestic juvenile justice systems.[17] Coalition-building between inter-governmental departments, NGOs and governments have revolutionized child protection in some instances. Local and regional NGOs have applied pressure on governments to make domestic legal changes that result in greater compliance with the UNCRC. Greater cooperation between different stakeholders has resulted in a pooling of resources, as partnerships have formed to carry out research and assessments in support of reform proposals. This can be seen in the Iranian cooperation with UNICEF considered above, and the increase in Advocacy and Social Mobilization groups in Turkey that work to realize the aims outlined at the World Fit for Children conference, ensuring full implementation of the UNCRC by translating Turkey's international commitments in the fields of child rights into action.[18] The operation of the child rights movement has became more sophisticated in influencing public policy, through providing training and running projects on child rights issues and sharing information. The movement has benefited from specializations by different NGOs, such as those that target issues for street children.[19]

V. DISPARITIES BETWEEN LAW AND PRACTICE

Despite great improvements in child rights law, the country reports show that in many jurisdictions, key concerns inhibit the full reach offered by the new protection measures.

As demonstrated by the Egypt case, while the law includes provisions for a specialized child court, in reality only two of Egypt's governorates, Cairo and Alexandria, possess a stand-alone Juvenile Court. In the remaining 28 governorates, temporary juvenile courts are held on a periodic basis presided over by judges not trained to deal with juvenile cases. Similarly in Iran, where there are roughly 120,000 police personnel in direct contact with children throughout Iran (according to the Education Deputy Chief of the Iranian Disciplinarian Forces), only 600 have had specialized training

---

[17] B Abramson, 'Juvenile Justice: The Unwanted Child: Why the Potential of the Convention on the Rights of the Child is Not Being Realized and What We Can Do About It' in EL Jensen and J Jepsen (eds) *Juvenile Law Violators, Human Rights and the Development of New Juvenile Systems* (Hart Publishing, Oxford, 2006) 17.

[18] 'Plus 5' Review of the 2002 Special Session on Children and World Fit for Children Plan of Action National Progress Report: Turkey (January 2007) 9 and http://www.unicef.org/turkey/pr/pd3.html.

[19] ibid.

with youths. Article 219 of the Iranian Code of Criminal Procedure provides that within each jurisdiction, one specific division of the public court should be dedicated for courts proceedings involving minors, however in practice when no such facilities are available the general courts hear youth offenders.

In the United Arab Emirates, despite the general observance of the UNCRC, there is still no special training for police officials, public prosecutors and government officials who come into contact with the juveniles in conflict with the law. This is indeed a failing and one which is common throughout this study. All States should ensure that those administering justice, particularly judges, have an understanding of child rights and psychology, especially when it comes to adjudication. The CRC also made a series of recommendations to the UAE[20] regarding the need for allocating resources to suitable training for juvenile justice stakeholders, as well as for a separate criminal justice system for juveniles with specialized courts with the speedy promulgation of the new law across the country. The overriding message of the CRC was that the UAE meets the legal substance of the UNCRC but that the practical implementation of the Convention needed greater care and accuracy. Pakistan also reflects this worrying dichotomy, with legislation upholding the values of the UNCRC but needing to 'develop effective resourced policies and programmes for a systematic and sustained training process', according to the CRC.[21]

In Turkey, Turkish Penal Code article 31(2) exempts from criminal liability children between the ages of 13 and 16 who have been identified as incapable of appreciating the legal meaning and consequences of their actions. However, in ascertaining the capability of children, doctors in charge of examining can abuse this safeguard by acting irresponsibly in making their diagnosis.

Similarly, it has been shown that the laws of all of the States provide that young offenders must be detained separately from adults, to protect them from direct contact with adult criminals. However, inconsistencies have been found in law and practice. For example, in Pakistan the CRC expressed its concern about the poor implementation of the Juvenile Justice System Ordinance 2000. Many of the authorities charged with its implementation, specifically within provincial governments and tribal areas, were found to be unaware of the law's existence. Apart from the poor conditions of the prisons, large numbers of children are often found detained with adult offenders and are vulnerable to abuse.[22] Juvenile offenders are also

---

[20] Concluding Observations of the Committee on the Rights of the Child: United Arab Emirates, CRC/C/15/Add.183, 13 June 2002, para 42.

[21] Committee on the Rights of the Child (34th Session) Consideration of Reports Submitted By States Parties Under Article 44 Of The Convention, CRC/C/15/Add.217 (27 October 2003) 5.

[22] ibid 18 para 80.

being found in the same detention and prison facilities as adults in Nigeria. The CRC noted frequent physical assault on juveniles by the police, excessive length of prosecution and detention and their trial in adult courts, and a lack of legal representation. The Committee also found serious overcrowding and poor conditions in juvenile centres.

Cases of keeping juveniles with adults have also been found in Malaysia, among other rights violations. In the case of Malaysian law, the representation of a child by a legal counsel is mostly conditional on the provision of legal counsel by the family; the conditions worsen in cases where a parent or guardian is not present at the proceeding. In these cases, the court may pass any order without paying attention to the needs of the child. This provision violates article 12 of the UNCRC, which provides a right to be heard. In these cases, filling the gaps as well as proper implementation of the laws is desperately required.

Although many juvenile justice systems lack specialized child courts, many States try juveniles in ordinary courts but under separate juvenile regulations and procedures. Nevertheless, some of the States have established independent juvenile courts. In Turkey there are 73 juvenile courts and 20 juvenile felony courts.[23] However, the number of the juvenile courts is still not enough to meet the needs of the population.[24] Long delays before cases go to trial, have an equally detrimental effect on preserving child rights. In several cases the average duration of proceedings has been found to be longer at juvenile courts than in others.[25]

This problem occurs in other jurisdictions. In Lebanon, some cases have resulted in juveniles waiting for many months before facing trial and trial periods lasting up to three years.[26] This conflicts with article 40 of the UNCRC, which provides that the children who come into conflict with the law should have the assurance 'to have the matter determined without delay'. Long detention periods have also been noted, which violates article 37 of the UNCRC.

Hence, along with the establishment of independent courts, there needs to be an adequate amount of specialized juvenile courts for the benefits of the UNCRC to take effect. There remain considerable gaps between the law and practice in relation to the rights of the child in the criminal justice system in these States. While lack of resources are clearly one factor in a number of the States, priorities in resourcing and provision of support for those working in these areas is needed in all States.

[23] As of 1 July 2009.
[24] See Final Report, in J Zermatten (ed), *Training Course On Juvenile Justice for Officials from Turkey*, Working Report 2-2003, 93.
[25] Commission of the European Communities, *2002 Regular Report on Turkey's Progress Towards Accession*, 21; the average duration of juvenile court cases is 517 days and for the cases before the Juvenile Aggravated Felony court, 619 days (2008).
[26] The CRC has addressed this concern in its recommendations following Lebanon's submission of its periodic report. Such reports have been submitted in 1994, 1998 and 2003.

VI. THE DEATH PENALTY

The UNCRC specifically prohibits the use of the death penalty against juvenile offenders. Article 37(a) explicitly states: 'Neither capital punishment nor life imprisonment without possibility of release shall be imposed for offences committed by persons below eighteen years of age.' Further, the imposition of death penalty on a person under 18 at the time of committing the offence has been declared 'contrary to customary international law'.[27] This is binding on all States, regardless of which treaties they have or have not ratified. Therefore, ratifying States are bound by two sources of international law not to impose the penalty on those younger than 18: from the Convention itself and under customary international law.

The study reveals trends on how States respond to the death penalty in regard to children. States can be roughly categorized as holding three broad positions. In the first are States which have completely abolished the death penalty, which include Spain, Turkey, and the UK. The second category is those States which have not completely abolished the death penalty, however, in order to make their laws conform with the UNCRC, have instead held children under 18 legally exempt from the death penalty. States in this category include Afghanistan, Egypt, Lebanon, Malaysia, Pakistan and the UAE. Their laws provide an alternative to the death penalty, with other measures available for punishing that taking into consideration the age of a child.

However, in some of these States, even if the juveniles are exempt from the death penalty, some loopholes mean that children can remain vulnerable to such a penalty. For example, in Malaysia juvenile offenders have to be placed in detention as an alternative to the death penalty. The period of their detention is left to the discretion of the ruler, which in itself could lead to arbitrary treatment and the abuse of the rights of child criminal offenders. Three criminal cases involving juvenile defendants cast an interesting light on the inconsistencies in child rights protection. In the murder trials for the killing of a person by eight 17–year-old boys and in the case where an 11-year old boy was killed by someone under 18, the convicted defendants were sentenced to detention at a facility for juvenile offenders. Yet in a case where a 14–year-old boy was charged under section 57 of Internal Security Act of 1960 for possessing firearms, because it was a security offence under Regulation 2 of Essential (Security Cases) Regulations 1975 (ESCAR), it meant that the Juvenile Courts Act 1947 did not apply and the defendant was sentenced to death, a verdict upheld at appeal. Only after

---

[27] D Weissbrodt et al, *International Human Rights: Law, Policy and Process* (3rd edn, Anderson, Ohio) 709–710; Amnesty International, 'Pakistan: Protection of Juveniles in the Criminal Justice System Remains Inadequate' http://www.amnesty.org/en/library/info/ASA33/021/2005/en, accessed 15 October 2009.

public outcry and the intervention of the King of Malaysia was the sentence commuted to imprisonment until the age of 21 years. Hence, this exception restricting the Juvenile Act in cases of security offences leaves children less protected and vulnerable to exploitation, which could lead to the death penalty for under-18s.

The third category is comprised of States that have retained the death penalty even for offenders younger than 18 years. This includes Nigeria and Iran. In 12 Northern states of Nigeria, the Child and Young Persons Act,[28] the Criminal Code and the Sharia Penal Codes allow for the imposition of the death penalty on persons under 18.[29] In this context, after examining the Nigerian report of 2005, the CRC raised some issues regarding discrepancies between the provisions of the UNCRC and the Sharia laws and juvenile justice system. The CRC particularly questioned the execution of a 17-year-old in 1997, after the UNCRC had been ratified into State law. Similarly, in January 2005, while considering Iran's second periodic report the CRC urged Iran:

> [T]o take the necessary steps to immediately suspend the execution of all death penalties imposed on persons for having committed a crime before the age of 18, to take the appropriate legal measures to convert them to penalties in conformity with the provisions of the Convention and to abolish the death penalty as a sentence imposed on persons for having committed crimes before the age of 18, as required by article 37 of the Convention.[30]

As States parties to the UNCRC, Iran and Nigeria are under a legal obligation to abolish the death penalty for the juveniles. In the case of Iran, it is hoped that a new set of legislations pertaining to child offenders will obtain the Guardian Council's approval allowing the new Act to offer juveniles in conflict with the law this measure of protection against the death penalty.

VII. GENDER DISCRIMINATION

Most national laws within States prohibit discrimination based on gender and other grounds. However, the UNCRC also obliges States parties to ensure that juveniles enjoy their rights without discrimination.

---

[28] Art 12.

[29] Art 319 (2). http://www.unhchr.ch/tbs/doc.nsf/898586b1dc7b4043c1256a450044f331/b06804b33ec4eadbc1257018002c82db/$FILE/G0541053.pdf,accessed 17 July 2009.

[30] Paras 30 and 72(b) of the Committee's Concluding Observations, UN Doc CRC/c/15/Add. 254.

Nevertheless, despite the large amount of legislation surrounding the issue, discrepancies and discrimination are still common in practice.

Egypt is among one of the States that have ratified the UNCRC, and its domestic Egyptian Child Law 2008 does not provide or condone gender discrimination. This study has shown that the Egyptian State fails to offer proper protection of female child defendants from discrimination. It has been found that girls over 15 years are not been kept in a separate custodial facility from adult prisoners and are likely to be imprisoned in the same cells as adult criminals.[31]

In some States, cases of assimilation of cultural practices with the religious law have operated without a coherent conceptualization of human rights. Within Afghanistan, a system of tribalism is still prevalent in many rural areas; murder cases, when adjudicated through the tribal jury system (*jirga*) can recommend that a girl to be married from the family of the murderer to a near relative of the victim, a practiced referred to as *bad*.[32] The national laws of Afghanistan prohibit such practices and the Sharia also protects young girls from such abuses of human rights. States are acting contrary to international and Islamic law for allowing such breaches of the law to take place under a semi-judicial system.

In Iran, article 49 of the Islamic Penal Code of 1991 requires that 'in the case of committing an offense, children are devoid of criminal responsibility.' Note 1 of this article states that 'a child is an individual who has not reached the age limit of legal maturity'. However, according to the Iranian Civil Code (article 1210), this age is nine years for girls and 15 years for boys. This difference constitutes discrimination between boys and girls, contravening the UNCRC.

VIII. THE APPLICATION OF *DIYAH*

The country reports demonstrate that throughout the States that apply Islamic criminal law, the current trend in the implementation of *diyah* (or 'blood money') is often distorted from the fundamental principle of the practice, as set out in Islamic law. This application and interpretation has resulted in many inequalities, at the same time failing to protect rights that were originally ensured.

On the payment of *diyah* the Quran says:

---

[31] Human Rights Watch, 'World Report 2003: Middle East and Northern Africa' available at http://www.hrw.org/wr2k3/mideast2.html 54, fn 3.

[32] See United State Agency for International Development (USAID), 'Afghanistan Rule of Law Project: Field Study of Informal and Customary Justice in Afghanistan and Recommendations on Improving Access to Justice and Relations between Formal Courts and Informal Bodies' (June 2005) 48.

And if something [of his guilt] is remitted to a guilty person by his brother, this [remission] shall be adhered to with fairness, and restitution to this fellowman shall be made in a goodly manner. This is alleviation from your Sustainer, and an act of his grace. And for him who none the less, wilfully transgresses the bounds of what is right there is grievous suffering in store.[33]

In the verse the phrase 'goodly manner' indicates that the payment of *diyah* should be in a way which demonstrates mercy and fairness along with empathy.[34]

Some sources of this practice are the sayings from the Prophet Muhammed (the *hadith*) and situations in which he reportedly specified the amounts or equivalent amounts that are available in *diyah* rulings. However it has been noted within the analysis of States reports, in several Muslim States which implement *qisas* and *diyah* laws, these Sharia provisions are marginalized and in practice over-inflated *diyah* payments have emerged. The Iranian case of Sina Paymard[35] provides an example where the victim's family accepted the pardon of the offender in exchange for a payment of US$160,000 in *diyah*, a substantial sum in Iran and far out of reach of the average person, so it was only met by the help of private donors. In the case of Nazanin Fatehi, the victim's family was very poor and could not meet the requested *diyah* requirements set by the victim's family.[36] This trend is also practised in Saudi Arabia, where it was reported that the suggested *diyah* amount has reached sums as high as 10 million Saudi Riyals (US$26 million) such as the case of Abd al Majid bin Mubark al-Anizi.[37] In February 2009, the Saudi Gazette pointed out that tribal leaders have urged the *Shoura* council to put rules aimed at governing the *diyah* cases as to put an end to exorbitant sums.[38]

In Pakistan, the Qisas and Diyah Ordinance provides for a minimum fixed amount of *diyah*, as the lack of determination of a maximum amount opens the way for the same kind of excessiveness in the requested *diyah* from the victim's family. Gottesman, commenting of the criminal laws of Pakistan, affirmed that the system serves to create a shift in the theory of

---

[33] Surah 2 verse 178, Muhammed Asad 47–48.

[34] See in this volume Chapter 3, section VI.B (Basis for Diyah and Islamic Law).

[35] See in Part II of this Volume Iran Country Report; Human Rights Watch Letter on Juvenile Death Penalty in Iran, 21 September 2006, available at: http://www.hrw.org/en/news/2006/09/21/human-rights-watch-letter-juvenile-death-penalty-iran, accessed 11 March 2010.

[36] Foreign Policy Centre, *From Cradle to Coffin: A Report on Child Execution In Iran*, 21 http://www.stopchildexecutions.com/Saved_Prisoners.aspx

[37] See Human Rights Watch 'Adults Before Their Time' (March 2008) available at,http://www.hrw.org/en/node/62308/section/6.

[38] http://www.saudigazette.com.sa/index.cfm?method=home.regcon&contentID=2009022330141&archiveissuedate=23/02/2009.

punishment by empowering the victim or the heirs.[39] These present-day practices can be considered to undermine the principles of Sharia. The reformation of domestic laws is necessary in the light of original established jurisprudential framework of detailed and proper codification of procedures and law. The resulting uniformity and codification should result in better protection. However, it is also worth noting that some case law in Pakistan shows that the codification by itself does not provide the ideal protection if the judiciary does not ensure a fair implementation in practice. In many cases, particularly where the offender and the victim belong to a same family, pressure was put in order to accept a *diyah* amount lower than the minimum amount provided by the law.[40]

The role of the State in the application of *diyah* is essential in ensuring better protection of juveniles. Although it does not seem that legislation in these States did provide for an involvement of judicial authorities in the determination of *diyah*, case law shows that the participation of the judges in the negotiations between the victim's family and the offender has helped to secure compromise. For example, in the last two years, the Iranian Department of Justice and many local judges have been active in seeking forgiveness of the child offender from the victim's family, such as the Moslem M[41] and many other cases.[42] According to Human Rights Watch, the Saudi Royal family engaged in negotiations and encouraged settlements in many cases.[43]

Another key question emerging from this research relates to the extent of the State's role in paying the funds when the offender's family cannot meet the requested amounts within the fixed period of time, particularly when the offender is a juvenile. Governments and public officials in Iran, Saudi Arabia and Pakistan actively participated in raising funds at many occasions where child offenders were sentenced to death. For example, in the case of Abd al Majid bin Mubark al-Anizi,[44] the Governor of Riyadh and the Crown Prince were directly involved in raising the necessary funds to meet the *diyah* requirements set by the family of the victim. Although the initiative by officials can only be commended at this level, particularly because their interventions have saved many lives, it is regrettable that there are no rules regulating this process, as they remain discretionary and only available to some people on a case-by-case basis. Defining the grounds based on which governments will intervene will bring more fairness and equality to the process.

---

[39] E Gottesman, 'The Reemergence of Qisas and Diyat in Pakistan' (1992) 23 Columbia Human Rights Law Review 2.

[40] See Pakistan Country Report Part II. Human Rights WatchReport, 'Crime or Custom? Violence Against Women in Pakistan' (August 1999).

[41] See Iranian Judicial Gazette, Maa'va, 30 November 2008.

[42] See Iranian Judicial Gazette, Maa'va, 2 June 2009.

[43] http://www.hrw.org/en/node/62308/section/6#_ftn93.   [44] ibid.

IX. THE AGE OF CRIMINAL LIABILITY

The age at which a child can be tried on criminal charges is a contentious issue and an area discussed at length within the country reports. Looking at the role of an established minimum age of criminal responsibility within criminal justice systems, the discussions recognize explicitly the diminished capacity for reasoning in very young children, due to their lack of development. In creating a minimum benchmark, States seek not to prosecute unfairly those who are deemed too young to have any understanding of the gravity of their actions and be criminally liable.

It is important to summarize the position of Islamic Law on the age of criminal responsibility: the latter is closely linked with a child's attainment of puberty and majority, coupled with their capability of perception and full understanding. If any of these components are missing, an individual would not be liable for the punishment for a specific crime which he or she has committed. This exemption of a child from the death penalty under *qisas* (retribution) and punishments of *hudood* is mentioned in the *hadith* (the recorded sayings and traditions of the Prophet Muhammed) in which he is reported to have said: 'three people are not accountable for their actions: a child until he reaches puberty; a person asleep until they wake and an insane person until they regain their sanity'.[45] Therefore, the schools of Islamic jurisprudence unanimously agree on this matter. Differences between Islamic schools of thought lie in what age a child is considered to have reached the age of puberty. Whether a child has reached mental maturity also should be a key consideration, however this area is often not given as much weight in adjudication.

Looking at the minimum age of criminal responsibility in each State within the study, there are huge differences between jurisdictions. Lebanon, the United Arab Emirates and Pakistan all set the minimum age of criminal responsibility at seven years old. Egypt sets it at 12 years. The United Nations Standard Minimum Rules for the Administration of Juvenile Justice (the Beijing Rules) state that: 'In those legal systems recognizing the concept of the age of criminal responsibility for juveniles, the beginning age shall not be fixed at too low an age level, bearing in mind the facts of emotional, mental and intellectual maturity'.[46] By setting a very low minimum age, children are unfairly punished for activities they do not understand as being criminal, greatly undermining the purpose of criminal law, which is to prosecute those who intentionally commit crimes. As the commentary of the Beijing Rules states, it would effectively make the

---

[45] Al-Hafiz Abi Essa Mohammed Bin Essa At Tirmazi. Sunnan At Tirmazi 'Chapter regarding persons exempted from Hudd punishments' vol 2, 64.

[46] United Nations Standard Minimum Rules for the Administration of Juvenile Justice (The Beijing Rules) (1985) art 4.1.

'notion of criminal responsibility meaningless'.[47] However the UNCRC does not prescribe a specific age,[48] and the Beijing Rules do not give specific guidance to what age is considered 'too low'.

Guidance on this matter can be found perhaps through the Committee on the Rights of the Child (CRC) reports. The UK was criticized by the CRC for retaining a low age of criminal responsibility (10 in England, Wales and Northern Ireland and eight in Scotland). However when brought to the attention of the European Court of Human Rights (ECtHR) in *A and T v United Kingdom*, the Court ruled that, although the UK had a low age of criminal responsibility, it did not violate the child defendants' rights under article 3 or 13 of the ECtHR (though this Convention does not include specific protection of the rights of the child).[49] Therefore it is arguable that States such as the United Arab Emirates and Pakistan do not violate child rights solely due to their comparatively low age of criminal responsibility. Rather a more nuanced, detailed investigation of juvenile justice systems is required to assess the effectiveness of child rights protection.

In the same case involving the UK, the Court found that, where criminal trials of juveniles charged with serious crimes are conducted in closed adult courts, not enough effort was being made to explain proceedings to child defendants, barring them from effectively taking part in them. The Court held: 'it is essential that a child charged with an offence is dealt with in a manner which takes full account of his age, level of maturity and intellectual and emotional capacities, and that steps are taken to promote his ability to understand and participate in the proceedings.'[50]

Comparing the treatment of child defendants within the Iranian juvenile justice system and those within the UAE system, Iran has an older age set for the minimum age of criminal responsibility, 15 years old for boys and nine years old for girls, and so it may arguably be less protective in general towards child rights. The UAE, although setting a low age of criminal responsibility, maintains the provision under article 7 of the Federal Law no 9 (1976) that where children between seven and 16 years old are found to have committed a crime, the authorities have the right to look into applying 'necessary disciplinary, educational or medical measures'. This is compared to the Iranian juvenile system where, although criminal responsibility starts at 15 years old, those juveniles may be subject to the death penalty.

---

[47] Commentary on United Nations Standard Minimum Rules for the Administration of Juvenile Justice (The Beijing Rules) (1985) art 4.1.

[48] Art 40(3)(a) of the UNCRC.

[49] Art 3 of the Convention provides: 'No one shall be subjected to torture or to inhumane or degrading treatment or punishment.' Art 14 prohibits discrimination in the enjoyment of Convention rights.

[50] *T and V v UK* (2000) 30 EHRR 121 para 86, 179.

While some States are heeding the suggestions made by the CRC and raising the minimum age of criminal responsibility, certain other factors must also be considered in order to make these actions effective in protecting child rights. For example, Egypt has increased the age of criminal responsibility to 12 years but this is subject to an exception which permits children from the age of seven years old to be referred to the Child Court, which effectively brings younger children into the juvenile justice system.[51] The prevailing view of law enforcement personnel, including judges and the police officers, is that this exception is essential; arguing that the committing of serious offences by young children is a continuous threat to society. This is part of the dual pressures on the State: to protect the rights of juveniles in conflict with the law, and to protect the interests of society as a whole from juvenile delinquent behaviour.

The analysis of some case law in the country reports raises the debate about the factors or the criteria on which judges rely in order to reach their decisions regarding young offenders. In some cases judges were reluctant to provide juveniles with further protection based on the nature of the crime and so do not take particular consideration of the age of the juvenile per se. Although in cases where the crime is of a less serious nature, courts do consider the age of juvenile defendants a key consideration. In cases where the crime is of a serious or grave nature the case law shows the age of juvenile defendants is of much less importance than the gravity of the crime itself.

In the *Sher Ali*[52] case, it seems that the brutality of the way in which the crime was committed determined the High Court of Pakistan's decision not to grant the juvenile offender any reduction of the sentence. This was also echoed in the UK Home Secretary's assertions in the James Bulger case,[53] where he pointed to the exceptional cruelty of the offence against a defenseless victim. Consequently, it appears that multiple factors determine the Courts' reasoning and decisions when handling cases. These factors pertain to the circumstances of the offenders and of the offence itself including the age, the level of understanding, the way the crime is committed and the gravity and seriousness of the crime itself.

In practical terms, in many States establishing the age of defendants is difficult due to the lack of proper birth registration. In Afghanistan, only around 10 per cent of births are registered.[54] In Pakistan, the CRC observed a substantial number of children were not registered at the time of birth.[55] This could be due to the fact that, even though birth registration is compul-

---

[51] See Egypt Country Report section IV.B.
[52] See Pakistan Country Report section IV.A.
[53] See UK Country Report section IV.A.
[54] See Afghanistan Country Report section IV.A.
[55] See Pakistan Country Report section III.

sory, a number of births still take place at home. Consequently, obtaining accurate birth dates is extremely difficult. Instead, to establish an approximate age for young offenders, medical examination or school registers are routinely used. However this practice in itself is not an accepted guaranteed alternative as the case law shows. For example, *In Muhammad Anwar and others v State,* 1976 P Cr.LJ 1325, the Pakistan court decided that in order to determine the child's age, medical opinion cannot override the evidence provided by the birth certificate.[56] Yet, in another case, the court preferred evidence of a radiologist to a school certificate and birth certificate.[57] In fact, for the determination of age, mere medical evidence, even if based on ossification tests and bone density, is not decisive.[58] Hence, no definite medical test exists that can determine age with certainty. This greatly discriminates against poor children and those born in rural areas without access to hospitals.

This uncertain situation may open doors for further exploitation. For example, children may be registered as adults (for employment purposes) and adults registered as children in order to avoid conviction. In both of these situations, the ends of justice can not be met since there would be lighter punishment for an adult and a harsher one for a child. Further, the child will be detained in an adult prison, and will remain at continuous risk of physical and sexual exploitation.[59] Consequently, without proper birth registration, even if the State parties raise the minimum age of criminal responsibility to international standards, not all children would be able to benefit from protections within the juvenile justice system.

Finally, it is important to highlight the following three conclusions this research has reached. First, although the minimum age of criminal responsibility has an essential role in establishing the limits upon which the juvenile criminal rules can apply, it is not a sole indicator of the protection provided for juveniles. The rights of the child in criminal matters are rather heavily dependent on the way the juvenile justice system is run in general, and the sentencing available, and not only on the fixed age of criminal liability per se. To some extent, it seems preferable to have a low age for criminal liability, complemented by a balanced and protective set of juvenile norms rather than a higher age with no specific protective framework for conducting trials for child offenders.

Second, this study has made efforts to demonstrate that Islamic criminal law does provide substantial protection for child offenders. Muslim jurists

---

[56] ibid.

[57] ibid.

[58] See I Khan, *Laws Relating to Children* (Pakistan Law House, Karachi, 2004) 16.

[59] UNICEF, 'South Asia and the Minimum Age of Criminal Responsibility' (Kathmandu, Nepal, July, 2005) http://www.unicef.org/rosa/Criminal_Responsibility_08July_05(final_copy).pdf, accessed 15 October 2009.

of different school of jurisprudence have interpreted and provided a basis, with reasoning, which could be used for developing a consensus of opinion to set a reasonable uniform minimum age to adopt in all Muslim States, which should neither be too low nor too high. Concerning the minimum age of penal majority, it would be safe to adopt a highest age limit, which according to some Muslim jurists should be 18. This can lead to a better juvenile justice system at both theory (legislations and regulations) and practice levels within Muslim jurisdictions.

Third, the protection for child offenders within both secular and religious criminal jurisdictions can become more effective when legislations allow judges who are involved in juvenile trials to have a large margin of power in assessing and implementing what 'the best interest of the child' is at the various stages from investigation through to sentencing.

Bibliography

INTERNATIONAL TREATIES

African Charter on the Rights and Welfare of the child
Convention on the Elimination of Discrimination Against Women
Convention on the Rights of the Child
International Covenant on Civil and Political Rights
The Bonn Agreement
United Nations Guidelines for the Prevention of Juvenile Delinquency (The Riyadh Guidelines) 1990
United Nations Standard Minimum Rules for the Administration of Juvenile Justice ('The Beijing Rules') 1985

NATION STATES' DOMESTIC LEGISLATION

Afghanistan
Afghan Penal Code (1976)
Juvenile Code of Afghanistan (2005)
The Constitution of the Islamic Republic of Afghanistan (January 3, 2004)
The Police Law of Afghanistan

Egypt
Egyptian Constitution
Egyptian Penal Code 58/1937

Iran
Iranian Constitution
The Islamic Penal Code
The Public Military Service Act 1984

Lebanon
Law No 422 of 6 June 2002

Malaysia
Act 468
Act 560
Act A902
Child Act 2001
Child Protection Act 1991

Criminal Justice Act, 1982
Domestic Violence Act 1994 (Act 521)
Guardianship of Infants Act, 1961
Juvenile Courts Act 1947
Malaysian Constitution
Penal Code by Legislative Decree No 112/83
Syariah Penal Code
The Adoption Act 1952
The Births and Deaths Registration Act 1957 (Act 299)
The Reformatory Schools Enactment (Cap. 37)
The Syariah Courts (Criminal Jurisdiction) Act 1965
The Syariah Criminal Offences (Federal Territories) Act 1997 (Act 559)
Women and Young Girls' Protection Act 1973

Nigeria
Child's Rights Act 2003
Children and Young Persons Law, Cap. 22 Laws of Sokoto State of Nigeria,
    1996
Criminal Procedure Code of Northern Nigeria
Kano Petty Trading Law
Kano State Juvenile Court Edict, 1987
Laws of Kano State of Nigeria, 1991
Laws of Northern Nigeria 1963
Laws of Sokoto State of Nigeria 1996
Sharia Criminal Procedure Code Law 2005, No 6 of 2005
Zamfara State Sharia Penal Code Law No 5 of 2005 (also known as
    Harmonized Sharia Penal Code)

Pakistan
Child Offenders Act (Bill), 1995
Constitution of the Islamic Republic of Pakistan
Enforcement of Hudood Ordinance, 1979 Ordinance VII of 1979
Juvenile Justice System Ordinance, 2000, No XXII
Offence Of Zina, Hudood Ordinance VII, 1979
Offences Against Property, Hudood Ordinance VI of 1979
Ordinance IV of 1990
Ordinance VII of 1990
PLD 1989, SC 633
Punjab Children Ordinance 1983
Qisas and Diyat Ordinance XII of 1993
Sindh Children Act 1955
The 'Protection of Women (Criminal Laws Amendment) Bill, 2006

Spain
The Spanish Constitution of 1978
The 1995 Penal Code
Organic Act 2/1979 of 3 of October
CRMA (Act 5/2000)

Turkey
Act No 2828 on Social Services and the Child Protection Agency, dated 24 May 1983
Children's Protection Law 2005 No 5395
Law No 4058
The Penal Code
The Turkish Constitution The Constitution is available in English at: http://www.anayasa.gov.tr/images/loaded/pdf_dosyalari/THE_ CONSTITUTION_OF_THE_REPUBLIC_OF_TURKEY.pdf, accessed 25 February 2010

United Arab Emirates
Law No 9 of 1976

United Kingdom
Children and Young Person Act 1933, Section 50 (amended by 1963 Act)
Criminal Justice and Immigration Act 2008
Powers of Criminal Courts (Sentencing) Act 2000
The Crime and Disorder Act 1998
The Justice (Northern Ireland) Act 2002
Youth Justice and Criminal Evidence Act 1999

CASES

Egypt
Appeal 1292, J.Y. 67 (2005); Court of Cassation
Appeal 17320, J.Y. 67 (2005); Court of Cassation
Appeal 25243, J.Y. 67 (1998); Court of Cassation
Appeal 50556, J.Y. 59 (1995); Court of Cassation
Appeal 5926, J.Y. 60 (1997); Court of Cassation
Appeal 7767, J.Y. 63 (1998)

Lebanon
Court of Cassation Plenary Assembly Decision No of 2000.
Beirut Labour Court (Conseil arbitral du travail), Decision No 46/95 of 19 December 1995, ASSAF v. National Social Security Fund. Unpublished.

Court of Cassation, Plenary Assembly, Decision No of 2002.

Beirut Court of First Instance (Chamber of Juvenile Justice), Decision dated 7 November 2007. Al ADL 2008, T.I p. 429.

Court of Cassation Decision No 56. 1968, Baz Compendium of Jurisprudence, 1968.

Decision No 7/85; Decision No 25/96. IDREL Case Law Data Base.

Criminal Court of Mount Lebanon. Decision No. 547/2003, 13 November 2003 IDREL Case Law Data Base. Juvenile Justice section.

Decision No 96/167, 10 July 1996; Decision 2001/1, 9 January 2001; Decision No 281/2001, 19 December 2001. IDREL Case Law Data Base. Juvenile Justice section.

Council of State Decision of 3 March 1971, 71: 630, ibid IDREL Index of Jurisprudence p. 2378.

Court of Cassation, No 59, 9 December 1973. A.A., 1974, p. 277.

Civil Court of Cassation, Decision of 5 March 1974. Judicial Journal 74: 166. Compendium Baz, N0 18, p. 2377.

Décret-loi n° 83/90 du 16.09.1983. IDREL Case Law Data Base.

Beirut Court of Appeal, No 121, 26 April 1988. Judicial Journal 1988 p. 692.

Conseil d'Etat No 130 of 29 November 1993.

Conseil d' Etat No. 239 of 10 February 1994.

Constitutional Council Decision No. 2/95 of 25 February 1995 and 395 of 18 September 1995 published in L' Orient-Le Jour newspaper of 22 September 1995.

Decision No 9/91, Decision N0 5/97 IDREL Case Law Data Base. Juvenile Justice section.

Decision No 98/69, 24 March 1998. IDREL Case Law Data Base. Juvenile Justice section.

Criminal Court of North Lebanon Decision No 11/98 of 8 January 1998.

Beirut Court of Appeals, Decision dated 27 May 2005, Proche-Orient Etudes Juridiques, 2005, p. 22.

Decision dated 23 April 2007 in Al Adl Law Journal 3/2009 p. 487.

Court of Cassation, Decision No 79 of 31 May 2007.

Beirut Juvenile Court Decision No 31 of 24.10.2007 Al Adl Law Journal 1/2008.

Al Nahar Beirut Daily, 27.10.2007.

Beirut Juvenile Court, Decision No 313/2008 of 14 July 2008.

Juvenile Court of Beirut, Decision dated 12 August 2008 published in Al Adl Law Journal 2009/1 p. 377.

Juvenile Court of Beirut Decision dated 28 August 2008 Al Adl Law Journal 3/2009.

Juvenile Court of Beirut Decision dated 19 November 2008 in Adl Law Journal 3/2009.

Mount-Lebanon Court of First Instance, Decision dated 8 February 2007, AL ADL 2007.T.3, p. 1358.

Malaysia
Balasundaram case
Deng Anak Ekom v Regina [1963] 1 MLJ 343
Meor Atiqulrahman Ishak v. Fatimah bte Sihi [2000] 5 MJL 375
Omar Che Soh v. Public Prosecutor [1988] 2 MLJ 55
PP v. Ben Ismail [1993] MLJU 25
PP v. Boy bin Islais [1993] MLJU 25,
PP v. Nur Hassan b Salib [1993] MLJU 241
Ramah v. Laton (1927) 6 FMSLR 128
See Tang Kong Meng v. Zainon [1995] 5 MLJ 408.
Shaik Abdul Latif and others v. Shaik Elias Bux (1915) 1 FMSLR 204 at 214

Nigeria
State v. Adamu Musa, Gusau Zamfara State, Case No. ZMS/GS/1c/2004

Pakistan
Farooq Ahmed v. Federation of Pakistan, PLD 2005, Lahore 15
Kashif Nadeem alias Pappi v. State: 1992 P Cr. L J 1799
Muhammad Akram v. The State (1992, ALD 383(2))
Muhammad Ashraf v. The State (1992 ALD 140)
Muhammad Nawaz v. The State (1998 MLD 1)
Muhammad Riaz v. The State PLD 1980 FSC 54
Sarwar Khan v. The State (1994 SCMR 1262)
Shabbir Ahmad v. The State (1991, ALD 265)
Sharafar Ali v. The State (1997 PCrLJ 199)

Spain
Audiencia Provincial of Ourense of 18 February 1998
Audiencia Provincial of Jaén No 3/2003 of 30 January
Constitutional Court judgement No 36/1991 of 14 February
Audiencia Provincial of La Rioja No 131/2003 of 7 July
The Constitutional Court judgment 38/1981 of 23 November

United Arab Emirates
Case 93/1997, Criminal, Juvenile, Supreme Court, Sunday 26 October 1997
Case 137/1996, Criminal, Juvenile, Supreme Court, 10 May 1997

United Kingdom

Ex parte V and T, HL [1997]

V v. United Kingdom, Application No. 24888/94, 30 EHRR 121, 16 December 1999

'The Afghan Interim Criminal Procedure Code for Courts' in the Official Gazette, Extraordinary Issue, Issue No 820, [2004], available online at http://www.afghanistantranslation.com/ last accessed 28 March, 2009

Abdel Satar, M *The Human Dimension in Designing Social Care Institutions for Children at Risk of Delinquency*. A study conducted under the auspices of the PDR project. Social Research Center, the American University in Cairo (2005)

Abghari, Adineh '*Introduction to the Iranian Legal System and the Protection of Human Rights in Iran*', British Institute of International and Comparative Law, London (2008)

Abubakar, MU (2005) '*Child's Rights Act: Critical Analysis from the Islamic Perspective*', a paper presented at the 7th Annual National Scientific Conference of Islamic Medical Association of Nigeria at Mambayya House, Kano Nigeria, 8th–10th July 2005 available at www.gamji.com

Abubakar, MU (2005) '*Unravelling the Knotty Areas in the Child's Rights Act 2003*' paper presented at a One day Interactive Session on Child's Rights Act 2003 organised by Zamfara State Ministry of Justice, Gusau, 12th May 2005 available at www.gamji.com

Abubakar, MU '*Accommodating Diversion in the Nigerian Juvenile Justice Regime*', a paper presented at a two-day interactive session with Juvenile Justice Administrators organised by LEADS in collaboration with Unicef Zone 'C'at Katsina Motel, Katsina State Nigeria, 21st–22nd November 2007

Abubakar, MU '*Gender and Islamic Criminal Law in Northern Nigeria*', LL.M Dissertation submitted to the School of Law, University of Warwick, United Kingdom (2004)

Afshini-Jan, N and Danesh, T *From Cradle to Coffin: A Report on Child Execution In Iran*, Foreign Policy Centre (2009)

Ahmed, L '*Women and Gender in Islam: Historical Roots of a Modern Debate*'. Yale University: London (1993)

Al Ahram Newspaper (Eygpt), 9/6/2007: Interview with Wafaa Al Mistikawi, Director General of the Social Defence Administration

Al Dostour Newspaper (Eygpt), 18/06/2009, *The merits of the case of El Torbini and his associates: the suspects committed the crimes of murder associated with sexual abuse*

Ali, Shaheen Sardar '*The United Nations Convention on the Rights of the Child, Islamic Law and Pakistan Legislation: A Comparative Study*' Shaheen Printing Press, Peshawer Pakistan (1994)

Ammar, N *'The Relationship Between Street Children and the Justice System in Egypt'*, in the International Journal of Offender Therapy and Comparative Criminology, OnlineFirst, published on July 29, 2008

Ansay and Wallace (ed) *Introduction to Turkish Law*, 5th edition, The Hague (2005)

Anwarullah, Dr Prof *'The criminal law of Islam'*. Kitab Bhavan: New Delhi (2006)

Ariffin, Nor Bee Bt *'The Child Act, 2001: How far is it fairing?'* paper presented at the 11th Malaysian Law Conference 2001, Kuala Lampur, 8–10 November, 2001.

Arshadi, Zohreh *Islamic Republic of Iran and Penal Codes: Restructuring society on the basis of violence and sexual apartheid, available at:* http://www.iran-bulletin.org/political_islam/punishmnt.html, accessed 11 March 2010

Asad, Mohamed *'The Message of the Qur'an'*, (Translation), Oriental Press: Dubai (2003)

Ashworth, A *Sentencing and Criminal Justice, Law in Context Series*, Fourth Edition, Cambridge University Press

Augi, M *Principles of Civil Law* Bahsoun Publishers (1992).

Awdah, Abdul Qadir *'Criminal Law of Islam vol 1–3'* International Islamic Publishers: Karachi, Pakistan (1987)

Ayua IA and Okagbue Isabella (eds), *The Right of the Child in Nigeria/* Nigerian Institute of Advanced Legal Studies: Lagos (1996)

Baderin, Mashood A *'International Human Rights and Islamic Law'*, Oxford University Press: New York (2003)

Badran, A (2005) *Evaluation of the Role and Impact of Social Care Institutions for Juvenile Delinquents. A study conducted under the auspices of the PDR Project.* Social Research Center, the American University in Cairo

Bassiouni, M Cherif *'The Islamic Criminal Justice System'* Oceana: New York (1982)

Bibars, I *'Street children in Egypt: from the home to the street to inappropriate corrective institutions'*, Environment and Urbanization, Vol 10, No 1, April 1998

Cipriani, D *Children's Rights and the Minimum Age of Criminal Responsibility*, Ashgate, London (2009)

Daily Trust Newspaper (Nigeria*) 'Jigawa Assembly Invalidates Circulated Child's Rights Law'* available at http://allafrica.com/stories/ 200903270547.html accessed 27/06/09

Dusuki, Farah Nini *'What Malaysia can Learn from the Experience of England and Wales to Protect Victims of Child Abuse and Neglect'*, PhD thesis, unpublished, Cardiff University (2002)

Dusuki, Farah Nini, *Implementation of Article 12 of the CRC within*

Juvenile Justice System in Malaysia, for UNICEF Malaysia, 11–21 July 2006. Input to the Day of General Discussion in Geneva, 15 September 2006 on the theme 'Speak, Participate & Decide—The Child's Right to be Heard' organised by the United Nation's Committee on the Rights of the Child available at www.crin.org/docs/GDD_2006_UNICEF_Malaysia2.doc accessed 9/7/2010

Edge, Ian (ed) *Comparative Law in Global Perspective,* New York (2000)

El-Awa, Mohamed S *'Punishment in Islamic Law'* American Trust Publications: Plainfield, IN 46168 (1993)

Fottrell, Deidre (ed) *'Revisiting Children's Rights: Ten Years on From the UN Convention on the Rights of the Child'.* Kluwer Law International: London (2001)

Friday, Paul C and Reng, Xin (eds), *Delinquency and Juvenile Justice Systems in the Non-Western World,* Criminal Justice Press: USA (2006)

Gottesman, Evan, The Reemergence of Qisas and Diyat in Pakistan' 14 Columbia Human Rights Law Review (1992)

Hood, Roger G *'The Death Penalty: a Worldwide Perspective'* 3rd edition Oxford, (2003)

Hussain, Dr Shaikh Shaukat H *'Human Rights in Islam'* Kitab Bhavan: New Delhi (2001)

Hussin, Dr Nasimah *'Juvenile Delinquencies in Malaysia: Legal Provisions and Prospects for Reform'* found at http://www.lawrights.asn.au/index.php?option=com_content&view=article&id=62 accessed 9 July 2010

Jensen, Eric L and Jepsen, Jorgen (ed) *Juvenile Law Violators, and the Development of New Juvenile Justice Systems,* the Onati International Institute for the Sociology of Law, Hart Publishing (2006)

Kalu, A and Osinbajo, Y (eds) *Women and Children under Nigeria Law* Federal Ministry of Justice: Lagos (1991)

Kandiyoti, Deniz *Between the Hammer and the Anvil: Post-Conflict Reconstruction, Islam and Women's Rights.'* Third World Quarterly, 28 (3) (1007)

Kassim, K, Hsien Jin T, Suan Lim Gaik & Azmi Z, *Juvenile Delinquency: A Study Report,* Malaysian Crime Prevention Foundation (2001)

Khan, Ilyas *'Laws Relating to Children'.* Pakistan Law House: Karachi, Pakistan (2004)

Khan, Tauqir Mohammad and Syed, MH *'Criminal Law in Islam'.* Pentagon Press, New Delhi (2007)

Lippman, M, McConville, S and Yerushalmi, M *'Islamic Criminal Law and Procedure'* Praeger: New York (1988)

Majid, Mimi Kamariah *Criminal Procedure in Malaysia,* 3rd edition, University of Malaya Press (1999)

Majid, Mimi Kamariah *Legislation on Social Ills,* Auditorium

Perdanasiswa, University of Malaya, 17 November (1997) Published within The Star Newspaper, 18 November, 1997 and Berita Harian, 18 November, 1997.

Mansoor, Farkhanda Zia (2005) *'Reassessing Packer in the Light of International Human Rights Norms'* in the University of Connecticut School of Law Connecticut Public Interest Law Journal, Vol 4, No 2, 2005

McLeod, Ian *Legal Method,* Fourth Edition, Palgrave Law Masters, MacMillian, London (2002)

Nyazee, Imran Ahsan Khan *'Theories of Islamic Law'*, Islamic Research Institute: Islamabad, Pakistan (1993)

Okagbue, I *'Children in Conflict with the Law: The Nigerian Experience'* available at http://www.unicef-irc.org/portfolios/documents/487_nigeria.htm accessed 9 July 2010

Packer, Herbert L *'The Limits of Criminal Sanction'*. Stanford University Press: California (1969)

Parekh, Vikram *Prison bound: the denial of juvenile justice in Pakistan* Human Rights Watch, New York, (1999)

Peters, R 'Islamic and Secular Criminal Law in Nineteenth Century Egypt: The Role and Function of the Qadi', in Islamic Law and Society, Vol 4, No 1 (1997), BRILL

Peters, Rudolph *'Crime and Punishment in Islamic Law Theory and Practice from the Sixteenth to the Twenty-first Century'*, Cambridge University Press, London (2005)

Price, Richard and Al Tamimi, Essam *United Arab Emirates Court of Cassation Judgments 1998–2003, Arab and Islamic Law Series*, Leiden: Brill, (2005)

Rutter, MJ *'The Applicable Law in Singapore and Malaysia'*, Malayan Law Journal (1989)

Sanders, Andrew and Young, Richard *'Criminal Justice'*. Oxford University Press: Oxford (2006)

Shah, Dr Nasim Hasan (Retd Chief Justice of Pakistan & President SAARC LAW), *Islamisation of Law in Pakistan*. Lecture delivered at the National Law School of India University, Bangalore, Dec 1994

Sloth-Neilsen, J (ed) *Children's Rights in Africa: A Legal Perspective*, Ashgate Publishing Limite: England (2008)

Smith, JC (ed) *Smith and Hogan Criminal Law*, 10th Edition

Spatz, Melissa, 'A Lesser Crime: A Comparative Study of Legal Defences for Men Who Kill Their Wives', 24 Columbia Journal of Law and Social Problems (1991)

Turner, JW Cecil (ed) *Kenny's outlines of criminal law*, 17th Edition

Van Bueren Professor Geraldine *Article 40: Child Criminal Justice (Commentary on the United Nations Convention on the Rights of the Child, 40)* Martinus Nijhoff Publishers, Leiden (2005)

Wasti, Tahir '*The Application of Islamic Criminal Law in Pakistan—Sharia in Practice*' BRILL, Leiden (2009)

Wolff, S & McCall Smith Alexander AR   *Child Homicide and the Law: Implications of the Judgements of Human Rights in the case of the children who killed James Bulger.* Child Psychology & Psychiatric Review, Vol 5.

Zermatten, J (ed), *Training Course On Juvenile Justice for Officials from Turkey, Working Report* 2-(2003) available at http://www. childsrights.org/html/documents/Publications/WRTurquie2003.pdf, accessed 25 February 2010.

REPORTS

Afghan Independent Human Rights Commission, '*A Call for Justice: A National Consultation on Past Human Rights Violations in Afghanistan*', Kabul, (January 2005). Available at: http://www.aihrc. org.af/pressreng28_1_05call.htm accessed 20 October 2010

Afghanistan Human Development Report 2007, '*Bridging Modernity and Tradition: Rule of Law and the Search for Justice*', Centre for Policy and Human Development, Kabul University. Available at: http://www. usip.org/resources/bridging-modernity-and-tradition-rule-law-and-search-justice-afghanistan, accessed 20 October 2010

Afghanistan Independent Human Rights Commission (AIHRC), *Justice for children. The situation of children in conflict with the law in Afghanistan*, 26 June 2008 available athttp://www.unhcr.org/refworld/ category,REFERENCE,AIHRC,,,47fdfae50,0.html

Afshini-Jan, N and Danesh, T *From Cradle to Coffin: A Report on Child Execution In Iran*, Foreign Policy Centre (2009)

Amnesty International, 'Amnesty *International's comments on the Lahore High Court judgment of December 2004 revoking the Juvenile Justice System Ordinance*', http://asiapacific.amnesty.org/library/Index/ ENGASA330262005?open&of=ENG-403, accessed 15 October 2009

Amnesty International: Country Report on Afghanistan 2008 available at http://www.amnesty.org/en/region/afghanistan/report-2008 accessed 20 October 2010

Bather, P Fitzpatrick, R and Rutherford, M '*Briefing 36: The Police and Mental Health*', Sainsbury Centre for Mental Health, 2008, available at http://www.scmh.org.uk/publications/police_and_mental_health.aspx?I D=583, accessed 4 March 2010

Berti, Stefano Rights of the Child in Pakistan, *Report on the implementation of the Convention on the Rights of the Child by Pakistan*, OMCT, Geneva, May 2003, available at www.omct.org/pdf/cc/ PakistanCRCreport.en.doc, accessed 9 July 2010

British Government Paper, '*Malaya: Statement of Policy for the Future Constitution of the Malayan Union and the Colony of Singapore*', January 1946.

Commission of the European Communities, 2002 Regular Report on Turkey's Progress Towards Accession, available at: http://ec.europa.eu/enlargement/archives/pdf/key_documents/2002/tu_en.pdf, accessed 26 February 2010

Community and Institutional Development (CID) *A Rights-based Analysis of Child Protection in Egypt Final Report*, report commissioned by Save the Children UK, Cairo, Egypt (2007)

Federal Ministry of Women Affairs (2004) *Nigeria: Convention on the Rights of the Child: Second Country Periodic Report* available at http://www2.ohchr.org/english/bodies/crc/docs/AdvanceVersions/CRC.C.70.Add.24.Rev.2.pdf, accessed 16 July 2009

General comment No 24 on Issues relating to reservations made upon ratification or accession to the Covenant adopted by the ICCPR Committee at its 52nd session in 1994, available at: http://www.unhchr.ch/tbs/doc.nsf/%28Symbol%29/69c55b086f72957ec12563ed004ecf7a?Opendocument accessed 18 October 2010

General Comment No 06: The right to life (art 6) Office for the Commissioner of Human Rights 04/30/1982 available at http://www.unhchr.ch/tbs/doc.nsf/0/84ab9690ccd81fc7c12563ed0046fae3 accessed 21 October 2010

General comment No 10 (Children's Rights in Juvenile Justice) of the Committee on CRC released February 2007 available at http://www2.ohchr.org/english/bodies/crc/docs/CRC.C.GC.10.pdf accessed 11 August 2009

General comment no. 10 (Children's Rights in Juvenile Justice) of the Committee on CRC released February 2007 available at http://www2.ohchr.org/english/bodies/crc/docs/CRC.C.GC.10.pdf accessed 11 August 2009

Human Rights Commission of Pakistan, *Slow March to the Gallows: Death Penalty in Pakistan*, January (2007) available at http://www.fidh.org/Slow-march-to-the-gallows-Death-penalty-in, accessed 20 October 2010

Human Rights Commission of Pakistan, *State of Human Rights in 2007* available at http://hrcp-web.org/5-2%20children.pdf, accessed 25 May 2008

Human Rights Watch '*Enforcing the International Prohibition on the Juvenile Death Penalty*' www.juvenilejusticepanel.org/.../HRWEnfIntProhibJuvDPenalty08EN.pdf accessed 15 October 2009

Human Rights Watch '*World Report Afghanistan*' (2008) available at http://www.hrw.org/en/node/87390 accessed 21 October 2010

Human Rights Watch Letter on Juvenile Death Penalty in Iran, 21

September 2006, available at: http://www.hrw.org/en/news/2006/09/21/human-rights-watch-letter-juvenile-death-penalty-iran, accessed 11 March 2010

Human Rights Watch Report, '*Crime or Custom? Violence Against Women in Pakistan*', August 1999 available at http://www.unhcr.org/ refworld/country,,HRW,,PAK,,45d314242,0.html accessed 18 October 2010

Ministry of Women, Family and Community Development, *Malaysia's First Country Report on the Implementation of the Convention of the Rights of the Child,* 2007 available at http://daccess-ods.un.org/TMP/3995074.03373718.html accessed 07/02/2010

National Association of Care and Resettlement of Offenders ,Youth Crime Briefing September 2005http://www.nacro.org.uk/data/files/nacro-2006071402-104.pdf, accessed 4 March 2010

National Human Rights Commission Nigeria, 2007 NHRC Prison Report at www.nigeriarights.gov.ng accessed 25 June 2009

Organisation Mondiale Contre la Torture. *The rights of the child in Egypt* Geneva, Switzerland (2001)

Police Services of Northern Ireland 'PSNI Section 75, Equality Impact Assessment, Youth Diversion Scheme'. Published March 2007, p 5, available at www.psni.police.uk/summary_of_youth_diversion_eqia.pdf, accessed 4 March 2010

Report by the Bureau of Democracy, Human Rights and Labor on events in Afghanistan published on 11th March 2008 available at

Report of Fact Finding Mission, 11-20 February 2008, Turkey, available at: http://www.unhcr.org/refworld/topic,45a5fb512,4652f4a02,489c167e2,0.html, accessed 26 February 2010

Report of the Juvenile Delinquency and Juvenile Welfare Committee, No 18, February 1947, c289 at c291-291, M.U. 3484/47 (Malaysia)

Report of the *Special Rapporteur on extra-judicial, summary or arbitrary executions* on his mission to the USA available at http://daccess-ods.un.org/access.nsf/Get?Open&DS=E/CN.4/1998/68/Add.3&Lang=E accessed 21 October 2010

Report of the Working Group on the Universal Periodic Review on Nigeria at http://www2.ohchr.org/english/bodies/hrcouncil/11session/reports.htm, accessed 28 July 2009

Report of the Working Group on the Universal Periodic Review on Nigeria at http://www2.ohchr.org/english/bodies/hrcouncil/11session/reports.htm, accessed 28 July 2009

Report presented by the Minister of Justice of Turkey, in: 28th Conference of European Ministers of Justice, Lanzarote (25–26 October 2007), available at http://www.coe.int/t/dghl/standardsetting/minjust/mju28/MJU-28%282007%2914E-Turkey.pdf, accessed 25 February 2010

Response of the Turkish Government to the report of the European Committee for the Prevention of Torture and Inhuman or Degrading Treatment or Punishment (CPT) on it visit to Turkey from 7 to 15 September 2003, p 7 and 22, available at: http://www.unhcr.org/refworld/country,,COECPT,,TUR,4562d8cf2,4718b94e2,0.html, accessed 26 February 2010

Sainsbury Centre for Mental Health, 'The Chance of a Lifetime—preventing early conduct problems and reducing crime', published 23 November 2009, available at: http://www.scmh.org.uk/publications/chance_of_a_lifetime.aspx?ID=604, accessed 10 January 2010

SUHAKAM, *Report of the Forum on Malaysia's Reservations to the Convention on the Rights of the Child*, 2008 available at http://www.suhakam.org.my

The Human Rights Association for the Assistance of Prisoners (HRAAP), *Detention and Detainees in Egypt 2004*, Conditions of Detainees and Detention Centers in Egypt. The Seventh Annual Report: HRAAP. Available at hrcap.org/.../Detention%20and%20Detainees%20in%20Egypt%202004%20(Final).rtf accessed 20 October 2010

The Scottish Law Commission Report No 185, 'Report on Age of Criminal Responsibility', January 2002, available at: www.chscotland.gov.uk/pdf/krcy.pdf, accessed 4 March 2010

UN Committee for the Rights of the Child Egypt's Third and Fourth Periodic Report to the International Committee on the Rights of the Child, period 2001–2008, (December 2008) accessed 21 October 2010

UN Committee of the Rights of the Child CRC/C/SR.795 Thirtieth session, Summary Record of the 795th Meeting 13 May 2002 available at http://www.unhchr.ch/tbs/doc.nsf/0/1de3ad4071c7c778c1256bd8002ce01c?Opendocument accessed 21 October 2010

UN Committee on the Rights of the Child Concluding Observations Pakistan, CRC/C/15/Add.217, 27/10/2003, available at www.unhchr.ch/tbs/doc.nsf/.../$FILE/G0344662.doc

UN Committee on the Rights of the Child for the UK the consolidated 3rd and 4th Periodic report available at: http://www.dcsf.gov.uk/everychildmatters/resources-and-practice/IG00249/, accessed 3 March 2010

UN Committee on the Rights of the Child, Concluding Observations: UK, CRC/C/15/Add.188, 9/10/2002, available at http://www.unhchr.ch/tbs/doc.nsf/898586b1dc7b4043c1256a450044f331/2f2744b7e0d015d6c1256c76004b3ab7/$FILE/G0245381.pdf, accessed 5 March 2010

UN Committee on the Rights of the Child, Concluding Observations, Islamic Republic of Iran, CRC/C/15/Add.254, 20/01/2005 http://www.unhchr.ch/tbs/doc.nsf/0/816601ca7398c9b3c1257021004d0583/$FILE/G0540872.pdf accessed 21 October 2010

UN Committee on the Rights of the Child, Concluding Observations Spain,

CRC/C/15/Add.153, 9/7/2001. Available at http://www.unhchr.ch/tbs/doc.nsf/(Symbol)/CRC.C.15.Add.149.En?Opendocument accessed 21 October 2010

UN Committee on the Rights Of The Child, Forty-Second Session, Summary Record of The 1129th Meeting (Chamber B) available at http://www.unhchr.ch/tbs/doc.nsf/898586b1dc7b4043c1256a450044f3 31/c0418bef762dfbefc1257185002e697c/$FILE/G0642246.pdf, accessed 25 February 2010

UN Committee on the Rights of the Child, General Comment No 10 (2007): Children's rights in Juvenile Justice, Forty-fourth session. Geneva, 15 January-2 February 2007 http://www.unhcr.org/refworld/type,GENERAL,,,4670fca12,0.html accessed 21 October 2010

UN Committee on the Rights of the Child, Periodic Reports of States Parties Spain 1999, available at http://www.unhchr.ch/tbs/doc.nsf/(Symbol)/7c388e71b37136cdc1256bb80035ddab?Opendocument, accessed 8 July 2009

UN Committee on the Rights Of The Child, Sixth Session, Summary Record Of The 134th Meeting: Pakistan, CRC/C/SR.134, 6/04/1992, available at http://www.unhchr.ch/tbs/doc.nsf/0/6d28f3c73f6e9beb802 565e1004e280f?Opendocument accessed 9 October 2009

UN Committee on the Rights of the Child: Concluding Observations, Lebanon, 8/06/2006, CRC/C/LBN/CO/3, available at http://www.unhcr.org/refworld/docid/45377ee70.html, accessed 2 March 2010

UN Committee on the Rights of the Child: Concluding Observations: Lebanon, CRC/C/15/Add.54, 7/06/1996   available at http://www.unhcr.org/refworld/docid/3ae6af5b28.html, accessed 02 March 2010

UN Committee on the Rights of the Child: Concluding Observations: UK, CRC/C/GBR/CO/4 20/10/2008, available at http://www2.ohchr.org/english/bodies/crc/docs/AdvanceVersions/CRC.C.GBR.CO.4.pdf, accessed 4 March 2010

UN Committee on the Rights of the Child: Concluding Observations: Malaysia, CRC/C/MYS/CO/1 25/06/2007 available at http://daccess-ods.un.org/TMP/650273.934006691.html, accessed 21 October 2010

UN Committee on the Rights of the Child: The Initial reports of States parties due in 1999: United Arab Emirates, CRC/C/78/Add.2, 24 October 2001 available at http://www.unhchr.ch/tbs/doc.nsf/(Symbol)/d5f09e6c6edb682cc1256b3b004d1a3e?Opendocumen t accessed 20 October 2010

UN Committee on the Rights of the Child:Concluding Observations: United Arab Emirates, CRC/C/15/Add.183 13/06/2002, available at http://www.unhchr.ch/tbs/doc.nsf/(Symbol)/CRC.C.15.Add.183.En?Ope ndocument accessed 20 October 2010

UN Security Council, Commission on Counter Terrorism, S/2003/280 http://daccess-ods.un.org/TMP/5814992.html accessed 21 October 2010

Ünal, Şeref, 'Turkish Legal System and the Protection of Human Rights', SAM (Stratejik Araştırmalar Merkezi) Papers, No. 3/99

UNICEF Nigeria report, *'Protection and Participation'* available at http://www.unicef.org/nigeria/protection_2169.html accessed 27/06/09

UNICEF *South Asia and the Minimum Age of Criminal Responsibility* Kathmandu, Nepal, July, (2005), http://www.unicef.org/rosa/Criminal_Responsibility_08July_05(final_copy).pdflast accessed 9 July 2010

UNICEF, The Situation of Egyptian Children and Women: A Rights Based Analysis, Arab Republic of Egypt and Unicef, Cairo: August 2002

United Nations Children's Fund Executive Board First regular session 2006, 16–20 and 23 January 2006, Revised country programme document, Turkey, p 3, available at: http://www.unicef.org/about/ execboard/files/Turkey-CPD_Rev1.pdf, accessed 26 February 2010

United Nations Committee On The Rights Of The Child, Forty-Second Session, Summary Record of The 1129th Meeting (Chamber B), available at http://www.unhchr.ch/tbs/doc.nsf/898586b1dc7b4043c1256a 450044f331/c0418bef762dfbefc1257185002e697c/$FILE/G0642246.p df, accessed 26 February 2010

United States Agency for International Development (USAID), 'Afghanistan Rule of Law Project: Field Study of Informal and Customary Justice in Afghanistan and Recommendations on Improving Access to Justice and Relations between Formal Courts and Informal Bodies' (June 2005) Available at pdf.usaid.gov/pdf_docs/PNADF590.pdf accessed 21 October 2010

White Paper: *No More Excuses—A New Approach to Tackling Youth Crime in England and Wales',* published November 1997, Home Office, available at: http://www.homeoffice.gov.uk/documents/jou-no-more-excusesa8cf.html?view=Html, accessed 04 March 2010

Zuberi, Danish *'Pakistan: Will the NCSW's latest recommendation to repeal the Hudood Ordinances finally put an end to the dreaded law?'* 4/11/2003, http://www.wluml.org/english/newsfulltxt.shtml?cmd [157]=x-157-27267 accessed 3 March 2010

INTERNET RESOURCES

Amnesty International, 'Denial of basic rights for child prisoners', http://www.amnesty.org/en/library/asset/ASA33/011/2003/en/4fb4b9fc-d698-11dd-ab95-a13b602c0642/asa330112003en.html accessed 9 July 2010

Amnesty International, 'Pakistan: Protection of Juveniles in the Criminal Justice System Remains Inadequate' http://www.amnesty.org/en/library/info/ASA33/021/2005/en accessed 15 October 2010

Article 'The Age of Criminal Responsibility' http://billofrights.nihrc.org/submissions/submission_323.pdf, accessed 9 July 2010

Crime and Society, Comparative Criminology Tour of the World: Pakistan http://www.rohan.sdsu.edu/faculty/rwinslow/asia_pacific/pakistan.html, accessed 9 July 2010

Figures for child rights indicators in Egypt http://www.unicef.org/infoby country/egypt_statistics.html accessed 09 July 2010

'Shirin Ebadi and Iran's women: in the vanguard of change' by Nazila Fathi, 30 October 2003, available a thttp://www.opendemocracy.net/people-irandemocracy/article_1557.jsp accessed 9 July 2010

Committee for the Defence of Iranian People's Rights: *'The gag is tightened'* by Saeed Kamali Dehghan, 6 January 2008, The Observer, available at http://www.codir.net/books/index.html, accessed 9 July 2010

For an overview of Iranian *Diyat* laws relating to women, see http://www.learningpartnership.org/resources/legislation/nationallaw/iran accessed 9 July 2010

Statistics on Iran http://www.unicef.org/infobycountry/iran_statistics.html, accessed 9 July 2010

Information on the prison system of England and Wales Her Majesty's Prison Service: http://www.hmprisonservice.gov.uk/adviceandsupport/prison_life/lifesentencedprisoners/ accessed 15 February 2010

Universal Periodic Review of Religious Freedoms in Kyrgyzstan http://treaties.un.org/Pages/ViewDetails.aspx?src=TREATY&mtdsg_no=IV-4&chapter=4&lang=en, accessed 9 July 2010

International Covenant on Civil and Political Rights http://www2.ohchr.org/english/law/ccpr.htm, accessed 9 July 2010

Child Rights Information Network: Turkey Campaign Against Children on Trial http://www.crin.org/resources/infodetail.asp?id=20056, accessed 9 July 2010

Safeguards guaranteeing protection of the rights of those facing the death penalty Approved by Economic and Social Council resolution 1984/50 of 25 May 1984 http://www2.ohchr.org/english/law/protection.htm, accessed 9 July 2010

Pakistan Legal System http://www.globalsecurity.org/military/world/pakistan/legal-system.htm

BBC News website country profile: Iran http://news.bbc.co.uk/1/hi/world/europe/country_profiles/790877.stm accessed 09/07/2010

Globalex: Guide to the legal system of Iran http://www.nyulawglobal.org/globalex/iran.htm#_System_of_Government accessed 9 July 2010

UK Youth Justice Board: http://www.yjb.gov.uk/en-gb/yjs/Sentences OrdersandAgreements/ParentingOrder/, accessed 4 March 2010

World Vision UK Summary on Afghanistan: http://www. worldvision.org.uk/server.php?show=nav.1897 accessed 9 July 2010

BBC News *James Bulger murderer Jon Venables returned to prison* http://news.bbc.co.uk/1/hi/england/merseyside/8546528.stm, accessed 9 July 2010

The Times Newspaper (UK) *Parents of Edlington torture brothers could face charges*, Jan 22nd 2010, Philippe Naughton and Andrew Norfolk, available at http://www.timesonline.co.uk/tol/news/uk/crime/article6998636.ece, accessed 15 February 2010

BBC News *Young brothers admit boys' attack*, 22nd Jan 2010, available at: http://news.bbc.co.uk/1/hi/england/south_yorkshire/8233822.stm, accessed 15 February 2010 http://www.guardian.co.uk/uk/2009/sep/03/brothers-plead-guilty-attack-schoolboys, accessed 15 February 2010

The Times Newspaper (UK) Full text of Mr Justice Keith's comments on Edlington case available at: http://www.timesonline.co.uk/tol/news/uk/crime/article6998667.ece, accessed 15 February 2010

The Times Newspaper (UK) *Brothers appear in court over Edlington 'torture'*, April 8 2009, available at: http://www.timesonline.co.uk/tol/news/uk/crime/article6053832.ece, accessed 15 February 2010

Criminal Justice and Immigration Act 2008 in full http://www.opsi.gov.uk/acts/acts2008/ukpga_20080004_en_1, accessed 15 February 2010

National Association for the Care and Resettlement of Offenders. Youth Crime Policy Officer, Tim Bateman, http://www.nacro.org.uk/news-and-resources/latest-news/nacro-responds-to-edlington-case,302,NAP.html, accessed 9 July 2010

Inquiry into case of 'torture boys', by Dave Higgens, Press Association, January 26 2010, available at: The Independent Newspaper (UK) http://www.independent.co.uk/news/uk/home-news/inquiry-into-case-of-torture-boys-1878803.html, accessed 15 February 2010

BBC News *Judge is refused care authorities' report in Edlington torture case*, Andrew Norfolk and Rosemary Bennett, Jan 22nd 2010, available at http://www.timesonline.co.uk/tol/news/uk/crime/article6997640.ece, accessed 15 February 2010

BBC News *How Edlington case follows course paved by Bulger trial*, by Martha Buckley, 22 Jan. 2010, available at: http://news.bbc.co.uk/1/hi/uk/8300034.stm, accessed 15 February 2010

UNICEF country profile Turkey. http://www.unicef.org/turkey/ut/ut2_2010.html#nt26, accessed 9 July 2010

Turkish Criminal Code http://www.legislationline.org/documents/action/popup/id/6872/preview, accessed 25 February 2010

European Twinning Project with Turkey on Rehabilitation of Juvenile Offenders http://ec.europa.eu/enlargement/pdf/turkey/ipa/tr_07_01_01_work_with_juveniles_victims_by_the_tk_probation_service_en.pdf, accessed 9 July 2010

Information on UK Magistrates Courts http://www.cjsonline.gov.uk/the_cjs/how_it_works/magistrates_court/, accessed 3 March 2010

Information on Court System of England and Wales Her Majesty's Court Services: http://www.hmcourts-service.gov.uk/infoabout/magistrates/index.htm, accessed 3 March 2010

Official Scottish Courts Homepage, available at: http://www.scotcourts.gov.ulk/district/index.asp, accessed 3 March 2010

UK Supreme Court Website http://www.supremecourt.gov.uk/about/the-supreme-court-and-europe.html, accessed 3 March 2010

Civil Code for the Islamic Republic of Iran http://www.alaviandassociates.com/documents/civilcode.pdf, accessed 9 July 2010

Juvenile Justice Initiatives in Lebanon http://www.unodc.org/pdf/crime/forum/forum3_note2.pdf, accessed 9 July 2010

The Centre for Islamic Legal Studies' Draft Harmonised Sharia Penal Code Annotated http://www.sharia-in-africa.net/media/publications/sharia-implementation-in-northern-nigeria/vol_4_4_chapter_4_part_ III.pdf?wb_session_id=233572382b1bd517663d60f1428d705c accessed 27 June 2009

Dr Faqir Hussian, the Judicial system of Pakistan, http://pklegal.org/resources/JUDICIAL_SYSTEM_OF_PAKISTAN-FAQIR_HUSSAIN.doc accessed 9 July 2010

Jahangir, Asma 'Women's Commission And Hudood Ordinances', http://www.peacewomen.org/news/Pakistan/newsarchive03/Zina.html, accessed 9 July 2010

Pakistan's Fiery Shame, Women Die in Stove Death http://www.womensenews.org/article.cfm/dyn/aid/1085/context/archive accessed 9 July 2010

Pakistan: Protection of juveniles in the criminal justice system remains inadequate, Amnesty International, http://www.amnesty.org/en/library/info/ASA33/021/2005/en, accessed 9 July 2010

Pakistan-the Death Penalty. http://asiapacific.amnesty.org/library/Index/ENGASA330101996?open&of=ENG-333 accessed 9 July 2010

Islamic Law Myths and Realities http://muslim-canada.org/Islam_myths.htm accessed 6 July 2010

Pakistan: Further information on: death penalty: Mutabar Khan, http://www.amnesty.org/en/library/asset/ASA33/023/2006/en/072fdc2a-d41d-11dd-8743-d305bea2b2c7/asa330232006en.html accessed 3 March 2010

Pakistan: Death penalty for juveniles reintroduced, 9 December 2004,

http://www.amnesty.ca/resource_ce/ntre/news/view.php?load=arcview&
article=2051&c=/esource+Centre+News accessed 18 October 2010

Middle East Online. 'UAE population topped four million in 2003,' 13
April 2004, available at http://www.middle-east-online.com/english/
?id=9623

Emirates Media Studies Centre http://www.emasc.com/content.asp?
ContentId=17839; accessed 18 October 2010

The Khaleej Times': Delinquents in detention separated from non-Arabs,'
Amira Agarib and Afkar Ali, 13 July 2009 Available at
http://www.khaleejtimes.com/DisplayArticle08.asp?xfile=data/theuae/20
09/July/theuae_July287.xml&section=theuae accessed 18 October 2010

Inter Press Service News Agency '*Call for innovative solutions to check
juvenile delinquency*' November 23 2004, WAM, (http://ipsnotizie.it/
wam_en/news.php?idnews=1587)

The Khaleej Times Newspaper (UAE), *Strict measures needed to curb juvenile delinquency*, Sadiq A. Salam, 22 June 2005 http://www.khaleejtimes.
com/DisplayArticleNew.asp?section=theuae&xfile=data/theuae/2005/ju
ne/theuae_june629.xml

The Khaleej Times Newspaper (UAE) '*Juvenile crimes on the rise*,' Lina
Abdul Rahman, 23 September 2005, available at: http://www.khaleej
times.com/Displayarticle.asp?section=theuae&xfile=data/theuae/2005/se
ptember/theuae_september707.xml, accessed 15 October 2010

The Khaleej Times Newspaper, (UAE)'*Domestic Instability May Push Girls
Towards Crime*,' 13 July 2009 Available at: http://www.khaleejtimes.
com/darticlen.asp?xfile=data/theuae/2009/July/theuae_July288.xml&sec
tion=theuae accessed 15 October 2010

Emirati Ministry of Social Affaires http://www.msa.gov.ae/MSA/AR/News/
Pages/NewsDetails.aspx?NewsID=194 accessed 9 July 2010

Carnegie Endowment for International Peace available at 'Arab Political
Systems: Baseline Information and Reforms – UAE, www.carnegie
endowment.org/arabpoliticalsystems accessed 15 October 2010

Dubai Courts website: http://www.dubaicourts.gov.ae/portal/
page?_pageid=53,72555,53_72567:53_78353&_dad=portal&_
schema=PORTAL accessed 15 February 2010

UAE Interacts '*UAE preparing comprehensive law on protection of children's rights: FNC member*'posted on 23 June 2009 and available at:
http://www.uaeinteract.com/docs/UAE_preparing_comprehensive_law_
on_protection_of_childrens_rights_FNC_member/36430.htm accessed
15 October 2010

UK Home Office Margaret Ayres and Liz Murray, 16th December 2005.
Research Developments and Statistics Directorate. Available at:
http://www.homeoffice.gov.uk/rds/pdfs05/hosb2105.pdf, accessed 3
March 2010

The Independent Newspaper (UK) *The Big Question: At what age should children be held responsible for their criminal acts?* Thursday, 5 February 2009, Nigel Morris http://www.inddependent.co.uk/news/uk/crime/the-big-question-at-what-age-should-children-be-held-responsible-for-their-criminal-acts-1546284.html accessed 9 July 2010

Arabic sources

Abd El-Khaleq Ebn Al-Mofaddal Ahmaddon, *'Qa'edat dar'e al hedood bel-Shobehat wa atharoha fi al fiqh al gena'ei al islami (translation: The Rule of Eliminating Penalty on Suspicion Criterion and Its Role in Islamic Penal Jurisdiction)*, 7 Contemporary Jurisprudence Research Journal 7–75 (1995)

Abu Dawood, Imam Suleman Bin Al-Ashhas, *'Sunnan Abi Dawood'*

Abu Yalla *'Al-Ahkam-Al-Sultania'* Dar-al Kutub al Ilmia: Beirut (1406AH, 1985)

Ahmed, Leila 'Women and Gender in Islam: Historical Roots of a Modern Debate'. Yale University: London (1993)

Ameen, Imam Mohammed *'Rad-al-Mohtar-Ala-Dur-al-Mukhtar (Hasheia-Ibn-e-Abedeen) Vol 5 '* Mustapha Al-Babi Al-Halbi (publisher): Cairo 3rd edition (1984)

Asad, Mohamed *'The Message of the Qur'an'* (Translation) 2003, Oriental Press Dubai

Al Asqalani, Mohammad-bin- Ismail (1959) *'Subal-Assalam-Sharah-Baloogh-Almaram'* Dar Al-Kutab Al Islamia (publishers): Pakistan and Maktabah Atif (publishers): Al Azhar: Egypt

Bin Masood, Imam Allaudin Abi-Baqar *'Badai-us-Sanaiy Vol 7'*, Educational Press Karachi and Egypt (1910)

Al-Bukhari, Abu Abdullah Bin Ismael 'Sahih Al Bukahari' (n.d)

Hemid, Dr.Ahamed *'Muqwamat-Al- Jareema-wa-Dawafiaohaa'* Amara Al-Sor: Kuwait (1982)

Ibn-e-Quddama *'Al Mughni vol 8'*. Maktabatul Quliat: Al-Azharia, Egypt (620 AH)

Ismael, Dr Muhammed Rushdi Muhammed *'Janayat fi Shariah Al Islamia'*. Dar ul Ansar (1983)

Al-Jaziri, *'Kitab al-Fiqh Ala al- Madahahib al-Arba'ah Vol 5 '* (1997)

Al Jowzia, Ibn-Al-Qayam *'AelamAl Moqeain Vol 2'*, Darul Jaleel: Beirut and Aotaba Al Kuliyat: Al Azhar, Egypt(1968)

Imam Mālik ibn Anas ibn Malik ibn 'Āmr al-Asbahi *'Muwatta ibn Malik'* (n.d)

Al Maward *'Al-Ahkam-Al-Sultania'* Dar-al Kutub al Ilmia: Beirut (1406AH, 1985)

Munir, Mohammad *'From Jinnah to Zia'*. Vanguard: Lahore, Pakistan (1980)

Muslim, Imam Bin Hijaj Al-Qashiri,' *Sahih Muslim'* (n.d)

An-Nisa'i, Ahmad Ibn Shu'ayb *'Sunan An-Nisa'i.'* Beirut: Dar al-Kitab al-'Arabi, (n.d.)

Ar-Ramali, Allamah Shamsh-ud-Din Muhammad Bin Abi-Al-Abbas Ahmed Bin Hamza Shahab-ud-Din *'Nihayat-ul-muhtaj ala-sharhil-minhaj vol 7'* Mustapha Al-Babi Al-Halbi (publishers): Cairo (1938)

Rishmawi, Marwat 'The Revised Arab Charter on Human Rights: A Step Forward?' In *Human Rights Law Review*, Vol 5, Num 2, (2005) pp. 361–376 at 371

Sabiq, Syed *'Fiqh us Sunnah vol 2'* Dar-ul-Fikr: Beirut, (1985)

As Sarkhsi, Shams-Al-Aiama *'Al Mabsut vol 4'.* Dar Al Mahrifah: Beirut (nd)

Shah, Sayed Sikandar, *Homicide in Islam: Major Legal Themes*, lecture delivered International Islamic University, Malaysia, 15 April 1999

Al Sharkawi, A. *Inhiraf al Ahdath*, Anglo-Egyptian Library: Cairo (1986)

At-Tirmazi, Al- Hafiz Abi Essa Mohammed Bin Essa *'Sunnan At Tirmazi'* (nd)

Utaiba, Mohammad Bajat *'Mohadarat -Fi-Alfiah-Al- Janai Al Islami'.* *Mahad Darasat al Islamia* (publishers) (1998)

Wahdan, A. 'Dawr Shortat al Ahdath fi Marhalat al Dabt al Qada'i ' in *Al Afaq al Jadida lel Adala al Jina'eya fi Majal al Ahdath*, Fifth conference of the Egyptian Criminal Law Association (Cairo, 18–20 April 1992: Dar al Nahda al Arabiya)

Ya'qub Ibn Ibrahim Abu Youssuf, *Kitab Al-Kharaj*, AlMatba'ah al-Salafiyah: Cairo (1933)

Zahara, Imam Abu *'Falsafah-tul-Aquba-fee-Fiqahl Islami'.* Mahad Darasat Al-Arabia Al Alamia (publishers): Beirut (1963)

Zahara, Imam Abu *'Jareema Wal Aqooba Fi-Al Fiq Al-Islami'.* Dar ul Fikr: Beirut (1974)

Al Zuhali, Dr Wahbah *'Fiqh-al-Isalami-wa-Adilatuhoo'.* Darul-Fiker: Beirut (1985)

Al Zuhali, Dr Wahbah, *'Al Fiqh Al -Hanbali Al Maiyser bi Addilah tihe, Wa Tatbeqat tihe, Al-Moaserah vol 4'.* Dar-Al-Qalam (publishers) (1997)

Sources in French

Zermatten, J., *Face à l'évolution des droits de l'enfant, quel système judiciaire: système de protection ou système de justice?* in Revue internationale de criminologie et de police technique, n° 2, Genève 1994.

Sources in Farsi

http://www.schrr.net/spip.php?page=sarticle&id_article=2531, accessed 11 March 2010

http://hright.iran-emrooz.net/index.php?/hright/more/16474/, accessed 9 March 2010 http://www.iranbar.org/pmm191.php, accessed 9 March 2010

http://www.ghazavat.com/ghazavat.com/ghezavat19/Selection.htm, accessed 09/03/2010

http://hoghoogh.online.fr/article.php3?id_article=375, accessed 9 March 2010

http://www.hawzah.net/Hawzah/Magazines/MagArt.aspx?id=41507, accessed 11 March 2010

http://www.siasatrooz.ir/CNewsRDetail.aspx?QSCNDId=10544&QSDNI d=235, accessed 11 March 2010

http://www.magiran.com/npview.asp?ID=1724043, accessed 9 March 2010

http://www.humanrightsiran.com/FA/Print.aspx?ID=3355, accessed 11 March 2010

http://www.siasatrooz.ir/CNewsRDetail.aspx?QSCNDId=10544&QSDNI d=235, accessed 11 March 2010

http://vekalat88.com/post-19.aspx, accessed 9 March 2010

http://pnu-8g.mihanblog.com/post/7, accessed 9 March 2010

Sources in Spanish

J Morant Vidal, 'La delincuencia juvenil', *Noticias Jurídicas*, 2003, online publication available at http://noticias.juridicas.com/ articulos/ 55-Derecho%20Penal/200307-58551523610332031.html [8 May 2009], 3

Manel Capdevila Capdevila paper 'Justicia juvenil y reincidencia: apuntes de los estudios de investigación en Cataluña' submitted to the *I Congreso Internacional de Responsabilidad Penal de Menores* conference, 212

C Rechea Alberola & AL Cuervo García, *Menores Agresores en el Ámbito Familiar (Estudio de Casos)* Report, 2009, available online at: http://www.uclm.es/criminologia/pdf/17-2009.pdf [8 July 2009]

C Rechea Alberola report elaborated under commission of the CGPJ (Judicial Power governmental organ) 'Conductas Antisociales y Delictivas de los Jóvenes en España', 2008, Available online at http://www.uclm.es/criminologia/pdf/17-2009.pdf [8 June 2009]

Memoria Fiscalía 2008 (Prosecution Service Annual Report 2008); A Andrés Pueyo, 'Violencia juvenil: realidad actual y factores psicológicos implicados' Revista ROL de Enfermería, Vol. 29, No 1, 2006

JM de la Rosa Cortina, 'El Fenómeno de la delincuencia juvenil: Causas y tratamientos', *Encuentros Multidisciplinares*, No. 13, 2003, p. 9-10, available online at http://www.encuentros-multidisciplinares.org/ Revistan°13/ José%20Miguel%20de%20la%20Rosa%20Cortina.pdf, [5 June 2009]

Luis González Cieza paper 'Programa de intervención por maltrato familiar ascendente de la Agencia de la Comunidad de Madrid para la reeducación y reinserción del menor infractor: resultados y proyectos' submitted to the *I Congreso Internacional de Responsabilidad Penal de Menores* conference, 149

J Sáinz-Cantero Caparrós, 'Fundamentos Teóricos y Antecedentes del Sistema de Responsabilidad Penal de los Menores' available online at: http://www.cej.justicia.es/pdf/publicaciones/secretarios_judiciales/SECJU D24.pdf [5 June], 5138-5152

JD González Campos et al, *Curso de Derecho Internacional Público*, (Servicio Publicaciones Facultad Derecho Universidad Complutense Madrid, 5th ed, 1992), 239

L Cosculluela Montaner, *Manual de Derecho Administrativo Tomo I*, 19th ed, (Thomson Civitas, Madrid, 2008), 71

Audiencia Provincial of Asturias judgement of 26 September 2002

JA Blanco Barea, 'Responsabilidad Penal del Menor: Principios y Medidas Judiciales Aplicables en el Derecho Penal Español', *Revista de Estudios Jurídicos n° 8/2008 (Segunda Época), (2008)*

Sources in Turkish

Hancı, Hamit/Eşiyok, Burcu/şimşek, Filiz/Ulukol, Betül, Cezaevinde Bulunan Çocukların Temel Özellikleri ve Suç Tipleri, in: III. Ulusal Çocuk ve Suç Sempozyumu, Bakım, Gözetme ve Eğitim, 22–25 Ekim 2003, Bildiriler (Akyüz/Uluğtekin/Acar/Öntaş, Ed.), Ankara (2005)

Dayıoğlu, Hatice/Dayıoğlu, Mehmet, in: Kriminoloji Dergisi (Turkish Journal of Criminologiy and Criminal Justice), C.I, S.I, Ocak (2009). http://bianet.org/english/english/children-of-turkey-in-2004, accessed 26/02/2010.

S. Çor, Yaşar, Aile İçi Şiddet, in: Suç Mağdurları, Halil İbrahim Bahar (Ed.), Ankara (2006).

Bahar, Halil İbrahim/Arıcan, Mehmet, Dünya'da ve Türkiye'de Çocuk Adaletinin Gelişimi: Temel Sorunlar, Modeller ve Arayışlar, in: Kriminoloji Dergisi (Turkish Journal of Criminology and Criminal Justice), C.I, S.I, Ocak 2009, 64-66. Also see: J. Zermatten, Introduction, in: Training Course On Juvenile Justice for Officials from Turkey, Jean Zermatten (Ed.), Working Report 2-2003, p. 3. http://conventions.coe.int/Treaty/Commun/ChercheSig.asp?NT=005&CM =&DF=&CL=ENG, accessed 25/02/2010.

Balo, Yusuf Solmaz, Teori ve Uygulamada Çocuk Ceza Hukuku, 2.B., Ankara (2005)

Yılmaz, Hasan, Çocuk, Suç ve Mağduriyet: Suçlu Olan Çocuk Yoktur, Suça İtilen Çocuk Vardır, in: Suç Mağdurları, Halil İbrahim Bahar (Ed.), Ankara (2006)

Yokuş-Sevük, Uluslar arası Sözleşmelerdeki İlkeler Açısından Çocuk Suçluluğu ile Mücadelede Kurumsal Yaklaşım